CONTENTS

THE ARTHURIAN PLACE
NAMES OF WALES

The
ARTHURIAN PLACE NAMES OF WALES

SCOTT LLOYD

UNIVERSITY OF WALES PRESS
2017

www.uwp.co.uk

British Library CIP Data
A catalogue record for this book is available from the British Library

ISBN   978-1-7868-3025-8
eISBN   978-1-7868-3026-5

The right of Scott Lloyd to be identified as author of this work has been asserted in accord-
ance with sections 77 and 79 of the Copyright, Designs and Patents Act 1988.

Published in cooperation with the Vinaver Trust.
The Vinaver Trust was established by the British Branch of the International Arthurian
Society to commemorate a greatly respected colleague and distinguished scholar, Eugène
Vinaver, editor of Malory's *Morte Darthur*. The Trust aims to advance study of Arthurian
literature in all languages by planning and encouraging research projects in the field, and
by aiding publication of the resultant studies.

MIX
Paper from
responsible sources
FSC   FSC® C013604
www.fsc.org

Designed and typeset by Chris Bell, cbdesign
Printed by CPI Antony Rowe, Melksham

For Susie

ACKNOWLEDGEMENTS

THIS PROJECT BEGAN over ten years ago and formed the basis for my MPhil thesis at Aberystwyth University in 2009. I would like to thank Michael Roberts and David Ceri Jones for their advice and supervision, and my examiner, Oliver Padel, for his constructive criticism. This book now supersedes that thesis. The two anonymous readers for University of Wales Press made many invaluable suggestions for improvement, and this book is all the better for them. The mistakes that remain are my responsibility alone. I would like to thank the Vinaver Trust for awarding a grant towards the publication of this book.

My time at Aberystwyth University was enhanced by the company of fellow postgraduates in the department, especially, Owen Collins and James Cooper. I am very grateful to everybody who came along to the Celtic Studies Reading Group in Aberystwyth and provided information on various lines of enquiry, in particular Simon Rodway who runs the group and has been generous with his advice, Barry Lewis for his in-depth discussions about many topics and Jenny Day for her help with medieval Welsh poetry. I have been a member of the International Arthurian Society since 2007 and was honoured to serve on the committee of the British Branch for a three-year term from 2010 to 2013. It is the most helpful, friendliest and encouraging group of scholars I know. David Dumville, P. J. C. Field, Marged Haycock, Ceridwen Lloyd-Morgan, Marieke Meelen, Thea Summerfield and Alex Woolf have all provided invaluable information and references. I would also like to thank the staff at the National Library of Wales, Hugh Owen Library, Bangor University Archives, Grays Inn Library and the Bodleian Library for their help and advice and Jon Dollery for his help with GIS mapping.

I would like to thank my parents, my sister Fay and her husband Liam and my nephews Jake and Elliot for all of their support over the years. I would also like to thank the following: Lucille and David Strachan, whose kindness and caravan will for ever be appreciated; my fellow booksellers, Stephen Whitaker and the late Jane Wolfe and all the customers who made Gildas Books in Chester a pleasure to own and run; Janet Bord and Tristan Gray Hulse, who have always been generous with their time and advice; Arnold Bantzer, James Crane and John Williams, who have been good friends for a long time; and colleagues, past and present, at the Royal Commission on the Ancient and Historical Monuments of Wales. The greatest gratitude goes to Gwilym and Ceinwen and, most importantly of all, Susie Fielding, without whom this book would never have been completed.

FIGURES AND MAPS

Figures

1 An aerial view of Carn Gafallt SW of Rhayader showing the numerous cairns on the summit, any one of which could be the heap of stones mentioned in the *Mirabilia*. ©Crown Copyright RCAHMW.

2 For her 1849 edition of the *Mabinogion* Lady Charlotte Guest 'prevailed upon a gentleman to undertake a pilgrimage to the summit of Cefn Carn Cavall'. His account included this sketch of a stone, 'two feet in length and not quite a foot wide', which he thought might be the stone noted in the *Mirabilia*.

3 An illustration from *L'Estoire del Saint Graal* (written *c*.1220) in Paris, Bibliothèque nationale de France, MS fr. 105, f. 103 (*c*.1320) showing Crudel, the king of Norgales (North Wales), imprisoning Joseph of Arimathea and his followers. This predates his association with Glastonbury by at least thirty years. © Bibliothèque Nationale de France.

4 A page from the Black Book of Carmarthen (written *c*.1250) showing a section of the poem about Arthur at Llongborth. His name can be seen two lines above the lacuna in the manuscript. By permission of Llyfrgell Genedlaethol Cymru / The National Library of Wales.

5 Aerial view of the Presceli Hills where Arthur hunted the Twrch Trwyth in Culhwch and Olwen. © Crown Copyright RCAHMW.

6 Maen Huail situated on the town square in Ruthin. A folktale preserved by Elis Gruffydd (*c*.1550) relates how Arthur beheaded Huail on this stone. © Scott Lloyd.

7 The name Pikel Arthur, given to a standing stone near Ro Wen in Carnarfonshire, is first attested in NLW Peniarth 267, p. 40 written by John Jones of Gellilyfdy (*c*.1635). By permission of Llyfrgell Genedlaethol Cymru / The National Library of Wales.

8 The hillfort of Moel Arthur in Flintshire. This is one of several Arthurian names first attested in the correspondence of Edward Lhwyd during his research for the 1695 edition of William Camden's *Britannia*. © Crown Copyright RCAHMW.

9 Map of Bardsey Island from 1748 by Lewis Morris, including a note referring to a reef called Gorffrydiau Caswennan, where Arthur's ship Gwennan was

supposedly wrecked. By permission of Llyfrgell Genedlaethol Cymru / The National Library of Wales.

10   Carreg Carn March Arthur, a stone marking the border between Flintshire and Denbighshire, from an extra-illustrated edition of Thomas Pennant's *A Tour in Wales*. By permission of Llyfrgell Genedlaethol Cymru / The National Library of Wales.

11   Maen Arthur, the name given to a rocking stone near Dolbenmaen, Caernarfonshire, from the unpublished 'Celtic Antiquites of Snowdonia' (1772) by the Rev. Richard Farrington (NLW 1118C, p. 180). By permission of Llyfrgell Genedlaethol Cymru / The National Library of Wales.

Maps

INTRODUCTION

I know something about place-names: it is one of my research interests.
But Arthurian place names! On Arthurian place-names I have no expertise
whatsoever. Neither has anyone else, as far as I can discover. I know of no
scholarly discussion on the subject [...] it needs to be done for Britain [...]
It would help to suppress a whole lot of nonsense.[1]

T HE INTERNATIONAL APPEAL of the Arthurian legend plays a prominent
role in popular culture, being the subject of Hollywood films, best-selling nov-
els, documentaries, video games, musicals, works of art and thousands of websites.
Wales has long had a prominent association with the legend. It is where the earliest
sources were written, and the legend, in varying degrees, has played a role in the
national identity of Wales since the medieval period. The Welsh landscape contains
more sites with an Arthurian association than anywhere else, and many of these
continue to attract both curious visitors and the attention of scholars. Surprisingly,
despite this interest, no comprehensive study of these sites and names exists. What
is the earliest notice of an Arthurian place name? Did the site have an earlier name?
Who first recorded the association? These are the questions that this work will examine. By surveying all the available sources it is possible to show how interest in the
legend has ebbed and flowed over the centuries and how fashions in antiquarian and
academic thought have combined to give us the Arthurian landscape we see today.

The academic study of the Arthurian legend falls broadly into two schools: the
study of medieval literatures from the twelfth to the sixteenth century from across
Europe; and the study of Arthur as a potential historical figure who flourished in the
early sixth century and fought against the Saxons. The first school produces most
of the published work, and university language departments all over the world run
courses on Arthurian literature while important authors such as Chrétien de Troyes
and Thomas Malory have become academic fields in their own right. Paradoxically,
the smaller second school is better known to the public at large and attempts to
prove, or disprove, the historical authenticity of a sixth-century Arthur continue to
attract attention.

The number of academic books and articles published on the subject is quite phenomenal. The annual *Bibliographical Bulletin of the International Arthurian Society* was first published in order to 'draw attention to all scholarly books and articles concerned with the *matière de Bretagne*'.[2] The first volume appeared in 1948 listing 145 items and the number steadily increased, (1955, 185 items; 1965, 198; 1975, 424; 1985, 739; 1995, 937) peaking with the volume from 2008, listing 1,365 items. When we consider that the bibliography excludes 'popular works, general surveys found in histories of literature and most studies which deal with the Arthurian tradition after the sixteenth century', the annual number of publications is actually considerably higher.[3] These 'popular works' are often better known to the general public and can be found on the shelves of most bookshops, unlike an expensive specialist academic monograph, only a few hundred copies of which may be published. This gap between popular works and academia is accentuated by the differing requirements of the two fields. Academia is rightly focused upon quality, but the number of people who read and can make use of this specialist research is often quite small. Most specialised research never makes media headlines, and delivering a paper to their peers at an academic conference is as close as academics get to a public appearance. The same is not true, however, for the author who claims to have discovered the 'true' whereabouts of Arthur's battles, courts and resting place. The priority for this market is visibility, with quality control less rigorously enforced. The publishers of these works cater to the large interest that exists for all things Arthurian, and if authors are willing to make exciting claims about their work, then substantial sales can often follow. That is not to say that all non-academic work is without merit, but the gap between the two audiences is rarely bridged successfully.

The internet has made a vast number of earlier and obscure works readily available, with two important consequences. First, it is now possible for anyone freely to access the earliest printed works through such sites as *Google Books* and *The Internet Archive*, and for a small subscription or via a major library, *Early English Books Online* and *Eighteenth Century Collections Online* provide further sources.[4] Electronic journals and digital archives make it possible to data-mine millions of pages for references, and this allows a more comprehensive picture to be formed. Rare books and unpublished doctoral theses, that would previously have been inaccessible without travelling to a major library, can now be downloaded from anywhere with an internet connection, enabling both writer and reader to get closer to the sources.[5] Second, the downside to this ready availability of older works is that the unwary can be led astray. Without any curation of older works it can be difficult to disentangle those that have been subsequently discredited, or that provide inaccurate texts and erroneous translations of important source materials. The internet can make it difficult to separate the good from the bad; this has led to thousands of websites devoted to King Arthur, which apart from a handful of notable exceptions, can be largely derivative or unreliable.

The tourism industry has long made use of the Arthurian legend, from the monks of Glastonbury Abbey attracting pilgrims in the late twelfth century, to both Welsh and Cornish tourist boards drawing upon the international appeal of the Arthurian legends in different campaigns over recent years. It is often happy to rely upon popular works for its information, and the publicity it gives to the Arthurian associations made in these works only ingrains them further on the landscape. The formation of the Welsh Assembly in 1998 heightened the ever-present strong sense of nationalism in some parts of Wales and it is not uncommon to find Arthur used alongside Owain Glyndŵr and Llywelyn ap Gruffudd as a figure of historical importance to Wales.

The aim of this work is not to make an identification of a historical Arthur, if such a thing is even possible, as the evidence has been discussed many times and until some new source comes to light, little progress is likely to be made. Many good surveys covering the relevant material already exist and I do not intend to rehearse it once more in this work.[6] Neither is it the intention of this book to discuss every source relevant to the Arthurian legend in Wales, as again this has been done admirably elsewhere.[7] My main aim is to focus on the Arthurian place names of Wales; a subject that always plays a role in studies of the Arthurian legend, but is rarely discussed at length. Therefore, the focus of this discussion dictates that some texts, crucial to the Arthurian legend in Wales, are dealt with only briefly, as they provide little evidence for this study, and more space has been given to lesser-known sources that provide the earliest attestation of an Arthurian place name. The aim of this work is to find the earliest attestation of each place name and look at those sources in context.

While restricting the geographical range of this book to sites in Wales it has been possible to survey sources, in whatever language they appear, from the ninth century to the present day. To undertake this for the whole of Britain is a much larger task, which I hope will be the subject of future publications. Focusing on one region has allowed a detailed overview of how the Arthurian legend has been used in Wales and how certain elements repeat themselves.

Research has been carried out on the Arthurian place names of other areas of Britain, but it is not extensive. A majority of the Arthurian place names claimed for Scotland originate in two works from the 1860s noted below, and the small number of names, however debatable, that do have a medieval origin have been discussed elsewhere.[8] In Scottish topography the figures of Fionn and Ossian are more prevalent than Arthur, and a detailed study of those names would be very welcome for comparative purposes.[9] Arthurian associations with Cornwall and the south-west of Britain have been looked at in detail by Oliver Padel.[10] The remainder of the Arthurian sites in England are located primarily in the west and north and still remain to be properly gathered together and analysed.

A second reason for restricting the geographical spread of this work is that many of what are considered to be the earliest Arthurian sources were composed in Wales, and this has led to a focus upon this landscape for clues to the origin of the legend. Major Arthurian sources, such as the *Historia regum Britanniae* by Geoffrey of Monmouth, play a prominent role in the historiography of Wales, and the fact that the country retained a degree of independence and a distinct literary culture until the late thirteenth century means that Wales has a crucial role to play in our under-standing of the development of the legend. For the purposes of this work I have not included sites associated with the figure of Merlin for two reasons. First, the Welsh Merlin, Myrddin, is renowned primarily for his prophecies, his association with Arthur is rarely used in later sources, and the character develops very differently. To discuss this alongside the development of Arthur would be a large undertaking for little return, as Merlin/Myrddin place names in Wales are comparatively few and have been discussed elsewhere.[11] Other characters associated with Arthur such as Cai, Bedwyr and Gwenhwyfar are discussed when relevant, but they make very few appearances in the Welsh landscape.[12]

In order to undertake this study a gazetteer was compiled of all the relevant sites across Wales, from a myriad of different sources. These sources span more than a millennium and consist primarily of Latin, French, Welsh and English texts. Arthu-rian place names can be found primarily in four types of sources:

- Literary, in prose or poetry.
- Administrative, such as charters and public records.
- Antiquarian and folkloric works.
- Ordnance Survey and earlier maps.

The place names found in these sources can then in turn be divided into two types, those which contain the name Arthur (Bryn Arthur, Coetan Arthur) and those asso-ciated with Arthur in literary or folkloric works (Lliwedd, Carn Gafallt). Illustrative examples will be used throughout the main discussion in this work, with the details of individual sites being confined to the Gazetteer in Appendix Two.

The first chapter will focus upon the Latin sources dating from the ninth to the thirteenth centuries, including the two most influential, Geoffrey of Monmouth's *Historia regum Britanniae* and its important source, the *Historia Brittonum*, as well as hagiographical texts and the works of Gerald of Wales. The next important develop-ment in the legend is the emergence of French Arthurian romances in the late twelfth century where Wales appears frequently, primarily as a setting for the Arthurian adventures. The names of castles, cities and topographical features located in Wales appear in a romanticised form, but a sufficient number of sites can be identified to show that the writers, at least occasionally, had real locations in mind when they wrote. Nearly all of the French Arthurian romances were written before the Edward-ian conquest of Wales in 1283, and they portray Wales as a wild, untamed land, full of marvels. A parallel development in the same period was the composition of Welsh Arthurian texts, including the prose tale *Culhwch and Olwen*, and Arthurian refer-ences in Welsh poetry. The dating of these poems will be discussed, in particular recent research which has questioned long-held views on early attestations. I have made an attempt to summarise these findings with a particular emphasis on their importance to Arthurian studies.

The twilight of the medieval era saw the emergence of works important to the historiography of Wales in the writings of John Leland, Sir John Prise and Elis Gruffydd. The Arthurian legend was discussed by all three, but in very different ways. These works defended the British history, as portrayed by Geoffrey of Monmouth, from the attack of Polydore Vergil and other critics in the early sixteenth century. The detailed topographical research undertaken by Edward Lhwyd at the end of the seventeenth century contains the earliest attestations of many new Arthurian names and represented a new era in understanding the past in Wales. The same period also saw an increased interest in non-Arthurian-orientated views of the past, and the figure of Arthur became far less prominent in published works as the eighteenth century progressed. The emergence of tourist literature between 1770 and 1830, alongside the first books to put medieval Welsh material in print, gave a new impetus and confidence to the study of Welsh history. Many Arthurian names are first attested during the nineteenth century, largely owing to the rise in publications concerning folklore studies, local history and archaeology. The main discussion will conclude with a survey of the role that the topography of Wales has played in recent Arthurian works, especially those by non-academic authors. The two appendices provide a chronological list of first attestations and a gazetteer containing information about each site.

Previous studies

Lady Charlotte Guest was one of the earliest authors (1849) to call explicitly for a study of the topography of Wales, with a view to a better understanding medieval Welsh texts, including those containing Arthurian material: 'There is one argument in favour of the high antiquity in Wales of many of the Mabinogion, which deserves to be mentioned here. This argument is founded upon the topography of the country.'[13]

Guest notes place names that contain interesting elements, such as Llyn y Morwynion (Lake of the Maidens) and Llyn Llynclys (Lake of the Sunken Court) and notes that it 'would be very interesting to pursue this branch of evidence in detail'.[14] At the end of her introduction she concludes

> Looking at the connexion between divers of the more ancient Mabinogion, and the topographical nomenclature of part of the country, we find evidence of the great, though indefinite, antiquity of these tales, and of an origin, which if not indigenous, is certainly derived from no European nation.[15]

Her notes to the tale of *Culhwch and Olwen* refer to other place names concerned with Arthur and despite Guest providing few references, her discussions have been influential.

The first concerted effort to deal with Arthurian place names in Britain was the work of John Stuart Glennie, a barrister, ethnologist and fellow of the Society of Antiquaries. His first contribution to Arthurian studies was an article printed in the

December 1867 edition of *Macmillan's Magazine*.[16] Glennie was convinced that most of the sites associated with King Arthur could be identified with locations in Scotland, and building upon W. F. Skene's *Four Ancient Books of Wales* (1868), he wrote a book entitled *Arthurian Localities: Their Historical Origin, Chief Country and Fingalian Relations with a map of Arthurian Scotland* (1869).[17] He refers to the Arthurian sites of England and Wales in a little over six pages and the rest of his 140-page book deals solely with Scotland. Nearly all of Glennie's identifications strain credibility, but his work has been influential and used by many writers, primarily because of a lack of any alternative study or readily available critique. A short query in the January 1872 edition of the journal *Archaeologia Cambrensis* drew attention to several places containing the element Camlan in the vicinity of Dinas Mawddwy and the query ends with an appeal for information about the name Llys Arthur, near Aberystwyth.[18] The query led to a list of twenty-three Arthurian place names to appear under the title 'Arthurian Localities in the Principality and the Marches' in the September 1872 part of the same volume and a call by the editor for 'further contributions on this interesting topic'.[19] The influence of Glennie's work is obvious in both the title and the notes to individual places. A longer and more detailed collection of names was printed in the 1874 volume, drawn mainly from earlier issues of the same journal and the notes to *Culhwch and Olwen* in Guest's *Mabinogion*.[20] Two further brief collections from the same sources followed, but by the end of 1875 the interest in Arthurian localities had ceased.[21]

The major collections of Welsh folklore that appeared in the period 1880–1930 deal with Arthurian material to varying degrees. Elias Owen's *Welsh Folklore* (1896) does not mention Arthur once in over 360 pages, and Wirt Sikes's *British Goblins* (1880) and Marie Trevelyan's *Folk-Lore and Folk-Stories of Wales* (1909) both contain less than a page concerning Arthur.[22] Two other works of note, John Rhŷs's *Celtic Folklore* (1901) and *Welsh Folklore and Folk-Custom* (1930) by T. Gwynn Jones, were both written by academics with an interest in Celtic Studies who had previously published works on Arthur.[23] Unsurprisingly, these works contain far more relevant material and have had considerable influence on later writers.

The first half of the twentieth century saw the publication of further works on the subject. *King Arthur in Cornwall* (1900) looked at place names in Cornwall from Geoffrey of Monmouth through to the folklore collections of the nineteenth century, although references are few and mainly to secondary works.[24] *The Lost Land of King Arthur* (1909), which focuses again on Cornwall, includes Glastonbury material and although it occasionally mentions sites in Wales, is again lacking in references to sources.[25] F. J. Snell's *King Arthur's Country* (1926) covers the whole of Britain, but the author spends much of his time discussing non-Arthurian materials and makes several errors.[26] *Arthur of Britain* (1927) by the Shakespearean scholar, E. K. Chambers devotes twenty pages to discussing topographical features associated with Arthur across Britain, but the bibliography shows that nearly all of the material was gleaned from either Glennie, Rhŷs or Snell.[27] Egerton Phillimore also drew attention to various Arthurian names in his voluminous footnotes to the four-volume edition of George Owen's *Description of Penbrokeshire*.[28] The early county inventories of the Royal Commission on the Ancient and Historical Monuments of Wales often mention megalithic monuments with Arthurian associations, and the Carmarthenshire volume, from 1917, seems to be the earliest source for at least three of them.

The unpublished DPhil dissertation by Ruth Eloise Roberts, 'Welsh Place-Names in the Earliest Arthurian Texts' (1957), is primarily concerned with the *Historia Brittonum*, *Culhwch and Olwen* and Geoffrey of Monmouth, although later traditions are mentioned at points throughout the work.[29] Melville Richards dealt with Arthurian names in his 1969 article 'Arthurian Onomastics', and although most of the article is concerned with personal names, Richards states in a footnote: 'I hope to provide a fully documented list of Arthurian names in a future article.'[30] Sadly no such list was ever published. The folklore of prehistoric sites across Britain has been discussed by Leslie V. Grinsell in his 1976 publication, where he lists twelve Arthurian sites in Wales and provides reliable sources, although not necessarily to the earliest notice of the name.[31]

The most widely referenced work on Arthurian sites in Britain, by both academic and popular writers, is Geoffrey Ashe's *A Guidebook to Arthurian Britain* (1980) as it contains more place names than any previous works and the author has attempted some clarification of ambiguous sites.[32] Ashe lists over 150 locations but, as with his predecessors, he gives few references to sources for individual sites and makes little attempt to evaluate the authenticity or age of the attestation. A detailed chapter in *Camelot Regained* (1990) by Roger Simpson, entitled 'The topographical Arthur', discusses the figure of Arthur in the tours and literature of the early Victorian period, and remains invaluable.[33] *The Giants of Wales* (1993) by Chris Grooms, examines the folklore of giants and features in the Welsh landscape associated with them. The author includes over fifty sites, primarily prehistoric monuments, associated with Arthur on the basis that he is sometimes depicted as a giant in Welsh folklore. It includes full references, often to obscure publications; however, the Arthurian material is only a secondary product of his research.[34] The same year also saw the appearance of *Arthur, Prehistoric Sites and Place-Names: A Comprehensive List* by John Godfrey Williams in which he gathers together over 300 names from across Britain, Ireland and Brittany that he considers to be associated with Arthur.[35] However, his methodology is somewhat erratic, as he also includes any place name in Wales containing the element *arth*, including, for example, *buarth* (cattle enclosure). The list is further compromised by the inclusion of any place name in Wales containing the word *Pegwn* (pole) in an attempt to justify his theory that Arthur can be interpreted as *Arth Fawr*, the Great Bear, and therefore associated with the Pole Star and the constellation of Ursa Major.[36]

Oliver Padel's important 1994 article, entitled 'The Nature of Arthur', examines how the earliest sources depict two different types of Arthur, one historical and the other mythical, and discusses several landscape features with Arthurian associations.[37] *A Gazetteer of Arthurian Onomastic and Topographic Folklore* by Thomas Green was originally a web-based document published in 1999, revised to supplement the publication of his 2007 work *Concepts of Arthur*, and is also available as part of his *Arthuriana: Early Arthurian Tradition and the Origins of the Legend* (2009).[38] As Green readily admits in his introduction, nearly all names noted for Wales were derived from either Ashe or Grooms. A useful bibliography of studies about individual place names associated with the Matter of Britain can be found as an appendix to *A Reader's Guide to the Place-Names of the United Kingdom* (1990).[39] Two works with an emphasis on the photography of Arthurian sites are Neil Fairburn's *Kingdoms of Arthur* and John K. Bollard and Anthony Griffiths, *Tales of Arthur: Legend and Landscape of Wales.*[40]

Place name studies in Wales are not as comprehensive as those in England, epitomised by the volumes of the English Place-Name Society. The foundation of the Place-Name Research Centre at Bangor by Hywel Wyn Owen in 1996 centralised work on the subject and two major projects have been completed. The Melville Richards Archive, consisting of over 300,000 slips, has now been computerised and this invaluable resource is now available online.[41] The *Dictionary of the Place-Names of Wales* was published in 2007 and it is to be hoped that further more detailed studies of smaller areas will follow.[42] A further project on Welsh place name studies, at the Centre for Advanced Welsh and Celtic Studies in Aberystwyth, has resulted in an extensive online bibliography of the topic by David Parsons.[43] Detailed studies have been published for some counties of Wales, notably B. G. Charles's *Place-Names of Pembrokeshire* (1992) and Iwan Wmffre's *The Place-Names of Cardiganshire* (2004).[44] In contrast, some counties of Wales are very poorly covered, Denbighshire being a notable example in this respect.

This book aims to provide a detailed list of the Arthurian place-names of Wales, accompanied by a date for the earliest attestation of each one and a discussion of the sources in which they first appear. The possibility that a name was in existence at an earlier date than the one given in this book should always be borne in mind throughout, and further research will undoubtedly uncover more names and earlier attestations. It is hoped that this work will reduce the need to assign an Arthurian place names in Wales to 'tradition', for the want of anything more secure.

Notes

1   Bedwyr Lewis Jones, 'Arthurian Place-Names: An End to Nonsense', *Amazing Quests: The Journey into Growth. A Special Issue of the Journal of Myth, Fantasy and Romanticism*, 4 (The Mythopoeic Literature Society of Australia, 1996), 1–9, based upon a lecture delivered in 1990 at the Aberystwyth Celtic Summer School, entitled 'The Arthur of the Welsh'. I am very grateful to Professor Peter Field for sending me a copy of this obscure article.

2   *The Bibliographical Bulletin of the International Arthurian Society*, 63 (2011), 13.

3   *The Bibliographical Bulletin of the International Arthurian Society*, 63 (2011), 13.

4   For further details, see *books.google.co.uk*; *www.archive.org*; *eebo.chadwyck.com/home* and *quod.lib.umich.edu/e/ecco/*

5   EThOS, hosted by the British Library at *ethos.bl.uk*, provides information on doctoral theses from across the UK and acts as a portal to downloadable copies.

6   N. J. Higham, *King Arthur: Myth-Making and History* (London, 2002) is particularly useful.

7   Rachel Bromwich, A. O. H. Jarman and Brynley F. Roberts (eds), *The Arthur of the Welsh* (Cardiff, 1991); and O. J. Padel, *Arthur in Medieval Welsh Literature* (Cardiff, 2000).

8   Scott Lloyd, 'Arthurian place names and later traditions', in Ceridwen Lloyd-Morgan and Erich Poppe (eds), *The Arthur of the Celtic Literatures* (Cardiff, forthcoming).

9   O. J. Padel, 'The Nature of Arthur', *Cambrian Medieval Celtic Studies*, 27 (1994), 1–31; and Dáithí ÓhÓgáin, *Fionn mac Cumhail Images of a Gaelic Hero* (Dublin, 1988).

10 O. J. Padel, 'Some south-western sites with Arthurian associations', in Bromwich et al., *Arthur of the Welsh*, pp. 229–48; and 'Geoffrey of Monmouth and Cornwall', *Cambridge Medieval Celtic Studies*, 8 (1984), 1–28. See also C. A. Ralegh Radford and Michael Swanton, *Arthurian Sites in the West* (Exeter, 2002).

11 Michael Dames, *Merlin and Wales: A Magician's Landscape* (London, 2002), although his interpretation of the figure of Merlin will not appeal to everybody. Owing to Merlin's medieval association with Carmarthen, a majority of names are found in that vicinity. It is worth noting that Merlin's Bridge near Haverfordwest appears in its earlier forms as Magdalene or Mawdlin, only becoming Merlin at the end of the eighteenth century; B. G. Charles, *The Place-Names of Pembrokeshire*, 2 vols (Aberystwyth, 1992), II, pp. 649–50.

12 Melville Richards, 'Arthurian Onomastics', *Transactions of the Honourable Society of Cymmrodorion* (1969), 261–3.

13 Charlotte Guest, *The Mabinogion from the Llyfr Coch o Hergest and Other Ancient Welsh Manuscripts with an English Translation and Notes*, 3 vols (London, 1849), I, pp. xviii–xix.

14 Guest, *The Mabinogion*, I, p. xx.

15 Guest, *The Mabinogion*, I, p. xxiii.

16 J. S. Stuart Glennie, 'A Journey through Arthurian Scotland', *Macmillan's Magazine* (December, 1867), 161–74.

17 J. S. Stuart Glennie, *Arthurian Localities: Their Historical Origin, Chief Country, and Fingalian Relations with a Map of Arthurian Scotland* (Edinburgh, 1869), pp. 101–7.

18 Anon., 'Arthurian Localities in the Principality and the Marches', *Archaeologia Cambrensis* (1872), 71–2.

19 *Archaeologia Cambrensis* (1872), 269–70. Reprinted in *Bye-Gones* (1871–3), p. 90.

20 *Archaeologia Cambrensis* (1874), 88–90.

21 *Archaeologia Cambrensis* (1874), 175 and (1875), 290.

22 Elias Owen, *Welsh Folklore* (Oswestry, 1896); Wirt Sikes, *British Goblins: Welsh Folk-Lore, Fairy Mythology, Legends and Traditions* (London, 1880) and Marie Trevelyan, *Folk-Lore and Folk-Stories of Wales* (London, 1909).

23 John Rhŷs, *Celtic Folklore* (Oxford, 1901) and T. Gwynn Jones, *Welsh Folklore and Folk-Custom* (London, 1930).

24 W. H. Dickinson, *King Arthur in Cornwall* (London, 1900).

25 J. Cuming Walters, *The Lost Land of King Arthur* (London, 1909).

26 F. J. Snell, *King Arthur's Country* (London, 1926).

27 E. K. Chambers, *Arthur of Britain* (London, 1927), pp. 183–204.

28 Owen, Henry (ed.), *The Description of Penbrokeshire by George Owen of Henllys*, 4 vols (London, 1892–1936). The bulk of the Arthurian notes appear in vol. IV, pp. 530–1. An index to

the place names discussed has been published: Nerys Ann Jones, 'An Index to the Discussions on Place Names by Henry Owen and E. J. Phillimore in *The Description of Penbrokshire* by George Owen of Henllys', *Studia Celtica*, 26–7 (1991/2), 214–25.

29   Ruth Eloise Roberts, 'Welsh place-names in the earliest Arthurian texts' (unpublished DPhil thesis, Columbia University, 1957).

30   Richards, 'Arthurian Onomastics', 262.

31   Leslie V. Grinsell, *Folklore of Prehistoric Sites in Britain* (Newton Abbot, 1976), pp. 36–40. See also his 'Notes on the Folklore of Prehistoric Sites in Britain', *Folklore*, 90/1 (1979), 66–70.

32   Geoffrey Ashe, *A Guidebook to Arthurian Britain* (London, 1980). Reprinted with corrections, but without the illustrations as *The Traveller's Guide to Arthurian Britain* (Glastonbury, 1997).

33   Roger Simpson, *Camelot Regained: The Arthurian Revival and Tennyson 1800–1849* (Cambridge, 1990), pp. 55–113.

34   Chris Grooms, *The Giants of Wales: Cewri Cymru* (Lampeter, 1993), pp. 113–28.

35   John Godfrey Williams, *Arthur, Prehistoric Sites & Place-Names* (Hay-on-Wye, 1993). Also of note from the same period is Charles Evans-Gunther, 'Arthur: The Clwyd Connection', *Journal of the Pendragon Society*, 24/1 (1994), 4–7.

36   Williams, Arthur, *Prehistoric Sites*, p. 3.

37   Padel, 'The Nature of Arthur'.

38   Thomas Green, *Concepts of Arthur* (Stroud, 2007) and *Arthuriana: Early Arthurian Tradition and the Origins of the Legend* (Lincoln, 2009). This work is also available as a download from the author's website *www.arthuriana.co.uk/book/index.htm* (accessed 25 June 2014).

39   Jeffrey Spittal and John Field, *A Reader's Guide to the Place-Names of the United Kingdom* (Stamford, 1990), pp. 290–8.

40   Neil Fairburn, *Traveller's Guide to the Kingdoms of Arthur* (London, 1983); and John K. Bollard and Anthony Griffiths, *Tales of Arthur: Legend and Landscape of Wales* (Llandysul, 2010).

41   *www.e-gymraeg.co.uk/enwaulleoedd/amr/* (accessed 25 June 2015).

42   Hywel Wyn Owen and Richard Morgan, *Dictionary of the Place-Names of Wales* (Llandysul, 2007).

43   *www.wales.ac.uk/en/CentreforAdvancedWelshCelticStudies/ResearchProjects/CurrentProjects/WelshNameStudies/WelshNamesSearch.aspx* (accessed 22 March 2015).

44   Charles, *Place-Names of Pembrokeshire*; and Iwan Wmffre, *The Place-Names of Cardiganshire*, 3 vols (Oxford, 2004).

ONE
ThE LATIN TEXTS

T HE POSSIBILITY that the Arthur of legend was a real historical figure has been a topic of debate for over 800 years, and various candidates have been suggested: these include the Roman general Lucius Artorius Castus, Artuir the son of the Áedán, a sixth-century king of Dalriata in Scotland, and Arthur map Petr, a member of the Dyfed dynasty, from the same period.[1] None of these candidates has found wide acceptance and a definitive answer to the question of the historicity of Arthur remains unlikely. This chapter will examine the place names from the earliest sources for the Arthurian legend, from the ninth-century battle list of the *Historia Brittonum* (*HB*), through the *vitae* of the Welsh saints, to the influential *Historia regum Britanniae* (*HRB*) of Geoffrey of Monmouth (*c.*1138). This last work was largely responsible for the huge popularity of the Arthurian legend in the twelfth and thirteenth centuries, and later chroniclers and romance writers used it frequently, but the earliest source for the figure of Arthur is the battle-list in the *Historia Brittonum*.

Historia Brittonum

The complex of manuscripts known to scholars as the *Historia Brittonum* (a title given in early printed editions, but rarely in the manuscripts themselves) is fundamental to our understanding of the development of the Arthurian legend, not just in Wales, but also the rest of Europe.[2] A dating clause to the fourth year of the reign of Merfyn Frych, the king of Gwynedd, is found in most manuscripts:

> A primo anno quo Saxones uenerunt in Brittanniam usque ad annum quartum Mermini Regis supputantur anni quadringenti uiginti nouem.[3]

> From the first year in which the Saxons came to Britain to the fourth year of King Merfyn are computed four hundred and twenty-nine years.[4]

This clause is widely accepted as denoting the year in which the text was first compiled; Merfyn came to power in Gwynedd following the death of Hywel ap Caradog in the year 825, making the fourth year of his reign 829/30.[5] A Gwynedd origin for the text has been widely accepted by most commentators, and the kingdom was a renowned place of intellectual activity in the ninth century.[6] In 2002, Higham put forward the argument that the text had been commissioned by Merfyn as a work of propaganda against the neighbouring dynasties of Powys and Mercia, to bolster his weak claim to the throne of Gwynedd.[7]

Following its first appearance, *HB* was adapted, abbreviated and combined with other texts on a regular basis over the following 350 years, and the forty or so surviving manuscripts have been classified into nine different Latin recensions and a Middle Irish translation.[8] The most detailed study of the complex textual transmission of *HB* remains Dumville's 1975 thesis and a series of accompanying articles.[9] Seventy-six different sections can be identified across the recensions, but only the Harleian, in British Library, Harley 3859, includes them all.

1–18	The six ages of the world in which are described the Trojan origins of the Britons and the alternative biblical origins. The arrival of the Picts and Scots in Britain.
19–30	A brief history of Roman Britain concerning the reign of nine emperors from Julius Caesar to Constantinus with particular attention given to Maximus and his removal of British soldiers to the continent.
31–49	The story of Vortigern, the coming of the Saxons to Britain, Ambrosius and the dragons beneath Dinas Emrys.
50–55	Abbreviated story of the life of St Patrick.
56	Arthurian battle list.
57–61	Anglian genealogies.
62–65	Wars between the Britons and the Angles, known as the 'Northern History'.
66	Calculi and 28 cities of Britain.
67–76	Mirabilia.

The first discussions and extracts in print date to the early sixteenth century, but it was not until 1691 that Thomas Gale published a version of the text.[10] The Vatican recension was printed by Gunn in 1819, the Harleian by Stevenson in 1838 and a confusing multi-recension version was edited by Theodore Mommsen in 1898.[11] A useful English translation of the Harleian text was published by Wade-Evans in 1938, and another by John Morris in 1980 is widely quoted despite its inadequacies.[12] Dumville proposed a ten-volume edition covering all recensions and variants, but to date only the Vatican recension volume has appeared and his 1975 thesis remains the most detailed discussion of the work.

The Harleian recension is considered to be closest to the original form of the text and is found amongst the 365 folios that make up London, British Library,

Harleian MS 3859, dated to *c.*1100.[13] This manuscript also preserves the earliest copy of the *Mirabilia*, often considered to be an integral part of *HB* and containing material of Arthurian interest, the *Annales Cambriae* (both discussed below) and a series of Welsh genealogies. The other manuscript that provides early evidence for the importance of *HB* is that of the Vatican recension: Rome, Bibliotheca Apostolica Vaticana, MS Reginensis Lat. 1964, dates from the second half of the eleventh century and originated at the church of Saint Médard in Soissons, sixty miles north-east of Paris.[14] It is the earliest securely datable manuscript to mention Arthur. It is a shorter text compared to the Harleian recension, as it omits the 'Northern History' and the *Mirabilia*.[15] For the purposes of studying the Arthurian material relating to Wales these two recensions are sufficient to establish its date and development; however, the other recensions provide material relevant to the reception of the Arthurian legend in Scotland and are important for the development of *HB* as a source for the history of Britain.[16]

The Battle List

The battle list from the Harleian recension is given below with the place names left in their original form and variant spellings from the Vatican recension given in parenthesis.

> Then it was that Arthur was wont to fight against them [the Saxons] in those days along with the kings of Britannia, but he himself was *Dux Bellorum*. The first battle was at the mouth of the river, which is called *Glein*. The second, third, fourth and fifth on another river, which is called *Dubglas* (*Duglas*) and is in the region of *Linnius* (*Linnuis*). The sixth battle on a river, which is called *Bassas*. The seventh was a battle in the wood of *Celidon*, that is *Cat Coit Celidon*. The eighth was the battle at *Castellum Guinnion*, in which Arthur carried the image of Saint Mary, the perpetual virgin on his shoulders, and the pagans were put to flight on that day and a great slaughter was upon them through the power of our Lord Jesus Christ and through the power of Saint Mary his holy virgin mother. The ninth battle was fought at *Urbes Legionis* (*urbe Leogis that in British is called Cair Lion*). The tenth battle was fought on the shore of the river, which is called *Tribruit* (*Treuroit*). The eleventh battle occurred on the mountain, which is called *Agned* (*Bregion*). The twelfth was the battle on the mountain of *Badon*, in which there fell in one day nine hundred and sixty men from one charge [of] Arthur; and no-one slew them except he alone, and in all battles he remained the victor.[17]

In this text Arthur is referred to as *dux bellorum* (leader in battles), not *rex* (king) as he became in later sources. The phrase *dux bellorum* occurs in earlier sources, primarily the Latin Vulgate of the Old Testament in the opening lines of the Book of Judges where Joshua is referred to as *dux belli* (leader in battle), and Bede later used the phrase in his 'Greater Chronicle', written in 725, to describe Germanus.[18] Higham has suggested that the apostolic number twelve may have influenced the number of battles described, despite four of them taking place at the same location.[19]

Is it possible to identify any of the battle sites? One of the first independent witnesses to the battle list is William of Malmesbury's *Gesta regum Anglorum* (1125), in which he mentions Arthur's victory at the siege of Mount Badon, where he wore the image of the Virgin on his armour, a fact associated with the battle of *Castello Guinnion* in all surviving manuscripts of *HB*.[20] The next earliest reference is by Henry of Huntingdon in his *Historia Anglorum* (1129), who notes that 'none of the places can be identified now'.[21] The fact that by the early twelfth century none of the battle sites could be located made Arthur into a mysterious heroic figure and, perhaps more importantly, a blank canvas on which a new view of the early history of Britain could be portrayed. Geoffrey of Monmouth grasped this potential and was the first author to place the battles into a recognisable geographical framework in his *Historia regum Brittaniae* (c.1138). He located the battles in areas across Britain, from Scotland to Cornwall, and his identifications gave rise to the idea that Arthur was a figure to be associated with the whole of the British Isles, not something obviously claimed in *HB*. Only two of the battle names can definitively be shown to derive from earlier sources, *Monte Badonis* from *De excidio Britanniae* by Gildas (c.540) and *Urbes legionis* from Bede's *Historia ecclesiastica gentis Anglorum* (731).[22] Another early attempt to identify one of Arthur's battles with a geographical site was by Ranulf Higden in his *Polychronicon* (c.1325) where he associates the battles at *Dubglas* with the river Douglas, near Wigan in Lancashire.[23]

A bibliography of discussions about the Arthurian battle list, published by Tolstoy in 1960, lists some eighty articles published after 1845.[24] These articles argue for identifications in one particular area of Britain, usually founded upon the idea that the sites must be located in an area where a British army would most likely encounter a Saxon army. Hence Skene identified all of the sites in Scotland, Collingwood located them all in the south-east of England and Anscombe placed them all in the Midlands.[25] Attempting to identify the exact location of all the battles and prove the involvement of Arthur is unlikely to produce a satisfactory answer. How do you identify such obscure names as *Glein, Tribruit, Bassas, Agned* and *Breguion* without further context and additional references from other sources? Attempts to locate the battle sites of Arthur continue to be made however, and armed with a better understanding of the complex origins of *HB*, some progress might be possible.[26] Exactly where the author of *HB* found the name Arthur and why he chose to use him in such a way, remains a major obstacle to our understanding of the origins of the Arthurian legend. We can only assume that it must have had, for whatever reason, some resonance in north Wales in the first half of the ninth century.

Mirabilia

The earliest copy of the *Mirabilia* (Marvels) is also found in Harleian 3859, separated from the main text of *HB* by the *Annales Cambriae* and a collection of Welsh genealogies.[27] Eighteen marvels are listed and eight of them can be securely located in south-east Wales and the English borders, about the river Severn. These include a reference to a tidal whirlpool on the Severn estuary called Llyn Lliwan, the Severn bore, a well in the region of Cynllibiwg between the Wye and the Severn, an ash tree that produces apples near the mouth of the river Wye, and a cave from which the wind blows in the region of Gwent.[28] The other marvels, slightly further afield, include the wells of salt at Droitwich, the hot springs at Bath, a levitating altar in Gower, a grave that changes its size each time it is measured on Crug Mawr in Ceredigion, and two of Arthurian interest discussed below. Lists of such marvels can also be found in Irish tradition preserved in collections known as *Dindshenchas* (lore of places) and they are also frequently found in hagiographical works where they are attributed to a particular saint, the levitating altar of St Illtud in Gower being a notable example.[29]

In Harleian 3859 the *Annales Cambriae* and the Welsh genealogies separate the *Mirabilia* from *HB* and it has long been assumed that they are an integral part of *HB* as they appear in all later recensions directly after the text. However, there is reason to doubt this assumption. They are not, and appear never to have been, present in any manuscripts of the Vatican recension, making it difficult to prove exactly when they were written.[30] The *Mirabilia* cannot therefore be relied upon as evidence for the origin of *HB* and, until further evidence is published, should be treated as a separate text that had become associated with *HB* by the early twelfth century. Despite this, there is little doubt that it is the earliest surviving text to associate Arthur with topographical features in in Wales, or indeed anywhere else:

> There is another wonder in the country called *Buelt* [Builth]. There is a heap of stones there, and one of the stones placed on top of the pile has the footprint of a dog on it. When he hunted Twrch Trwyth, Cafal, the warrior Arthur's hound, impressed his footprint on the stone, and Arthur later brought together the pile of stones, under the stone in which was his dog's footprint, and it is called Carn Cafal. Men come and take the stone in their hands for the space of a day and a night, and on the morrow it is found upon the stone pile.[31]

The cantref of Builth gave its name to the modern town of Builth Wells, and the hilltop concerned is Carn Gafallt, south-west of Rhayader. The hilltop has three large Bronze Age cairns upon it, any of which could have been the one intended. An illustration of the stone bearing the footprint appeared in Charlotte Guest's 1849 edition of the *Mabinogion*, although she is rather sceptical as to its authenticity. The tale of

Figure 1. *An aerial view of Carn Gafallt SW of Rhayader showing the numerous cairns on the summit, any one of which could be the heap of stones mentioned in the* Mirabilia.
©Crown Copyright RCAHMW.

Arthur hunting the Twrch Trwyth (the boar called Trwyth) is also found in *Culhwch and Olwen*, and he also appears, in a non-Arthurian context, in the 'Gorchan Cynfelyn' from the Book of Aneirin discussed in chapter 3.

The second site of Arthurian interest from the *Mirabilia* concerns Arthur's son, Amir, who is rarely mentioned in later texts:[32]

> There is another wonder in the country called *Ercing* [Erging]. There is a tomb there by a spring, called *Licat Amr* [Llygad Amr]; the name of the man who is buried in the tomb was Amr. He was a son of the warrior Arthur, and he killed him there and buried him. Men come to measure the tomb, and it is sometimes six feet long, sometimes nine, sometimes twelve, sometimes fifteen. At whatever measure you measure it on one occasion, you never find it again of the same measure, and I have tried it myself.[33]

The border region of Erging (now in Herefordshire) was a part of Wales in the early medieval period. The Norman name for the region was Archenfield and the entry for the region in Domesday Book (1086) preserves the name *Lagedamr*, almost certainly the same place as the *Licat Amr* in the *Mirabilia*.[34] *Licat* is a Latinised form of the Welsh word *Llygad* meaning 'eye' and is sometimes used to denote a spring at the source of a river. The river in question is likely the Gamber, which flows through the village of Llanwarne and then becomes Garren Brook before joining the Wye near Goodrich. The charters in the twelfth-century Book of Llandaf, refer to properties owned by the diocese of Llandaf, and one of them, 'Hen Lenhic near Llangwern in Erging', is situated *super ripam amhyr fluminis* 'on the banks of the river Amyr'.[35] This charter has been dated to *c*.758, although the charters in the Book of Llandaf have been the centre of much academic discussion as to whether they contain authentic records or were created in the twelfth century.[36] The source, or eye, of the Gamber must be upstream of Llanwerne, and two options are possible: firstly, the highest point from which water runs down to the Gamber on Orcop Hill to the west, and secondly, the fields around a house called Gamber Head, a suggestive name in its own right. Gamber Head is very near the site of Wormelow Tump, a large earthen mound, now destroyed, which is a strong candidate for the site of Amir's tomb.[37] The Book of Llandaf also records the personal name Amir in charters regarding Erging, and it is possible that the *Mirabilia* records an aetiological story based upon a local personal name and an impressive mound near the source of a river with a similar sounding name.[38] The association with Arthur could be a secondary development. The fact that the author tells us that he has visited this site and that many of the others are in the surrounding area, provides valuable evidence as to where he may be from. If the *Mirabilia* is a separate text from the main *Historia Brittonum* and therefore not tied to the ninth-century date, the possibility arises that there may be a link to the early twelfth-century hagiographical writing from the same area discussed below.

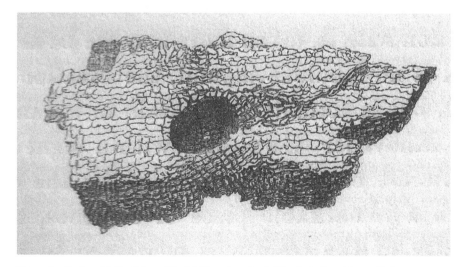

Figure 2. *For her 1849 edition of the* Mabinogion, *Lady Charlotte Guest 'prevailed upon a gentleman to undertake a pilgrimage to the summit of Cefn Carn Cavall'. His account included this sketch of a stone, 'two feet in length and not quite a foot wide', which he thought might be the stone noted in the* Mirabilia.

Annales Cambriae

The collection of Welsh annals preserved in Harleian MS 3859 are known today by their Victorian title, *Annales Cambriae (AC)*.[39] The *AC* consist of brief entries next to *an'*, standing for *Anno*, with every tenth year marked off in Roman numerals, and the start date must be worked out, placing it at AD 445. The Harleian Chronicle extends to the year 977, suggesting that a framework based on the Dionysian Easter Cycle of 532 years was intended.[40] Similar annals are also found on the flyleaves of the Breviate Domesday in London, TNA, MS E. 164/1 (B text or Breviate Chronicle) and in British Library, Cotton Domitian A.i (C text or Cottonian Chronicle), both dating from the end of the thirteenth century and extending the annals up to 1286 and 1288 respectively.[41]

The annals contain two entries regarding Arthur, alongside historical events known from other sources, which have led some to argue that they are proof of a historical Arthur. The first entry seemingly shows a familiarity with *HB*, but the second is unique to *AC*:

> [516] Bellum Badonis, in quo Arthur portavit crucem Domini nostri Jhesu Christi tribus diebus et tribus noctibus in humeros suos et Brittones victores fuerunt.
> [537] Gueith Camlann, in qua Arthur et Medraut corruerunt.[42]

> [516] Battle of Badon, in which Arthur carried the cross of our lord Jesus Christ for three days and three nights on his shoulders and the Britons were victors.
> [537] The battle of Camlan, in which Arthur and Medraut fell.[43]

The first entry is a conflation of the twelfth battle at Badon and the ninth at *Castellum Guinnion* from the battle list in *HB*, but the second introduces two names that played an important role in the development of the Arthurian legend.[44] The introduction of the battle at Camlan between Arthur and Medrawd became one of the key events in the story of Arthur under the influence of Geoffrey of Monmouth and went on to play a prominent part in later Arthurian literature, as the site of Arthur's last battle. The annal merely states that Arthur and Medrawd fell at a place called Camlan, it does not provide any context about who Medrawd was or whether he was fighting against Arthur, or alongside him. The name Camlan consists of two elements: *Cam* meaning crooked and *Lan* which is either *Glan*, meaning a river bank, or less likely, *Llan* meaning a sacred enclosure, such as a church. Geoffrey of Monmouth later located the battle on the river Camel in Cornwall, but the annal provides no evidence to support this location or any other. The location of Camlan has been discussed many times, and as with the battles in *HB*, the conclusions have been largely dependent on the idea that it must be situated in an area where a British ruler would most likely encounter a Saxon army. This approach has been influenced by the fictional account of the battle by Geoffrey of Monmouth, for in Welsh tradition the battle is not associated with the Saxons and Medrawd is not considered a villain, in fact quite the opposite.

The poet Meilyr Brydydd (*fl.* 1100–57), in an elegy to Gruffudd ap Cynan, king of Gwynedd (d. 1137), describes him as having *eissor Medra6d* 'the nature of Medrawd', and Gwalchmai ap Meilyr (*fl.* 1130–80) praises Madog ap Maredudd, king of Powys (d. 1160) for having *Arthur gederyd, menwyd Medra6d* 'Arthur's strength, the good nature of Medrawd'.[45] Neither description suggests that Medrawd was viewed in a negative light in twelfth-century Wales, and he seems to be an exemplary figure renowned for his good nature. Later poets sometimes used Camlan as a proverbial expression for a fierce conflict.[46] The information supplied by *AC* fills an obvious gap in the life of Arthur as portrayed in *HB*, namely the date and place of his death. The question of whether or not this information can be considered historical has been frequently debated and it is not possible to say anything more certain than it was current in the first quarter of the twelfth century when it was copied into Harleian 3859 and possibly during the original composition of *AC* in the mid-ninth century.[47]

Vitae of the Welsh Saints

The production of Latin hagiography for Welsh saints falls into two distinct periods, with a substantial gap in between, where we have little evidence for the production of such texts. The earliest period (sixth to the ninth century) saw the production of *vitae* (Lives) for St Samson, St Paul Aurelian, St Guenole, St Malo and the first life of St Gildas, all of whom had associations with Wales, although their *vitae* were composed in Brittany.[48] The earliest evidence of hagiography written in Wales is found in two sections of *HB* (*c*.830). The first, concerning St Patrick, was probably derived from an earlier *vita* in the Book of Armagh, and the second deals with events in the life of St Garmon claimed to be derived from *Liber beati Germani*, an earlier work now lost.[49] Apart from minor references to saints in *AC*, little more is known to have been produced in Wales until the late eleventh century. This lack of hagiographical activity was not just restricted to Wales, as a similar state of affairs also existed in England and Ireland. As John Reuben Davies notes, 'a lack of interest in Latin hagiography therefore appears to have been an insular phenomenon in the first half of the eleventh century.'[50]

In late eleventh-century Wales two saints' *vitae* appeared: that of St David by Rhygyfarch ap Sulien from Llanbadarn Fawr, in Ceredigion; and that of St Cadog by Lifris of Llancarfan, in Morgannwg.[51] The *Vita David* is important for the dating of the other *vitae* and for contextual reasons, but it plays no part in the development of the Arthurian legend of Wales, unlike the *Vita Cadoci*, which is of fundamental importance. Davies notes that 'these two authors were the vanguard of a literary trend: taking in the Book of Llandaf on the way, it culminated in a substantial corpus of Lives of Welsh saints, now preserved in British Library as part of MS Cotton Vespasian A. xiv'.[52]

London, British Library, Cotton Vespasian A. xiv is a composite manuscript consisting of three different works bound together and written in a number of Anglo-Norman hands of about 1200, 'all of the same general type and period, but of varying accomplishment'.[53] The first 105 folios contain a collection of saints' *vitae* (fourteen Welsh and two Irish), a liturgical calendar of mostly Welsh saints, a Latin–Old Cornish glossary and a genealogical tract known as *De situ Brecheniauc*.[54] The *vitae* are all concerned with south Wales and were likely written at (or for) Monmouth Priory and based upon texts from Gloucester Abbey, which owned the church of Llancarfan, from where some of the material seems to have originated.[55] Of the sixteen *vitae* in the manuscript, only four contain references to Arthur, those of Cadog, Carannog, Padarn and Illtud. The last three were all written by Caradog of Llancarfan (*fl.* 1130–60), but the *Vita Cadoci* was originally written by his predecessor, Lifris of Llancarfan (d. 1104), although Caradog did later write a version of his own.[56]

Vita Cadoci

The earliest and longest of the Welsh *vitae* in the Vespasian manuscript to mention Arthur was written by Lifris of Llancarfan *c.*1090 and a later abbreviated version was undertaken by Caradog of Llancarfan *c.*1150.[57] Unfortunately, the Vespasian version of the *Vita Cadoci* is a composite of both texts, meaning that the original *vita* by Lifris must be reconstructed.[58] The prologue of the *Vita Cadoci* relates the kidnapping of Gwladus, the virgin daughter of Brychan, from her father's court at Talgarth by Gwynllyw (the eponymous ruler of Gwynllŵg). Brychan then pursues Gwynllyw

> as far as the hill, which is on the confines of either country, which in the Britannic tongue takes the name Boch Rhiw Carn [*Bochriucarn*], which means the cheek of the stony way. But when Gwynllyw had arrived at the borders of his land, safe in body with the aforesaid virgin, although sorrowful at the very great slaughter in the fight with his adversaries, lo, three vigorous champions, Arthur and his two knights, to wit, Cai and Bedwyr, were sitting on top of the aforesaid hill playing with dice.[59]

The hill of Boch Rhiw Carn is also named in a now lost land grant from Margam Abbey, datable to between 1158 and *c.*1174; a good example of how the *vita* is concerned with ecclesiastical lands, and names boundaries and notable landscape features also mentioned in land grants.[60] The site in question is the hill known today as Mynydd Fochriw, overlooking Merthyr Tydfil, the summit of which is dominated by a large cairn.[61] If we accept the date of composition as *c.*1090, then it is the earliest landscape feature to be associated with Arthur himself, rather than his dog or son, which can also be securely located.

Chapter 22 of the *Vita Cadoci*, also considered to be part of the original composition by Lifris and therefore datable to the final decade of the eleventh century, opens with the following sentence: 'In that same time a certain very brave leader of the British, called Ligessauc ap Eliman also named Llaw Hir, that is Long Hand, slew three soldiers of Arthur, most illustrious king [*regis*] of Britannia.'[62] This is the earliest source to refer to Arthur as *rex*, in contrast to the *dux bellorum* of the earlier *HB*, and also to give him a kingdom, *Britannia*. The Cambro-Latin usage of the term Britannia has been the cause of much confusion, as evidenced by Asser's *Life of King Alfred* (893), which refers to Offa of Mercia, 'who had a great dyke built between Britannia and Mercia from sea to sea.'[63] It is clear that the earthwork known today as Offa's Dyke is meant and that Britannia was west of the Saxon king-dom of Mercia and therefore denoted Wales, approximately as we know it today. However, later in the same text Asser uses *Britannia* in its more usual sense, to denote the whole of the island of Britain.[64] This dual sense of Britannia has been the cause of much uncertainty, and in the early twelfth century Cambro-Latin authors used it alongside the terms that eventually replaced it, such as *Gualia*, *Wallia* and *Cambria*, to denote their country. Huw Pryce notes: 'The chronology of this shift no doubt varied according to author and intended audience, but the earliest known instances occur at the end of the second decade of the twelfth century.'[65] The term *Cambria* does not seem to have been widely used in Wales, and its usage in Cam-bro-Latin documents is sparse and confined primarily to works originating in south-west Wales.[66] As *Cambria* does not appear in the Vespasian manuscript, it is clear, unless the context suggests otherwise, that all the references to Britannia can be equated with Wales. The *Vita Cadoci* is the earliest source to make Arthur a king and in doing so describes him specifically as the 'king of Wales', a title not widely attributed to him in later sources.

Chapter 22 concludes with Ligessauc finding refuge with St Cadog for seven years, before being betrayed and his location being revealed. Arthur arrives with a great force at the river Usk to seek his revenge on Ligessauc, but the nobles award Arthur one hundred head of cattle to spare Ligessauc's life. When Arthur, Cai and Bedwyr try to take the cattle the creatures miraculously turn into bundles of ferns, and Arthur, humbled by this miracle, prolongs the period of refuge at Cadog's sanc-tuary to seven years and seven months: 'For from that day that place in British speech is called Tredunnock [*Tref Redinauc*], that is fern homestead. Also that ford, about which the pleading (or action at law) took place, is called Rhyd Gwrthebau [*Rith Guurtebou*].'[67] Tredunnock is a small village to the west of the river Usk, four miles north-east of Caerleon, in Monmouthshire. The name Rhyd Gwrthebou (Ford of Responses) no longer survives and does not appear in any other source, but was probably near the site of Newbridge on Usk, 500 metres east of Tredunnock.

Vita Carantoci

The remaining three *vitae* in the Vespasian manuscript that mention Arthur, although important in the development of the legend, can, from a topographical point of view, be dealt with briefly. The *Vita Carantoci* survives in two versions, and both date from the early twelfth century.[68] St Carannog was a saint from Ceredigion and is commemorated at Llangrannog on the coast, north of Cardigan.[69] Arthur makes an appearance in the first Life, which states that he was ruling with Cadwy at a place called *Dindraithov*, a site situated on 'the far side of the Severn Sea'.[70] As the *vita* is primarily concerned with the church of Carhampton (*Carrum*) in Somerset, it is logical to place *Dindraithov* nearby as well, and therefore outside Wales. The exact location of *Dindraithov* is uncertain, but the name is probably derived from the *Cair Draithou* in the list of cities attached to *HB* in Harleian 3859.[71]

Vita Iltuti

The *Vita Iltuti* can be dated by the reference to 'Dubricius bishop of the church of Llandaf' as later than 1121, probably in the late 1120s.[72] Chapter 2 states that Illtud was a cousin to Arthur and visited his court, but no geographical clues are given as to its location, although the context of the story would suggest south Wales, probably Glamorganshire. The Vespasian *vita* is almost certainly based upon earlier material about Illtud, but the brief reference to Arthur is probably an addition, contemporary with the final recension of the *vita*, as the main subject of the chapter is King Poulentus of Glamorgan. This is the earliest text to depict Arthur as a king with a court, and may have influenced Geoffrey of Monmouth, who mentions Illtud in association with Arthur's court at Caerleon.[73]

Vita Paterni

The *Vita Paterni* was written *c.*1120 at Llanbadarn Fawr, near Aberystwyth in Ceredigion. The Arthurian section of the narrative is very brief and takes place whilst Padarn is resting at his church in *Mauritana* in Ceredigion, identified as Llanbadarn Fawr, when 'a certain tyrant (*tirannus*), Arthur by name' comes to his cell.[75] Arthur asks if he can have Padarn's tunic which had been given to him in Jeruslaem, but Padarn refuses. Arthur leaves the monastery in a rage and 'returns in wrath, that he might take away the tunic against the counsels of his own companions'. One of Padarn's disciples runs into the monastery to warn Padarn of Arthur's return and Padarn replies, 'Nay rather, may the earth swallow him.' With this, the earth immediately opens and swallows Arthur up to his neck, Acknowledging his guilt Arthur begs forgiveness, is then released, makes Padarn his continual patron and leaves.[76] Later in the *vita*, Padarn comes into conflict with other well-known names from sixth-century Wales, including Maelgwn Gwynedd and Caradog Freichfras; his encounter with Arthur is very minor and of no importance to the rest of the *vita*. The description of Arthur as a tyrant is unique and his behaviour and failure to listen to his companions reminds us of the prologue in the *Vita Cadoci*.[77]

Vita Gildae

Caradog of Llancarfan was also responsible for the *Vita Gildae* which mentions Arthur, but was not included in the Vespasian collection. An earlier *vita* of Gildas dating from *c*.1045, or possibly as early as the ninth century, written by a monk of Rhuys in Brittany, makes no mention of Arthur.[78] The later *vita* survives in Cambridge, Corpus Christi College, MS 139 (written 1164) alongside a copy of the Sawley recension of *HB*.[79] Although events do not take place in Wales, the text is important for two developments. Firstly, it depicts Huail, Gildas's eldest brother, as a ruler who had defeated Arthur in battle but was later slain by him on the island of *Minau* (it appears the Isle of Man is meant).[80] The enmity between Huail and Arthur is also mentioned in *Culhwch and Olwen*, and again, in an expanded form, by Elis Gruffydd in the mid-sixteenth century, a tradition that will be discussed in chapter 4. Secondly, the *vita* relates the earliest form of the tale regarding the abduction of Gwenhwyfar by Melwas, an episode also found in the French romance *Lancelot* (*c*.1180) by Chrétien de Troyes.[81] Although the narrative takes place in Somerset, an association between Gwenhwyfar and Melwas was known to Dafydd ap Gwilym (*c*.1350) and later poets of north-east Wales, namely Gruffydd Hiraethog and Sion Tudur, who associated Melwas with the cantref of Maelor.[82] It is not impossible that some local tradition was known to them, but the poetic alliteration of the names Melwas and Maelor is likely the main reason for their becoming associated.[83]

The Gazetteer in Appendix 2 shows that three Arthur place names originate as boundary markers in the charters of Welsh monastic sites. *Vadum Arturi* (Arthur's Ford), is the name given to a boundary marker near Cardigan in a lease from Chertsey Abbey, written sometime between 1165 and 1197.[84] Two wells associated with the name Arthur are also mentioned as boundary markers: *Fontem Arthur* in a charter for Cwmhir Abbey in Radnorshire dated 1200, and *Ffynnon Arthur* in Glamorganshire as a site on the boundary between the lands of the abbeys of Margam and Caerleon in 1203.[85] It is by no means certain that the Arthur named in these boundary markers is the Arthur of legend, but the name was not common in Wales in the medieval period and the fact that both Caerleon and Cardigan had already appeared in earlier Arthurian sources is perhaps worthy of note.[86]

The *vitae* of the south Wales saints are the earliest texts to show a development of the figure of Arthur beyond that depicted in the *HB* battle list, as he becomes for the first time a king with a kingdom and a court. It is also the first time that Arthur himself becomes associated with specific and identifiable locations in Wales, rather than his dog or his son, as in the *Mirabilia*. It is clear that these sites were on lands owned by the church associated with the saint in question, and that this factor is of more importance than any association with Arthur. The locations are either boundary markers, as seems the case with Boch Rhiw Garn, or the mother church of the saint, as shown with Llanbadarn Fawr and Llancarfan in the *Vita Paterni* and *Vita Cadoci* respectively. Arthur is much less important than the place, a point reinforced by the role that Maelgwn Gwynedd plays in the *vitae* by fulfilling a similar purpose.[87] The fact that Arthur was well known enough to be used in this role, suggests that *HB* was a text known to the hagiographers of south Wales in the late eleventh century. However, it is noteworthy that he was not considered important or useful enough to be mentioned in that other great work of south Wales ecclesiastical pseudo-history of the early twelfth century, *The Book of Llandaf*. The embryonic King Arthur figure portrayed in the *vitae* soon became known to writers outside Wales and within a few years had been turned into the most prominent legendary figure in Europe.

Geoffrey of Monmouth

The years between 1120 and 1140 are notable for the number of works that were either written or translated into Latin, and Neil Ker notes that 'existing books suggest that in many of the great Benedictine abbeys the scriptorium was at its best in the second quarter of the twelfth century'.[88] Ker also highlights the west of England, centred upon Gloucester, as an area of particular note for book production in this period, and it is from this area that the first notable references to Arthur from outside Wales occur. The *Gesta regum Anglorum* (Deeds of the Kings of England, written *c.*1125) of William of Malmesbury covers the history of England from the Romans to the reign of Henry I and notes that Arthur 'deserves to be the subject of reliable history rather than of false and dreaming fable'.[89] William is also the source of the unique and early reference to a grave of Gawain in Wales, that can be identified with Walwyn's Castle in the cantref of Rhos (Roose), in Pembrokeshire.[90] In conjunction with the *vitae* discussed above, this is the best evidence that an early form of the legend surrounding Arthur was in existence in south Wales by the first quarter of the twelfth century.

Henry of Huntingdon, in his *Historia Anglorum*, bemoaned the fact that there was so little evidence available to him for the pre-Roman period, but in January 1139 he was shown, much to his amazement, a copy of a work that related the history of the Britons back to 1170 BC. This work was the *Historia regum Britanniae* (History of the Kings of Britain, henceforth *HRB*) written by Geoffrey of Monmouth, and Henry was so impressed by the work that he wrote an epitome of it and sent it to his friend Warin the Breton.[91] In later versions of his chronicle, Henry incorporated some minor additions to his text, based upon *HRB*, mostly concerning place names, and there is no obvious evidence to suggest that Henry thought *HRB* to be an unreliable source. The appearance of *HRB* in 1138 is the single most important event in the dissemination of the Arthurian legend. Following its publication Arthur was transformed from a minor hero in Wales into the central figure of the most popular legendary cycle of the Middle Ages.[92] Without *HRB* Arthur would probably have remained little more than an interesting footnote in the history of early medieval Britain.

What little we know of Geoffrey of Monmouth comes from his own writings and the appearance of his name as a witness to seven charters associated with property near Oxford.[93] His use of Monumentis suggests that he was from Monmouth, and references to places near the town in *HRB*, notably Ganerew and Erging, would seem to confirm this.[94] He first appears in the historical record in 1129 as a signatory to a charter for Osney, and would seem to have spent most of his time in Oxford at the church of St George. In one of the charters, he signs his name as *magister Galf. Arcturus* 'Galfridi Arthur', the term *magister* indicating that he was a teacher of some kind.[95] William of Newburgh, writing in 1180, however, had a rather more cynical suggestion for his use of the name Arthur:

> He is called Geoffrey, surnamed Arthur, from having given, in a Latin version, the fabulous exploits of Arthur, drawn from the traditional fictions of the Britons, with additions of his own, and endeavoured to dignify them with the name of authentic history.[96]

Geoffrey was ordained at Westminster on 16 February 1152 and consecrated as bishop of St Asaph eight days later. It is uncertain that he ever visited St Asaph owing to the ongoing conflict in the area with Owain Gwynedd, but the last work he wrote, the *Vita Merlini* (*c*.1150), contains a probable reference to St Kentigern, the supposed founder of the see.[97] The Welsh chronicle *Brut y Tywysogion* states that he died in 1154.[98]

Three versions of the text of *HRB* have been identified. The Vulgate text is the earliest (*c*.1138), survives in a majority of the manuscripts and forms the basis for the most recent edition. The First Variant Version (compiled *c*.1150 and surviving in eight manuscripts) introduces further references from the Bible and classical authors, as well as editing some of the material found in the Vulgate.[99] The Second Variant Version removes some material from the second half of the text and survives in eighteen manuscripts. The date for the creation of this version is not certain, but it was probably in place by the mid-twelfth century; this version has not yet been edited.[100] At present 219 manuscripts, including the two Variant Versions, of *HRB* are known, making it one of the most copied texts in the medieval period.[101] As a comparison, Bede's popular *Historia ecclesiastica* survives in 164 manuscripts.[102] Although *HRB* was first printed in 1508, a reliable edition did not exist until 1929.[103] A new single-manuscript edition by Neil Wright in 1985, and a catalogue and discussion of the dissemination of the text by Julia Crick in 1989, cleared up many of the problems faced by earlier scholars, although some still remain.[104]

John Gillingham's 1992 article on the historical context of *HRB* built upon the work done by Neil Wright and Julia Crick and began to overturn some long-held views regarding the text.[105] These views are best exemplified by Tatlock's 1950 book, which was so comprehensive that it caused a virtual hiatus in Galfridian studies for a generation.[106] Building upon Gillingham's work was Schichtman and Finke's 1993 article, which by applying a postcolonial approach to *HRB*, provided many intriguing new insights and was in turn itself built upon by Michelle Warren in 2000.[107] Later articles by Michael Faletra and Paul Dalton both exemplify how far our knowledge of Geoffrey's reasons for writing his work has progressed since Tatlock wrote.[108]

Sources of *HRB*

Geoffrey claimed that he was able to write *HRB* because he was simply translating 'a very old book in the British tongue'.[109] At the end of the work he mentions it again, with the additional information 'which Walter the Archdeacon of Oxford brought from Britannia'.[110] In the medieval period it was a common feature to claim to have an ancient or obscure source, which is now conveniently lost. Whether such a book actually existed has been the cause of much scholarly debate, and those who allow that such a source may have existed have been divided over the location of Britannia: did Geoffrey mean Brittany or Wales? For his basic historical framework, Geoffrey used *De excidio* by Gildas, Bede's *Historia ecclesiastica*, and *HB*, and he was also aware of Welsh genealogical material, similar to that found in Harleian 3859 and possibly the *vitae* of the Welsh saints discussed above. The ambiguous meaning of the term Britannia in the first half of the twelfth century has already been discussed, but for much of Geoffrey's source material the balance of evidence favours a Welsh origin. If Geoffrey did have access to 'a very old book', it was probably something similar to Harleian 3859 and written in Latin rather than Welsh, although possibly of Welsh origin.[111]

Amongst the 219 manuscripts of *HRB* four different dedications exist, the most important being to Robert of Gloucester; the others are to Waleran of Worcester, King Stephen and Alexander, bishop of Lincoln. References to Llandaf and the saints associated with that see are found throughout *HRB* and Robert of Gloucester was also involved, to some extent, with an earlier work of pseudo-history, the Book of Llandaf, a work composed in the 1130s to bolster the claims of Bishop Urban and his newly created diocese of Llandaf.[112]

Geoffrey's epilogue to *HRB* implores the reader to continue the history of the Saxons by reading Henry of Huntington and William of Malmesbury, and for the history of the Britons the work of his 'contemporary' Caradog of Llancarfan.[113] The *Historia Anglorum* (1129) of Henry of Huntington was dedicated to Alexander, bishop of Lincoln, to whom Geoffrey also dedicated the *Prophecies of Merlin*, and William of Malmesbury's *Gesta regum Anglorum* (1125) was dedicated to Robert of Gloucester. By 1138, the works of these three authors along with the Book of Llandaf are strong evidence for a concerted effort to manipulate the past, and Robert of Gloucester, even if not directly responsible, was certainly aware of all of them.

Caerleon

It is notable that in the story of Arthur, as told in *HRB*, he has nothing to do with Wales apart from the location of his court at Caerleon, which leads us to the obvious question: why did Geoffrey choose Caerleon as the site of Arthur's court? In 1135, despite the best efforts of Henry I to ensure the succession of his daughter Matilda, his death, after thirty-five years of comparative calm, brought chaos. His nephew

Stephen seized the throne, and a protracted civil war broke out between Stephen's forces and those loyal to Matilda and her half-brother Robert of Gloucester.[114] The descent into anarchy on the death of Henry I also led to the Welsh confronting the Anglo-Norman lords, who had taken their lands, in battle. This period was termed the 'great revolt' by Sir John Lloyd, and the Welsh inflicted substantial defeats upon the Normans right across Wales.[115]

In his important article on the historical context of Geoffrey's work, Gillingham draws attention to the status of Caerleon during this period of Welsh success and suggests that this may lie behind Geoffrey's choice for the location of Arthur's court.[116] In 1136 Morgan and Iorwerth, the sons of Owain Wan of Gwynllŵg, ambushed and murdered the powerful Marcher lord Richard de Clare and shortly afterwards captured the castle at Caerleon. The conquest of an Anglo-Norman stronghold in Glamorgan, an area ruled over by Geoffrey's patron Robert of Gloucester, would no doubt have come as a sobering example of how powerful the Welsh could be.[117] It is against the backdrop of this event that the association of King Arthur with Caerleon should be considered, and the extensive remains of the Roman fortress on the site no doubt added an air of authenticity to this newly created facet of the legend. It now seems clear that Geoffrey wrote *HRB* as a pacificatory text to warn his patrons (the major protagonists) that if they did not stop their civil war they would be defeated, just as the Britons had been in the past, by outside forces, this time by the Britons themselves.

Geoffrey's interest in south Wales is apparent elsewhere in *HRB*: he mentions Llandaf (once), Margam (once), Llanbadarn (once) and St David's (three times). Carmarthen is mentioned once in relation to Merlin, and Monmouth, with the nearby hills of Ganerew and Little Doward, appears in association with Vortigern.[118] Gwynedd is named twice in the *Prophecies of Merlin* and again in relation to the later kings, Maelgwn and Cadwaladr. The monks from Bangor-is-y-Coed, slaughtered by the English in the early seventh century, are mistakenly relocated to Bangor in Arfon, and the mountains of Snowdonia are associated with the demise of Vortigern. Whereas the *vitae* had made Arthur *rex Britanniae* (king of Wales) and placed events associated with him in Wales, Geoffrey of Monmouth expanded his sphere of influence to encompass all of the British Isles and continental Europe. This claimed sphere of influence soon caught the attention of chronicle writers and led them to ask the obvious question: if Arthur was so powerful and had fought many battles on the continent, why did none of the continental chronicle writers ever mention him? This line of questioning began to cast doubt on the authenticity of *HRB* and by the late twelfth century, some considered the work of Geoffrey of Monmouth to be an unreliable fantasy.

Gerald of Wales

In 1188 Gerald of Wales accompanied Archbishop Baldwin on a tour around Wales in order to gather support for the second crusade, and in 1191 he published his account of that journey as *Itinerarium Kambriae* (The Journey through Wales).[119] Gerald subsequently revised the work on two occasions, in 1197 and 1214.[120] It has often been argued, on the basis of one much-quoted incident in the *Itinerarium Kambriae*, that Gerald had no love for Geoffrey of Monmouth and his work. Gerald relates the story of Meilyr, who could explain the future and had occult powers, in an incident where he exorcised a man possessed by demons.

> When he was harassed beyond endurance by these unclean spirits, Saint John's Gospel was placed on his lap, and then they all vanished immediately, flying away like so many birds. If the Gospel were afterwards removed and the History of the Kings of Britain by Geoffrey of Monmouth was put there in its place, just to see what would happen, the demons would alight all over his body, and on the book, too, staying there longer than usual and being even more demanding.[121]

Julia Crick has shown that although Gerald may not have liked Geoffrey the person, he was not averse to using his material when it suited him.[122] Throughout his works about Wales, frequent references to people, places and events only otherwise found in *HRB* occur and his campaign for the priority and antiquity of St David's as an archbishopric relied to some extent upon that work, especially the *Prophecies of Merlin*.[123] Two of the three references to Arthur in the *Itinerarium Kambriae* rely upon HRB, referring to Arthur holding his court at Caerleon and St David being his uncle.[124] The remaining reference contains the earliest example of a landscape feature in Wales to be named explicitly after King Arthur:

> To the south by a range of hills the chief of which is *Cadair Arthur*, or Arthur's Chair, so called from two peaks which rise up in the form of a throne. This summit is a very lofty spot and most difficult of access, so that in the minds of simple folk it is thought to have belonged to Arthur, the greatest and most distinguished King of the Britons.[125]

This reference, no doubt due to its early appearance in print in 1585, has been quoted by nearly every author to describe the topography of Wales or discuss the historicity of Arthur. However, despite this reference being so well known, it is rarely discussed in its proper context. [126] Gerald would often write of the Welsh in disparaging terms, no doubt to appeal to the Anglo-Norman world in which he thrived and looked to for promotion.[127] The extract above comes from a section of the *Itinerarum Kambriae* in which Gerald depicts the natives of this area of Breconshire as a superstitious and violent people. Although Gerald may have preserved some sort of native tradition, it is also possible that he was emphasising the image of a superstitious Welsh folk used elsewhere in this work.

Gerald's later work *Descriptio Kambriae* (The Description of Wales), written in 1193, revised in 1215 and again a few years later, is divided into two books, the first describing the geography and people of Wales in a positive manner and the second focusing on the negative aspects of the Welsh.[128] There are thirteen differences, mostly additions, between the first and second editions; one of these refers to Arthur and is important evidence for the use of the Arthurian legend in Wales in the early thirteenth century.[129]

> The Britons maintain that, when Gildas criticized his own people so bitterly, he wrote as he did because he was so infuriated by the fact that King Arthur had killed his own brother, who was a Scottish Chieftain. When he heard of his brother's death, or so the Britons say, he threw into the sea a number of outstanding books, which he had written in their praise and about Arthur's achievements. As a result you will find no book which gives an authentic account of that great prince.[130]

One of the most vexing problems for Arthurian scholars, over many centuries, has been the fact that Gildas's *De excidio*, the only historical text contemporary with the supposed life of Arthur, fails to provide any reference to him. The above extract is one of the earliest attempts to explain this absence. Gerald is also the primary source for another important event in Arthurian scholarship: the exhumation of Arthur's body at Glastonbury in 1191, which he describes in his *De instructione principis* (written between 1193 and 1198) and again in an expanded form in his *Speculum ecclesiae* (*c*.1215).[131] A detailed study of this event is outside the scope of this work, but it does have an impact upon the next text under consideration.

Vera historia de morte Arthuri

The description of Arthur's exhumation by Gerald of Wales was the first to associate the Isle of Avalon, first mentioned in *HRB*, with Glastonbury, in Somerset. A few years later an alternative claim for the location of Avalon was made, in a little-known and peculiar Latin text originating in north Wales. The text, entitled *Vera historia de morte Arthuri* (The True History of the Death of Arthur, henceforth *Vera*), written *c*.1200, survives in London, Grays Inn MS 4 (*c*.1300), originating from the Franciscan friary at Chester.[132] In place of Geoffrey's single and enigmatic line about Arthur's fate, 'he was taken away to the island of Avalon to have his wounds tended', the *Vera* provides a detailed narrative of events during the battle of Camlan, Arthur's journey to Avalon and his subsequent funeral.[133] The alternative identification for the location of Avalon appears with Arthur lying wounded at Camlan: 'At length the king, slightly restored by an improvement in his condition, gives orders to be taken to Gwynedd, since he had decided to sojourn in the delightful Isle of Avalon.'[134] Arthur is then visited by the archbishop of London, Urien of Bangor and Urbegen of Glamorgan to whom he confesses his sins, before settling the rule of Britain on Constantine. The author of the *Vera* then describes the funeral rites of the deceased king after his body was taken to a small chapel dedicated to St Mary. The chapel was so small that his body had to be left outside during the funeral and whilst it was taking place, a great storm occurred. When the mist had cleared, Arthur's body was missing and the tomb that had been prepared for him appeared to be sealed, but nobody knew where his body had gone.

The *Vera* is the only text to locate the Isle of Avalon in Gwynedd and to describe Arthur's funeral, thereby filling an obvious gap in the narrative of his life as described by Geoffrey, for which reason at least one copy has been found inserted at the relevant place in a manuscript of *HRB*.[135] References within the text to St David's as an archbishopric suggest that the *Vera* was composed during the campaign by Welsh ecclesiastics for the see of St David's to be recognised as an archbishopric, independent of Canterbury.[136] The most important witness to this claim is Gerald of Wales, who made three trips to Rome to promote the cause during the years 1199–1203, and letters of support survive from Llywelyn ap Iorwerth showing that there was interest in this matter in Gwynedd.[137] A connection to Llywelyn ap Iorwerth and the presence of an abbreviated version of the text in a manuscript from Hailes Abbey in Gloucestershire, has led to the suggestion that the text was written at the Cistercian abbey of Aberconwy on the north Wales coast, which is known to have had connections with Hailes in the thirteenth century.[138] The Cistercian monastery of Aberconwy was founded by Llywelyn ap Iorwerth in 1198, and there is evidence that both the Cistericans and the mendicant orders in Gwynedd were often involved in diplomatic meetings on his behalf.[139] The *Vera* provides strong evidence that there was an interest in the Arthurian legend amongst the ecclesiastical orders in north Wales at the turn of the thirteenth century, but the fact that so few manuscripts exist, and those that do survived in England and Italy, may account for the lack of reference to the material elsewhere in Welsh sources.

The Latin Arthurian Romances

Dozens of Arthurian romances were composed in the medieval period, but only four survive that were written in Latin.[140] In common with the romances written in French and German, the court of Arthur acts primarily as a backdrop against which events unfold and Arthur himself only appears in a supporting role to the main hero of the tale. The *Historia Meriadoci regis Cambrie* is the only one to provide any details of Welsh topography beyond the references to Caerleon derived from *HRB*.[141] The reader is left in no doubt that Wales is the setting for the first part of the tale, as Meiriadoc is called the king of *Cambria*, instead of the ambiguous *Britannia*. Only two Welsh place names occur: the snow-capped peak called *Snawdown*, which is easily identifiable as Snowdon, and the forest of *Arglud*. Day associates *Arglud* with *Alclud*, a Welsh term used for Dumbarton on the river Clyde in Scotland, but the internal geography of the tale (if such a thing can be relied upon) states that the site could be reached in less than a day from Snowdon.[142] This suggests that the forest of *Arglud* may have been intended to have some connection with the river Clwyd, referred to in Domesday Book and documents from the twelfth and thirteenth century as the *Clud* or *Clut*, and only a day's journey from Snowdon.[143] The date of the romance remains controversial, with some suggesting it could date from *c*.1150, whilst others have suggested that a date in the first half of the thirteenth century is more likely.[144]

Conclusion

The Latin texts discussed in this chapter are amongst the earliest sources of the Arthurian legend and are responsible for the place names that form the spine of the Arthurian legend: the twelve battles, Camlan and Caerleon. *HB* originated in north Wales and then there was a gap of over 250 years before Arthur reappeared in the *vitae* of four saints from south Wales. These hagiographical texts were written at a time when the Norman Church was encroaching into Wales and the major churches needed to justify the lands they claimed. The need to record the details of their properties and their boundaries is one of the main reasons behind the composition of the hagiographical texts at this time. Arthur's role in these works is to come into conflict with the saints and, following his inevitable defeat, grant the Church lands.

The *vitae* are also the earliest source to depict Arthur as a king and, along with the references in William of Malmesbury and Henry of Huntingdon, show that the legend of Arthur was already developing beyond that found in the ninth-century *Historia Brittonum*. Geoffrey of Monmouth was the first to create a biography of Arthur and place his activities in a firm geographical setting, spanning from Cornwall to Scotland and ultimately most of western Europe. Considering how important *HRB* was to become to the Welsh in later centuries, it is ironic that it only associates Arthur with one place in Wales, the remains of the Roman fortress at Caerleon. Gerald of Wales also reflects the south Wales bias of these twelfth-century sources in his reference to Cadair Arthur: he makes no such associations in north Wales. The *Historia Meriadoci* is the only one of the four Latin Arthurian romances to refer to north Wales, but as the next chapter will show, the region was to play an important role in the French Arthurian Romances that came to dominate the image of Arthur in the early thirteenth century.

Notes

1   N. J. Higham, *King Arthur: Myth-Making and History* (London, 2002), pp. 74–7, discusses the various suggestions.

2   David N. Dumville, '*Historia Brittonum*: An Insular History from the Carolingian age', in Anton Scharer and Georg Scheibelreiter (eds), *Historiographie im frühen Mittelalter* (Institut für Österreichische Geschichtsforschung, Veröffentlichungen, 32) (Vienna, 1994), pp. 415–17.

3   David Dumville, 'Some Aspects of the Chronology of the *Historia Brittonum*', *Bulletin of the Board of Celtic Studies*, 25 (1972–4), 439.

4   A. W. Wade-Evans, *Nennius's The History of the Britons* (London, 1938), p. 43.

5   T. M. Charles-Edwards, *Wales and the Britons 350–1064* (Oxford, 2013), pp. 467–79.

6   Ben Guy, 'The Origins of the Compilation of Welsh Historical Texts in Harley 3859', *Studia Celtica*, 49 (2015), 45–55; Nora K. Chadwick, 'Early culture and learning in north Wales', in Nora K. Chadwick, Kathleen Hughes, Christopher Brooke and Kenneth Jackson (eds), *Studies in the Early British Church* (Cambridge, 1958), pp. 29–120.

7   N. J. Higham, *King Arthur*, pp. 98–169. For an alternative view, see Charles-Edwards *Wales and the Britons*, pp. 450–2.

8   David Dumville (ed.), *The Historia Brittonum, 3: The Vatican Recension* (Cambridge, 1985), p. 3 outlines the various recensions.

9   David N. Dumville, 'The textual history of the Welsh-Latin *Historia Brittonum*' (unpublished DPhil thesis, University of Edinburgh, 1975); *idem*, 'The Corpus Christi "Nennius"', *Bulletin of the Board of Celtic Studies*, 25 (1972–4), 369–80; *idem*, 'The Textual History of "Lebor Bretnach": A Preliminary Study', *Éigse: A Journal of Irish Studies*, 16 (1975/6), 255–73; *idem*, 'An Irish Idiom Latinised', *Éigse: A Journal of Irish Studies*, 16 (1976), 183–6; and *idem*, 'Celtic-Latin Texts in Northern England c.1150–c.1250', *Celtica*, 12 (1977), 19–49. Articles reprinted with additional notes and the same pagination in David Dumville, *Histories and Pseudo-Histories of the Insular Middle Ages* (Aldershot, 1990).

10   John Prise, *Historiae Brytannicae Defensio* (London, 1573), pp. 114–19; Thomas Gale (ed.), *Historiae Britannicae, Saxonicae, Anglo-Danicae scriptores*, XV (Oxford, 1691), pp. 93–139.

11   Rev. W. Gunn (ed. and trans.), *The "Historia Brittonum" commonly attributed to Nennius, from a manuscript lately discovered in the library of the Vatican Palace at Rome; edited in the tenth century by Mark the Hermit; with an English version* (London, 1819); Joseph Stevenson (ed.), *Nennii Historia Britonum ad fidem codicum manuscriptorum* (London, 1838); Theodor Mommsen (ed.), *Monumenta Germaniae Historica, Auctores Antiquissimi, xii: Chronica Minora saec IV, V, VI, VII*, vol. 3 (Berlin, 1898), pp. 111–222. This work is now available online at *www.dmgh.de*

12   Wade-Evans, *Nennius*; John Morris (ed. and trans.), *Nennius, the British History and the Welsh Annals* (Chichester, 1980).

13   Guy, 'Origins', 21–2.

14   Dumville, *Vatican Recension*, pp. 24–9.

15   Dumville, *Vatican Recension*, p. 4

16   Dumville, 'The Corpus Christi "Nennius"'.

17   Wade-Evans, *Nennius*, p. 75 with minor alterations and variants in parenthesis from Dumville, *Vatican Recension*, pp.103–4.

18   Higham, *King Arthur*, p. 142; Judith McClure and Roger Collins (eds and trans. *Bede: The Ecclesiastical History of the English People, The Greater Chronicle and Bede's Letter to Egbert* (Oxford, 1994), p. 327.

19   Higham, *King Arthur*, pp. 141–4.

20   R. A. B, Mynors, R. M. Thomson and M. Winterbottom (eds), *William of Malmesbury: Gesta Regvm Anglorvm, The History of the English Kings*, I (Oxford, 1998), p. 27. The association with Badon is also found in the *Annales Cambriae*.

21   Diana Greenway (ed. and trans.), *Henry, Archdeacon of Huntingdon: Historia Anglorum: The History of the English People* (Oxford, 1996), pp. 99–101.

22   Michael Winterbottom (ed. and trans.), *Gildas: The Ruin of Britain and Other Documents* (London, 1978), p. 98; and B. Colgrave and R. A. B. Mynors (eds), *Bede's Ecclesiastical History of the English People* (Oxford, 1992), p. 54.

23   C. Babington and J. R. Lumby (eds), *Polychronicon Ranulphi Higden monachi Cestrensis*, 9 vols, Rolls Series, 41 (1865–86), V, p. 328.

24 Nikolai Tolstoy, 'Nennius, Chapter Fifty-Six', *Bulletin of the Board of Celtic Studies*, 19 (1960–2), 118–62; the extensive bibliography can be found on 154–6. The best overview of the various ideas up to 1945 can be found in Kenneth Jackson, 'Once Again Arthur's Battles', *Modern Philology*, 43 (1945), 44–57, and most modern ideas as to the location of the battles are frequently based on works discussed there.

25 William F. Skene, *The Four Ancient Books of Wales*, 2 vols (Edinburgh, 1868), I, pp. 52–8; W. G. Collingwood, 'Arthur's Battles', *Antiquity*, 3 (1929), 292: 'The rest of Arthur's battle-sites listed by Nennius are incredible, as placed up to the present, not so much because Nennius is suspect as because they have been located in districts where Arthur – if he existed – could not have fought Saxons'; A. Anscombe, 'Local Names in the "Arthuriana" in the "Historia Brittonum"', *Zeitschrift für Celtische Philologie*, 5 (1904), 103–23.

26 Andrew Breeze, 'The Historical Arthur and Sixth Century Scotland', *Northern History*, 52 (2015), 158–81, is a recent attempt.

27 Mommsen, *Chronica Minora*, III, pp. 213–19; Wade-Evans, *Nennius*, pp. 116–21, provides a translation and also places the *Mirabilia* in their correct position in relation to the text of *HB* in Harleian 3859.

28 Andrew J. Evans, John Nettleship and Steven Perry, '*Linn Liuan / Llynn Llyw*: The Wondrous Lake of the *Historia Brittonum's de Mirabilibus Britanniae* and *Culhwch ac Olwen*', *Folklore*, 119/3 (2008), 295–318.

29 Edward J. Gwynn (ed. and trans.), *The Metrical Dindshenchas*, 4 vols (1903–6).

30 Dumville, 'The Historical Value of the *Historia Brittonum*', *Arthurian Literature*, 6 (1986), 22, notes that an unpublished study by Kenneth Jackson of the Welsh forms in the *Mirabilia* suggests that they date from the ninth century, like the rest of the text, but our understanding of the development of Welsh in this period is now much improved.

31 Wade-Evans, *Nennius*, pp. 119–20: 'Est aliud mirabile in regione que dicitur Buelt. Est ibi cumulus lapidum, et unus lapis superpositus super congestum cum uestigio canis in eo. Quando uenatus est porcum (Troyt), impressit Caball qui erat canis Arthuri militis uestigium in lapide; et Arthur postea congregauit congestum lapidum sub lapide in quo erat uestigium canis sui, et uocatur carnn Caball. Et ueniunt homines et tollunt lapidem in manibus suis per spatium diei et noctis; et in crastino die inuenitur super congestum suum'; Mommsen, *Chronica Minora*, p. 217.

32 Peter C. Bartrum, *A Welsh Classical Dictionary* (Aberystwyth, 1993), p. 13.

33 Wade-Evans, *Nennius*, p. 120: 'Est aliud miraculum in regione que uocatur Ercing. Habetur ibi sepulchrum iuxta fontem qui cognominatur Licat A(m)r. Et uiri nomen qui sepultus est in tumulo sic uocabatur A(m)r; filius Arthuri militia erat, et ipse occidit eum ibidem et sepeliuit. Et ueniunt homines ad mensurandum tumulum – in longitudine aliquando sex pedes, aliquando nouem, aliquando duodecim, aliquando quindecim. In qua mensura metieris eum in ista uice, iterum non inuenies eum in una mensura. Et ego solus probaui'; Mommsen, *Chronica Minora*, pp. 217–18.

34 Frank and Caroline Thorn (eds), *Domesday Book*, XVII: *Herefordshire* (Chichester, 1982), 1.50.

35 J. Gwenogvryn Evans and John Rhys (eds), *The Text of the Book of Llan Dâv* (Oxford, 1893), p. 174; Jonathan Baron Coe, 'The place-names of the Book of Llandaf' (unpublished PhD thesis, University of Wales, Aberystwyth, 2001), 297–8.

36 Wendy Davies, *The Llandaff Charters* (Aberystwyth, 1979).

37 For a detailed discussion of other possibilities and information about all of the *Mirabilia*, see *www.wondersofbritain.org* (accessed 22 March 2016).

38   Evans and Rhys, *Book of Llan Dâv*, p. 277.

39   Egerton Phillimore, 'The *Annales Cambriae* and Old Welsh Genealogies from *Harleian MS. 3859*', *Y Cymmrodor*, 9 (1888), 141–83, remains the best edition.

40   Guy, 'Origins', discusses the development of the annals in detail and suggests that they were initially compiled at Abergele *c*.858, then supplemented with material at St David's *c*.954 before being copied into Harley 3859 at Canterbury *c*.1100.

41   The B and C texts have been re-edited by Henry Gough Cooper and are available at *http://croniclau.bangor.ac.uk/editions.php.en* (accessed 12 January 2016). Important discussions of the annals can be found in Kathleen Hughes, 'The Welsh Latin chronicles: *Annales Cambriae* and related texts', in David Dumville (ed.), *Celtic Britain in the Early Middle Ages* (Wood-bridge, 1980), p. 68, and Kathryn Grabowski and David Dumville (eds), *Chronicles and Annals of Mediaeval Ireland and Wales: The Clonmacnoise-Group* (Woodbridge, 1984), pp. 209–26. For an English translation see, Paul Martin Remfry (trans.), *Annales Cambriae: A Translation of Harleian 3859: PRO E. 164/1: Cottonian Domitian, A1: Exeter Cathedral Library MS. 3514 and MS Exchequer DB Neath, PRO E. 164/1* (n.p. 2007).

42   Phillimore, 'The Annales Cambriae', 154.

43   Wade-Evans, *Nennius*, p. 86.

44   The reference to Arthur carrying the image on his shoulder may have arisen due to a misun-derstanding of the Welsh words *scuit* for shield and *scuid* for shoulder.

45   J. E. Caerwyn Williams and Peredur I. Lynch (eds), *Gwaith Meilyr Brydydd a'i Ddisgynyddion* (Cardiff, 1994), p. 71, line 25 and p. 142, line 8.

46   Rachel Bromwich, *Trioedd Ynys Prydein*, third edn (Cardiff, 2006), pp. 169–70.

47   Guy, 'Origins', 55.

48   John Reuben Davies, 'The saints of south Wales and the Welsh Church', in A. Thacker and R. Sharpe (eds), *Local Saints and Local Churches in the Early Medieval West* (Oxford, 2002), pp. 361–95.

49   St Patrick can be found in sections 50–5, and Garmon in sections 32–5, 39 and 47 of *HB*. The Life of St Patrick from the *Book of Armagh* can be read in Ludwig Bieler (ed. and trans.), *The Patrician Texts in the Book of Armagh: Scriptores Latini Hiberniae*, X (Dublin, 1979).

50   Davies, 'The saints of south Wales', p.384.

51   Richard Sharpe and John Reuben Davies, 'Rhygyfarch's Life of St David', in J. Wyn Evans and Jonathan M. Wooding (eds), *St David of Wales: Cult, Church and Nation* (Woodbridge, 2007), pp. 107–55.

52   John Reuben Davies, *The Book of Llandaf and the Norman Church in Wales* (Woodbridge, 2003), p. 76.

53   A. W. Wade-Evans (ed. and trans.), *Vitae sanctorum Britanniae et genealogiae* (Cardiff, 1944; reprint edn Cardiff, 2013), pp. viii–xi.

54   Silas M. Harris, 'The Calendar of the Vitae Sanctorum Wallensium', *Journal of the Historical Society of the Church in Wales*, 3 (1953), 3–53; and P. C. Bartrum, *Early Welsh Genealogical Tracts* (Cardiff, 1966), pp. 14–16.

55   Kathleen Hughes, 'British Library MS. Cotton Vespasian A. XIV (*Vitae Sanctorum Wallen-sium*): its purpose and provenance', in Dumville (ed.), *Celtic Britain in the Early Middle Ages*, pp. 53–66.

56   Davies, *Book of Llandaf and the Norman Church*, pp. 132–42.

57   P. Grosjean, 'Vie de Saint Cadoc par Caradoc de Llancarfan', *Analecta Bollandiana*, 60 (1942), 35–67.

58   Hywel D. Emanuel, 'The Latin Life of St Cadoc: a textual and lexicographical study'

(unpublished MA dissertation, University of Wales, 1950); Hywel D. Emanuel, 'An Analysis of the Composition of the "Vita Cadoci"', *National Library of Wales Journal*, 7 (1951–2), 217–27.

59   Wade-Evans, *Vitae Sanctorum*, pp. 26–7.

60   Huw Pryce (ed.), *Acts of the Welsh Rulers 1120–1283* (Cardiff, 2005), p. 813.

61   Pryce, *Acts of the Welsh Rulers*, p. 814. See Gazetteer GLA for more information.

62   Wade-Evans, *Vitae Sanctorum*, pp. 68–9: 'In eodem igitur tempore dux quidam Britannorum fortissimus, uocabulo Ligessauc, filius Eliman, cognomento quoque Lau hiir, id est, longa manus, tres milites Arthurii, regis illustrissimi Brittannie, trucidauit.'

63   'qui uallum magnum inter Britanniam atque Mercian de mari usque ad mare fieri imperauit'; William Henry Stevenson (ed.), *Asser's Life of King Alfred* (Oxford, 1959), p. 12. Translation in Simon Keynes and Michael Lapidge, *Alfred the Great, Asser's Life of King Alfred and Other Contemporary Sources* (Harmondsworth, 1983), p. 71.

64   Keynes and Lapidge, *Alfred the Great*, p. 74.

65   Huw Pryce, 'British or Welsh? National Identity in Twelfth-Century Wales', *English Historical Review*, 115 (2001), 780.

66   Pryce, 'British or Welsh?', 797–8.

67   Wade-Evans, *Vitae Sanctorum*, pp. 72–3: 'Ab illo enim die ille Brittannico fatu Tref redinauc i[d est], uilla filicis, uocatur, Illud quoque uadum, circa quod placitum erat, Rith guurtebou nuncupatur.'

68   Wade-Evans, *Vitae Sanctorum*, p. xiii.

69   For a modern discussion of Carannog see, Karen Jankulak, 'Carantoc alias Cairnech? British saints, Irish saints, and the Irish in Wales', in Karen Jankulak and Jonathan M. Wooding (eds), *Ireland and Wales in the Middle Ages* (Dublin, 2007), pp. 116–48.

70   Wade-Evans, *Vitae Sanctorum*, p.145.

71   Wade-Evans, *Nennius*, p. 116.

72   Wade-Evans, *Vitae Sanctorum*, p. 215; Davies, *The Book of Llandaf*, p. 133.

73   This assumes that a date in the 1120s is secure; for an 1140 date see Wade-Evans, *Vitae Sanctorum*, p. xii. The forced nature of the Arthurian episode makes a post-Geoffrey of Monmouth date more likely.

74   Wade-Evans, *Vitae Sanctorum*, p. xiv. Charles Thomas and David Howlett, 'Vita Sancti Paterni: The Life of Saint Padarn and the Original Miniu', *Trivium*, 33 (2003), 76, argue for a date of c.1080.

75   Wade-Evans, *Vitae Sanctorum*, p. 261.

76   Wade-Evans, *Vitae Sanctorum*, p. 261.

77   Wade-Evans, *Vitae Sanctorum*, p. 27.

78   Hugh Williams (ed. and trans.), *Gildas*, Cymmrodorion Record Series No. 3, 2 vols (London, 1899–1901), I, pp. 317–21 for a discussion on the dating of the text.

79   Dumville, 'The Corpus Christi "Nennius"'. The text was printed by Mommsen in 1898 and reprinted with a facing translation in 1901 in Williams, *Gildas*, II, pp. 390–413.

80   Williams, *Gildas*, II, p. 403.

81   For a detailed discussion of this motif, see K. T. Webster, *Guinevere: A Study of Her Abductions* (Milton, 1951).

82   Bromwich, *Trioedd Ynys Prydein*, p. 379.

83   A Welsh poem known as 'The Dialogue of Melwas and Gwenhwyfar', found in two late manuscripts, the earliest dating from the mid-sixteenth century, associates Melwas, Gwenhwyfar and Cei, although not Arthur, in a similar story. See Evan D. Jones, 'Melwas, Gwenhwyfar, a Chai', *Bulletin of the Board of Celtic Studies*, 8 (1937), 203–8.

84   Pryce, *Acts of the Welsh Rulers*, p. 168.

85   B. G. Charles, 'An Early Charter of the Abbey of Cwmhir', *Radnorshire Society Transactions*, 40 (1970), 68–74; G. T. Clark (ed.), *Cartae et alia munimenta quae ad dominium de Glamorgancia pertinent*, 6 vols (Cardiff, 1910), II, p. 289.

86   Cardigan was mentioned by Chrétien de Troyes in the 1170s and is discussed in chapter 2.

87   Elissa Henken, *Traditions of the Welsh Saints* (Woodbridge, 1987), pp. 301–6.

88   Neil Ker, *English Manuscripts in the Century after the Norman Conquest: The Lyell Lectures 1952–3* (Oxford, 1960), p. 8.

89   Mynors, Thomson and Winterbottom (eds), *Gesta Regvm Anglorvm* (Oxford, 1998), I, p. 27.

90   Mynors and Winterbottom (eds), *Gesta Regvm Anglorvm*, p. 521. The critical apparatus shows that Rhos was not named in the earliest version of the text.

91   Michael D. Reeve (ed.) and Neil Wright (trans.), *Geoffrey of Monmouth, The History of the Kings of Britain: An Edition and Translation of De Gestis Britonum [Historia Regum Britanniae]* (Woodbridge, 2007); Neil Wright, 'The place of Henry of Huntingdon's *Epistola ad Warinumin* in the text-history of Geoffrey of Monmouth's *Historia regum Britannie*: a preliminary investigation', in Gillian Jondorf and David N. Dumville (eds), *France and the British Isles in the Middle Ages* (Woodbridge, 1991), pp. 71–113.

92   Christopher N. L Brooke, *The Church and the Welsh Border in the Central Middle Ages* (Woodbridge, 1986), p. 106.

93   J. C. Crick, 'Monmouth, Geoffrey of (d. 1154/5)', *Oxford Dictionary of National Biography* (Oxford, 2004).

94   J. P. S. Tatlock, *The Legendary History of Britain* (Berkeley, 1950), pp. 72–3. This monumental work is an essential starting point for any detailed study of the life and works of Geoffrey of Monmouth.

95   H. E. Salter, 'Geoffrey of Monmouth and Oxford', *English Historical Review*, 34 (1919), 383.

96   Online edition at *www.fordham.edu/halsall/basis/williamofnewburgh-one.html#epistle* (accessed 1 July 2014); 'Gaufridus hic dictus est, agnomen habens Arturi, pro priscis Britonum figmerio auctas, per superductum Latini sermonis colorem honesto historiae nomine palliavit'; R. Howlett (ed.), *Chronicles of the Reigns of Stephen, Henry II and Richard I*, I (London, 1884), p. 11.

97   Basil Clarke (ed. and trans.), *Life of Merlin* (Cardiff, 1973); John Reuben Davies, 'Bishop Kentigern amongst the Britons', in Steve Boardman, John Reuben Davies and Elia Williamson (eds), *Saints' Cults in the Celtic Worlds* (Woodbridge, 2009), pp. 66–90.

98   Thomas Jones (ed. and trans.), *Brut y Tywysogyon: The Chronicle of the Princes, Red Book of Hergest Version* (Cardiff, 1955), p. 132.

99   Neil Wright (ed.), *Historia Regum Britannie of Geoffrey of Monmouth II: The First Variant Version: A Critical Edition* (Cambridge, 1988).

100 For a discussion of the Second Variant see, H. D. Emanuel, 'Geoffrey of Monmouth's *Historia Regum Britannie*: A Second Variant Version', *Medium Ævum*, 35 (1966), 103–8.

101 Reeves and Wright, *Geoffrey of Monmouth*, pp. vii–viii.

102 Julia Crick, *Historia Regum Britannie of Geoffrey of Monmouth III: A Summary Catalogue of the Manuscripts* (Cambridge, 1989), p. 9; Reeves and Wright, *Geoffrey of Monmouth*, pp. vii–viii, gives a brief overview of new manuscripts discovered since the publication of Crick's catalogue.

103 Reeves and Wright, *Geoffrey of Monmouth*, pp. lxii–lxiv, for a discussion of the printing history of the text.

104 Neil Wright (ed.) *Historia Regum Britannie of Geoffrey of Monmouth I: Bern, Burgerbibliothek, MS 568* (Cambridge, 1985); and Crick, *A Summary Catalogue*.

105 John Gillingham, 'The Context and Purposes of Geoffrey of Monmouth's History of the Kings of Britain', *Anglo-Norman Studies*, 13 (1992), 99–118.

106 Tatlock, *Legendary History*.

107 Martin Schichtman and Laurie Finke, 'Profiting from the Past: History as Symbolic Culture in the *Historia Regum Britanniae*', *Arthurian Literature*, 12 (1993), 1–35; and Michelle A. Warren, *History on the Edge: Excalibur and the Borders of Britain, 1100–1300* (Minneapolis, 2000).

108 Michael A. Faletra, 'Narrating the Matter of Britain: Geoffrey of Monmouth and the Norman Colonization of Wales', *Chaucer Review*, 35 (2000), 60–85; and Paul Dalton, 'The Topical Concerns of Geoffrey of Monmouth's *Historia Regum Britannie*: History, Prophecy and Peacemaking, and English Identity in the Twelfth Century', *Journal of British Studies*, 44 (2005), 688–712.

109 Reeves and Wright, *Geoffrey of Monmouth*, p. 4: 'quendam Britannici sermonis librum uetustissimum'.

110 Reeves and Wright, *Geoffrey of Monmouth*, p. 280: 'quem Gualterus Oxenfordensis archidiaconus ex Britannia aduexit'. Walter the Archdeacon of Oxford is often confused with Walter Map, deacon to Henry II some fifty years later; they are *not* the same person.

111 Stuart Piggott, 'The Sources of Geoffrey of Monmouth', *Antiquity*, 15 (1941), 269–86.

112 Davies, *The Book of Llandaf*, passim.

113 Reeves and Wright, *Geoffrey of Monmouth*, p. 280.

114 Marjorie Chibnall, 'Matilda (1102–1167)', *Oxford Dictionary of National Biography* (Oxford, 2004).

115 John E. Lloyd, *A History of Wales: From the Earliest Times to the Edwardian Conquest*, third edn (London, 1939), pp. 469–80.

116 Gillingham, 'Context and Purposes', 112–16.

117 David Crouch, 'The Slow Death of Kingship in Glamorgan, 1067–1158', *Morgannwg*, 29 (1985), 33.

118 Tatlock, *Legendary History*, pp. 66–70.

119 James F. Dimock (ed.), *Giraldi Cambrensis Opera*, VI: *Itinerarium Kambriae et descriptio Kambriae* (London, 1868), pp. 3–152; and an English translation in Lewis Thorpe (trans.), *Gerald of Wales, The Journey through Wales and The Description of Wales* (Harmondsworth, 1978), pp. 63–209.

120 Thorpe, *Gerald of Wales*, pp. 37–9.

121 Thorpe, *Gerald of Wales*, pp. 117–18.

122 Julia Crick, 'The British Past and the Welsh Future: Gerald of Wales, Geoffrey of Monmouth and Arthur of Britain', *Celtica*, 23 (1999), 70.

123 Crick, 'The British Past', 71.

124 Thorpe, *Gerald of Wales*, pp. 115 and 160.

125 Thorpe, *Gerald of Wales*, p. 96. The Latin text actually reads *Kair Arthur*, but the subsequent reference to Arthur's Chair, suggests that *Kadeir Arthur* was intended; Dimock, *Opera*, VI, p. 36.

126 First printed as David Powel (ed.), *Pontici Virunnii viri doctissimi Britannicae historiae libri sex magna et fide et diligentia conscripti: ad Britannici codicis fidem correcti, & ab infinitis mendis liberati: quibus praefixus est catalogus regum Britanniae* (London, 1585) with *Itinerarii Cambriae* on pp. 49–230 and *Cambriae Descriptio* on pp. 231–77.

127 Robert Bartlett, *Gerald of Wales: A Voice of the Middle Ages* (Stroud, 2006), pp. 147–53.

128 Dimock, *Opera*, VI, pp. 144–227; and an English translation in Thorpe, *Gerald of Wales*, pp. 211–74.

129 Thorpe, *Gerald of Wales*, pp. 278–9.

130 Thorpe, *Gerald of Wales*, p. 259.

131 The exact date of *De instructione principis* remains uncertain; Crick, 'The British Past', 72. For more on Arthur at Glastonbury see the collection of articles gathered together in James P. Carley (ed.), *Glastonbury Abbey and the Arthurian Tradition* (Cambridge, 2001).

132 M. Lapidge, 'The *Vera historia de morte Arthuri*: a new edition', in Carley, *Glastonbury Abbey*, pp. 115–41.

133 Reeves and Wright, *Geoffrey of Monmouth*, p. 252.

134 Lapidge, '*Vera historia*', p. 137, 'denique rex, parumper melioracioni restitutus, iubet se tran-suehi ad Venedociam, quia in Auallonis insula delectabili propter loci amenitatem.'

135 Richard Barber, 'Addendum on the *Vera historia de morte Arthuri*', in Carley, *Glastonbury Abbey*, p. 143.

136 Lapidge, '*Vera historia*', p. 125.

137 Pryce, *Acts of the Welsh Rulers*, pp. 368–71.

138 Lapidge, '*Vera historia*', p. 128.

139 Glyn Roberts, *Aspects of Welsh History* (Cardiff, 1969), p. 230.

140 For an edition and translation of the texts see Mildred Leake Day (ed. and trans.), *Latin Arthurian Literature* (Cambridge, 2005), and for a broader discussion, Sian Echard, *Arthurian Narrative in the Latin Tradition* (Cambridge, 1998).

141 Day, *Latin Arthurian Literature*, pp. 122–207.

142 Day, *Latin Arthurian Literature*, p. 132 and note on p. 261.

143 The Clwyd was variously spelt in the medieval period as *Clud*, *Clut*, *Cloit*, *Cluyt* and *Cluit*; see Ellis Davies, *Flintshire Placenames* (Cardiff, 1959), p. 36, and for further examples the index entry for Dyffryn Clwyd in Pryce, *Acts of the Welsh Rulers*, p. 840.

144 Day, *Latin Arthurian Literature*, pp. 2–11. For opposing views see, Helen Nicholson, 'Following the Path of the Lionheart: The *De Ortu Walwanii* and the *Itinerarium Peregrinorum et Gesta Regis Ricardi*', *Medium Ævum*, 69 (2000), 21–33; and Martin Aurell, 'Henry II and Arthurian legend', in Christopher Harper-Bill and Nicholas Vincent (eds), *Henry II: New Interpretations* (Woodbridge, 2007), p. 369.

TWO
The FRENCh ARThURIAN ROMANCES

T HIS CHAPTER WILL EXAMINE the references to Welsh place names in French Arthurian romances, with occasional reference to those written in Anglo-Norman, Middle English and German, in the period from 1170 to 1485. Over 500 medieval manuscripts of Arthurian romance survive in French alone, which gives an indication of the popularity of the material. When we also consider the large number of translations and adaptations into German, Old Norse, Spanish, Middle Dutch, Portuguese and Italian, the surviving manuscripts number more than 800 and reveal an audience that covered western Europe.[1] Nearly all of the surviving French romances refer to *Gales* (Wales) as a kingdom or region and many also mention towns, castles and topographical features within it, yet little work exists that examines these topographical clues in detail. A detailed study of this topic requires a volume in its own right and this chapter is only intended as an introduction to the material and to highlight the potential for further study. The possibility that Arthurian place names, first attested during this period, on the lands owned by the Marcher lords may have arisen because of their interest in Arthurian matters will also be discussed. The medieval Arthurian material in Welsh will be dealt with separately in the following chapter.

Before discussing the French Arthurian romances, it is important to understand their source material. The rise of Henry II to the throne in 1153 seems to have been the catalyst for the production of an adaptation of *Historia regum Britanniae* (*HRB*) by Geoffrey of Monmouth into the Anglo-Norman vernacular by Wace, a poet originally from Jersey and active in the town of Caen in Normandy.[2] His *Roman de Brut* appeared in 1155 and adapted the narrative written by Geoffrey of Monmouth into rhyming octosyllabic lines. Wace also made many minor additions to his text, including an expanded note on the origin of the name of Wales, a reference to the British prophet Taliesin and, perhaps most famously of all, the first mention of the Round Table.[3] The work of Wace is an important transitional step from the pseudo-history of *HRB* to the courtly romances of Chrétien de Troyes.

In the latter half of its Arthurian narrative, *HRB* briefly notes that Arthur reigned in peace for twelve years, before the wars with the Romans and his final battle at Camlan.[4] It is during this period of peace that the adventures of the Knights of the Round Table and the Grail quest take place. Wace expands upon the brief reference in *HRB* and notes that

> In this time of great peace I speak of – I do not know if you have heard of it – the wondrous events appeared and the adventures were sought out which, whether for love of his generosity, or for fear of his bravery, are so often told about Arthur that they have become the stuff of fiction: not all lies, not all truth, neither total folly nor total wisdom. The raconteurs have told so many yarns, the story-tellers so many stories, to embellish their tales that they have made it all appear fiction.[5]

French Arthurian Romances

The French Arthurian romances were produced in a period from the early 1170s to *c.*1280. The earliest works were written solely in verse, but after the turn of the thirteenth century, they became increasingly written in prose form. The focus of this chapter is to discuss the earliest appearance of a place name and its context. It is not intended to discuss the appearance of the place name in later texts in any detail, as that discussion is beyond the scope of this work.

Nearly all of the French Arthurian romance material has now been edited, and the most important texts have been translated, although some can only be consulted in antiquated editions.[6] The references to British geography in medieval French literature were studied by Rickard in his 1956 book on the subject, but Wales was dealt with only briefly.[7] The most detailed works on the topic, relevant to Wales, are a monograph and two articles by J. Neale Carman focusing upon *Perlesvaus* and *Mort Artu*, an article by Rosemary Morris concerned primarily with topography in the works of Chrétien de Troyes, and the influential place-name identifications of Roger S. Loomis.[8] The French Arthurian verse romances were indexed by G. D. West in *An Index of Proper Names in French Arthurian Verse Romances 1150–1300* (1969).[9] The slightly later, but more extensive, prose romances received a similar treatment in 1978, and both works are invaluable.[10]

French Verse Romances

The earliest French Arthurian romances were written in verse, and *Erec et Enide*, dating from the early 1170s, by Chrétien de Troyes is considered the first major work of the genre. Many of the later French verse romances built upon the work of Chrétien, often at great length, some of them running to over 30,000 lines, until abruptly ending with Girart d'Amiens's *Escanor c.*1280.[11] Although these romances were written in French, it is important to remember that the nobility in England was predominately

French-speaking in the twelfth and thirteenth centuries and, as Keith Busby notes, 'to define English and French literature in merely linguistic terms corresponds to modern preconceptions of ethnic and national identity and creates a highly distorted view of the medieval reality.'[12] The likelihood that many of the Arthurian verse romances were intended for an English, or perhaps more accurately, Anglo-Angevin, audience, makes the references to Wales within them all the more relevant.[13] As Michael Faletra notes, 'Anglo-Norman ambitions and fantasies about colonizing and annexing Wales were a critical impetus behind the sudden flourishing of the Matters of Britain as a literary and courtly phenomenon.'[14]

The verse romances also make reference to a region called Estre Gales (Beyond Wales), but the exact location intended by this term is uncertain and varies between different tales.[15] Ceridwen Lloyd-Morgan notes that 'although events in French Arthurian romances are often localised in what purports to be Wales, the geography, as indeed the descriptions of Welsh life and customs, undoubtedly owes more to French literary imaginations than to any historical or geographical reality.'[16]

Chrétien de Troyes

The first French reference to an Arthurian location in Wales, not originating in the works of either Geoffrey of Monmouth or Wace, is found in Chrétien de Troyes's *Erec et Enide*. The poem opens:

> One springtide, on Easter Day, King Arthur held at his stronghold of *Caradigan* a court more lavish than had ever been seen; for it was attended by many good, bold, brave and proud knights and rich ladies and maidens, fair and noble daughters of kings.[17]

Caradigan can be identified as the town of Cardigan in west Wales, but there is nothing in any earlier source to associate Arthur with Cardigan, so why did Chrétien choose to locate Arthur's court there? Loomis suggested that the name had been transmitted to France by a Breton storyteller who had visited Wales in the mid-twelfth century, but a more likely scenario centres on the relationship between Lord Rhys, the ruler of Deheubarth (south-west Wales) and King Henry II.[18] In 1172 Henry II appointed Lord Rhys to be 'justice on his behalf in all of Deheubarth', and they remained on good terms until the death of Henry in 1189.[19] This friendship was noted by English chroniclers and coincided with Rhys reconstructing the castle at Cardigan, the first stone, as opposed to timber, castle built by a Welsh prince.[20] It seems possible therefore that Chrétien was aware of these developments in west Wales when he made use of the name Cardigan in his poem. Another notable event at Cardigan, a bardic competition in 1176, has also been suggested as a reason for its appearance in a French romance.[21] This event is often referred to in modern works as the first ever *eisteddfod*, although J. E. Caerwyn Williams has argued that Rhys was adapting a French *puys*, a festival of the arts held across France in the twelfth century, rather than continuing any Welsh tradition.[22] It is possible that Chrétien visited England on more than one occasion, and his use of such places as *Guallingford*, an allusion to Wallingford near Oxford, where Henry II held a competition in 1157, suggests some knowledge of the court of Henry II.[23]

The poems of Chrétien de Troyes became very popular in the last quarter of the twelfth century and *Erec et Enide* in particular, was translated into Old Norse, Swedish and German. His final unfinished tale, *Perceval*, is notable for introducing the Holy Grail into the Arthurian legend and by the first decade of the thirteenth century at least four lengthy continuations to this unfinished work had been written.[24] The tale of *Perceval* opens in Wales and refers to the Welsh customs of the protagonist, but it does not specifically refer to any locations in Wales.[25]

Beyond the works of Chrétien de Troyes, further place names can be identified in the verse romances with a good degree of certainty. The cathedral town of Bangor in north-west Wales appears as 'Bangort, cite en Gales' in *Durmart le Galois* (*c.*1220) and the strategic town of Rhuddlan, on the river Clwyd, is Rouëlent, the town where Arthur assembles his army before invading Ireland in *La vengeance Raguidel* (*c.*1220–30).[26] A further interesting reference to Wales can also be found in the German Grail verse romance *Parzival*, written by Wolfram von Eschenbach, sometime between 1210 and 1225 and surviving in over eighty manuscripts. *Parzival* is famed for its exotic geography and in one section Arthur laments that Parzival has been robbed by another knight of his rightful lands of Waleis (Wales), along with Norgals (north Wales) and its capital city of Kingrivals.[27] This name is unknown elsewhere, and the location of the capital city is difficult to determine, but the knight who took it from Parzival is named Lähelin; could this be a reference to Llywelyn ap Iorwerth, who was in control of north Wales from 1200–40, or just a fascinating coincidence?[28]

Prose romances

At the turn of the thirteenth century prose began increasingly to replace verse as the medium for French Arthurian romances. The later prose romances, which built upon Chrétien's work, make up nearly three-quarters of the remaining medieval manuscripts (approximately 350) and were the most popular Arthurian works in medieval England and France.[29] The prose romances took many themes, names and ideas from the earlier verse romances and in a review of West's 1978 *Prose Index*, Armel Diverres compared it with the author's earlier *Verse Index* and noted:

> What is striking in comparison between the two indexes is the sharp decrease in the proportion of names of British origin in the prose romances, accompanied by an increase in names borrowed from the *romans d'antiquité* and the *chansons de geste*, by the creation of entirely fictitious names and by the adoption for new characters of names of established ones.[30]

This increase in fictitious names is particularly evident in the prose romances. Whereas many of the place names related to Wales in the verse romances can be identified, in the prose romances it is much more difficult, as many of the castles, rivers and kingdoms are located only in the vaguest of terms.

One of the earliest prose romances to be inspired by Chrétien's *Perceval* was the *Perlesvaus* (written 1200–10).[31] The work was evidently known in Shropshire in the early fourteenth century, as the opening episode was later used by the author of the Anglo-Norman poem, *Fouke le Fitz Waryn* (*c*.1330).[32] One place name that is unique to *Perlesvaus* and appears nowhere else in French Arthurian romance, is a castle called Clef de Gales (Key to Wales). In the notes to their edition of the text, Nitze and Jenkins tried, unconvincingly, to associate the name with the town of Oswestry, and Carman later suggested Abergavenny as a possible site.[33] Neither of these suggestions takes into account the fact that the term 'Key to Wales' also exists in a set of Latin annals known as *Cronica Wallia*, in Exeter Cathedral Library, MS 3514 (late thirteenth century). The entry for the year 1200 reads, *Mailgun filius Resi castellum de Aberteiui, clauem et custodiam tocius Kambrie*, 'Maelgwn the son of Rhys sold Cardigan castle, the key and defence of all Wales.'[34] The French text gives no clues as to where *Clef de Gales* was situated, but Cardigan is not otherwise mentioned and the similarity of usage is striking. With the exception of Caerleon, originating in Geoffrey of Monmouth's *HRB*, Cardigan was one of the most famous courts of Arthur in the early thirteenth century and was known across Europe, before being forced from the limelight by the rise of the later and unlocatable Camelot.[35]

Out of the 500 or so French manuscripts that predate 1450, 340 consist of two lengthy prose works, the *Lancelot-Grail* cycle (220 manuscripts) and the *Prose Tristan* (120 manuscripts).[36] Although the *Prose Tristan* does contain material of interest (Norgales and places within it are often mentioned), it is less important as a source for the earliest appearance of place names than the *Lancelot-Grail* cycle (1215–30).[37] The *Lancelot-Grail* cycle consists of five tales: *L'Estoire del Saint Graal* (History of the Holy Grail), *The Story of Merlin, Lancelot Proper, La Queste del Saint Graal* (The Quest for the Holy Grail) and *La Mort le roi Artu* (The Death of King Arthur). Together, these tales provide a familiar narrative that begins with Joseph of Arimathea laying Christ's body in his tomb just after the crucifixion, his subsequent travels bringing Christianity and the Grail to Britain, the many chivalric adventures of the Knights of the Round Table, the love affair between Guinevere and Lancelot, the grail quest of Galahad and ending with the death of Arthur in his final battle with Mordred.

The importance of north Wales as a location within the cycle is set out towards the end of the *Estoire*, when Joseph of Arimathea, his son Josephus and over 150 followers arrive in Britain and according to the text, 'preach here and there, until they arrived in North Wales'.[38] On finding the Christians in his land, Crudel, the king of north Wales, described as 'the cruellest and most traitorous pagan ever known', imprisons them without any food and with only the Holy Grail to sustain them.[39] During the first night of their incarceration, King Mordrains in Egypt, who had

Figure 3. *An illustration from* L'Estoire del Saint Graal *(written c.1220) in Paris, Bibliothèque nationale de France, MS fr. 105, f. 103 (c.1320) showing Crudel, the king of Norgales (North Wales), imprisoning Joseph of Arimathea and his followers. This predates his association with Glastonbury by at least thirty years.* © Bibliothèque Nationale de France.

earlier been converted to Christianity by Joseph, has a dream in which Christ appears to him with the wounds of the crucifixion. Mordrains asks him how this happened and Christ replies:

> This was done by King Crudel, the lord of North Wales, who has crucified Me thus. It was not enough for him that I was put on the cross once, but he has done it again. Get up and take your armour and your wife, Nascien's wife, and King Label's daughter and go to the sea and cross over to Great Britain. There avenge Me against King Crudel, who has thus tortured Me.[40]

This startling passage has received very little comment by literary scholars or historians of medieval Wales. The fifth crusade to the Holy Land (1217–21) had just ended when the *Lancelot-Grail* cycle was written and the excerpt given above, in which

Jesus Christ himself advocates attacking pagan north Wales, should perhaps be best understood in this context.[41] Attacks on north Wales were frequent at this time, King John was often in conflict with Llywelyn ap Iorwerth, the ruler of Gwynedd (north Wales) until his death in 1216, and regular battles between English forces and Llewelyn continued throughout the 1220s.[42]

Soon after arriving in Britain, Mordrains decides to act on his dream and takes his army to north Wales, where he demands that Joseph and his followers be released. King Crudel is outraged at such a request, and because of this Mordrains 'began at once to ravage the land of North Wales, burning cities, castles and houses'.[43] King Crudel gathers his armies together at a city, called Languetoune and the two armies meet in battle nearby. Crudel is killed and the Christian army pursue the remains of the pagan Welsh army back to Languetoune and kill them all. Following the battle, Joseph, Mordrains and their respective followers move to a castle called Galefort in *la marche de Norgales* 'the march of north Wales', a site that becomes a focal point for the early Christians throughout the rest of the story. The two towns of Languetoune and Galefort are depicted as being either in, or near, north Wales, but neither site can be identified any more securely.

Occasionally, the geographical confusion clears and a coherent description is provided that enables the reader to locate events in the real world. The kingdom of Sorelois plays an important role in the story and makes its first appearance in the shorter, pre-cyclic *Lancelot* (composed *c.*1210), which provides the following information as to its location:

> Galehaut and his companion journeyed until at length they came to the land of which he was lord, the land of Sorelois, which is situated between Wales and the distant Isles.[44]

> On the side toward King Arthur's land, the kingdom of Sorelois was completely cut off by a single body of water, very broad and swift and deep, and it was called Ausurne; on the other side it was entirely surrounded by sea ... from King Arthur's land no one could enter Sorelois except by first crossing the Ausurne. This was not fresh water, for its larger end came from the sea, and the other flowed into it.[45]

Later on in the narrative, Gawain asks for directions to Sorelois and a hermit tells him that it is 'at the end of North Wales, in the direction of the setting sun'.[46] The geographical description of an island, separated from north Wales by a river running into the sea at both ends, must surely relate to the Isle of Anglesey and the Menai Strait. It appears then, that in the mind of the author of the pre-cyclic *Lancelot*, in the early thirteenth century, the kingdom of Sorelois was located on the Isle of Anglesey. Aside from the occasional moments of clarity noted above, the geography of the prose romances is very obscure, the romanticised names seemingly defy identification, and it is perhaps a fruitless task to attempt to do so.

The story of Joseph of Arimathea bringing Christianity to Britain was only absorbed into Glastonbury's ever-growing mythology *c.*1250 and went on to play a prominent role in medieval ecclesiastical matters: the fact that the story's earliest association was with north Wales has received little attention.[47] In order to understand why north Wales played such a prominent role in French Arthurian romances it is worthwhile to take a brief look at the history of the area during the period in which they were written.

The dominant force in Welsh politics in the early thirteenth century was Llywelyn ap Iorwerth, often referred to in official documents as *princeps Norwallie* 'Prince of North Wales', mirroring the terms used in the *Lancelot-Grail* cycle.[48] Llywelyn made frequent raids into the Marcher regions and in 1215 reached as far east as Shrewsbury.[49] The Marcher region was semi-autonomous during the period in which the romances were written, and the various lordships were regularly involved in conflicts with both the Crown and native Welsh rulers. The Marcher kingdoms of the late twelfth and early thirteenth centuries included territory in what we would now regard as south Wales. The region from Pembroke, east through Gower into Glamorgan and across to England, was in the control of Marcher lords, and references to lands bordering Gales or Norgales could just as well be in this area as in the better-known Marcher regions along the English border. The fact that south Wales was primarily in English hands at this time may also explain the paucity of references to Sorgales, for south Wales, in the romances.[50] The level of the region's independence can be gauged to some degree by the fact that Magna Carta recognised Marcher law as being separate from both the English and Welsh laws.[51] Dynastic marriages between the Marcher families and the native Welsh rulers were commonplace, most notably the marriage of Llywelyn's daughter Gwladus to Roger Mortimer in 1230.[52] The projection of current issues onto the past, even a fictional one, is common in medieval works and the frequent small-scale conflicts in the Marcher regions could, possibly mirror sections of the narrative in the romances. A detailed study of both sets of sources may provide some parallels, but that is a mammoth task not helped by the fact that, as R. R. Davies points out, 'A fully documented check-list of the descent and control of castles and lordships is an urgent desideratum of Welsh medieval scholarship.'[53] The continuing interest of the Marcher lords in Arthurian matters is discussed below.

Wales continued to act as a setting for Arthurian adventures throughout the thirteenth century until the appearance of *Escanor* by Girart d'Amiens (*c.*1280), composed for Eleanor of Castile, wife of Edward I, and generally considered to be the final French Arthurian romance to be written. The latest editor of the tale, Richard Trachsler, has suggested that the figure of *Escanor de Blanche Montaigne* is based on Llywelyn ap Gruffudd and his stronghold in Snowdonia.[54] In the text, King Arthur has great trouble trying to defeat Escanor, mirroring the campaigns by Edward I against Llywelyn. At one point in the text, a list of rulers and their heraldic arms is given, two of which relate to Alexander II of Scotland and Llywelyn ap Gruffudd, reinforcing the contemporary concerns of the author.[55]

There has been much discussion about the Arthurian interests of Edward I since Roger Loomis first brought together the evidence in an article entitled 'Edward I, Arthurian Enthusiast' in 1953, and events that took place during the period of Edward's campaigns in Wales offer some support to the idea.[56] Edward forced Llywelyn ap Gruffudd to do homage before him at Aberconwy Abbey on 11 November 1277, having inflicted a heavy defeat on the Welsh.[57] On 19 April 1278, Edward and his queen were at Glastonbury Abbey, where the monks were ordered to exhume the remains of Arthur and Guinevere. According to the two medieval records of this event, the bones were then kept in the treasury until the new tomb could be built to house them. Subsequent writers have tried to associate this event with Edward's recent victory over Llywelyn, and claim that the event was staged primarily, to show the defeated Welsh forces that King Arthur was dead and would not return to help them.[58] Despite this oft-cited view, the medieval texts offer no evidence to support it. If this was the reason, it was more likely done to appeal to those immersed in the propaganda that the Welsh believed in the return of King Arthur to help them in their time of need, which, as we shall see in the next chapter, has been overplayed.

Following his final conquest of Wales, Edward I came to Aberconwy Abbey again in June 1283 and received there the regalia of the Welsh, including the sacred relic of the *Croes Naid* (a fragment of the true cross) and a crown, that according to some chroniclers had belonged to Arthur, but to others was the crown of Llywelyn.[59] 'The famous crown of King Arthur, which had been held in the greatest honour by the Welsh for a long time [...] was presented to the king [...] thus the glory of the Welsh passed, although unwillingly, to the English.'[60] In 1284 Edward I held a Round Table tournament at Nefyn, on the coast of the Llŷn peninsula in north Wales, to celebrate his victory over the Welsh. Why he chose to hold such an event at Nefyn is uncertain, but the fact that the church and surrounding lands had been owned by the English abbey of Haughmond, near Shrewsbury, since 1141, probably played a part in the decision.[61] For those attending the celebration, getting to Nefyn would have been something of an adventure in itself, through lands previously too dangerous to cross. Later that year Edward returned to London where the *talaith* (crown) of Llywelyn was presented to the shrine of Edward the Confessor at Westminster Abbey as a sign of supremacy over the Welsh. As noted above, some English chroniclers referred to this *talaith* as the crown of Arthur, further enhancing his Welsh associations, but records of the king's goldsmith from the time, show that the item was simply known as the crown of Llywelyn and was regilded and enlarged before the presentation, no doubt to make it look more impressive as a crown that had supposedly befitted the figure of Arthur.[62] No Welsh source ever refers to a crown of Arthur. Having conquered Wales, Edward I moved on to his next project, the conquest of Scotland, and in a similar move he took the Stone of Scone in 1296, and the crown of John Balliol in 1299, to demonstrate his supremacy over Scotland.

The production of French Arthurian verse romances came to a halt c.1280, and the fact that this coincides with the final conquest of Wales, where many of the tales are set, is worthy of attention. Throughout the thirteenth century, whilst it preserved a degree of independence, Wales was consistently portrayed as an Arthurian setting, but with the final conquest by Edward I, the need to portray it as such vanished. This romanticised view of a new frontier finds an analogy in literature concerning the Wild West in America, or the limits of the British Empire in Afghanistan in the nineteenth century, as epitomised in such works as Rudyard Kipling's *Kim*. The French Arthurian romances acted as the '*Boy's Own*' adventure books of their day, encouraging knights to engage in the chivalric Arthurian adventures to be had in the untamed Welsh landscape. The place names first attested in these sources are frequently vague and difficult to identify, but the occasional moments of clarity, noted above, suggest that, to the authors of these works, Wales was a suitable place to set their tales, both geographically and politically.

As the fourteenth century progressed, English began to replace French as the dominant language in England, and this change is also reflected in the production of Arthurian romances. As with the earlier French poets, those writing in English had access to *HRB* and the *Roman de Brut* of Wace, but they may also have had access to the Middle English translation of Wace, written by Layamon c.1205. Layamon's *Brut* is one of the earliest major pieces of Middle English to have been composed (although it only survives in two manuscripts) and, like Wace, some fifty years earlier, translated the Arthurian narrative of *HRB* into the vernacular.[63] Layamon lived near Worcester on the border of Wales and shows an awareness of Welsh traditions, but he did not add any new Arthurian Welsh place names.[64] Only a handful of Middle English Arthurian tales survive in a small number of manuscripts, and although they do add new Arthurian names for England, notably Tarn Wathelyne in northern England, a survey of Robert Ackerman's *Index of Arthurian Names in Middle English* shows that no new names were added for sites in Wales.[65] However, the best-known Middle English Arthurian tale, *Sir Gawain and the Green Knight* (c.1400) does refer to north Wales and has Gawain crossing over to the Wirral from the a place called 'Holy Head'.[66] The location of the place from which Gawain crossed over to the Wirral has led to much speculation.[67]

The Marcher Lords

The most influential family to propagate Arthurian literature in the Welsh Marches was undoubtedly the Mortimer family of Wigmore in Herefordshire. The dynasty first established itself on the Welsh borders at the turn of the twelfth century and proceeded to build castles and to grant lands to monastic establishments in the middle Marches until the fifteenth century.[68] John Thompson, in his study of the surviving manuscripts of Middle English Arthurian romances, draws attention to three manuscripts with links to the Mortimer family.

It is striking that the best examples of literary collections preserving Middle English Arthurian items for a roughly contemporary polyglot readership are all regional products. These are BL MS Harley 2253 and the two other codices to which its main scribe-compiler contributed, BL MS Harley 273 and Royal 12.c. xii, all three of which can be associated with reading audiences on the Welsh borders […].[69]

Neil Ker in his detailed study of Harley 2253 (compiled *c*.1325) has shown that the scribe was based in or near Ludlow in Shropshire and had links to the Mortimers of Wigmore.[70] Harley 2253 incudes the Harley Lyrics and also contains several works of Arthurian interest, whereas Royal 12.c.xii contains the unique copy of *Fouke le fitz Waryn*, mentioned above, with its narrative centred on Ludlow. Thompson notes that 'its scribe-compiler combined a serious scholar's interest in Arthur and British history with an obvious desire to celebrate Mortimer power and influence at a number of different local, regional and national levels'.[71]

During the period 1326–30, Roger Mortimer of Wigmore and his mistress Isabella, Edward II's queen consort, ruled England as regents for her son, the underage Edward III. The keeper of the Privy Wardrobe accounts for this period notes books given to members of the court and romances appear frequently, although the term 'romance' is used in a broad sense and is no guarantee of the existence of an Arthurian text.[72] The accounts also note that a number of books, including romances, were moved to London from Mortimer's own collection at Wigmore.[73] Isabella is known to have been interested in the story of Perceval and the Holy Grail and just before she died had scribes produce a copy of a grail romance.[74] Further evidence of Mortimer enthusiasm for Arthurian matters can be found in the Wigmore manuscript (Chicago, University of Chicago Library, MS 224).[75] It was written sometime after 1376 in support of the ongoing Mortimer claims to the English throne and contains a unique abbreviation of the *Prose Brut*, although the main focus of the work is a detailed genealogical roll showing the descent of the Mortimer family from Brutus, through Arthur, to Cadwaladr and focusing upon the marriage between Ralph Mortimer and Gwladus Du, the daughter of Llywelyn ap Iorwerth, in 1230. Accompanying the genealogy are accounts of Round Table tournaments held in 1279 and 1328. The 1279 Round Table, organised by Roger Mortimer (first baron) at Kenilworth, was attended by Edward I and nobles from all over England and caught the attention of contemporary chroniclers.[76] Mary Giffen suggests that 'it is possible that Roger de Mortimer used Arthurian legend to point out what might be done for England by a prince of the Welsh blood who was also loyal to the king'.[77] A poem by the Welsh poet Iolo Goch, celebrating the life of the sixth Roger Mortimer (d. 1398), offers him 'the grace of Arthur and his cross to you', refers to him as a 'second Galahad' and also as the 'Earl of Caerleon, brave warrior'.[78] The town of Caerleon was in the possession of the Mortimer dynasty at this time and these Arthurian comparisons were obviously considered a suitable subject for a poem celebrating the life of a member of that dynasty.

During her discussion of the Wigmore manuscript, Giffen draws attention to further Arthurian associations in Wales on lands owned by the Mortimer family.[79] She notes the following names (I have added the date of the earliest attestation for each name in brackets): Cadair Arthur in the Brecon Beacons (1188); Coetan Arthur in Dyffryn Ardudwy (1795); and Llygad Amr, near Rhayder in Radnorshire (1100). It seems unlikely that either Cadair Arthur or Llygad Amr has anything to do with the Mortimer dynasty, and the Coetan Arthur in question does not appear in the record until 1795. Although the examples used by Giffen provide no firm evidence for a Mortimer link to an Arthurian place name, the gazetteer in Appendix 2 does provide at least five potential candidates. Roger Mortimer (d. 1214) granted lands to the Cwm-Hir abbey, in Radnorshire and in a document from 1200 one of the boundary markers is given the name 'Fontem Arthur' (Arthur's Well).[80] The town walls of Montgomery were built in the 1280s and the name 'Arthur's Street', which still survives, appears in documents relating to the town from 1300 onwards, where a mortgage from 1336/7 refers to one of the town gates as 'Arthur's Gate'.[81] A prehistoric burial chamber called Arthur's Stone, five miles east of Hay-on-Wye, in Herefordshire, is recorded in the late thirteenth century, and the township of Ffynnon Arthur in Montgomeryshire enters the record in 1309, both of which lay in lands under Mortimer control.[82] It is not possible to say, with any certainty, that the interest shown in Arthurian matters by the Mortimer family had any influence on these names, but the coincidence is certainly worthy of attention.

During the reign of Edward IV Sir Thomas Malory (1415–71), whilst imprisoned in Newgate Prison between 1468 and 1471, wrote the most famous and influential English work in the Arthurian canon. *Le Morte Darthur* is a text that runs to nearly a thousand pages in its printed form. The author states throughout the text that he was translating from 'the Frenshe Book', and studies have shown that he drew heavily upon the *Lancelot-Grail* cycle, as well as earlier English Arthurian sources such as the *Alliterative Morte Arthur*.[83] Malory's work was only known from the edition printed by William Caxton (d. 1492) at his press in Westminster in 1485, until the discovery of an earlier manuscript version in the Winchester College Library in 1934.[84] Despite its place as one of the most studied texts in the Arthurian canon, its contents provide few new names for the purpose of this work, as the names associated with Wales are almost all, with one exception, found in the earlier sources discussed above.

In his preface to the 1485 edition of *Le Morte Darthur*, Caxton describes the Arthurian relics still extant in England in his day as proof of Arthur's former existence. Following his discussion of the relics in England, Caxton refers to the Arthurian remains in Wales.

> And yet of record remayne in wytnesse of hym in Wales, in the toune of Camelot, the grete stones and mervayllous werkys of yron lyeng under the grounde, and ryal vautes, which dyvers now lyvyng hath seen. Wherfor it is a mervayl why he is no

more renomed in his owne contreye, sauf onelye it accordeth to the word of God, whyche sayth that no man is accept for a prophete in his owne contreye.[85]

This notice of the ruins of Camelot being visible in Wales is likely to be a reference to the Roman remains at either Caerleon or Caerwent, whereas Malory himself equates Camelot with Winchester. Eugene Vinaver, in his edition of *Le Morte Darthur*, draws attention to the fact that Malory would often introduce 'Wales and Welsh knights contrary to his sources'.[86] The towns of Cardiff, Caernarfon and Cardigan are occasionally used where the earlier French sources had a romantic name which cannot be located, and it would seem that Malory was attempting to give his story a more realistic geography.[87] Malory himself depicts Wales as divided into two parts: the south, centred on Caerleon, which is loyal to Arthur; and the north, which is hostile to him. It would have been difficult for Malory to have depicted Wales in any other way, as he relied on the French sources that often depicted north Wales as a land beyond the control of Arthur.[88] There is little evidence that *Le Morte Darthur* had any real impact upon the poetry and prose of Wales.

Conclusion

The French Arthurian romances were an important development that expanded upon the material first introduced by Geoffrey of Monmouth in 1138, and are a sign of how popular and influential his work became. The poems of Chrétien de Troyes became equally influential and his references to locations in Wales, both real and imagined, soon found themselves as an essential part in the new romance genre. The likelihood that much of what was written in French was intended for an audience in England gives the Welsh material a contemporary relevance that has not always been considered and goes some way to explaining the continued portrayal of Wales as an Arthurian setting. The manuscripts of the major prose cycles were produced in incredible numbers for medieval texts; more manuscripts of the *Lancelot-Grail* cycle survive than of the *HRB* of Geoffrey of Monmouth, were produced within a shorter time period and have more to say about Wales and Arthur. It can be shown that Geoffrey of Monmouth reflected upon contemporary events in the writing of his work, but a similar approach to the intent of the compilers of the *Lancelot-Grail* cycle has yet to be fully considered.[89] The many references to Gales, Norgales and locations associated with them in French Arthurian romances need to be studied with contemporary events in mind. The possibility that the interest shown in Arthurian material by the Mortimer family may have led to place names with an Arthurian association, is also an avenue for further research.

Notes

1   For a detailed discussion of the French manuscripts see Roger Middleton, 'The manuscripts', in Glyn S. Burgess and Karen Pratt (eds), *The Arthur of the French* (Cardiff, 2006), pp. 1–92. This collection of essays is an essential starting point, and this chapter is indebted to it.

2   Judith Weiss (ed.), *Wace's Roman De Brut: A History of the British: Text and Translation* (Exeter, 1999). A precursor to Wace was *L'Estoire des Engles* written by Geffrei Gaimar in 1140; Ian Short (ed. and trans.) *Estoire des Engleis: History of the English* (Oxford, 2009).

3   Weiss, *Roman de Brut*, p. 32, ll. 1238–40, for the origins of the name Wales, and pp. 122–3, ll. 4855–76 for the reference to Taliesin. For a detailed discussion of the Round Table see Beate Schmolke-Hasselmann, 'The Round Table: Ideal, Fiction, Reality', *Arthurian Literature*, 2 (1983), 41–75.

4   Michael D. Reeve (ed.) and Neil Wright (trans.), *Geoffrey of Monmouth, The History of the Kings of Britain: An Edition and Translation of De Gestis Britonum [Historia Regum Britanniae]* (Woodbridge, 2007), p. 204.

5   Weiss, *Roman de Brut*, pp.246–7, ll. 9785–98.

6   For detailed discussions of these texts, see the relevant chapters in Burgess and Pratt, *The Arthur of the French*.

7   P. Rickard, *Britain in Medieval French Literature 1100–1500* (Cambridge, 1956).

8   Neale, J. Carman, *A Study of the Pseudo-Map Cycle of Arthurian Romance* (Kansas, 1973); idem, 'The *Perlesvaus* and the Bristol Channel', *Research Studies*, 32 (1964), 85–105; and idem, 'South Welsh geography and British history in the *Perlesvaus*', in Norris J. Lacy (ed.), *A Medieval French Miscellany: Papers of the 1970 Kansas Conference on Medieval French Literature* (Kansas, 1972), pp. 37–59; Rosemary Morris, 'Aspects of Time and Place in the French Arthurian Verse Romances', *French Studies*, 42 (1988), 257–77; Roger S. Loomis, *Arthurian Tradition and Chrétien de Troyes* (New York, 1949), his most detailed work on the topic.

9   G. D. West, *An Index of Proper Names in French Arthurian Verse Romances 1150–1300* (Toronto, 1969).

10   G. D. West, *An Index of Proper Names in French Arthurian Prose Romances* (Toronto, 1978).

11   Richard Trachsler (ed.), *Girart d'Amiens, Escanor: roman arthurien en vers de la fin du XIIIe siècle*, 2 vols (Geneva, 1994).

12   From his Foreword to Beate Schmolke-Hasselmann, *Evolution of Arthurian Romance: The Verse Tradition from Chrétien to Froissart* (Cambridge, 1998), p. xi.

13   Schmolke-Hasselmann, *Evolution of Arthurian Romance*, pp. 219–81.

14   Michael A. Faletra, *Wales and the Medieval Colonial Imagination: The Matters of Britain in the Twelfth Century* (London, 2014), p. 173.

15   West, *Verse Index*, p. 60 provides a list of references.

16   Ceridwen Lloyd-Morgan, 'Crossing the borders: literary borrowing in Wales and England', in Ruth Kennedy and Simon Meecham-Jones (eds), *Authority and Subjugation in Writing of Medieval Wales* (New York, 2008), p. 160.

17   D. D. R. Owen (trans.), *Chrétien de Troyes, Arthurian Romances* (London, 1993), p. 1. 'Un jor de Pasque, au tans novel, / A Caradigan son chastel / Ot li rois Arthur cort tenue. / Einz si riche ne su veüe; / Car mout i ot buens chevaliers, / Hardiz et corageus et fiers, / Et riches dames et puceles, / Filles de rois, jantes et beles'; Wendelin Foerster (ed.), *Erec und Enide von Christian von Troyes* (Halle, 1890), p. 2, lines 27–34.

18   Loomis, *Arthurian Tradition and Chrétien de Troyes*, p. 29.

19   Thomas Jones (ed. and trans.), *Brut y Tywysogyon or The Chronicle of the Princes: Peniarth MS 20 Version* (Cardiff, 1952), p. 68.

20   John Gillingham, 'Henry II, Richard I and the Lord Rhys', *Peritia*, 10 (1996), 225–36.

21   Roger Middleton, 'Studies in the textual relationships of the Erec/Geraint stories' (unpublished DPhil thesis, University of Oxford, 1976), 18.

22   J. E. Caerwyn Williams, 'Yr Arglwydd Rhys ac "Eisteddfod" Aberteifi 1176', in Nerys Ann Jones and Huw Pryce (eds), *Yr Arglwydd Rhys* (Cardiff, 1996), pp. 116–19.

23   Constance Bullock-Davies, 'Chrétien de Troyes and England', *Arthurian Literature*, 1 (1981), 1–61.

24   Rupert T. Pickens, Keith Busby and Andrea M. L. Williams, 'Perceval and the Grail', in Burgess and Pratt (eds), *The Arthur of the French*, pp. 222–47; and Nigel Bryant, *The Complete Story of the Grail: Chrétien de Troyes' Perceval and its Continuations* (Cambridge, 2015).

25   K. Busby (ed.), *Chrétien de Troyes, Le Roman de Perceval ou Le Conte du Graal: édition critique d'après tous les manuscrits* (Tübingen, 1993).

26   J. Gildea (ed.), *Durmart le Galois, roman arthurien du treizième siècle*, 2 vols (Villanova, 1965–6), l. 5064 and G. Roussineau (ed.), *Raoul de Houdenz, La Vengeance Raguidel* (Geneva, 2004), l. 3.

27   Cyril Edwards (trans.), *Parzival with Titurel and the Love Lyrics: Wolfram von Eschenbach* (Cambridge, 2004), p. 45.

28   Edwards, *Parzival*, p. 41.

29   Middleton, 'Manuscripts', p. 2.

30   A. H. Diverres, Review of G. D. West, *An Index of Proper Names in French Arthurian Prose Romances*, *French Studies*, 35 (1981), 63–4.

31   William A. Nitze and T. A. Jenkins (eds), *Le Haut Livre du Graal: Perlesvaus*, 2 vols (Chicago, 1932–7).

32   E. J. Hathaway, P. T. Ricketts, C. A. Robson and A. D. Wilshere (eds), *Fouke le Fitz Waryn*, Anglo-Norman Text Society, 26–8 (Oxford, 1975). For an English translation see Thomas E. Kelly, 'Fouke fitz Waryn', in Thomas H. Ohlgren (ed.), *Medieval Outlaws: Ten Tales in Modern English* (Stroud, 1998), pp. 106–67.

33   Nitze and Jenkins, *Perlesvaus*, II, p. 206; Carman, 'South Welsh geography', 42.

34   Thomas Jones (ed.), *Cronica de Wallia and Other Documents from Exeter Cathedral Library MS. 3514* (Cardiff, 1946), p. 6. The same phrase *allwed holl Kymry*, 'the key to all Wales' is also found in Thomas Jones (ed. and trans.), *Brut y Tywysogyon: The Chronicle of the Princes, Red Book of Hergest Version* (Cardiff, 1955), p. 183.

35   The first appearance of Camelot is in Chrétien de Troyes's *Lancelot*; Owen, *Chrétien de Troyes*, p. 185. It should be noted that it does not appear in all of the surviving manuscripts, suggesting that it may not have been a part of the original composition.

36   Roger Middleton, 'Manuscripts of the *Lancelot-Grail* cycle in England and Wales: some books and their owners', in Carol Dover (ed.), *A Companion to the Lancelot-Grail Cycle* (Woodbridge, 2003), p. 220.

37   For a detailed summary of the text and the current state of scholarship regarding this tale see Emmanuèle Baumgartner, 'The Prose *Tristan*', in Burgess and Pratt (eds), *The Arthur of the French*, pp. 325–41.

38   Carol Chase (trans.), *Lancelot-Grail 1: The History of the Holy Grail* (Cambridge, 2010), p. 245: 'Si alerent preechant d'une part et d'autre tant qu'il vindrent el roiaume de Norgales'; Jean-Paul Ponceau (ed.), *L'Estoire del Saint Graal* (Paris, 1997), p. 453.

39   Chase, *History of the Holy Grail*, p. 245: 'Il plus fels et li plus delloiaus paiens del monde'; Ponceau, *L'Estoire*, p. 454.

40   Chase, *History of the Holy Grail*, pp. 245–6: 'Ce m'a fet li rois Crudex, li sires de Norgales, qui einsi m'a crucifié: il ne li sofisoit mie ce que ge i fui une foiz mis, ainz me r'a ore clofichié tot de novel. Lieve sus, si pren tes homes et ta feme et la feme Nascien et la fille au roi de Label, puis t'en va droit a la mer et la passe et arriveras en la Grant Bretaigne et iluec me venge del roi Crudel, qui einsint m'a tormenté'; Ponceau, *L'Estoire*, p. 455.

41   D. A. Trotter, *Medieval French Literature and the Crusades (1100–1300)* (Geneva, 1987), pp. 153–9.

42   J. Beverley Smith, *Llywelyn ap Gruffudd: Prince of Wales* (Cardiff, 1998), pp. 11–29.

43   Chase, *History of the Holy Grail*, p. 252: 'Il comença maintenant a forfaire a cels de Norgales et a ardoir viles et chasteaus et mesons'; Ponceau, *L'Estoire*, p. 469.

44   Samuel N. Rosenberg and Carleton W. Carroll (trans.), *Lancelot-Grail 3: Lancelot Parts I and II* (Cambridge, 2010), p. 288; 'Ce dit li contes que antre Galehot et son conpaignon errerent par lor jornees, que il vint en la terre dom il estoit sires. Ce fu la terre de Sorolois qui siet antre Gales et les Estranges Illes'; Elspeth Kennedy (ed.), *Lancelot do Lac: The Non-Cyclic Old French Prose Romance*, 2 vols (Oxford, 1980), I, p. 356. The non-cyclic or *Prose Lancelot* is the name given to the earlier and stand-alone Lancelot story (c.1210) before it was incorporated into the *Lancelot-Grail* cycle

45   Rosenberg and Carroll, *Lancelot-Grail 3*, p. 288: 'Li reiaumes de Sorelois par devers la terre lo roi Artu estoit toz clos d'une sole aigue qui mout estoit roide et granz et parfonde, si estoit apelee Assurne. Et d'autre part estoit tote avironee de la mer. Et aprés i avoit chastiaus et citez et forz et delitables et de murs et de bois et de montaignes, et d'autres aives avoit assez en la terre, do li plus an cheoit an Assurne et cele cheoit an mer, si que de la terre lo roi Artu ne pooit nus antrer an Sorelois qui par Assurne ne passant avant. Ne ce n'estoit mie aive douce, car li premiers chiés s'isoit de mer'; Kennedy, *Lancelot do Lac*, I, pp. 356 –7.

46   Rosenberg and Carroll, *Lancelot-Grail 3*, p. 386: 'Sire, fait li hermits, an la fin de Norgales, devers solau cochant'; Kennedy, *Lancelot do Lac*, I, p. 478.

47   Valerie M. Lagorio, 'The evolving legend of St Joseph of Glastonbury', in James P. Carley (ed.), *Glastonbury Abbey and the Arthurian Tradition* (Cambridge, 2001), pp. 55–81.

48   Huw Pryce, *The Acts of the Welsh Rulers* (Cardiff, 2005), pp. 75–8.

49   Jones, *Brut y Tywysogyon: Red Book of Hergest Version*, p. 203.

50   West, *Prose Index*, p. 282.

51   Kevin Mann, 'The March of Wales: A Question of Terminology', *Welsh History Review*, 18 (1996), 1.

52   J. J. Crump, 'The Mortimer Family and the Making of the March', *Thirteenth Century England*, 6 (1997), 117–26.

53   R. R. Davies, *Conquest Co-existence and Change* (Cardiff, 1987), p. 466. Progress has been made with Max Lieberman, *The Medieval March of Wales: The Creation and Perception of a Frontier, 1066–1283* (Cambridge, 2010) and Brock W. Holden, *Lords of the Central Marches: English Aristocracy and Frontier Society, 1087–1265* (Oxford, 2008).

54   Trachsler (ed.), *Girart d' Amiens*, p. 34.

55   Gérard Brault, 'Arthurian Heraldry and the Date of *Escanor*', *Bibliographical Bulletin of the International Arthurian Society*, 11 (1959), 81–8.

56   Roger S. Loomis, 'Edward I, Arthurian Enthusiast', *Speculum*, 28 (1953), 114–27.

57   J. Beverley Smith, *Llywelyn ap Gruffudd*, pp. 438–45.

58   John Carmi Parsons, 'The second exhumation of King Arthur's remains at Glastonbury, 19 April 1278', in Carley, *Glastonbury Abbey and the Arthurian Tradition*, pp. 179–83.

59   W. C. Tennant, 'Croes Naid', *National Library of Wales Journal*, 7 (1951–2), 102–15.

60 Juliet Vale, 'Arthur in English society', in W. R. J. Barron (ed.), *The Arthur of the English*, p. 188 translating the Waverley Annals in H. R. Luard (ed.), *Annales Monastici*, II (London, 1865), p. 401.

61 Huw Pryce, *The Acts of Welsh Rulers 1120–1283* (Cardiff, 2005), pp. 329–31. The king stayed at Nefyn again in January 1295; Una Rees (ed.), *The Cartulary of Haughmond Abbey* (Cardiff, 1985), pp. 159–63, nos. 784–803.

62 Smith, *Llywelyn ap Gruffudd*, pp. 332 and 584.

63 W. R. J. Barron and S. C. Weinberg (eds), *Lawmans Brut* (Harlow, 1995).

64 Arthur C. L. Brown, 'Welsh Traditions in Layamon's "Brut"', *Modern Philology*, 1 (1903), 95–103; and Françoise Le Saux, *Layamon's Brut: The Poem and its Sources* (Woodbridge, 1989), pp. 118–54.

65 Robert W. Ackerman, *An Index of Arthurian Names in Middle English* (Stanford, 1952). See W. R. J. Barron (ed.), *The Arthur of the English*, revised edition (Cardiff, 2001), p. 124 for a discussion of the manuscripts. Attention should also be drawn to the mention of Kardyf (Cardiff) in Sir Cleges; see Walter Hoyt French and Charles Brockway (eds), *Middle English Metrical Romances* (New York, 1930), p. 880, line 87. For further discussion of how Wales was viewed in Middle English works see, Tony Davenport, 'Wales and Welshness in Middle English romances', in Ruth Kennedy and Simon Meecham-Jones (eds), *Authority and Subjugation in Writing of Medieval Wales* (New York, 2008), pp. 137–58.

66 W. R. J. Barron (ed.), *Sir Gawain and the Green Knight* (Manchester, 1998) p. 68, ll. 697–701.

67 P. L. Heyworth, 'Sir Gawain's Crossing of Dee', *Medium Ævum*, 41 (1972), 124–7; and J. Eadie, 'Sir Gawain's Travels in North Wales', *The Review of English Studies*, 34 (1983), 191–5.

68 Charles Hopkinson and Martin Speight, *The Mortimers, Lords of the March* (Logaston, 2002).

69 John J. Thompson, 'Authors and audiences', in Barron (ed.), *The Arthur of the English*, p. 389.

70 Thompson, 'Authors and audiences', p. 379.

71 Thompson, 'Authors and audiences', p. 381.

72 For a detailed study of the romances mentioned in this manuscript (London, British Library MS Add. 60584) see Carter Revard, 'Courtly romances in the Privy Wardrobe', in Evelyn Mullally and John Thompson (eds), *Court and Cultural Diversity* (Woodbridge, 1997), pp. 297–308.

73 Revard, 'Courtly romances in the Privy Wardrobe', p. 306.

74 Revard, 'Courtly romances in the Privy Wardrobe', p. 305. For further information on French Arthurian romances in the Welsh Marches, see Middleton, 'Manuscripts of the *Lancelot-Grail* cycle', pp. 219–35.

75 Mary E. Giffin, 'Cadwalader, Arthur and Brutus in the Wigmore Manuscript', *Speculum*, 16 (1941), 109–20.

76 Giffin, 'Cadwalader, Arthur and Brutus', 111–12.

77 Giffin, 'Cadwalader, Arthur and Brutus', 113.

78 Dafydd Johnston (trans.), *Iolo Goch Poems* (Llandysul, 1993): '*Gras Arthur a'i groes wrthyd*', p.87, line 103; '*ail Galäath*', p. 87, line 111; '*Iarll Caerllion, dragon drud*', p. 84, line 47.

79 Giffin, 'Cadwalader, Arthur and Brutus', 116.

80 B. G. Charles, 'An Early Charter of the Abbey of Cwmhir', *Radnorshire Society Transactions*, 40 (1970), 68–74.

81 Melville Richards, 'Arthur's Gate at Montgomery', *Archaeologia Cambrensis*, 114 (1965), 181–2. See Gazetteer MTG Arthur's Gate.

82 H. C. Maxwell Lyte (ed.), *A Descriptive Catalogue of Ancient Deeds in the Public Record Office*, I (London, 1890), no. B. 1275 equating to TNA E326/1275. Situated at SO 31884312; see Gazetteer MTG Ffynnon Arthur for further details.

83   Ralph Norris, *Malory's Library: The Sources of Morte Darthur* (Woodbridge, 2008).

84   London, British Library, Additional MS 59678.

85   A facsimile of the Caxton edition can be viewed on The Malory Project website at *www.maloryproject.com*. The reference to Wales is on Sig. IIv and IIIr.

86   Eugene Vinaver (ed.), *The Works of Thomas Malory*, third edn, revised by P. J. C. Field, 3 vols (Oxford, 1990), I, pp. 126–7.

87   Richard R. Griffith, 'The authorship question reconsidered', in Toshiyuki Takamiya and Derek Brewer (eds), *Aspects of Malory* (Woodbridge, 1981), p. 163.

88   Cory James Rushton, 'Malory's divided Wales', in Ruth Kennedy and Simon Meecham-Jones (eds), *Authority and Subjugation in Writing of Medieval Wales* (New York, 2008), 175–89.

89   John Gillingham, 'The Context and Purposes of Geoffrey of Monmouth's *History of the Kings of Britain*', *Anglo-Norman Studies*, 13 (1990), 99–118.

ThRЄЄ
The WЄLSh TЄXTS

THE PREVIOUS TWO CHAPTERS have had the luxury of discussing texts and manuscripts that can be reliably dated, to within a decade in some instances, show a natural development of ideas from one to the next, and in some cases even refer to each other. The situation with medieval Welsh material could not be more different. A majority of medieval Welsh manuscripts can only be dated on palaeographical grounds, as colophons and other dating evidence appear only rarely, but fortunately the work of Daniel Huws has provided us with a series of research articles that enable a good workable chronology to be constructed.[1] In some instances it is possible to show that two or more manuscripts were written by the same scribe and likely locations have also been suggested for their place of writing. Very few medieval Welsh manuscripts can be associated with a single individual, and on the whole they remain anonymous, making it difficult to understand their provenance and reasons for being written. Just over 150 manuscripts written in Welsh survive from the period before 1540, and the earliest one dates from c.1250, over a century after Geoffrey had portrayed Arthur as the most important ruler of early medieval Britain.[2] The small amount of relevant material relating to the Arthurian topography of Wales in medieval Welsh manuscripts is found primarily in poetry and prose literary texts, as Latin remained the preferred language for official documents.

The medieval Welsh Arthurian sources consist primarily of: a small number of poetic references; five prose tales, three of which are adaptations of Chrétien de Troyes's earlier poems; some references in the collection of triadic texts known as *Trioedd Ynys Prydein* and *Brut y Brenhinedd*; a Welsh translation of *Historia regum Britanniae* (*HRB*). A small number of very minor texts and fragments found in later manuscripts also contain occasional topographic references of interest. Although the earliest manuscripts only date from the mid-thirteenth century, there seems little doubt that they contain material composed earlier, but exactly how much earlier remains a controversial point.

Poetry

The earliest poetry is found primarily in three medieval Welsh manuscripts, the Black Book of Carmarthen, the Book of Aneirin and the Book of Taliesin, discussed individually below. Since the fourteenth century this early poetry has been referred to as *hengerdd* (literally 'old songs') and the writers of these works have been known, since the seventeenth century, as the *cynfeirdd* (early poets).[3] A single sentence, found only in the Harleian recension of the *Historia Brittonum*, has led some to claim that sections of the *hengerdd* could date back, in origin, to the sixth century. The sentence in question is situated between material regarding the mid-sixth-century Saxon kings, Ida, reigning in Bernicia, and Maelgwn, ruling in Gwynedd, and names five poets who supposedly wrote at that time: 'Then Talhaearn Tad Awen gained renown in poetry, and Aneirin and Taliesin and Bluchbard and Cian, who is called Gwenith Gwawd, gained renown together at the same time in British poetry.'[4]

On the basis of this evidence, a consensus emerged in the early nineteenth century that any poem that referred to Arthur, especially those associated with either Aneirin or Taliesin, but showed no obvious influence of Geoffrey's *HRB*, should be dated to '*c*.1100' or earlier. The small collection of texts that fit these criteria have therefore been seen as representative of a supposed earlier, pre-*HRB*, Arthurian tradition and have dominated discussions about the earliest sources for the Arthurian legend. However, since the early 1990s the publication of modern editions of medieval Welsh texts has enabled a better understanding of the material and this view has come under increasing scrutiny.

Historiography

The earliest works of scholarship to discuss the *hengerdd* were focused primarily on drawing the attention of those outside Wales to the very existence of early Welsh poetry, and only secondarily on preserving a different view of Arthur from that portrayed in *HRB*. The existence of this, supposedly, earlier view of Arthur was also used to reinforce the argument that Geoffrey had used a Welsh source for his *HRB*, as discussed in chapter 1. The earliest printed examples of *hengerdd* are found in Sir John Prise's posthumous 1573 publication, *Historiae Brytannicae Defensio*, in which is printed four stanzas, including one naming Arthur, from the poem 'Geraint fil Erbin', in the Black Book of Carmarthen.[5] John Lewis, who owned the Book of Taliesin, used extracts from it in his *History of Great Britain* (written 1611, but not published until 1729) and Robert Vaughan (d. 1667), who owned many of the most important manuscripts in his library at Hengwrt, discussed the *hengerdd* on several occasions in his correspondence and notebooks.[6] Despite this awareness of the *hengerdd* amongst Welsh antiquaries, the texts remained virtually unknown beyond their owners and the small handful of scholars who were fortunate enough to gain access to them. It was not until the eighteenth century that further examples were printed.

The publication of a printed text, including all the *hengerdd* and the later court poetry, in the first volume of *The Myvyrian Archaiology* in 1801, made the medieval texts widely available to those outside Wales for the first time.[7] One of the earliest historians to consider this poetry, primarily in an Arthurian context, was Sharon Turner, who in 1803 noted the idea that any Welsh poem about Arthur, that showed no influence from Geoffrey of Monmouth, must predate his influential *HRB* of 1138:

> My argument then is this, that if these poems had been forged in the twelfth century, they would have betrayed themselves by their panegyrics on Arthur. Some of them would have been devoted to this favourite of fame. In some the miraculous feats of Jeffrey's history would have appeared. The very contrary, however is found. Not a tittle of this vast celebrity appears. He is just mentioned and no more, and mentioned as any other warrior.[8]

> Can any one believe, that Welshmen would have forged the works of the contemporaries of Arthur and not have taken the opportunity of celebrating their favourite chieftain? Would not this be contrary to human nature?[9]

This basic argument, in one form or another, has been repeated many times, primarily owing to a lack of an alternative way of interpreting the dating of the texts.[10] W. F. Skene's *Four Ancient Books of Wales* (1868) was the first publication to provide accurate texts of the poetry, edited for the first time from the earliest manuscript witnesses and not later copies, as in previous works. It also included English translations by D. Silvan Evans and Robert Williams that, although competent by the standards of the day, are not reliable enough for the modern reader.[11] Skene also argued that some of the earliest poetry should be associated with Scotland rather than Wales, including material associated with Arthur. This will be discussed in more detail in chapter 5.

Between 1886 and 1916, Skene's work was superseded by the publication of photographic facsimile and printed diplomatic editions of each manuscript by J. Gwenogvryn Evans.[12] His editions were a major step forward as they reproduced the manuscript page in every detail and many are still in use today. The same, however, cannot be said of his attempts at editing and interpreting the texts, which can be best described as over-enthusiastic. The idea that much of this poetry dated from the sixth century was firmly entrenched by the turn of the twentieth century, and Evans is notable for being a rare dissenting voice, referring to the whole idea as 'the sixth century legend'.[13] In the introductions to his diplomatic editions of *The Book of Taliesin* (1910) and *The Book of Aneirin* (1922) he claimed that both bodies of poetry showed points of contact with the work of the *Gogynfeirdd* (literally 'not so early bards'), 1100–1300, and on that basis that they actually related to events of the early twelfth century.[14] Although he was mistaken in many of his conclusions and compounded his mistakes by using his amended texts to back up his arguments, his comparison with the work of the *Gogynfeirdd*, especially in the case of the Book of Taliesin, has recently been revisited in a much more thorough manner.

The founding text for modern ideas about *hengerdd* is a review of Gwenogvryn Evans's 1915 publication, *The Poems of Taliesin*.[15] The article, 'Taliesin' by Sir John Morris-Jones, is a cruel review running to nearly 300 pages and filling an entire volume of the periodical *Y Cymmrodor* for the year 1918, in which Morris-Jones set out his ideas on the 'historical' poems found in the Book of Taliesin and his reasons for dating them to the sixth century.[16] His ideas quickly became the standard interpretation of these texts and were impressively built upon by his student Ifor Williams in his ground-breaking editions of the *hengerdd*, published between 1938 and 1959 and in a series of articles from the same period.[17] Graham Isaac, in a thought-provoking article, has drawn attention to the reasons why such an early date was promoted so forcefully by Morris-Jones and Williams:

> Ifor Williams and John Morris-Jones, the two scholars who contributed above all others in the twentieth century to our understanding and awareness of the old Welsh poetry, were inspired by a deep and intense patriotism. They had a clear vision of the place of Hengerdd within Welsh culture, in Welsh literary tradition. And to them it was certainly a matter of great pride that the Welsh could point to a literary tradition that extended back to a period as long ago as the sixth century.[18]

The arguments for, or against, a sixth-century date for some of the *hengerdd* obviously have an impact upon the small number of Welsh poetic references to Arthur. In regard to the Welsh Arthurian poems, the most widely quoted views are those of Patrick Sims-Williams, from his chapter in the collaborative *The Arthur of the Welsh*, published in 1991.[19] This collection of articles has acted as the best single volume on Welsh Arthurian material for over twenty-five years and the opinions expressed therein have been widely quoted in studies into the origins of the Arthurian legend. Owing to its definitive position, however, more recent research, found only in specialist journals, can often be overlooked by those operating outside Welsh academic circles. In 1991 Sims-Williams provided a comprehensive overview of the poetic material, drawing attention to parallels and associations elsewhere in medieval Welsh sources. On the question of the dating of Arthurian poems in the Black Book of Carmarthen he noted the consensus pre-1100 view, but also noted that a later date may be possible:

> Pre-1100 dates have been claimed for some of them, but while these are quite credible, the linguistic and metrical criteria by which they might be confirmed have still to be found. There is no obvious influence from Geoffrey of Monmouth and the French romances. On the other hand, since there may be one case where material deriving

from Geoffrey (via the Brut) has been transmuted almost beyond recognition, one suspects that there could be other *unobvious* borrowings [italics in original].[20]

The Arthur of the Welsh portrayed the consensus view of Welsh Arthurian literature in 1991, but the same year also saw the publication of the first volume of a new edition of the poetry of the princes (1100–1282), composed by the *Gogynfeirdd* entitled *Cyfres Beirdd y Tywysogion* (*CBT*). The seventh and final volume was published in 1996, and with it a better understanding of the linguistic and metrical criteria required to date the Arthurian poems became available.[21] The importance of the *CBT* corpus is that it 'represents the earliest externally datable corpus of work in the Welsh language' large enough to provide sufficient examples for linguistic analysis.[22] The availability of a reliable and heavily annotated edition of datable medieval Welsh poetry has meant that the dates put forward by earlier scholars have come under closer scrutiny, and the implications for the medieval Welsh Arthurian poems have been significant.

The texts available in the *CBT* corpus have led to a better understanding of the linguistic development of the Welsh language during the twelfth century, notably by Simon Rodway, who has shown that many of the verbal forms considered early by Ifor Williams and his student Kenneth Jackson were still in regular use in the later twelfth century.[23] This means that the *c*.1100 dates suggested for some of the Arthurian poems by earlier scholars look increasingly unlikely. Marged Haycock's edition of the legendary poems from the Book of Taliesin has shown that some features found in the poetry, previously thought to date from pre *c*.1100, are also found in the work of the court poets, most notably in the work of Prydydd y Moch (1175–1220).[24] These 'unexpected findings' affect the Arthurian material from the Book of Taliesin, and Haycock notes:[25]

> It has been said, echoing T. J. Morgan, that the court poets in their praise poems were knitting the same socks with the same wool, but making them to a more complicated pattern. However, it may in some cases be masking another possible scenario – that some of the putative *hengerdd* or old poetry, traditionally kept in its separate pre-c.1100 box by scholars, overlaps with, or is in a somewhat more complicated relationship with the compositions of the twelfth and thirteenth-century court poets.[26]

Manuscripts and texts

The greatest claims for antiquity have been made regarding 'Y Gododdin' on the basis that its author, Aneirin, is named as one of the sixth-century poets in the sentence from the *Historia Brittonum* (page 58).[27] The surviving text is unusual in that the manuscript preserves two different versions of the same poem in two different hands, known as A and B. A single passing reference to Arthur is found only in the B text and is entirely absent from the A text.

gochore brein du ar uur	He fed black ravens on the rampart of a fortress
caer ceni bei af arthur	Though he was no Arthur
rug ciuin uerthi ig disur	Among the powerful ones in battle
ig kynnor guernor guaurdur	In the front rank, Gwarddur was a palisade.[28]

This stanza contains no topographical material and therefore does not associate Arthur with the landscape of Wales in any way. The date of the poem's composition has dominated recent scholarship, and if the earlier dates put forward are accepted then it would contain the first reference to Arthur anywhere in world literature. Kenneth Jackson, following the lead of Ifor Williams, dated the poem to 'about 600'; John Koch in his reconstruction of the text dates it to soon after the battle at Catraeth, which he dates to *c.*570; Higham has suggested that the mention of Arthur is a reference to the *Historia Brittonum*, thereby dating it to post-830; and Isaac has argued that a date as late as 1050 should not be ruled out.[29] The matter remains unresolved. However, the poem is almost certainly older than 1100 and therefore remains the earliest reference to Arthur in a Welsh text.

The Black Book of Carmarthen (Aberystwyth, NLW, Peniarth 1, *c.*1250) is the earliest manuscript of length written in Welsh and contains three poems of Arthurian interest.[30] All three poems have been dated to pre-*c.*1100, but in light of the developments outlined above, later dates are quite possible. The 'Englynion y Beddau' (Stanzas of the Graves) is a collection of seventy-three stanzas noting the burial places of heroes from Welsh tradition and containing a wealth of place names and topographical details.[31] The text refers to Arthurian names, such as Gwalchmai buried 'in Peryddon', Bedwyr 'on the slopes of Tryfan' and 'the grave of Osfran's son at Camlan'.[32] The reference to the burial place of Arthur, however, is frustratingly cryptic: *anoeth bid bet y arthur* (Difficult to attain in this world, a grave for Arthur).[33] This vague reference has been interpreted by some as a reference to the belief that Arthur was not dead, but sleeping in a cave. However, there is no native evidence for a belief in such a tradition in Wales until the sixteenth century. The lack of topographical detail in regard to the grave of Arthur suggests that, although the Welsh author of the 'Englynion y Beddau' knew of Arthur, he did not have the same detailed traditions about him as he did for the other heroes he wrote about.

The second poem, entitled *Gerient fil' Erbin*, is a eulogy to a warrior called Geraint and notes his death in battle at a place called Llongborth. It includes the stanza:

En llogporth y gueleis e. y Arthur	In Llongborth I saw to Arthur
guir deur kymynint a dur.	brave men – (they) used to slay with steel –
ameraudur llywiaudir llawur.	the emperor, the leader (in the) toil (of battle).[34]

Figure 4. (opposite) *A page from the Black Book of Carmarthen (written c.1250) showing a section of the poem about Arthur at Llongborth. His name can be seen two lines above the lacuna in the manuscript.* By permission of Llyfrgell Genedlaethol Cymru / The National Library of Wales.

Llongborth can be understood in one of two ways; either as a word meaning 'sea-port' or as a place name. Modern commentators seem content to identify it with Langport in Somerset, recorded as *langport*, the Old English for 'long market-place' as far back as Domesday Book.[35] Theophilus Evans, in his 1716 publication, *Drych y Prif Oesoedd*, proposed that it should be identified with Llanborth, near Aberporth in Ceredigion, an identification that is discussed in more detail on page 112. The true location of the site remains uncertain.

The final poem of Arthurian interest from the Black Book of Carmarthen is the most important of the three and is known to scholars, from its opening line, as 'Pa gur yv y porthor?' (What man is the Gatekeeper?). It consists of a dialogue between Arthur and a gatekeeper, in which Arthur is asked to name his men and their exploits before they can pass. The poem runs to ninety lines and contains the names of the Arthurian characters, Cai, Bedwyr and Uthyr Pendragon;

Kei win a aeth von	Cai the fair went to Mon
y dilein lleuon.	to destroy lions.
y iscuid oet mynud	His shield was polished
erbin cath paluc.[36]	against Palug's Cat.[36]

Palug's Cat also appears in the collection of triadic texts, collected together as *Trioedd Ynys Prydein*, at the end of an extended triad about the three powerful swineherds of the Isle of Britain.

> And at Llanfair in Arfon under the Black Rock she brought forth a kitten, and the powerful swineherd threw it from the Rock into the sea. And the sons of Palug fostered it in Mon, to their own harm: and that was Palug's Cat, and it was one of the three Great Oppressions of Mon.[37]

The association with Mon in both sources suggests that a more detailed tradition of Palug's Cat may have once existed in Welsh. Another possibility is that the tale was influenced by an episode in the Merlin section (written *c*.1230) of the *Lancelot-Grail* cycle, in which Arthur fights a monstrous cat near Lausanne in Switzerland.[38] Earlier still, is the poem, *Romanz des Franceis*, written *c*.1200, in which Arthur is killed by a cat called *Capalu*, which then goes on to conquer all of England.[39] Once again, the uncertainty over the date of the Welsh material makes it very difficult to ascertain which way the influence may have travelled.

The other Arthurian place name in the poem is *Tryfrwyd*, which appears on two occasions in the context of conflict and is almost certainly derived from the *Tribruit* of the battle list in the *Historia Brittonum*. The location of the battle is made no clearer in the poem.

Neus tic manauid	Manawyd brought
Eis tull o trywruid.[40]	Shattered spears back from Tryfrwyd.[41]

Ar traethev trywuid.	On the shores of Tryfrwyd,
in amvin a garvluid	fighting with Rough Grey,
Oet guychir y annuyd	furious was his nature
o cletyw ac yscuid.[42]	with sword and shield.[43]

In his discussion of this poem, Sims-Williams draws attention to the unusual topographical reference in the line '*Vythneint Elei*/vultures of Elei' and suggests that the *Elei* in question is linked to the modern-day river Ely, near Cardiff and might be an indication of the locality in which the poem was written. This possibility is supported by several references to *Elei* in the twelfth-century Book of Llandaf.[44] Two further references to Arthur exist in the Black Book of Carmarthen: one to Llacheu, the son of Arthur and another in a poem comparing the *teulu* (war band or family) of Madog ap Maredudd to that of the *teulu* of Arthur. Both show that Arthur was a useful comparative name, but neither provides any topographical associations.[45]

The manuscript known as the Book of Taliesin (Aberystwyth, NLW, Peniarth 2, *c*.1325) contains sixty-one, often obscure, poems attributed to a poet named Taliesin.[46] The handful of references to Arthur in this manuscript have been the source of much discussion, since they first became known to the wider world in the eighteenth century, and many claims have been made as to their antiquity. Arthur is named in five of the poems, although four of them only refer to him very briefly, e.g. 'Druids of the wise one / Prophesy to Arthur'[47] or 'It was I who shared my strong hold / Arthur has a mere ninth of my valour.'[48] Haycock, as noted above, has called into question the *c*.1100 dates attributed to them by earlier scholarship, and has also identified comparanda in the work of the court poet Prydydd y Moch (Llywarch ap Llewelyn) in all five poems that refer to Arthur. She also suggests a possible date of the 'second decade of the thirteenth century' for the poem 'Kat Godeu'.[49]

The longest and most widely discussed Arthurian poem in this manuscript is 'Preideu Annwfyn' ('The Spoils of Annwn') that describes a raid on *Annwn* (the otherworld) by Arthur and his men, in a ship called *Prytwen*, a name given to Arthur's shield in *HRB*.[50] The poem consists of sixty lines and provides eight place names, but seven of them are so obscure as to be of little use in trying to identify any real locations: *Caer Sidi* (Fort of the Sidi, *Sid* being an Irish term for the other world), *Caer Vedmit* (Mead-feast fort), *Gaer Rigor* (Petrification fort), *Caer Wydyr* (Glass fort), *Caer Golud* (Fort of impediment), *Caer Ochren* (Angular fort) and *Caer Vandwy* (Vandwy's fort). The only place name that seems worthwhile, from a topographical point of view, is *Doleu Defwy* (meadows of *Defwy*), which suggests that *Defwy* is a river name. *Defwy* is also mentioned in another poem from the same manuscript, in the line *Vn yw yn Deuwy pan ofwy y weirin* 'Delightful in Defwy, when he visits his people', but again without a topographical context from which to identify its location.[51]

The poem has been variously dated by scholars: John Koch suggests 'the poem probably dates to the eighth or ninth century'; Kenneth Jackson thought it to be 'probably of pre-Norman date'; but Patrick Sims-Williams notes that 'the date of composition cannot easily be narrowed further than *c*. 850-1150'.[52] In her notes to the poem, Haycock draws attention, yet again, to similarities with the work of Prydydd y Moch and thinks that an early date is debatable in a poem 'which purports to be spoken by a primordial poet reminiscing about his adventures in the distant Arthurian past'.[53]

The chronological boundary between the works of the *Cynfeirdd* and the *Gogynfeirdd* is seemingly not as clear cut as earlier scholarship would have us believe and what were previously considered to be almost two separate bodies of work may overlap by a century or more. This overlap brings the references to Arthur in the *CBT* corpus under closer scrutiny. Arthur is referred to in *CBT* on sixteen occasions, almost exclusively as a comparative figure, with the subjects of the poem having 'Arthur's Strength' etc.[54] Only six of the references pre-date 1200 and all of them are associated with princes of either Powys or Gwynedd, there being no references in association with Deheubarth or the south of Wales. Prydydd y Moch refers to Arthur on five occasions, more than any other poet, and if we accept the possible attribution of the Taliesin poetry to him, as noted above, then this would rise to ten.[55] All the poetry of Prydydd y Moch is concerned with Gwynedd, and in the latter half of his career, with Llywelyn ap Iorwerth in particular. The only *Gogynfeirdd* reference that provides a topographical context of any sort is found in a poem by Bleddyn Fardd (*c*.1258–84) to the three sons of Gruffudd ap Llywelyn:

Gwaed raeadyr baladyr, o lin Beli,	Blood-dripping lance, of Beli's lineage,
Gwae6ddur ual Arthur 6rth Gaer Uenlli	Steel-speared, like Arthur, at Caer Fenlli.[56]

The line compares the valour of Dafydd with that of Arthur. Caer Fenlli can be identified with the Iron Age hill fort on the summit of Foel Fenlli in the Clwydian Hills, overlooking the town of Ruthin. The problem with the line is that the syntax does not make it clear who was at Caer Fenlli, whether Arthur or Dafydd. The fact that Dafydd ruled Dyffryn Clwyd, and Foel Fenlli is a prominent landmark visible from most places in the area, suggest that the reference to Caer Fenlli should be associated with Dafydd, rather than understood as a reference to an otherwise unknown tradition of Arthur fighting at the hill fort. This is further reinforced by the genealogy of Dafydd, which does trace his lineage back to Beli Hir; no such claim can be made for Arthur.[57] Foel Fenlli is also the probable location for the site of the court of Benlli Gawr where, according to the *Historia Brittonum*, a lowly servant called Cadell defeated Benlli and became the founder of the Powys dynasty.[58] Benlli also appears, in a similar sense to Arthur, as a comparative figure in the work of the *Gogynfeirdd* on six occasions, as does Maelgwn Gwynedd (nine times), and most importantly his son Rhun (twenty-one times). All four figures are used for comparative purposes and originate in earlier sources, in particular the ninth-century *Historia Brittonum*, a source that was obviously known to, and used by, the *Gogynfeirdd* of the twelfth and early thirteenth century. There is no evidence of any topographical associations with Arthur in this corpus of poetry.

The lack of references to Arthur, in anything other than a comparative sense, continues into the later poetry. The *Beirdd yr Uchelwyr* (Poets of the Nobility), 1300–1540, also used Arthur as a hero to whom they could compare their patrons, focusing on his strength and prowess in battle, but as the influence of Geoffrey of Monmouth, via *Brut y Brenhinedd*, is obvious throughout their work, this is hardly surprising. A survey of this body of poetry finds no examples of any topographical association with Arthur, or any mention of his supposed messianic return.[59] A similar situation is also found in the mass of prophetic poetry of the same period, Arthur is very rarely mentioned and when he is, the reference is based upon *HRB*. There is no evidence for a Welsh belief in the messianic return of Arthur in these texts, the emphasis being on the heroic figures of Cynan, Cadwaladr and Owain.[60]

In the light of developments in dating Welsh linguistic changes, it is difficult to prove that any of the medieval Welsh poems to mention Arthur are earlier than Geoffrey of Monmouth in origin, with the probable exception of 'Y Gododdin'. As noted in chapter 1, Geoffrey of Monmouth probably had access to some Welsh traditions apart from those in the *Historia Brittonum*, and it is possible that the poetry under discussion here may also have had access to this material. A more likely scenario, though, is that it was the portrayal of Arthur in *HRB*, combined with his appearance in the *Historia Brittonum*, that informed the poets of twelfth- and early thirteenth-century Wales.[61]

Prose Tales

The most important medieval Welsh prose texts have been collectively known for the last two centuries as the *Mabinogion*.[62] The texts are found primarily in two medieval manuscripts, the White Book of Rhydderch (Aberystwyth, NLW Peniarth 4 and 5, *c*.1350) and the Red Book of Hergest, (Oxford, Jesus College 111, *c*.1400), although earlier fragments of some of the texts survive in thirteenth-century manuscripts.[63] The collection has been divided, for the sake of convenience, into three sections: the 'Four Branches' consisting of *Branwen*, *Pwyll*, *Manawydan* and *Math vab Mathonwy*; the 'Three Romances', *Owain*, *Peredur* and *Geraint*; and the 'Four Native Tales', *Culhwch and Olwen*, *Lludd and Llevelys*, *Dream of Rhonabwy* and the *Dream of Macsen Wledig*. This division does not represent the order of the tales in the earliest manuscripts. Arthur is completely absent from the 'Four Branches', and they will therefore not be discussed here.[64] The 'Three Romances' all show influence from the French Arthurian texts of Chrétien de Troyes, discussed in the previous chapter and are discussed below. Of the 'Four Native Tales' only *Culhwch and Olwen* and *Dream of Rhonabwy* are of Arthurian interest, and between them they contain a majority of the Arthurian topographical material that originates in medieval Welsh sources.

Culhwch and Olwen has long been recognised as the earliest and most extensive Arthurian prose text in Welsh and has been subjected to much scholarly discussion. The tale tells of Culhwch's quest to gain the hand of Olwen, the daughter of a giant called Ysbaddaden, with the help of Arthur and his men. The most recent editors of the text break it down into three sections.

> The first part tells of the hero's birth and the quest imposed upon him by the ill will of his jealous stepmother which brings him to Arthur's court. The second part describes the reception given to Culhwch and his companions at the fortress of Ysbaddaden, and it lists the *anoethau* or difficult tasks imposed on them by the giant. The final part is made up of tales of the accomplishment of some ten of these tasks.[65]

The tale is notable for placing Arthur's court at a place called Gelliwig, its breathtakingly long list of the names of people at Arthur's court and for its detailed description of Arthur and his men hunting the Twrch Trwyth (the Boar called Trwyth) across the mountains of south Wales. The tale shares names and themes with the poems 'Pa Gur' and 'Preiddeu Annwfn' discussed above, and together they provide us with the best evidence for understanding how Arthur was perceived in Wales before the Edwardian conquest of 1282.

The earliest text of *Culhwch and Olwen* is found in the White Book of Rhydderch, but the final third is missing owing to the lack of a folio.[66] The only medieval manuscript to contain the full text of the tale is the Red Book of Hergest which was written for Hopcyn ap Tomas sometime after 1382, but before his death in 1405.[67] The text in the Red Book has undergone a degree of modernisation, with the orthography updated and the meaning of the text clarified in places.[68] The text was first published by Lady Charlotte Guest in 1842 (based only on the Red Book of Hergest) with an accompanying English translation and notes.[69]

The first serious detailed study of the tale was undertaken by Sir Idris Foster in his unpublished MA thesis of 1935, in which he argued that the tale dated from c.1100.[70] He based his conclusion upon a linguistic analysis and the supposed similarities between historic events of that period and events in the tale, especially the boar hunt. Foster's views gained a wider audience from his article in the collaborative *Arthurian Literature in the Middle Ages* (1959).[71] Foster had been preparing a text for publication for many years, but it remained unpublished at his death in 1984.[72] In 1988, Rachel Bromwich and D. Simon Evans published Foster's text with minor changes, accompanied by a Welsh introduction and notes.[73] A revised and enlarged English edition was published in 1992 and this remains the standard text for any serious study.[74] Although Bromwich and Evans agreed in general with the c.1100 date proposed by Foster, suggestions that they thought the text may be of a later date occasionally find their way into their introduction.[75] As with the poetry discussed above, it was not until the publication of the *CBT* corpus that a comparative study of linguistic features found in the securely dated *Gogynfeirdd* poetry could be undertaken. In his 2005 article on the text, Simon Rodway showed that the earlier linguistic arguments used by Foster for his c.1100 date need to be revised in the light of advances in scholarship since the 1930s.[76] He also notes that the supposed historical events alluded to in the text that Foster identified were also, on closer examination, wishful thinking.[77] The long-held view that a lack of influence from *HRB* meant that the tale must pre-date *HRB* is also called into question by Rodway, and he concludes, 'there has been a reluctance to accept that an Arthurian text would have been composed in the post-Galfridian period without referring to it.'[78]

The first possible example of influence from *HRB* on Welsh literature appears in poetry from the 1220s, although the first definitive influence is not found until 1260.[79] Simply put, if none of the poetry that dates from the twelfth century contains any reference to *HRB*, why should we use this very same absence in the prose works to insist upon a date of composition before *HRB* in 1138? The first references to *HRB* in the poetry only appear following the translation of the Latin text into Welsh in the early thirteenth century (more of which below), which suggests that Welsh prose texts need not show any Galfridain influence before that date. Rodway concludes that the version of *Culhwch and Olwen* that has come down to us was written in the latter half of the twelfth century.[80] In considering the question of the likely author of the tale he suggests that, 'A court poet seems to me to be an eminently suitable candidate.'[81]

Although Arthur appears throughout *Culhwch and Olwen*, two sections in particular have dominated Arthurian studies, and these sections also contain the most detailed topographical material. The first is a list that names over 250 men and women at Arthur's court, running to nearly 200 lines in the printed text and nine columns in the White Book of Rhydderch. The list comprises a sixth of the tale in total, and some of the names are also found in 'Pa Gur', 'Y Gododdin' and the 'Four Branches', as well as the *Ulster Cycle*.[82] Several commentators have noted that the court list is most likely an accretion to the tale, added at some point before the earliest surviving manuscripts, and that it may have inspired similar, albeit shorter, lists in *The Dream of Rhonabwy* and *Geraint*.[83] Despite the large number of persons named, several of whom are described as Arthur's relatives, there are only three place names possibly relevant to Wales in the list: Camlan, Ehangwen and Caer Dathyl.[84] Camlan has been discussed in chapter 1, and although Arthur's hall of Ehangwen is mentioned elsewhere by later poets, at no point is it ever localised.[85] The remaining place name occurs after listing the six sons of Iaen: 'Gwyr Kaer tathal oedynt, kenetyl y Arthur o pleit y tat' (Men of Caer Dathyl were they, kindred to Arthur on his father's side).[86]

The location of Caer Dathyl is not made clear in *Culhwch and Olwen*, but fortunately it is also mentioned in the fourth branch of the Mabinogi, *Math Uab Mathonwy*, as the court of Math at 'Caer Dathyl in Arfon'.[87] The medieval cantref of Arfon was centred upon the town of Caernarfon and contained the important ecclesiastical centres of Bangor and Clynnog Fawr, but the name Caer Dathyl no longer survives. W. J. Gruffydd in his study of the tale thought that the Iron Age hill fort at Tre'r Ceiri was the most likely site, whereas Ifor Williams suggested the Roman settlement at Segontium.[88] The exact location remains obscure, but somewhere near the coast, in the vicinity of the hill fort of Dinas Dinlle is likely intended. The reference in *Culhwch and Olwen* is unique in that it not only associates Arthur with a family line by suggesting some sort of kindred with his father, Uthyr Pendragon, but also names where that family is from.[89]

The Boar Hunt

Arthur's hunt for the *Twrch Trwyth* (The Boar called Trwyth), contains the most detailed topographical material in *Culhwch and Olwen*, but, because of the missing folios in the White Book of Rhydderch, this episode only survives in the later Red Book of Hergest.[90] This well-known onomastic episode lists over thirty place names in south Wales that are visited during the journey that the Boar took across south

Wales, before crossing the Severn estuary to the south-west peninsula and disappearing into the sea off Cornwall.[91] To discuss every geographical place name visited by Arthur in this section individually would require many pages. Therefore each place name has been dealt with in turn in the Gazetteer in Appendix 2. The episode has been discussed in detail many times since it was first published by Charlotte Guest in 1842, and different interpretations have been put forward to try and explain it.[92] Apart from this episode in *Culhwch and Olwen*, the Twrch Trwyth is also mentioned in the *Mirabilia* associated with the *Historia Brittonum*, discussed in chapter 1 and in the poem 'Gwarchan Cynfelyn' from the Book of Aneirin.[93] It also appears on one occasion in the *CBT* corpus and on five occasions in the work of the later poets, but it is not clear whether these are references to *Culhwch* or the other sources.[94]

At the outset I had hoped that I might be able to find some association between the place names from *Culhwch and Olwen* in land grants, charters and other documents that might give some clue as to who may have been responsible for the tale, but frustratingly no concrete correspondences were found. Despite this, it is possible to put forward some observations in more general terms. It has long been thought, primarily due to a lack of any sensible alternative, that many of the medieval Welsh manuscripts were written at Cistercian abbeys.[95] With this in mind it is worth noting that none of the place names in the text lie on lands owned by the Cistercian Order. In fact, when compared against the maps in David Williams's *Atlas of Cistercian Lands in Wales*, it is noticeable how the route taken by the boar studiously avoids all Cistercian lands; however, it is impossible to say whether this is deliberate or just a coincidence.[96] The only place name mentioned during the Boar Hunt episode that can be associated with the lands of any monastic house is Cwm Cerwyn.[97] The abbey of the Tironensian Order at St Dogmaels near Cardigan was founded by Robert Fitzmartin in 1118 and endowed with lands in south Wales and Devon, including Combkaro (Cwm Cerwyn) and the nearby *Nigra Grangia* (Mynachlog Ddu) in the Prescelli hills.[98] Three confirmations of these endowments by Henry I are given in the *Cartulary of Tiron*, and the boundaries of the properties also survive in another confirmation from the time of Edward III.[99] Another intriguing possibility surrounds the lands owned by the Premonstratensian abbey at Talley in Carmarthenshire, founded by the Lord Rhys in 1185, which cover areas described in the Boar Hunt, but again a survey of the surviving documents did not reveal any references to places named in the tale.[100] These findings give rise to the possibility that the episode may have had some sort of secular purpose in origin and further research, with a later date for the text in mind, may bring more evidence to light.

Gelliwig

Apart from the detailed geography of the boar hunt the other prominent Arthurian feature of *Culhwch and Olwen* is the location of his court at *Gelliwig yn Cernyw* (usually translated as Gelliwig in Cornwall) that the author mentions on five occasions.[101]

Figure 5. *Aerial view of the Presceli Hills where Arthur hunted the Twrch Trwyth in Culhwch and Olwen.* © Crown Copyright RCAHMW.

Although Geoffrey of Monmouth places Arthur's final battle in Cornwall, he never mentions his having a court there, nor do any of the continental Arthurian romances. Gelliwig is only associated with Arthur in two Welsh sources, *Culhwch and Olwen* and *Trioedd Ynys Prydein*.[102] The earliest examples of this body of legendary triadic material are preserved in NLW Peniarth 16 (*c.*1275) and the closely related NLW Peniarth 45 (*c.*1300). Bromwich has shown that the triads were in existence by the mid-twelfth century and that they share many names and themes with the *Gogynfi-erdd* poetry and the prose texts, especially *Culhwch and Olwen*.[103] In the ninety-seven triads published by Bromwich, Arthur is mentioned in twenty-two of them, but for the purposes of this work only four of them contain any place-name evidence. Three are concerned with Gelliwig and will be discussed below; the remaining triad (no. 52) describes Arthur being imprisoned in two places, Caer Oeth ac Anoeth and Llech Echeifyeint, neither of which can be identified.[104] The three triads (nos. 1, 54 and 85) that mention Gelliwig, all locate it in Cernyw and name the site as Arthur's Court, therefore sharing the same tradition as *Culhwch and Olwen*.

The fact that medieval Welsh sources locate Arthur's court in Cornwall has been discussed many times, most notably by Oliver Padel, who notes that 'It demands identification and there have numerous attempts to do so', before going on to summarise the efforts of Cornish antiquarians and scholars over the last 250 years.[105] Padel refers to the two other instances of the name recorded in Wales, one near Botwnnog and the other near Llanvetherine in Monmouthsire, but makes no reference to the non-Arthurian medieval Welsh sources that also mention Gelliwig; indeed they appear to have received very little attention at all.[106] The earliest Welsh reference to a place called Gelliwig, in a non-Arthurian context, can be found in an elegy to Owain Gwynedd written shortly after his death in 1170 by Cynddelw Brydydd Mawr. In the poem Cynddelw compares Owain's court at Llanbeblig, near Caernarfon, with that of Gelliwig in the line;

> *Kyrt kertynt, mal kynt Kelliwyc*   Hosts would travel, as once [in] Celliwig.[107]

Another early non-Arthurian reference is found in a charter for the Cistercian abbey of Cymmer, near Dolgellau, dating from 1209. It names several sites owned by the abbey in, or bordering, the commote of Neigwl, on the Llŷn peninsula, including *ynyskellywyc* (ynys is being used here to denote a dry spot in a marshy place, rather than an island) which can be identified with the modern day Plas Gelliwig, near Botwnnog.[108] Further references to this non-Arthurian Gelliwig can be found in the later poetry.[109] The only other site named Gelliwig in Wales is referred to in fourteenth-century manorial records as Gelli-Wig and refers to a location, today named Gelli (SO 3609 1691), near Llanvetherine in Monmouthshire.[110]

The Arthurian association of Gelliwig with Cornwall is only to be found in *Culhwch and Olwen*, the Triads and the recently discovered Cornish play, *Bewnans Ke*.[111] The association is not found in other Welsh sources, and the reasons for this separate development are as yet uncertain. A potential crux to this problem is the exact meaning of the word *cernyw*. It is the modern Welsh term for Cornwall and has been understood in this context in the Arthurian sources. However, it has been suggested that the word may also once have been used to mean a peninsula, making the phrase *Gelliwig yn Cernyw* equally applicable to the site on the Llŷn peninsula.[112] With the exception of Caer Dathyl, there are no place names identifiable in north Wales, but in some instances references in the text to *y gogledd* (the north) could relate to this region.

As noted previously, Rodway has suggested that a court poet would be a likely candidate for the author of the tale, but stops short of naming any particular individual. With this in mind, it should be pointed out that the poem 'Marwnad Owain Gwynedd', written by Cynddelw (*c*.1170), refers to seven names from the court list, including Dilus fab Efrai, not named elsewhere, and is the only poem in the *CBT* corpus to mention the place names Caer Dathyl and Gelliwig.[113] The same poet is also responsible for the sole *Gogynfeirdd* reference to the Twrch Trwyth. Cynddelw flourished between 1155 and 1200, the period in which Rodway suggests that the tale might have been written, and wrote poems for the rulers of Powys, Gwynedd and Deheubarth during his career. If a court poet was the author of the tale, then Cynddelw Brydydd Mawr is certainly the strongest candidate for that role.

With the exception of an allusion to the tale by Dafydd ap Gwilym (*fl.* 1340–70), the personal names Culhwch and Olwen do not appear in the index to the works of the *Beirdd yr Uchelwyr*, suggesting it was unlikely that the tale was ever widely known.[114] Aside from a very brief passing mention in the catalogue of Welsh manuscripts produced by Edward Lhwyd in his *Archaeologia Britannica* (1707), the earliest modern reference to the tale is in the *Cambrian Biography* (1803) of William Owen Pughe.[115] The amount of attention the tale has received in the twentieth century can give the impression that the tale has always been well known, but this seems not to have been the case. The tale has long been used as a cornerstone for the dating of Welsh Arthurian texts and the compelling suggestion by Rodway that it may date from a later period has called much of the earlier scholarship on the dating of the text into question.

Three romances

The three tales of *Geraint, Owein* and *Peredur* are all derived, to a greater or lesser extent, from the three poems, *Yvain, Erec et Enide* and *Perceval* written by Chrétien de Troyes, and are often referred to for convenience' sake as *Y Tair Rhamant* (The Three Romances).[116] The Welsh texts are derived from the French, although, as with many other medieval Welsh texts, they are not translations in the strictest sense of the word. *Geraint* and *Owein* are closest to the French sources, whereas the relationship of *Peredur* to the French is much more complex. Unlike *Culhwch and Olwen*, fragments of all three texts can be found in manuscripts earlier than the White Book of Rhydderch.[117] All three tales have been dated to the first half of the thirteenth century, but the questions of where and for whom the tales were written, remain unanswered.[118] Unfortunately they contain very few place names relevant to Wales.

Geraint follows its French source, *Erec et Enide*, very closely and from a topographical point of view is the most interesting of the three tales.[119] *Erec et Enide*, as discussed in the previous chapter, has a close connection with Cardigan, but in the opening lines of *Geraint* Arthur's court is held instead at Caerleon on Usk. The reason for this change is unclear, but may perhaps have something to do with the ownership of Cardigan Castle at the time of composition, as it changed hands between Welsh and Norman ownership on at least three occasions in the thirteenth century.[120] The author seems to have had some knowledge of south-east Wales, as he has Geraint travelling to 'the town that is now called Caerdyf' by crossing the Usk and then again on his return. Cardiff is only mentioned on one occasion in French Arthurian romances, as a bishopric (most likely Llandaf is meant) in Gerbert de Montreuil's *Perceval Continuation* (1225–30), while it also appears in some later Middle English Arthurian poems and Malory's *Le Morte Darthur*.[121]

The entire text of *Owein* contains only three place names, and the only one relevant to Wales is again Caerleon on Usk.[122] The author of *Owein* has also replaced the name of Arthur's court in the French text, in this instance 'Carduel en Gales', with Caerleon on Usk. Although Carduel is described as '*en Gales*', most commentators have identified it with the English city of Carlisle, but in some romances it does appear to have been confused with Carleon on Usk.[123]

Peredur survives in four different manuscripts and in two different versions. The relationships between the two versions are complex, making it difficult to agree upon a standard text or date of composition.[124] The tale has obvious parallels with Chrétien de Troyes's *Perceval* (1180) and the *First Continuation* (1190), but despite its interesting textual history, *Peredur* is not helpful from a topographical perspective, as the only place mentioned in Wales is, again, Caerleon on Usk.

Y Seint Greal

The three texts discussed above show how medieval Welsh authors adapted earlier French Arthurian material in such a way as to make the tales more acceptable to their intended audience. Further evidence of the Welsh adaption of French Arthurian romance is found in the Welsh text *Y Seint Greal*, a translation of two French grail romances: the *Queste del Saint Graal* from the *Lancelot-Grail* cycle, and the *Perlesvaus*. The translation was made for Hopcyn ap Tomas, the owner of the Red Book of Hergest, and the oldest surviving manuscript, Aberystwyth, NLW Peniarth 11 (*c.*1400), is written by the same scribe, Hywel Fychan.[125] Later manuscripts of the text survive and give some indication of its popularity, but with the exception of a fragment in Peniarth 15, all are copies of Peniarth 11.[126] Guto Glyn refers to a manuscript of the text in one of his poems (written *c.*1480), where he asks to borrow it from Trahearn ap Ieuan of Pen Rhos, near Caerleon, on behalf of Dafydd ab Ieuan, the abbot of Valle Crucis Abbey near Llangollen in Denbighshire.[127] As with the three romances noted above, the Welsh text adapts the proper names for its intended audience and gives the Welsh form for place names in England. Ceridwen Lloyd-Morgan, in her study of the text, notes only one instance where a Welsh place name is added that does not derive from the French text. The French text of *Perlesvaus* refers to 'an island which lies in the sea', whereas *Y Seint Greal* replaces this with, 'an island that is called Lanoc'.[128] Glannog is the medieval Welsh name for Ynys Seiriol, the island off the east coast of Anglesey, better known today as Puffin Island, and Lloyd-Morgan notes that 'The most likely explanation for the inclusion of this name is that the translator had lived in northern Caernarfonshire or eastern Anglesey and chose this island as he was familiar with it.'[129]

From the early thirteenth century onwards, many popular European texts were translated into Welsh, often in the same manuscripts as the Arthurian romances – *Beves of Hampton*, *Seven Sages of Rome*, *The Songs of Charlemagne*, etc.[130] These later Welsh texts are far removed from the Arthurian material discussed at the beginning of this chapter, and show that the nobility of Wales had a keen interest in continental literature and, in the case of Arthur, an opportunity to merge it with earlier Welsh material.[131] The existence of Arthurian romances in Welsh should perhaps be viewed as a part of this general interest in continental literature, rather than any particularly strong interest in the Arthurian legend alone.

The Dream of Rhonabwy

The Dream of Rhonabwy, unlike the other Mabinogion texts, is only found in the Red Book of Hergest, and then in isolation from the other tales.[132] The centrepiece of the tale has Arthur and Owain playing a game of *gwyddbwyll* (a type of chess) while a battle rages around them. The tale is also notable for a list of forty-two of Arthur's warriors, which includes names originating from *HRB* and a reference to the battle of Camlan.[133] Native material is interwoven with these names, and the tale has been described by Lloyd-Morgan as, 'something new, a completely original Arthurian tale, lacking any close parallels, and composed in a satiric rather than heroic vein, with a highly complex interplay of ambiguities and ironies.'[134] The date of composition for *The Dream of Rhonabwy* is still uncertain, with suggested dates ranging from 1160, through to the late fourteenth century.[135] As with *Culhwch and Olwen*, *The Dream of Rhonabwy* was not well known among the later poets; a solitary reference to '*ail Rhonabwy*' (a second Rhonabwy) can be found in a poem by Madog Dwygraig, who also wrote for Hopcyn ap Tomas, for whom the Red Book of Hergest was written.[136] The text seems to have been virtually unknown until it was first published, along with an English translation and notes, by Lady Charlotte Guest in 1843.[137]

The introduction to the tale sets it very clearly in Powys and associates it with the reign of Madog ap Maredudd (d. 1160). The main character, Rhonabwy, has a dream about King Arthur and the battle of *Gwaith Faddon*, the Welsh rendering of Badon, the important British victory first mentioned by Gildas c.540 and then associated with Arthur in the *Historia Brittonum*, c.830.[138] This Arthurian section of the tale is set, on the evidence of three place names that are mentioned, in a small area near Welshpool. The first, Rhyd y Groes, is situated on the River Severn, in the vicinity of the village of Buttington and was the site of a battle in 1039 in which Gruffudd ap Llewelyn defeated the Saxons.[139] The second name, Digoll, is found associated with an earthwork on the high ground of Long Mountain known as Caer Digoll or Beacon Ring (SJ 265 058).[140] A battle of Digoll was fought by the seventh-century Welsh ruler Cadwallon and is mentioned in a poem, of uncertain date, in the Red Book of Hergest.[141] It is also mentioned in a twelfth-century poem by Cynddelw Brydydd Mawr and was associated with the 1295 revolt of Madog ap Llewelyn, by Humphrey Lhwyd in his *Cronica Wallia* (1559).[142] *Argyngroeg* is named in early fourteenth-century records as a place where a market was held just north of Welshpool, and survives today in the form Gyngrog.[143] The author of the *Dream of Rhonabwy* also places *Gwaith Faddon* in the same area, a localisation not found in any other Welsh source.[144] This confined area, north of Welshpool, does not play any further role in Welsh Arthurian sources and the reasons for locating the narrative in this area remain uncertain.

Brut y Brenhinedd

Chapter 1 discussed the near-immediate impact of Geoffrey of Monmouth's *HRB* (1138) on the history and literature of England and the continent, but in Wales, as noted above, the impact was not felt until *c.*1200. Over sixty manuscripts of *Brut y Brenhinedd* (Chronicle of the Kings), the Welsh translation of *HRB*, survive, about a third of which are medieval.[145] Modern scholarship relies heavily upon the work of Brynley F. Roberts for its understanding of the different versions of the text and how they relate to one another.[146] No comprehensive edition of the texts has yet been published. Roberts identifies three independent early translations and dates their composition to the early thirteenth century: *Brut Dingestow* (NLW MS 5266B), the incomplete NLW Peniarth 44 and NLW Llanstephan 1, both written in the same hand.[147] Although they are all independent translations, they show signs of having borrowed from one another, and the fact that all three are contemporaneous has led Roberts to suggest: 'These relationships, together with the similarity in the forms of personal names, seem to suggest, if not some element of co-operation, at least the possibility that an early Welsh translation of the *Historia* quickly became known at other centres.'[148]

The texts are close translations of the Latin, but the translators made changes to make the work more suitable to Welsh audiences. Similar changes can be found in the First Variant Version of *HRB*, and Charlotte Ward has shown how the Welsh translators toned down the military might of the Saxons, omitted references to courtly behaviour and heightened Arthur's military prowess, bringing the text closer to the world depicted in other medieval Welsh prose tales.[149] *Brut y Brenhinedd*, like *Y Seint Greal* discussed above, was further adapted for a Welsh audience by the use of alternative Welsh proper names, prompting Brynley Roberts to note:

> The *Historia* seems to reflect existing Welsh tradition in only a few sections and consequently these were the only opportunities for differences between the two to arise. For the most part, Geoffrey was accepted by his translators, who changed very little in the content of the *Historia*. Their versions of proper names, in general, do not point to the use of antecedent Welsh traditions by Geoffrey to any great extent. The trend, in fact was in the opposite direction. By replacing the proper names by genuine Welsh forms, sometimes related to the Latin, frequently not, they made the *Historia* even more acceptable to a Welsh audience.[150]

Throughout most of the twelfth century Geoffrey's pseudo-history seems to have had little impact on Welsh poetry or prose, and Bromwich notes that 'we are consequently drawn to the conclusion that the bards made no use of Geoffrey's narrative until after this had become available to them in a Welsh dress.'[151] The delayed influence of HRB upon Welsh literature is crucial for our understanding of when Welsh Arthurian material, that shows no influence from *HRB*, was written. Texts which have often been referred to as pre-Geoffrey and therefore pre-1138, should perhaps be more accurately described as pre-*Brut y Brenhinedd* and therefore pre-1200.

As shown in chapter 1, with the exception of Caerleon, Geoffrey has few geographical references to Arthur in Wales, and even though *Brut y Brenhinedd* makes many minor changes to the Latin text, it does not change this situation. The text adds nothing to the Arthurian topography of Wales, but it does provide us with a scenario that may explain the limited use of Arthur in medieval Welsh sources. The first attempts at unifying the Welsh kingdoms into a single nation can be found in the reign of Gruffudd ap Llywelyn who, through conquest, was ruler of Gwynedd, Powys and Deheubarth from 1055 until his death in 1063.[152] It was not until the invasion of Wales by Henry II in 1165 that the Welsh princes gathered together again under the command of a single leader, namely Owain Gwynedd, to fight a common enemy.[153] It is at this time that Owain refers to himself in letters as 'king of Wales' (*rex Walie*) and 'Prince of Wales' (*Waliarum princeps*), the first time that any Welsh ruler had used such titles.[154] Owain's claim to be the ruler of all Wales was only short-lived, as he died in 1170 and the kingdom of Gwynedd descended into chaos as his sons fought for supremacy.[155]

By 1201 Llywelyn ap Iorwerth, Owain's grandson, had wrested control of Gwynedd from his uncles, and in the July of that year he negotiated a peace accord with King John in which he used the title 'Prince of North Wales' (*princeps Northwallie*).[156] Now recognised as the ruler of north Wales by the king, Llywelyn cemented his position by marrying John's daughter Joan in the spring of 1205, but by 1210 the relationship had soured and John launched the first royal military incursion into Wales since the aborted attempt of his father Henry II in 1165.[157] The incursion continued until the spring of 1211, when Llywelyn, realising he could not win, accepted the humiliating terms of surrender set by John.[158] The terms included the loss of all of north Wales east of the River Conwy, the return of Merioneth to Hywel ap Gruffudd and the promise that the remaining lands of Gwynedd would pass to the Crown on his death if he did not produce a male heir with Joan.[159] By August 1212, Llewelyn spoke on behalf of all the princes of Wales in an alliance with Philip, the ruler of France, against King John, and by 1215 had secured three Welsh concessions in Magna Carta.[160] With his new status securely established, Llywelyn called an assembly of the princes of Wales at Aberdyfi, and as Turvey notes, 'the foundations of a greater Venedotian state were laid by Llewelyn at Aberdyfi in 1216, when he largely succeeded in binding the other lords and princes of Wales by ties of client-ship and dependence which involved the swearing of oaths of fealty.'[161] Despite the occasional setback, Llewelyn retained the position he had established in 1216, as the most powerful ruler in Wales, until his death in 1240. Llywelyn's desire to establish a united Wales with a national identity is evident in the literary output of Gwynedd during his reign, and, as Rees Davies notes, 'it is certainly noteworthy that the law texts, chronicles and official correspondence of the thirteenth century all partake of the phraseology of a Welsh national identity.'[162]

It was during Llywelyn's reign that the historical mythology of a pre-Norman, and therefore pre-colonial, Wales was actively promoted through the prologues to the Law Books, the production of literary texts such as the Four Branches and, perhaps most importantly, the translation of *HRB* into Welsh as *Brut y Brenhinedd*.[163] *HRB* provided something very important to the Gwynedd dynasty: it portrayed Wales as a single nation with an ancient past, in terms that would resonate with the English and complement their own fledgling historical mythology. This image was further reinforced by Geoffrey's claim that he found his information in 'a very old book in the British tongue', and a proven descent from Brutus became more relevant and important than any association with Arthur.[164] In medieval Welsh poetry notable heroes from the Welsh past, such as Maelgwn Gwynedd and his son Rhun, are frequently claimed as ancestors, but Arthur remains a merely comparative figure. Outside the *Brut* tradition, nobody claimed descent from him and, apart from allusions to his prowess in battle, he played no part in the works promoting Gwynedd's supremacy within Wales. The likely reason for Arthur's absence is the fact that the English Crown had periodically used Arthur as a figure to represent its own wished-for hegemony over the whole of the British Isles since the reign of Henry II, thereby making him an unattractive figurehead for the Gwynedd dynasty. According to *HRB*, Arthur was succeeded by rulers called Malgo (Maelgwn), Run (Rhun) and Caduanus (Cadfan), all names well known to Welsh tradition and not figures the English Crown could lay claim too. By emphasising their links to these kings, the Welsh, to all intents and purposes, abandoned Arthur to the English propaganda machine, only showing an interest in him again in the Tudor period.

Conclusion

The amount of scholarly attention lavished upon the small number of medieval Welsh texts that mention Arthur can often give the impression that Arthur played a prominent role in the medieval literature of Wales. The long-held consensus that certain texts must have predated Geoffrey of Monmouth's *HRB* of 1138, because they show no influence from it, has been responsible for much of the published work, but the two basic arguments behind this position have been challenged by more recent scholarship. A better understanding of the development of the Welsh language in the medieval period has evolved since the publication of *CBT*, and the results of this new understanding are increasingly being applied to prose texts and the difficult-to-date *cynfeirdd* poetry. *HRB* may have had an immediate impact on Latin and Anglo-Norman literature, but it was not until it was translated into Welsh *c*.1200, that it began to have any noticeable impact upon Welsh literature.

The lack of references to the prose tales, *Culhwch and Olwen* and the *Dream of Rhonabwy*, in medieval poetry suggests that they were only known to a very small literary circle, and the possibility that they represented a widely known Arthurian tradition seems very unlikely. These two prose texts contain identifiable Welsh place names associated with Arthur, the Boar Hunt from *Culhwch and Olwen* being the outstanding example, but none of these associations are mentioned elsewhere until the rediscovery of the text in the nineteenth century. In over 400 years of Welsh poetry there is only one possible association of Arthur with an identifiable location, at Foel Fenlli, and even that is doubtful. The poetry also makes no mention of the 'well-known' tradition of Arthur's return, the role of a returning hero being filled by Owain Lawgoch and Owain Glyndŵr in the fifteenth century. Arthur is only notable by his absence from such works.

The lack of a role for Arthur in the Gwynedd propaganda, produced during the attempt by the dynasty to gain hegemony over the whole of Wales, is illustrative of his minor role in the national consciousness of medieval Wales. It is only when the authenticity of Geoffrey of Monmouth's *HRB* was called into question in the early sixteenth century that Welsh authors, fired by a renewed sense of nationalism under the Tudor dynasty, began to claim the figure of Arthur as their own.

Notes

1   Daniel Huws, *Medieval Welsh Manuscripts* (Aberystwyth, 2000) is a compilation of his most important articles on the matter and an essential work. Currently in an advanced state of preparation is the same author's *Repertory of Welsh Manuscripts and Scribes*, which will describe over 3,000 Welsh manuscripts as well as identifying over 100 scribal hands.

2   Huws, *Medieval Welsh Manuscripts*, pp. 57–64, provides a chronological list of medieval Welsh manuscripts (1250–1540) and also identifies those written by the same scribe.

3   G. J. Williams and E. J. Jones, *Gramedegau'r Penceirddiaid* (Cardiff, 1934), p. 49.

4   A. W. Wade-Evans, *Nennius's History of the Britons* (London, 1938), p. 80: 'Tunc Talhaern Tataguen in poemate claruit; et Neirin, et Taliessin, et Bluchbard, et Cian, qui vocatur Gueinth Guaut, simul uno tempore in poemate Brittannico claruerunt'; E. Faral (ed), *La légende arthurienne: études et documents, les plus anciens textes*, 3 vols (Paris, 1929), III, p. 42.

5   John Prise, *Historiae Brytannicae Defensio* (London, 1573), p. 122; Ceri Davies (ed. and trans.), *John Prise: Historiae Britannicae Defensio/A Defence of the British History* (Oxford, 2015), pp. 214–15. This work provides a new edition and translation of the *Defensio*.

6   Both Vaughan and Lewis will be discussed in more detail in the next chapter.

7   Owen Jones, Edward Williams and William Owen Pughe (eds), *The Myvyrian Archaiology of Wales*, 3 vols (London, 1801–7), I, pp. 1–118.

8   Sharon Turner, *A Vindication of the Genuineness of the Ancient British Poems of Aneurin, Taliesin, Llywarch Hen, and Merdhin, with Specimens of the Poems* (London, 1803), pp. 160–1.

9   Turner, *A Vindication of the Genuineness*, p. 163.

10 Brynley F. Roberts, 'Culhwch ac Olwen, The triads, saints' Lives', in Rachael Bromwich, A. O. H Jarman and Brynley F. Roberts (eds), *The Arthur of the Welsh* (Cardiff, 1991), pp. 73–4.

11   William F. Skene, *The Four Ancient Books of Wales*, 2 vols (Edinburgh, 1868).

12   The exact publication dates of these works are uncertain, as the date on the introduction frequently differs from that on the copyright page and the facsimiles seem to have been available before the published edition; see Angela Grant, 'Gwenogvryn Evans and Cyfraith Hywel', *The National Library of Wales Journal*, 36 (2014), 5.

13   J. Gwenogvryn Evans, 'Taliesin or the Critic Criticised', *Y Cymmrodor*, 34 (1924), 7; David Nash, *Taliesin or the Bards and Druids of Britain* (London, 1858) had also earlier dismissed the idea that the poetry could date from the sixth century.

14   J. Gwenogvryn Evans, *The Book of Taliesin* (Llanbedrog, 1910) and *The Book of Aneirin* (Llanbedrog, 1922).

15   J. Gwenogvryn Evans, *Poems from the Book of Taliesin* (Llanbedrog, 1915).

16   John Morris-Jones, 'Taliesin', *Y Cymmrodor*, 28 (1918). Morris-Jones was renowned for his cutting reviews and was particularly angry with Evans for questioning the date of the poetry.

17   Ifor Williams (ed.), *Canu Aneirin* (Cardiff, 1938); idem, *Canu Taliesin* (Cardiff, 1958). His most important articles are collected together in Rachel Bromwich (ed.), *The Beginnings of Welsh Poetry: Studies by Sir Ifor Williams* (Cardiff, 1972).

18   Graham R. Isaac, 'Scholarship and Patriotism: The Case of the Oldest Welsh Poetry', *Studi Celtici*, 1 (2002), 75.

19   Patrick Sims-Williams, 'The early Welsh Arthurian poems', in Bromwich et al., *The Arthur of the Welsh*, pp. 33–71.

20   Sims-Williams, 'The early Welsh Arthurian poems', p. 38.

21   The seven-volume series, under the general editorship of R. Geraint Gruffydd, is entitled *Cyfres Beirdd y Tywysogion* (Cardiff, 1991–6), hereafter *CBT*. References to this work will be to the individual volumes.

22   Simon Rodway, 'A Datable Development in Medieval Welsh', *Cambrian Medieval Celtic Studies*, 36 (1998), 74.

23   Rodway, 'A Datable Development'. See also idem, 'Absolute Forms in the Poetry of the Gogynfeirdd: Functionally Obsolete Archaisms or Working System?', *Journal of Celtic Linguistics*, 7 (1998), 63–84; and *Dating Medieval Welsh Literature: Evidence from the Verbal System* (Aberystwyth, 2013).

24   Marged Haycock (ed. and trans.), *Legendary Poems in the Book of Taliesin* (Aberystwyth, 2007), pp. 27–36 and reinforced in the same authors' *Prophecies from the Book of Taliesin* (Aberystwyth, 2013), p. 6.

25   Haycock, *Legendary Poems*, p. 31.

26   Haycock, *Legendary Poems*, p. 26. The work of T. J. Morgan referred to in this quote can be found in 'Dadansoddi'r Gogynfeirdd (1)', *Bulletin of the Board of Celtic Studies*, 13 (1948–50), 169–74; and 'Dadansoddi'r Gogynfeirdd (2)', *Bulletin of the Board of Celtic Studies*, 14 (1950–2), 1–8.

27   Williams, *Canu Aneirin*. Since 2011 the manuscript has been housed at the National Library of Wales in Aberystwyth. For a digital copy of the manuscript see *www.llgc.org.uk/discover/digital-gallery/manuscripts/the-middle-ages/book-of-aneirin/* (accessed 31 December 2016).

28   Williams, *Canu Aneirin*, p. 49, ll. 1241–4.

29   Kenneth Jackson, *The Gododdin: The Oldest Scottish Poem* (Edinburgh, 1969), p. 63; Koch, *The Gododdin of Aneurin*, p. xci; N. J. Higham, *King Arthur: Myth-Making and History* (London, 2002), pp. 183–5; and Graham R. Isaac, 'The History and Transmission of the "Gododdin"', *Cambrian Medieval Celtic Studies*, 37 (1999), 65.

30 For a detailed discussion of the manuscript see A. O. H. Jarman, 'Llyfr Du Caerfyrddin: The Black Book of Carmarthen', *The Proceedings of the British Academy*, 71 (1985), 333–56. *Idem, Llyfr Du Caerfyrddin* (Cardiff, 1982) is an edition of the entire manuscript and will be used for all quotations. For a digital facsimile of the manuscript see *www.llgc.org.uk/ discover/digital-gallery/manuscripts/the-middle-ages/the-black-book-of-carmarthen/* (accessed 31 December 2016).

31 Thomas Jones, 'The Black Book of Carmarthen "Stanzas of the Graves"', *The Proceedings of the British Academy*, 53 (1967), 97–136; Jarman, *Llyfr Ddu*, pp. 36–44.

32 Jones, 'Stanzas of the Graves', 119: '*Bet Gwalchmei ym Peryton*'; and 121, '*Bet Bedwir in alld Tryvan*' and '*Bet mab Ossvran yg camlan*'.

33 Jones, 'Stanzas of the Graves', 127, corresponding with Jarman, *Llyfr Du*, p. 41, l. 135.

34 Sims-Williams, 'The early Welsh Arthurian poems', p. 47; Jarman, *Llyfr Du*, p. 48.

35 Michael Swanton (ed. and trans.), *The Anglo-Saxon Chronicle* (London, 1996), pp. 14–15.

36 Sims-Williams, 'The early Welsh Arthurian poems', p. 45; Jarman, *Llyfr Du*, p. 68.

37 'Ac yn Llanueir yn Aruon adan y maen du y dotwes are geneu kath, ac y ar y maen y b6ryoed y g6rueichat yn y mor, a meibion Paluc yMon a'e magassant yr dr6c vdunt'; Rachel Bromwich (ed. and trans.), *Trioedd Ynys Prydein* (Cardiff, 2006), p. 52, and further discussion on pp. 473–6; Lister M. Matheson, 'The Arthurian Stories of Lambeth Palace Library MS 84', *Arthurian Literature*, 5 (1985), 86–9.

38 Rupert T. Pickens (trans.), *Lancelot-Grail 2: The Story of Merlin* (Cambridge, 2010), pp. 470–4.

39 Bromwich, *Trioedd Ynys Prydein*, pp. 474–5 and references therein.

40 Jarman, *Llyfr Du*, p. 66.

41 Sims-Williams, 'The early Welsh Arthurian poems', p. 40.

42 Jarman, *Llyfr Du*, p. 67.

43 Sims-Williams, 'The early Welsh Arthurian poems', p. 42.

44 J. Gwenogvryn Evans and John Rhys, *The Text of the Book of Llan Dâv* (Oxford, 1893), p. 397 for index entry to *Elei*. See also Jonathan Baron Coe, 'The place-names of the Book of Llandaf', (unpublished PhD thesis, University of Wales, Aberystwyth, 2001), 261.

45 Jarman, *Llyfr Du*, pp. 73 and 77 respectively.

46 The only edition of the entire manuscript is still Evans, *The Book of Taliesin*. See *www.llgc.org. uk/discover/digital-gallery/manuscripts/the-middle-ages/book-of-taliesin/* (accessed 31 December 2016) for a digital copy of the manuscript.

47 Haycock, *Legendary Poems*, p. 186.

48 Haycock, *Legendary Poems*, p. 505.

49 Haycock, *Legendary Poems*, p. 173.

50 Haycock, *Legendary Poems*, pp. 433–51; Michael D. Reeve (ed.) and Neil Wright (trans.), *Geoffrey of Monmouth, The History of the Kings of Britain: An Edition and Translation of De Gestis Britonum* (Woodbridge, 2007), p. 198.

51 Evans, *Book of Taliesin*, p. 55, l. 21, translation from Thomas Clancy (trans.), *The Triumph Tree: Scotland's Earliest Poetry AD 550–1350* (Edinburgh, 1998), p. 87.

52 John T. Koch, *The Celtic Heroic Age* (Malden, 1995), p. 290; Kenneth Jackson, 'Arthur in early Welsh verse', in Roger Loomis (ed.), *Arthurian Literature in the Middle Ages* (Oxford, 1959), p. 15; and Sims-Williams, 'The early Welsh Arthurian poems', p. 54.

53 Haycock, *Legendary Poems*, p. 434. See pp. 27–36 for a detailed discussion of similarities between the poetry in the Book of Taliesin and the work of Prydydd y Moch.

54 For an index of all proper names in *CBT* see Ann Parry Owen, 'Mynegai i Enwau Priod ym Marddoniaeth Beirdd y Tywysogion', *Llên Cymru*, 20 (1997), 25–45. The index entry for

Arthur gives eleven references, but five references found in vol. V seem to be missing: 11.53, 12.8, 20.5, 23.64 and 26.96.

55   It is worth noting that Cynddelw, who wrote a generation earlier and composed forty-eight poems, compared to the thirty of Prydydd y Moch, mentions Arthur on only two occasions.

56   R. M. Andrews, N. G. Costigan (Bosco), Christine James, Peredur I. Lynch, Catherine McKenna and Morfydd E. Owen (eds), *Gwaith Bleddyn Fardd a Beirdd Eraill Ail Hanner y Drydedd Ganrif ar Ddeg* (Cardiff, 1996), p. 619, l. 30. Translation in Joseph P. Clancy, *Medieval Welsh Poems* (Dublin, 2003), p. 171.

57   David Ewan Thornton, 'A Neglected Genealogy of Llywelyn ap Gruffudd', *Cambrian Medieval Celtic Studies*, 23 (1992), 9–23.

58   Wade-Evans, *Nennius*, pp. 55–8.

59   Ann Parry Owen, 'Mynegai i Enwau Priod yng Ngwaith Beirdd y Bedwaredd Ganrif Ar Ddeg', *Llên Cymru*, 31 (2008), 35–89. I would like to thank Barry Lewis for his help with this poetry. A new survey of all the Arthurian names in medieval Welsh poetry came to my attention at the very last minute: Xiezhen Zhao, 'Arthurian personal names in medieval Welsh poetry' (unpublished MPhil thesis, Aberystwyth University, 2015).

60   For a more detailed discussion see Margaret Enid Griffiths, *Early Vaticination in Welsh with English Parallels* (Cardiff, 1937); Manon Bonner Jenkins, 'Aspects of the Welsh prophetic verse tradition' (unpublished PhD thesis, University of Cambridge, 1990); Helen Fulton, *Welsh Prophecy and English Politics in the Late Middle Ages* (Aberystwyth, 2008); and Aled Llion Jones, *Darogan: Prophecy, Lament and Absent Heroes in Medieval Welsh Literature* (Cardiff, 2013).

61   A similar claim has been put forward for the Myrddin poetry in *Llyfr Du Caerfyrddin* in O. J. Padel, 'Geoffrey of Monmouth and the Merlin Legend', *Cambrian Medieval Celtic Studies*, 51 (2006), 37–65.

62   The translation used for all quotations is Sioned Davies (trans.), *The Mabinogion* (Oxford, 2007).

63   Huws, *Medieval Welsh Manuscripts*, p. 245. The three earlier manuscripts are Aberystwyth, NLW Peniarth 6 in four parts, Peniarth 7 and Peniarth 14.

64   For an overview of the scholarship and issues regarding these texts see Simon Rodway, 'The Where, Who, When and Why of Medieval Welsh Prose Texts: Some Methodological Considerations', *Studia Celtica*, 41 (2007), 47–89.

65   Rachel Bromwich and Simon D. Evans (eds), *Culhwch and Olwen: An Edition and Study of the Oldest Arthurian Tale* (Cardiff, 1992), pp. xxxii–xxxiii.

66   For a detailed discussion of the manuscript and its history see Huws, *Medieval Welsh Manuscripts*, pp. 227–68.

67   Huws, *Medieval Welsh Manuscripts*, p. 60 for a convenient list. The most detailed discussion of the manuscript is Daniel Huws, 'Llyfr Coch Hergest', in Iestyn Daniel, Marged Haycock, Dafydd Johnston and Jenny Rowland (eds), *Cyfoeth y Testun: Ysgrifiau ar Lenyddiaeth Gymraeg yr Oesoedd Canol* (Cardiff, 2003), pp. 1–30.

68   Simon Rodway, 'The Red Book Text of *Culhwch and Olwen*: A Modernising Scribe at Work', *Studi Celtici*, 3 (2004), 93–161.

69   Charlotte Guest (ed. and trans.), *Kilhwch and Olwen* (Llandovery, 1842). The earlier text was not available until the diplomatic edition of the White Book of Rhydderch was published in J. Gwenogvryn Evans (ed.), *The White Book Mabinogion* (Pwllheli, 1907).

70   Idris Foster, 'Astudiaeth o Chwedl Culhwch ac Olwen' (unpublished MA dissertation, University of Bangor, 1935), 306–7.

71 Idris Foster, 'Culhwch and Olwen and Rhonabwy's Dream', in Loomis (ed.), Arthurian Literature in the Middle Ages, pp. 31–43.

72 Aberystwyth, NLW, Idris Foster papers, box 19, contains all of his notes and correspondence concerning the tale and includes a printed version of the text, dated to 1978, very similar to the 1988 edition.

73 Rachel Bromwich and Simon D. Evans (eds), Culhwch ac Olwen: testun Syr Idris Foster (Cardiff, 1988).

74 Bromwich and Evans, Culhwch and Olwen.

75 Bromwich and Evans, Culhwch and Olwen, pp. xxvii–xxviii.

76 Simon Rodway, 'The Date and Authorship of Culhwch ac Olwen: A Reassessment', Cambrian Medieval Celtic Studies, 49 (2005), 25–38.

77 Rodway, 'The Date and Authorship', 38.

78 Rodway, 'The Date and Authorship', 21.

79 J. E. Caerwyn Williams and Peredur I. Lynch (eds), Gwaith Meilyr Brydydd a'i Ddisgynyddion (Cardiff, 1994), p. 348, and further discussion in Bromwich, Trioedd Ynys Prydein, p. lxvi; Rodway, 'The Date and Authorship', 41.

80 Rodway, 'The Date and Authorship', 43.

81 Rodway, 'The Date and Authorship', 44. For an alternative view on the date of the text see T. M. Charles-Edwards, 'The date of Culhwch ac Olwen', in W. McLeod, A. Burnyear, D. U. Stiùbhairt, T. O. Clancy and R. O. Maolalaigh (eds), Bile ós Chrannaibh: A Festschrift for William Gillies (Ceann Drochaid, 2010), 45–56.

82 Bromwich and Evans, Culhwch and Olwen, pp. xxxvii–xlvi for a detailed discussion of the names.

83 Bromwich and Evans, Culhwch and Olwen, p. xliv and references therein.

84 For a convenient collection of the references to Arthur's relatives in Welsh texts see Steve Blake and Scott Lloyd, Pendragon: The Origins of Arthur (London, 2002), pp. 84–100.

85 Bromwich and Evans, Culhwch and Olwen, p. 10, l. 264.

86 Bromwich and Evans, Culhwch and Olwen, p. 8, l. 205; Davies, Mabinogion, p. 184.

87 Kaer Dathyl yn Aruon: Ian Hughes (ed.), Math Uab Mathonwy (Dublin, 2013), p. 1, l. 8 and notes on pp. 28–30; Davies, Mabinogion, p. 47.

88 For a concise discussion of the various suggestions see Colin Gresham, 'Archbishop Baldwin's Journey through Merioneth in 1188', Journal of the Merioneth Historical and Record Society, 10 (1985–9), 186–7.

89 Davies, Mabinogion, p. 184. The only other reference is found in a genealogical tract entitled 'Bonedd yr Arwyr', in Peter C. Bartrum, Early Welsh Genealogical Tracts (Cardiff, 1966), p. 85.

90 Bromwich and Evans, Culhwch and Olwen, ll. 1057–1204

91 Bromwich and Evans, Culhwch and Olwen, pp. lxiv–lxx and notes therein.

92 For example, John Rhŷs, 'Notes on the Hunting of the Twrch Trwyth', Transactions of the Honourable Society of Cymmrodorion (1894–5), 1–34 and 146–8.

93 Williams, Canu Aneirin, p. 53, l. 1340.

94 Nerys Ann Jones and Ann Parry Owen (eds), Gwaith Cynddelw Brydydd Mawr II (Cardiff, 1995), p. 122, l. 206 and note on p. 148; Owen, 'Mynegai i Enwau Priod yng Ngwaith Beirdd y Bedwaredd Ganrif Ar Ddeg', 73, once each in the works of Casnodyn, Gruffudd ap Maredudd, Iolo Goch and Rhys Goch Eryri.

95 Huws, Medieval Welsh Manuscripts, p. 52.

96 David Williams, Atlas of Cistercian Lands in Wales (Cardiff, 1990), pp. 91 and 98–101.

97 Bromwich and Evans, Culhwch and Olwen, p. 39, l. 1112.

98   Emily M. Pritchard, *The History of St. Dogmaels Abbey: Together with her Cells, Pill, Caldey and Glascareg and the Mother Abbey of Tiron* (London, 1907), p. 28.

99   Lucien Merlet, *Cartulaire de l'abbaye de la Sainte-Trinité de Tiron*, 2 vols (Chartres, 1882–3), I, numbers XXV, p. 41; XXVI, p. 42 and XXXI, pp. 49–51; Pritchard, *St Dogmaels*, pp. 46–7.

100   J. R. Daniel-Tyssen, *Royal Charters and Historical Documents Relating to the Town & County of Carmarthen and the Abbeys of Talley and Tygwyn-ar-Daf* (Carmarthen, 1878), pp. 60–72.

101   Bromwich and Evans, *Culhwch and Olwen*, ll. 261, 351, 975, 1024 and 1204.

102   Bromwich, *Trioedd Ynys Prydein*.

103   Bromwich, *Trioedd Ynys Prydein*, pp. xci–xcix and lxix–xcix.

104   Bromwich, *Trioedd Ynys Prydein*, pp. 146–9.

105   O. J. Padel, 'Some south-western sites with Arthurian associations', in Rachel Bromwich, A. O. H. Jarman and Brynley F. Roberts (eds), *The Arthur of the Welsh* (Cardiff, 1991), p. 234.

106   Padel, 'Some south-western sites', p. 237. Attention was also drawn to these two sites in Melville Richards, 'Arthurian Onomastics', *Transactions of the Honourable Society of Cymmrodorion* (1969), 250–64.

107   N. A. Jones and A. P. Owen, *Gwaith Cynddelw Brydydd Mawr II*, p. 52, line 167. I would like to thank Jenny Day for her translation of this line and helpful discussion about this poem.

108   Huw Pryce (ed.), *The Acts of the Welsh Rulers 1120-1283* (Cardiff, 2005), p. 381.

109   Dafydd Johnston (ed. and trans.), *Iolo Goch Poems* (Llandysul, 1993), pp. 12–13 and 24–5; E. Bachellery (ed. and trans.), *L'oeuvre poétique de Gutun Owain*, 2 vols (Paris, 1950–1), II, p. 251, l. 18.

110   TNA GB/NNAF/M172542. The manorial records can be searched at *http://discovery. nationalarchives.gov.uk/manor-search* (accessed 12 January 2016).

111   Graham Thomas and Nicholas Williams, *Bewnans Ke: The Life of St Kea* (Exeter, 2007). *Kyllywyk* appears on two occasions: pp. 131–3, ll. 1270 and 1286.

112   Iwan Wmffre, *The Place-Names of Cardiganshire* (Oxford, 2004), p. 1116.

113   N. A. Jones and Owen, *Gwaith Cynddelw Brydydd Mawr II*, pp. 44–86 at p. 45. Cynddelw rhymes *Dilius fab Eurfai* with *Cai* (p. 53, ll. 206–7), as does the *englyn* sung by Arthur in Bromwich and Evans, *Culhwch and Olwen*, p. 35, ll. 978–80, which may also suggest a possible connection.

114   Bromwich and Evans, *Culhwch and Olwen*, p. lxxvi; Dafydd Johnston et al. (eds), *Cerddi Dafydd ap Gwilym* (Cardiff, 2010), p. 130, ll. 16–20 and note on p. 620.

115   Lhuyd, *Archaeologia Britannica*, p. 265; William Owen Pughe, *The Cambrian Biography* (London, 1803), pp. 57–9.

116   This term has been contested as misleading by Ceridwen Lloyd-Morgan, 'Medieval Welsh Tales or Romances? Problems of Genre and Terminology', *Cambrian Medieval Celtic Studies*, 47 (2004), 41–58.

117   Huws, *Medieval Welsh Manuscripts*, p. 245.

118   Rodway, 'The Where, Who, When and Why', 61.

119   R. L. Thomson (ed.), *Ystorya Gereint uab Erbin* (Dublin, 1997). See also Roger Middleton, 'Studies in the textual relationships of the Erec/Geraint stories' (unpublished DPhil thesis, Oxford University, 1976).

120   Cardigan Castle was in Norman hands during the periods, 1197–1215, 1223–31 and from 1240 onwards.

121   P. J. C. Field, 'Malory and Cardiff', *Arthuriana*, 16/2 (2006), 45–8.

122   R. L. Thomson (ed.), *Owein or Chwedyl Iarlles y Ffynnawn* (Dublin, 1986).

123 The name is spelt in a variety of different ways: Cardoel, Kardoil, Cardueilh etc.; see G. D. West, *An Index of Proper Names in French Arthurian Prose Romances* (Toronto, 1978), p. 61; and J. Neale Carman, 'South Welsh geography and British history in the *Perlesvaus*', in Norris J. Lacy (ed.), *A Medieval French Miscellany: Papers of the 1970 Kansas Conference on Medieval French Literature* (Kansas, 1972), pp. 37–59.

124 For an edition of the texts see Glenys Goetnick (ed.), *Historia Peredur vab Efrawc* (Cardiff, 1976); and Anthony M. Vitt, 'Peredur vab Efrawc: edited texts and translations of the MSS Peniarth 7 and 14 versions' (unpublished MPhil Thesis, Aberystwyth University, 2010). See also Sioned Davies and Peter Wynn Thomas (eds), *Canhwyll Marchogion: Cyd-destunoli Peredur* (Cardiff, 2000); and an English summary in Paul Russell, 'Texts in Contexts: Recent Work on the Medieval Welsh Prose Tales', *Cambrian Medieval Celtic Studies*, 45 (2003), 60–72.

125 Ceridwen Lloyd-Morgan, 'Breuddwyd Rhonabwy and later Arthurian literature', in Rachel Bromwich, A. O. H. Jarman and Brynley F. Roberts (eds), *The Arthur of the Welsh* (Cardiff, 1991), p. 196.

126 Ceridwen Lloyd-Morgan, 'The Peniarth 15 Fragment of *Y Seint Greal*: Arthurian Tradition in the Late Fifteenth Century', *Bulletin of the Board of Celtic Studies*, 28 (1978), 73–82.

127 The poetry of Guto Glyn is now available online, poem 114, lines 53–62 at *www.gutorglyn.net/gutorglyn/poem/?poem=114* (accessed 25 May 2014).

128 Nigel Bryant, *The High Book of the Grail: Perlesvaus* (Woodbridge, 1978), pp. 116–17, corresponding to 'une ille qui est en ceste mer' in William A. Nitze, and T. A., Jenkins (eds), *Le Haut Livre du Graal Perlesvaus*, 2 vols (Chicago, 1932–7), I, p. 178, l. 3933; R. Williams (ed. and trans.), *Y Seint Greal* (London, 1876), p. 616: 'ynys yrhonn aelwir Ianoc', p. 276.

129 Ceridwen Lloyd-Morgan, 'A study of *Y Seint Greal* in relation to *La Queste del Saint Graal* and *Perlesvaus*' (unpublished DPhil thesis, Oxford University, 1978), 167–8.

130 Ceridwen Lloyd-Morgan, 'French texts, Welsh translators', in Roger Ellis (ed.), *The Medieval Translator*, II (London, 1991), pp. 45–63. See also Erich Poppe and Regine Reck, 'A French Romance in Wales: *Ystorya Bown o Hamtwn*. Processes of Medieval Translations' [Part I], *Zeitschrift für Celtische Philologie*, 55 (2006), 122–80 and [Part II] in *Zeitschrift für Celtische Philologie*, 56 (2008), 129–64.

131 Ceridwen Lloyd-Morgan, 'Nodiadau Ychwanegol ar yr Achau Arthuraidd a'u Ffynonellau Ffrangeg', *National Library of Wales Journal*, 21 (1980), 329–39.

132 Melvile Richards, *Breudwyt Ronabwy* (Cardiff, 1948); translation in Davies, *Mabinogion*, pp. 214–26.

133 John Bollard, 'Traddodiad a Dychan yn *Breudwydd Rhonabwy*', *Llên Cymru*, 13 (1985), 155–63, contains a useful table highlighting the cross-references to names and events in other medieval Welsh tales.

134 Lloyd-Morgan, '*Breuddwyd Rhonabwy* and Later Arthurian Literature', p. 185.

135 T. M. Charles-Edwards, 'The Date of the Four Branches of the Mabinogi', *Transactions of the Honourable Society of Cymmrodorion* (1970–1), 266 suggests a pre-1160 date; Helen Fulton, 'Cyd-destun Gwleidyddol *Breudwyt Ronabwy*', *Llên Cymru*, 22 (1999), 42–56 proposes a date in the first half of the thirteenth century, and Mary Giffin, 'The Date of the *Dream of Rhonabwy*', *Transactions of the Honourable Society of Cymmrodorion* (1958), 33–40, argues for a late fourteenth-century date.

136 Huw Meirion Edwards (ed.), *Gwaith Madog Dwygraig* (Aberystwyth, 2006), p. 10, l. 69.

137 Charlotte Guest (ed. and trans.), *Breuddydd Rhonabwy* (Llandovery, 1843).

138 The name is also found in the works of the *Gogynfeirdd*; see Jones and Owen, *Gwaith Cynddelw Brydydd Mawr II*, poems 1.40, 4.238, 6.99 and 13.19.

139   Richards, *Breudwyt Ronabwy*, p. 3, l. 28; Thomas Jones (ed. and trans.), *Brut y Tywysogyon or the Chronicle of the Princes: Peniarth MS. 20 Version* (Cardiff, 1952), p. 13.

140   Richards, *Breudwyt Ronabwy*, p. 9, l. 9.

141   R. Geraint Gruffydd, 'Canu Cadwallon ap Cadfan', in Rachel Bromwich and R. Brinley Jones (eds), *Astudiaethau ar yr Hengerdd Studies in Old Welsh Poetry* (Cardiff, 1978), pp. 34–41.

142   N. A. Jones and A. P. Owen, *Gwaith Cynddelw Brydydd Mawr I* (Cardiff, 1991), p. 224; Henry Owen, *The Description of Penbrokeshire by George Owen of Henllys*, 4 vols (London, 1892–1936), pp. 666–8; Ieuan M. Williams (ed.), *Humphrey Llwyd: Cronica Walliae* (Cardiff, 2002), p. 224.

143   Richards, *Breudwyt Ronabwy*, p. 3, l. 27; *Calendar of Inquisitions Post Mortem*, V (London, 1898), p. 145; Richard Morgan, *A Study of Montgomeryshire Place-Names* (Llanrwst, 2001), p. 100 (Grid Ref SJ 2309).

144   Richards, *Breudwyt Ronabwy*, p. 8, l. 24.

145   Edmund Reiss, 'The Welsh Versions of Geoffrey of Monmouth's *Historia*', *Welsh History Review*, 4 (1968), 97–127. For a detailed study of the major medieval versions see Patrick Sims-Williams, *Rhai Addasiadau Cymraeg Canol o Sieffre o Fynwy* (Aberystwyth, 2011).

146   His important articles are all now well over thirty-five years old: Brynley F. Roberts, 'Ymagweddau at Brut y Brenhinedd hyd 1890', *Bulletin of the Board of Celtic Studies*, 24 (1971), 122–38; 'The Treatment of Personal Names in the Early Welsh Versions of *Historia Regum Britanniae*', *Bulletin of the Board of Celtic Studies*, 25 (1972–4), 274–90; 'Fersiwn Dingestow o Brut y Brenhinedd', *Bulletin of the Board of Celtic Studies*, 27 (1977), 331–61; 'The Red Book of Hergest Version of *Brut y Brenhinedd*', *Studia Celtica*, 12/13 (1977/8), 147–86; and *Brut Tysilio* (Swansea, 1980). The most detailed treatment remains Brynley F. Roberts, 'Astudiaeth destunol o'r tri chyfieithiad Cymraeg cynharaf o Historia Regum Britanniae Sieffre o Fynwy: ynghyd ag "argraffiad" beirniadol o destun Peniarth 44' (unpublished PhD thesis, University of Wales, Aberystwyth, 1969).

147   An edition of the Dingestow text can be found in Henry Lewis (ed.), *Brut Dingestow* (Cardiff, 1942). Extracts from Llanstephan 1 can be found in Brynley F. Roberts, *Brut y Brenhinedd* (Dublin, 1971). See Huws, *Medieval Welsh Manuscripts*, p. 58 for the dates of all three manuscripts.

148   Roberts, 'The Treatment of Personal Names', 289.

149   Charlotte Ward, 'Arthur in the Welsh *Bruts*', in Cyril J. Byrne, Margaret Harry and Pádraig Ó Siadhail (eds), *Celtic Languages and Celtic Peoples: Proceedings of the Second North American Congress of Celtic Studies, Held in Halifax, August 16–19, 1989* (Halifax, 1992), pp. 383–90. See also Michael Faletra, *Wales and the Medieval Colonial Imagination: The Matters of Britain in the Twelfth Century* (London, 2014), p. 26. This important work only came to my attention at a very late stage in writing.

150   Roberts, 'Treatment of Personal Names', 288.

151   Bromwich, *Trioedd Ynys Prydein*, pp. lxvi–lxvii.

152   Charles-Edwards, *Wales and the Britons*, pp. 552–69.

153   Paul Latimer, 'Henry II's Campaign against the Welsh in 1165', *Welsh History Review*, 14 (1988), 523–52.

154   Pryce, *Acts of the Welsh Rulers*, pp. 325 and 329.

155   Pryce, *Acts of the Welsh Rulers*, pp. 24–6.

156   I. W. Rowlands, 'The 1201 Peace between King John and Llywelyn ap Iorwerth', *Studia Celtica*, 34 (2000), 149–66.

157 Louise J. Wilkinson, 'Joan, Wife of Llywelyn the Great', *Thirteenth Century England*, 10 (2005), 81–93.

158 I. W. Rowlands, 'King John and Wales', in S. D. Church (ed.), *King John: New Interpretations* (Woodbridge, 1999), pp. 273–87.

159 Pryce, *Acts of the Welsh Rulers*, pp. 386–8.

160 Pryce, *Acts of the Welsh Rulers*, pp. 392–3; J. Beverley Smith, 'Magna Carta and the Charters of the Welsh Princes', *English Historical Review*, 99 (1984), 344–62.

161 Roger Turvey, *Llywelyn the Great: Prince of Gwynedd* (Llandysul, 2007), p. 117. See also Morfydd E. Owen, 'Royal propaganda: stories from the law-texts', in T. M. Charles-Edwards, Morfydd E. Owen and Paul Russell (eds), *The Welsh King and his Court* (Cardiff, 2000), pp. 232–8.

162 R. R. Davies, 'Law and national identity in thirteenth-century Wales', in R. R. Davies, Ralph A. Griffiths, Ieuan Gwynedd Jones and Kenneth O. Morgan (eds), *Welsh Society and Nationhood* (Cardiff, 1984), p. 56.

163 Huw Pryce, 'The Context and Purpose of the Earliest Welsh Law Books', *Cambrian Medieval Celtic Studies*, 39 (2000), 39–63. Studies that focus on the likely Gwynedd provenance of these works include, Patrick Sims-Williams, 'Clas Beuno and the Four Branches of the Mabinogion', in Bernard Maier and Stefan Zimmer with Christine Bakte (eds), *150 Jahre "Mabinogion"*: *Deutch-Walische Kulturbeziehungen* (Tübingen, 2001), pp. 111–27; Brynley F. Roberts, 'Where were the Four Branches of the Mabinogi written?', in Joseph Falaky Nagy (ed.), *The Individual in Celtic Countries: CSANA Yearbook 1* (Dublin, 2001), pp. 61–73; and Helen Fulton, 'The *Mabinogi* and the education of princes in medieval Wales', in Helen Fulton (ed.), *Medieval Celtic Literature and Society* (Dublin, 2005), pp. 230–47.

164 Reeves and Wright, *Geoffrey of Monmouth*, p. 4.

FOUR
ḤUMANISTS AND ANTIQUARIANS

THE PREVIOUS THREE CHAPTERS have considered the Arthurian place names of Wales first attested in medieval manuscripts, whereas the following chapters will focus upon names first attested in the post-medieval period and how authors made use of these place names in arguing for the historicity of Arthur. The earliest works to address this subject appear during the reign of the Tudors and it is worthwhile to briefly consider what use the Tudors made of the legend and, perhaps more importantly, how modern historians have dealt with this matter.

The prophetic poetry of Wales during the fifteenth century was focused upon the role of the *mab darogan* (Son of Prophecy; predicting the return of Welsh sovereignty), and by the time of the brief reign of Richard III (1483–5) the Welsh bards had focused upon Henry Tudor as the man to fulfil this role.[1] It is notable that the same bards who wrote *cywyddau brud* (prophetic poems) in praise of Edward IV, did much the same for Henry and often used the same poetic imagery.[2] Henry's victory at Bosworth in 1485 was hailed, by some, as the culmination of the long-held hope for a British ruler on the throne and, perhaps more importantly, an opportunity for the Welsh nobility to gain influence. More than 200 prophetic poems survive from the period following the Glyndŵr revolt (1400–15) and the names of past heroes, Cynan, Cadwaladr and Owain, are frequently invoked, but never Arthur.[3] As discussed at the end of the previous chapter, the figure of Arthur was probably considered tainted in Welsh eyes as he had been used by the Norman rulers in their own propaganda efforts for nearly 200 years. Hence they put their energies into building a mythological past around the figure of Maelgwn Gwynedd, his son Rhun and their supposed court at Deganwy. Following the Edwardian conquest of Wales, Arthur continued to be used by English kings in their propaganda, although less so than previously, and was therefore not uniquely Welsh, unlike the established earlier heroes, Cynan, Cadwaladr and Owain. Why express your hopes for regaining your sovereignty around the same heroic figure used by the people who had taken it away, especially when you have several well-attested traditional heroes to choose from that were uniquely Welsh? It is primarily the high profile of the Arthurian legend that makes the lack of reference to Arthur in Welsh prophetic poetry appear surprising.

At Winchester in 1486, with its Arthurian Round Table hanging in the Great Hall, a son was born to Henry VII and named Arthur. The choice of the name is suggestive of some attempt to make use of the figure of Arthur for propaganda purposes, but as David Carlson observes,

> What calls for explanation is why Henry made as little use of the Galfridian prophecies and King Arthur as he did. The poetic evidence for use of the Arthur myth during the early months of Henry's reign poses this question insistently: the poets who wrote in celebration of the birth of Henry's first son Arthur made remarkably little out of the Arthurian legends that the occasion seems to have been deliberately designed to provide them.[4]

The idea that the early Tudors had encouraged a cult of King Arthur has often been repeated and relies heavily upon two works published in America in 1932. Millican's *Spenser and the Round Table* and Greenlaw's *Studies in Spenser's Historical Allegory*, both treat the matter at length, and their conclusions have been quoted by most writers on the subject ever since, if only indirectly through the pages of T. D. Kendrick's influential *British Antiquity*.[5] Anglo, in his studies of the use of Arthur and other characters in Tudor pageantry, argued that the oft-repeated view that the Tudors were obsessed with the Arthurian legend has arisen by looking at the available sources out of context.[6] Following the premature death of Prince Arthur in 1502, the figure of King Arthur, perhaps understandably, was rarely used at the royal court, but as Anglo notes, 'the Trojan descent, the prophecy of Cadwaladr, and Arthurianism were not abandoned; they were simply no longer emphasized.'[7] The legend continued to be used on occasion by King Henry VIII, primarily to impress overseas dignitaries, and it was during his reign that the battle over the authenticity of the British History led to the earliest appearance of Welsh Arthurian material in print.[8]

Polydore Vergil

The first printed edition of Geoffrey of Monmouth's *HRB* in 1508 was the catalyst for a new wave of criticism of the text, which would dominate antiquarian discussion in England for the next century, and in Wales for even longer.[9] It was this discussion that would lead to the first use of Welsh manuscripts and place names in the defence of the historicity of Arthur. The Italian, Polydore Vergil (1470–1555), had established himself as a scholar before he came to Britain in 1502 as the deputy collector of Peter's pence, and soon found favour at the court of Henry VII.[10] His first publication concerning the history of Britain was a forty-five page edition of *De excidio* by Gildas, based upon a collation of two manuscripts, published at Antwerp in 1525.[11] This was the first time that a critical edition of a British historical source had been published. Vergil, however, is better known for his *Anglica historia*, a history of England that he was encouraged to undertake by Henry VII in 1506. The work remained in manuscript until its publication at Basel in 1534 and almost immediately became the centre of controversy.[12] Whereas earlier chroniclers had been rather credulous towards their sources, Vergil was much more critical.

> I first began to spend the hours of my night and day in searching the pages of English and foreign histories ... I spent six whole years in reading these annals and histories during which, imitating the bees which laboriously gather their honey from every flower, I collected with discretion material proper for a true history.[13]

In following this approach, Vergil had rejected the Trojan origin myth of the Britons and most of what had appeared in Geoffrey of Monmouth's *HRB*. It is during his discussion of *HRB* that he draws upon the reference by Gildas to the Britons being 'feeble and cowards' and launches into his famous attack on the authenticity of Arthur, that was to cause such a reaction from the supporters of the British History and fuel the writings of Welsh antiquarians through to the nineteenth century:

> But on the other side there hathe appeared a writer in owre time which, to purge these defaultes of Brittains feinings of them things to be laughed at, hathe extolled them above the nobleness of Romains and Macedonians, enhauncinge them with most impudent lyeing. This man is cauled Geffray, surnamed Arthure, bie cause that oute of the old lesings of Brittons being somewhat augmented bie him, hee hathe recited manie things of this King Arthure, taking unto him bothe the coloure of Latin speech and the honest pretext of an Historie.[14]

Vergil mentions Arthur only once more. In a single paragraph, he casts doubt on his historicity, especially his supposed grave at Glastonbury, and in doing so called into question the very existence of what had been, to many, an important symbol of national identity.[15] His logical, if simplistic, approach offended those who supported the British History, especially in Wales, and as Kendrick notes, 'the extreme sensitiveness of the British to the Italian's rather mild twitting of their traditional history is one of the curiosities of the Tudor period.'[16]

John Leland

One of the earliest critics of Vergil's work was the English antiquarian John Leland (*c*.1503–52), who was given a Royal Commission by Henry VIII in 1533 to search the libraries of England and Wales for manuscripts of historical interest.[17] Many of the manuscripts Leland found during his travels were unknown to Vergil and this led him to write a short tract in 1536, although not published until 1715, entitled *Codrus, sive Laus et defensio Gallofridi Arturii Monumetensis contra Polydorum Vergilium*, the earliest work to make use of the archaeology and place names of Wales to argue for a historical Arthur.[18] Leland refers to the Roman remains at Caerleon as evidence for a settlement in Arthur's day and also discusses the reference by Gerald of Wales to *Kadair Arthur* in Breconshire, neither of which had been mentioned by Polydore. His reference to 'other surviving Welsh records' is of interest, as we know from his extant manuscripts that he was familiar with Asser's Latin *Life of King Alfred*, the *Historia Brittonum* and its confusion with Gildas, the works of Gerald of Wales and *Brut y Tywysogion*.[19] The argument put forward in *Codrus* was later expanded into a longer and much more detailed work, *Assertio inclytissimi Arturii regis Britanniae* (1544), which was in turn translated into English by Richard Robinson in 1582.[20] According to his friend John Bale, Leland was also familiar with the Welsh language and in the *Assertio* there are several attempts at Welsh phonology.[21]

The *Assertio* attacked the negative evidence approach of Polydore and other authors critical of Geoffrey of Monmouth, such as William of Newburgh and the Scottish chronicler Hector Boece.[22] Leland had gathered together a wealth of evidence from various sources to prove Arthur's existence, but he was less critical of his sources than Vergil and relied on quantity, rather than quality, to make his point. His argument was detailed and although ultimately in error, he analysed in over one hundred pages a matter that Vergil had dismissed in a single paragraph.

Leland also left behind a disjointed set of notes, known as his *Itinerary*, concerning his travels around England and Wales during the late 1530s, some of which had informed his arguments in *Codrus* and *Assertio*. These were never published in his lifetime, but were well known to later scholars and constitute one of the earliest topographical records of Britain. The material is spread over several different manuscripts and was first gathered together and published by Thomas Hearne in nine volumes (1710–12).[23] Although Wales played an important role in Leland's Arthurian studies, the *Itinerary* only refers to three sites in Wales with Arthurian associations.[24]

The first site is a burial mound in Ceredigion, which according to a local informant contained the body of a giant killed by Arthur.[25] This is the earliest reference to associate Arthur, in his role as a giant slayer, with a specific site in Wales, a theme that appears consistently in later Welsh folklore and is discussed further below (page 101). The second site is a note of Arthur's Gate at Montgomery, which is also mentioned in his *Assertio*, although, as shown in chapter 2, the name had been in use since 1336.[26] The third site is a rocky feature with twenty-four gaps in it, on a hilltop near Llansannan in Denbighshire, and Leland notes that 'Sum calle it the round table.'[27] Further Arthurian material is found in the English part of his *Itinerary*, at Glastonbury, Winchester, Dover and Westminster, and in the Scottish part a reference to the fragments of an image of the Virgin Mary brought back from Jerusalem by Arthur, in Melrose Abbey, all of which he used in his *Assertio*. His most famous Arthurian identification associates the Iron Age hill fort of South Cadbury in Somerset with Arthur's court of Camelot, an association later publicised to great effect by Leslie Alcock during his archaeological dig at the site in the late sixties.[28] Leland died in 1552 but his manuscripts and the evidence he had collated were regularly used by later authors to prove that Arthur was a historical figure.[29]

Sir John Prise

Sir John Prise (1501/2–55) from Brecon was, in contrast to the uncritical enthusiasm of Leland, the most sensible of Geoffrey's defenders. He was made the registrar-general in ecclesiastical causes in 1534, and was appointed by Thomas Cromwell to visit monasteries in 1535 and 1539.[30] It was during his visits to these monasteries that he started to collect manuscripts, his main interest being historical materials, especially relating to Wales, and at his death he had amassed an impressive library.[31] This collection meant that Prise had access to manuscripts in Welsh referring to Arthur that were unknown to Leland and more importantly for his argument, Vergil. Prise had written the first draft of his *Historiae Brytannicae Defensio* (A Defence of the British History), dedicated to Henry VIII, by 1545, and a second revised version, dating from *c.*1550, is very close to the text published posthumously by his son in 1573.[32] It remains the most eloquent and sensible of all of the works written in defence of the British History.

The *Defensio* published the Arthurian battle list from the author's own manuscript of the *Historia Brittonum* (now lost) that he had discovered in Brecon Priory, a cell of Battle Abbey where Leland had seen the same manuscript some years earlier.[33] Leland refers to this manuscript in his *Assertio*, and it would be interesting to know more about the relationship between these two scholars.[34] In a detailed chapter defending the authenticity of Arthur, Prise introduces extracts from the poem in the Black Book of Carmarthen concerning Arthur at Llongborth and Coed Celyddon, the site of one of Arthur's battles in the *Historia Brittonum*.[35] The remainder of the chapter draws together further evidence from Wales, including a note to the crown of Arthur (see page 47), and is one of the earliest printed works to discuss medieval Welsh manuscripts. Prise notes the presence of a grant to St Dubricius for land in *Penalyn* (Penally near Tenby) by 'Noe filius Arthur' in the twelfth-century Book of Llandaf, a work unknown to Vergil, and concludes that as St Dubricius is named as the archbishop who crowned Arthur in *HRB*, this grant is independent evidence of his historical existence.[36] The first use of the *Annales Cambriae* (discussed in chapter 1) as evidence for a historical Arthur also derives from the *Defensio* and thanks to Prise's detail about his manuscript coming from St David's, we know that it was the C-text of the *Annales*, which was also in his library.[37] Prise concludes his chapter on Arthur by summarising the evidence collected by Leland in his *Assertio* and then notes Arthur's Stone on the Herefordshire border:

> Likewise there are, throughout Wales, any number of other sites and rocks of this kind which have long held the name of Arthur given to them. Thanks to their very substance they are more inured against being worn down, and they will preserve the name of Arthur for a longer time than other memorials made by hand.[38]

A later chapter of the *Defensio*, concerned with the failure of Gildas to mention Arthur in his *De excidio*, built upon the reference in the second recension of Gerald's *Description of Wales*, a thirteenth-century manuscript of which Prise owned, to Gildas throwing away his works of Arthur because he had killed his brother Huail.[39] Prise notes that 'A place in North Wales still preserves the memory of this murder, and a huge stone there bears the name of Huail: it has been erected, as was the custom of men of old, to keep alive the memory of events of this kind.'[40] The traditions surrounding this stone at Ruthin are described in more detail by Elis Gruffydd, discussed below, but this is the first reference to the tradition in print. By drawing attention to the existence of early manuscripts concerning Arthur in Welsh that were unknown to Vergil, Prise supported the idea that Geoffrey had simply translated an earlier work into Latin. He had also shown that Vergil had been unaware of these Welsh texts and therefore his argument was incomplete. In drawing attention to the importance of the material found in Welsh manuscripts, the arguments set forth by Prise became an important foundation for subsequent Welsh antiquarian scholarship.

Elis Gruffydd

Elis Gruffydd (1490–1556) was born at Gronant Uchaf, in Flintshire, to a minor branch of the gentry. He joined the English Army and by 1518 was in Calais working for Sir Robert Wingfield, accompanying him on diplomatic missions in France and beyond.[41] Between 1524 and 1529 Gruffydd was in London, and it is during this period that he copied a tract of minor Arthurian interest, known as *Pedwar Marchog a farnwyd yn gadarnaf* (the twenty-four knights judged to be the strongest), which draws upon the list of kings in *Brut y Brenhinedd*.[42] His most important work was his Chronicle, which survives in four codices: NLW 5276Di–ii, covering the years from the Creation to 1066; and NLW 3054Di–ii, covering the period 1066–1552.[43] The Arthurian material is a narrative based largely upon *HRB*, but Gruffydd crucially includes many unique details not found elsewhere.[44] He brings together material from other chronicles, notably that of Robert Fabyan and other interesting medieval material in his Arthurian narrative, especially the prophecy concerning Thomas Becket and the Holy Oil used by Joseph of Arimathea to anoint the kings of England.[45] The most important section of the Chronicle, for the purposes of this work, is the story of Huail ap Caw, an onomastic tale explaining the name Maen Huail (Huail's Stone), a large stone still extant in the town square of Ruthin in Denbighshire. This section of the Chronicle has been edited and discussed by Thomas Jones and is an important source for Welsh Arthurian place names.[46] The section begins with a reference to Sorelois from the French *Lancelot-Grail* cycle.

> In this place [North Wales] and time there were many marvels in this part of the realm, especially in the island the French book calls Surloes, that which the story professes is called today Ynys Mon [Anglesey]. In the time, as the story shows, there

was a bridge [or causeway] over the Menai around about the place that is today called Bon y Don; at that place there were certain of men in armour guarding it all the time. And the king of this island made many cruel battles against Arthur, those which would be too long to relate at this time. Those who lamented of reading this story worked to read the book of the conquest, *Y Sang Reial.*[47]

As discussed in chapter 2, the identification of Sorelois with Anglesey does appear to fit the description in the French original. The addition of Moel y Don, a ferry crossing point since at least the twelfth century, is a good example of how Gruffydd would use his local knowledge to reinforce and add colour to his identifications. The causeway is named as *Pont Norgalois* in the original French text and one wonders whether Gruffydd had in mind the bridge of boats that was built over the Menai in 1282 by the English forces attacking Bangor.[48] Exactly which 'French book' Gruffydd used is difficult to identify with confidence, but the *Sorelois* description had previously appeared in printed editions of *Lancelot du Lac*, in 1488 and 1494, making either of these a possible source.[49]

The next section of the text relates a story of Huail being in love with one of Arthur's mistresses. Arthur, on becoming aware of this, has a sword fight with Huail in which he is wounded in his knee. They are reconciled, and Huail agrees never to mention the fact that he has wounded Arthur, who then goes home to his court 'that

Figure 6. *Maen Huail situated on the town square in Ruthin. A folktale preserved by Elis Gruffydd (c.1550) relates how Arthur beheaded Huail on this stone.* © Scott Lloyd.

was in a town which the story of the Sangreal calls Caerhass, that which the story professes is today called Caerwys'.[50] Caerhass appears as Karahais, a residence of King Arthur, in the *Prose Lancelot* and is most likely to be identified with Carhaix, in Finistère, Brittany.[51] The small town of Caerwys in Flintshire would have been known to Gruffydd, being only a few miles from his birthplace, but his Chronicle is the only source to make an Arthurian connection with the place.

The story continues and sees Arthur dancing with women in the town of Ruthin, dressed in women's clothes; the reason for this is never made clear. Huail sees him and shouts out, 'the dancing were very good were it not for the knee.' Arthur hears this and claims that Huail has broken his agreement and as a punishment takes him 'to the market of the town and caused his head to be cut off on the stone that was lying on the ground of the road ... And because of this, to remember this deed the stone was called from then to today, Maen Huail [the Stone of Huail].'[52]

As no parallel exists for this tale in the French romances, and neither does the place name Ruthin or anything similar appear in French sources, it appears that Gruffydd was drawing upon some native oral tradition. There is some evidence that an earlier tradition about Huail was known, as he is named on several occasions in Welsh poetry. A poem by Lewis Glyn Gothi compares the grave of 'Master Watkin, lord of Herast' to the grave of *Huail e hun* 'Huail himself', suggesting that Huail's grave was renowned in some way, and perhaps he too was aware of Maen Huail in Ruthin.[53] Gruffydd continues his text with the following passage.

> And at that time, according to some of the stories, Arthur made a court in that place now called Nannerch. And even now the spot is called Llys Arthur. And it is said that the church was his chapel and was for long afterwards called Capel Gwial [the Wicker chapel].[54]

The village of Nannerch is only three miles from Caerwys, although no spot called Llys Arthur is known today. However, the name Capel y Gwial, although no longer in use, is noted in a reply to Edward Lhuyd's *Parochialia* of 1696 which states that 'some say that the church was formerly called Capel y Gwail yn Rhos'.[55] These identifications are again unique to Gruffydd. Traces of a tradition concerning enmity between Arthur and Huail can also be seen in earlier texts: the *Descriptio Kambriae* of Gerald of Wales (1188); *Culhwch and Olwen* (twelfth century); and also the *Vita Gildae* of Caradoc of Llancarfan (*c.*1150).[56] No other example of Arthurian folklore in Wales can lay claim to have its roots in three, very different twelfth-century sources, making it a unique and intriguing survival. Elsewhere in his narrative Gruffydd relates the story of Arthur's dream, in which he loses his fingers, toes and hair, also originating in the *Prose Lancelot*.[57] In the French text the dream is dismissed as meaningless, but Gruffydd adds a tale whereby Arthur goes hunting in Denbighshire and is captured by a family of giants and is only released after passing a test, where he has to pronounce *tri gair gwir* 'three true words'.[58] Both the tale and the location are again unique and could derive from an earlier oral tradition, or may simply have been added by Gruffydd to give the story a local setting.

Non-Welsh writers often accused the Welsh of believing in the return of Arthur, despite the complete lack of evidence for such a belief in native Welsh sources. Elis Gruffydd encapsulates the situation during his discussion of the authenticity of the work of Geoffrey of Monmouth, and as Ceridwen Lloyd-Morgan notes,

> He complains that the English criticise the Welsh 'am *ynn* hryuig, *ni* am Arthur' [for *our* presumption about Arthur] (my emphasis), but in fact 'mae yn vwy j son *wyntt* amdano ef no nnyni' [NLW MS 5276Dii, fol. 342r: *they* talk much more about him then we do] (my emphasis).[59]

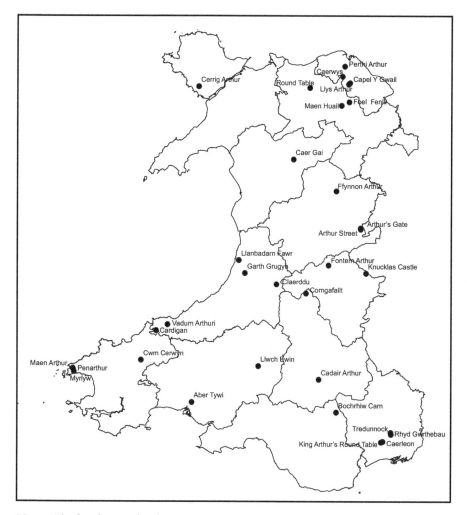

Map 1. *The distribution of Arthurian names first attested pre-1550*

Gruffydd was prepared to defend the British History, but he was not prepared to allow that the Welsh believed in the return of Arthur, and insisted that the supposed belief was an English creation, used to criticise the Welsh.[60]

We know from their printed books that John Leland and John Prise were aware of each other's works, and it has also been suggested that Elis Gruffydd may have come into contact with John Leland.[61] All three died within four years of each other, and enthusiasm for Welsh Arthurian material seems to have died with them; it would be nearly 250 years before such a keen interest would be shown again. In many ways the Chronicle of Elis Gruffydd signifies the end of a medieval view of the past, as the next generation of Welsh historians took a more critical, albeit still nationalistic, approach to the history of Wales.

Humphrey Llwyd

Described by William Salesbury, the author of the first Welsh–English Dictionary, as 'the most famous antiquarius of all our countreye', Humphrey Llwyd (1527–68) has a pivotal role in Welsh historiography.[62] He entered the service of Henry Fitzalan, Earl of Arundel, in 1553 and remained a member of his household until his death. One aspect of Llwyd's job was looking after the Fitzalan library at Nonsuch in Surrey and acquiring new titles for its expansion.[63] It was during this period that he wrote his *Cronica Walliae*, a history of Wales from the year 689, where *HRB* ended, to 1295.[64] Llwyd based his text on an English translation he had made of the Welsh chronicle *Brut y Tywysogion*, and added material from such medieval chroniclers as Nicholas Trivet and Matthew Paris, copies of which were available to him in the library at Nonsuch. Llwyd had finished the work by 1559 and five manuscript copies still survive.[65] The *Cronica Walliae* does not cover the period in which Arthur supposedly ruled, so it only mentions the supposed discovery of his bones at Glastonbury, misdated to 1179,[66] but Llwyd was also notable for his topographical interests, and it is here that we find the earliest attestation of an Arthurian association. The *Cronica Walliae* opens with a description of Wales and during the description of the cantref of Merioneth Llwyd notes, 'And not ferre frome this pound [Llyn Tegid, near Bala] is a place called Caergay, which was the house of Caye, Arthures foster brother.'[67] The site is the Roman fort of Caer Gai, near the village of Llanuwchllyn, at the southern end of the lake. Llwyd gives no indication as to where he found this information, but references to the place name, if not specifically the tradition, can be found in the poetry of the preceding century.[68] Although Llwyd notes the Arthurian association with the site, he makes nothing of it and has nothing else to say about Arthur. It is notable that the leading expert on Welsh place names and topography in the mid-sixteenth century, who shared along with Leland, Prise and Gruffydd, a dislike of the views of Polydore Vergil, saw no need to make use of any Arthurian evidence in his arguments.

One of the manuscripts of Llwyd's *Cronica Walliae*, London, British Library, Cotton Caligula A vi, passed through the hands of the famed Elizabethan magus Dr John

Dee, who also took an interest in Welsh history and Arthurian matters. Dee wrote a tract in 1577 entitled *Brytanici Imperii Limites* (Limits of the British Empire), which claimed that King Arthur had travelled to the Arctic and had eventually reached America, thus justifying the claims of Elizabeth in America.[69] He also made use of the legend which claimed that Prince Madog, the son of Owain Gwynedd, had reached America and set up a Welsh colony there in the twelfth century, which first appears in Llwyd's *Cronica Walliae*.[70] Dee travelled to Wales and northern England in 1574, and a manuscript account of his journey entitled 'Certaine verie rare observations of Chester and some parts of Wales' notes two sites with Arthurian connections in northern England, Mayborough castle and Ternython in Cumberland, but no such connections are noted in Wales.[71]

Another of the *Cronica Walliae* manuscripts came into the hands of Sir Henry Sidney, who then passed it to his chaplain, David Powel (*c*.1550–98) to prepare it for publication.[72] Powel duly undertook this task, also adding material from other sources, and in 1584 *The Historie of Cambria* was published.[73] The book became the major source for the history of Wales until the nineteenth century, and was reprinted and expanded on several occasions, the last being in 1832. It was also used as a source by many poets, notably Edmund Spenser, who refers to the Caer Gai tradition in his best-known work, *The Faerie Queen* (1590).[74] In the following year Powel continued his interest in Welsh history with the publication of an omnibus volume containing Ponticus Virunnius' *Historia Britannica* (an abridgment of *HRB*), Gerald of Wales's *Itinerarium Cambriae* and *Descriptio Cambriae* (but without Gerald's negative comments about the Welsh) and a short letter entitled *De Britannica Historia Recte Intelligenda*. Powel also annotated the texts, but did not include anything of Arthurian interest.[75] Powel's view of the British History is outlined in *De Britannica*, and like many subsequent authors who dealt with the subject were to do, he focused his attention on trying to prove the antiquity of the Welsh language rather than the authenticity of Arthur. Powel's publications gave scholars, for the first time, a history of medieval Wales and a good edition of one of its most important sources. A generation on from the works of Leland, Prise and Gruffydd, historical writing had become more focused upon the uniqueness of the Welsh language, the Welsh laws of Hywel Dda and the history of Wales before 1282.

Early Topographical Works

Arthur may have been marginalised from the history books, but references to landscape features bearing his name can be found amongst the topographical works and county histories that began to appear in the last quarter of the sixteenth century. The year 1576 saw the first detailed county history published in Britain, *A Perambulation of Kent* by William Lambarde (1536–1601).[76] A short time later, Rice Merrick (sometimes referred to as Rhys Meurig), a lawyer by profession and inspired by Lambarde's work, set about writing a history of his home county of Glamorganshire. The work was fundamentally complete by 1578 and is now known under the title *Morganiae Archaiographia*.[77] Merrick was a good scholar and made it very clear which sources he had used, amongst them the Red Book of Hergest, the Book of Llandaf, a manuscript copy of the works of Giraldus Cambrensis, a compilation of Welsh poetry known as *Y Cwta Cyfarwydd* (NLW Peniarth 50) and the now lost Register of Neath Abbey.[78] In his work, Merrick notes two sites of Arthurian interest, both in the parish of Ynysafan (now Cwmafan). The first refers to two stones said to mark the grave of one of Arthur's knights at Bwlch y Gyfylchi, and the second to a burial mound on the summit of Mynydd Tor y Bedol, named after the giant killed there by Arthur.[79] Merrick is notable for being the first writer to attempt a county history in Wales, yet he is never mentioned by Kendrick or Levy in their influential studies of the period, and his place in antiquarian studies has often been unfairly overlooked.[80]

William Camden

The most important topographical work to be published in the late sixteenth century was *Britannia* by William Camden (1551–1623) in 1586, which described, county by county, the topography and antiquities of Britain.[81] Camden included historical material in his work, but unlike Llwyd he was no adherent of the British History and dismissed the Brutus story at every opportunity. For the section on Wales Camden built upon the previous work of Leland, Prise and Llwyd, and although he was not averse to noting Arthurian antiquities, as shown by his discussion of the material associated with Glastonbury, Camden ignored most of the evidence that had been put forward by Prise and Leland.[82] The first edition of 1586 noted only two Arthurian sites in Wales, both from Breconshire: the ever-present *Cadair Arthur* from Gerald of Wales, quoted from Powel's 1585 edition; and a reference to the stone bearing the footprint of Arthur's dog in the region of Builth, taken from the *Mirabilia* associated with the *Historia Brittonum*, of which he owned an early manuscript copy.[83]

The *Britannia* was a great success, and this enabled Camden to continue his travels around Britain, gathering more material to be incorporated in the numerous editions of the work that followed. He travelled to Wales in 1590, accompanied by his friend Francis Godwin (who later became the bishop of Llandaf), researching antiquities for an enlarged edition of *Britannia* in 1594.[84] By the time Philemon Holland published the first English translation of *Britannia* in 1610 the work had grown considerably, with more illustrations and the inclusion of maps for each county. The section concerning Wales had also grown, and one of the additions was a reference to the Roman fort of *Caer Gai* at Llanuwchllyn, first mentioned by Llwyd. Camden makes no mention of any Arthurian connection, preferring to suggest that the name was derived from a Roman leader called Caius.[85]The huge success of Camden's *Britannia* set the standard for topographical works in Britain and attracted contributions from many notable antiquaries, but his views on the authenticity of the British History were not allowed to pass without comment in seventeenth-century Wales.

Siôn Dafydd Rhys

The last notable work of the Elizabethan period to draw attention to Arthurian place names in Wales and make a defence of the British History was written by Siôn Dafydd Rhys (1534–1609), referred to by William Camden as the 'most renowned and most learned' of the Welsh humanists.[86] His best-known work was *Cambrobrytannicae Cymraecaeve Linguae Institutiones et Rudimenta* (The Elements and Rudiments of the Cambro-British and Welsh Language) published in 1592, but much of his writing still remains in manuscript.[87] Rhys wrote a long treatise defending the authenticity of Geoffrey's *HRB* in 1597, a section of which is concerned with the idea that Britain was once inhabited by a race of giants, the last surviving members of which were killed by Brutus and his followers when they first arrived in Britain.[88] At the end of the section is a collection of references to Welsh giants, with a particular emphasis on the places where they supposedly lived, usually Iron Age hill forts.[89] Amongst the seventy or so Welsh giants mentioned by Rhys, eleven were killed by Arthur, thereby associating him with their respective hill forts. This depiction of Arthur as a killer of giants almost certainly originates from a chapter of Geoffrey of Monmouth's *HRB* where Arthur defeats an unnamed Spanish giant at Mont St Michel in France and then goes on to say that 'he had never encountered anyone of such strength since he had killed upon Mons Aravius the giant Ritho, who had challenged him to a duel.'[90]

Geoffrey states that the reason for the duel was due to Ritho demanding that Arthur shave off his beard and give it to him for his cloak, made up of the beards of kings he had already vanquished, but Arthur, of course, refused. Geoffrey himself never makes the exact location of Mons Aravius explicit, but does mention it a second time in the Prophecies of Merlin, where it appears separated by one word from *Venedotia*, the Latin term for Gwynedd.[91] It is possible that the proximity of the two names led the composer of the *Brut y Brenhinedd* to turn Mons Aravius into Eryri, the Welsh name for Snowdon.[92] The Merlin section of the *Lancelot-Grail* cycle repeats the story and makes Rion the king of Denmark, Ireland and the 'land of grasslands and giants'.[93] The episode is also found in the *Post-Vulgate Merlin* which makes Ritho the Lord of Norgales, a title that later found its way into Malory's *Le Morte Darthur* (1471), where he is called the king of north Wales.[94] Rhys records two slightly different localised traditions of this tale, placing the duel between Arthur and Ritho at Bwlch y Groes, a high pass in the Aran Mountains, perhaps identifying the Latin Aravius with Aran.[95] In his study of the tract, Grooms gathered together further poetic references to Rhita, dating back to the fifteenth century, which suggests that some sort of tradition was current in north Wales long before Rhys recorded his versions of the tale.[96]

Rhys also notes a brief tale associating Arthur with Knucklas castle, where he beheads a giant in order to rescue the three brothers of Gwenhwyfar, who had been held captive by him. He then throws the giant's head into the river Teme, where it turns into stone. According to William of Worcester, writing in 1478, Knucklas

Castle had been founded by King Arthur, but there is no direct evidence that Rhys had any knowledge of his work, which suggests that an Arthurian tradition may have been current in the area at an earlier date.[97] The remaining references to Arthur are very brief, like a majority of the references to the Welsh Giants, and only serve an onomastic purpose, for example, 'And in the parish of Penderyn, Dynas the giant was killed by Arthur. And the place in which he dwelt is still called Craig Dynas Gawr.'[98] Grooms goes on to make the interesting observation that many of the hill forts that Rhys names are close to the houses of gentry that he stayed with on his travels around Wales as a physician. In some instances, they actually share a name; for example, the giant Cerddan of Gogerddan, a notable mansion near Aberystwyth.[99] This fascinating tract is an important source of Welsh traditional lore, much of it apparently collected orally by Rhys during his travels around Wales. However, his main aim was to defend Geoffrey's claim that giants lived in Britain before the arrival of Brutus and his references to Arthur are used primarily to reinforce his rebuttal.

The earliest maps of Wales to be based upon a thorough survey were those of Christopher Saxton (1540–1610), engraved 1576–9 and printed in 1580.[100] None of his working notes have survived, and the only evidence of his time in Wales is an open letter, dated June 1576, to all of the Justices of the Peace, mayors and others 'to set forth and describe in coats [maps] p[ar]ticulerlie all the shieres of Wales.'[101] Two names of Arthurian interest appear on his maps of Wales. The first is the name Rowndtable Hill, given to the Iron Age hill fort in the parish of Llanfihangel-din-Sylwy in Anglesey, better known today as Bwrdd Arthur. It is likely that Saxton was recording a name that was used by sailors in the area, for the hill fort was a useful navigational marker when seen from the sea and is mentioned amongst a list of the harbours of Wales, written in 1562.[102] The second name of Arthurian interest is the depiction of a hill labelled Arthors Buttes Hill near Pentyrch, to the north of Cardiff, but the origin of this name remains uncertain. There is no evidence that Saxton made up the name, but it is not mentioned in Merrick's contemporaneous *Morganiae Archaiographia*, which notes many of the hill names in the area. The name continued to appear on maps until the early nineteenth century, when it was replaced by Garth Hill, the name by which the hill is known today.

Lesser-Known Sites

The personal name Arthur was surprisingly rare in medieval Wales, and the medieval Welsh genealogies, published by Peter Bartrum, note only one pre-sixteenth-century use, Arthur ap Pedr of Dyfed, from the genealogies preserved in Harleian 3859. The name does not appear again until the mid-sixteenth century, and then on only four occasions.[103] This led Bartrum to suggest that some superstition may have surrounded the name and that the early death of Prince Arthur in 1502 only strengthened it.[104] By the second half of the sixteenth century, the name begins to appear more frequently, noticeably in legal documents concerning land and property. Nearly every county in the gazetteer in Appendix 2 contains names such as Tir Arthur, Maes Arthur and Llain Arthur that can be first attested in the period 1550–1750. These minor place names, not otherwise associated with the legend of Arthur, have been included as they provide a small, but sufficient, statistical base to show that many of the names first attested to in this period are more likely to be associated with an individual named Arthur, rather than the figure of King Arthur.

The chronological list in Appendix 1 shows many place names containing the name Arthur from 1550 to1750 not recorded by antiquarians, but found in legal documents, such as mortgages and land surveys. A good example is the name Maen Arthur, near Pontrhydygroes in Ceredigion, which first appears as the name of a township *Manarthyr* in 1568. The names Coed Maen Arthur (1568) and Melin Maen Arthur (1601) appear near by, and Nant Arthur first appears on the parish register in 1829, showing the continued local influence of the name. None of the early sources give any specific location to Maen Arthur, and later writers seem to have had differing views as to its whereabouts.[105]

Many of these lesser-known names are associated with either a stone/rocky outcrop (*carreg*, *cist*, *craig*, *llech*, *maen*) or a well (*ffynnon*), while the remaining names refer to either a land measure (*acre*, *cae*, *tir*) or to a type of landscape feature (*coed*, *wern* or *gardd*). In some instances these features are compounded, for example, *Cae Maen Arthur* (1633), *Cae Carreg Arthur* (1636), or *Ffynnonau Craig Arthur* (1610). None of these sites have any recorded associated folklore, and despite some of them surviving onto modern maps, for example *Ffynnon Arthur* in Montgomeryshire, the rest have only come to light as the result of place name research, primarily that done by Melville Richards.[106] There is a sufficient number of these, otherwise unknown, Arthur names to suggest that they were concerned with individuals named Arthur who lived on, or owned, these plots of land and, unless evidence to the contrary exists, there seems little reason to associate them with King Arthur.

The Seventeenth Century

The shift in historiographical thought away from the traditional British History towards a more critical humanist approach was hotly debated following the publication of the *Anglica Historia* by Polydore Vergil in 1534. The debates continued throughout the sixteenth century, and the British History was only used by those critical of it when it could fill a gap for which there was no other source, such as the pre-Roman period, where some record was considered better than none, despite its dubious authenticity. The works of Geoffrey of Monmouth increasingly became a source for playwrights and poets, rather than historians. However, with the death of Elizabeth I and the ascension to the throne of James VI of Scotland, to become James I of Great Britain, the British History was used once more to help justify the claim of the new monarch. One outcome of this resurgence was the appearance of several influential literary works depicting Wales as a land steeped in the British past, most notably Michael Drayton's long chorographical poem *Polyolbion* (1612) and the accompanying notes by John Selden.[107] The popularity of this work and *The Faerie Queen* (1590) by Edmund Spenser did much to popularise the idea that places associated with the British History and King Arthur could be found within the landscape of Wales.[108]

During these developments, works defending the British History continued to be written in Wales, notably *The History of Great Britain* by John Lewis of Llynwene in Radnorshire, written in 1611, but not printed until 1729.[109] Lewis was a friend of both Camden and Rhys, and was able to make use of Welsh manuscripts not previously used in defending the reliability of *HRB*, most notably the Book of Taliesin, sections of which he translated.[110] Throughout his work Lewis shows an awareness of other writers who had previously defended the British History, including the *Historiarum Britanniae* (1597–1602) by the Catholic scholar, Richard White (Vitus) of Basingstoke.[111] This detailed work contains references to a great number of obscure sources and in Europe enjoyed an even greater prestige than Camden's *Britannia*, yet despite this, it seems, with the exception of Lewis who was also Catholic, to have gone otherwise unnoticed by Welsh antiquarians.[112] White took an interest in Arthurian matters and was the first to suggest that Arthur could be identified with the British king Riothamus, who had invaded Gaul in the fifth century, a theory that was later suggested by Geoffrey Ashe in 1981.[113]

Lewis was concerned to merge the British History view of the past, still popular in Wales, with the Scottish *Brut* tradition of Hector Boece and George Buchanan in an attempt to provide a single unified history of the British Isles.[114] The need to provide a coherent view of the past for the new monarch of Great Britain, meant that the different interpretations had to be reconciled, and in doing so Lewis took the opportunity to introduce material from a previously unknown source, the Book of Taliesin. The poetry in the manuscript, concerning Urien Rheged and his son Owain, was interpreted by Lewis as belonging to southern Scotland and northern England, perhaps in an attempt to incorporate it into an area otherwise bereft of sources for the period. His interpretation of this poetry was subsequently followed by Robert Vaughan and has dominated research ever since.[115]

Robert Vaughan

Robert Vaughan (1592–1667) of Hengwrt near Dolgellau was a Justice of the Peace for Merionethshire and is best known for his important collection of medieval Welsh manuscripts; indeed, over half of the medieval Welsh manuscripts that survive today came from his library.[116] He acquired the Book of Taliesin from John Lewis of Llynwene (d. 1616), the Black Book of Carmarthen and the White Book of Rhydderch from Jasper Gryffyth (d. 1614), the Hendregadredd Manuscript from Rhys Cain (by 1617) and the Book of Aneirin, from an unknown source by 1658.[117] These important

Arthurian sources, discussed in chapter 3, were therefore only available to those who could visit Vaughan at Hengwrt, or were lucky enough to be able to borrow a manuscript or receive extracts through correspondence with him.

Vaughan had started collecting early on in life. By 1616 he had transcribed the *Brut y Tywysogion* from NLW Peniarth 20 and was well aware of the works of the *cynfeirdd* and *gogynfeirdd*. Like many other antiquarians in Wales, Vaughan was well aware of the great topographical work of Camden and took issue with his lack of belief in the British History. Drawing inspiration from Camden, Vaughan wrote a work in a similar vein for his home county in the early 1620s, entitled 'The Survey of Merioneth'. The text gives details of parishes and townships in Merionethshire and also adds historical detail when the author thought something of interest could be said. There is no reference to anything directly Arthurian in this text, but in listing the townships of Dinas Mawddwy, Vaughan notes a township called Camlan, though he fails to draw any attention to this important Arthurian name, the site of Arthur's final battle.[118] The British History view that Arthur had died at the river Camel in Cornwall was well established, and as Vaughan was busy defending the authenticity of Geoffrey, it was unlikely that he was going to draw attention to a site that could cast doubt upon it. The nearby mountain pass between Dolgellau and Dinas Mawddwy is also called Camlan, while not two miles from Hengwrt is Afon Gamlan, yet at no point does Vaughan mention a possible Arthurian connection to these sites.[119] Vaughan continued in the tradition of Prise and Lewis in defending the authenticity of Geoffrey, but unlike them, did not focus his arguments upon Arthur, preferring to draw attention to the antiquity of the Welsh language.

Vaughan was close friends with John Jones of Gellilyfdy, near Ysgeifiog, in Flintshire, who had also amassed an impressive collection of Welsh manuscripts but regularly had money problems and spent frequent spells in gaol.[120] Like Vaughan, Jones showed no particular interest in Arthurian matters and following his death in 1658 his library came to Vaughan at Hengwrt. Amongst the many manuscripts, both originals and transcriptions of material now lost, one Arthurian name can be attested for the first time. NLW Peniarth 267 is a miscellany of short tracts on Welsh history and topography and provides the earliest reference to the name Pikel Arthur, associated with a still extant standing stone near Ro Wen, in the parish of Caerhun, in Caernarfonshire.[121]

Many of Vaughan's notes were used by other authors, but few had his insight and knowledge of Welsh manuscript sources.[122] Following his death, several attempts were made to sell the library at Hengwrt, but none ever reached fruition, and the collection lay practically neglected for over a century. Access to the library was notoriously difficult, and those that did gain entry seem to have been responsible for many manuscripts being removed, the Book of Aneirin and the Hendregadredd Manuscript being the most notable. Welsh scholarship suffered greatly through this lack of access to the largest collection of medieval Welsh manuscripts, and the Arthurian material that had been used by Sir John Prise in the 1540s was now virtually

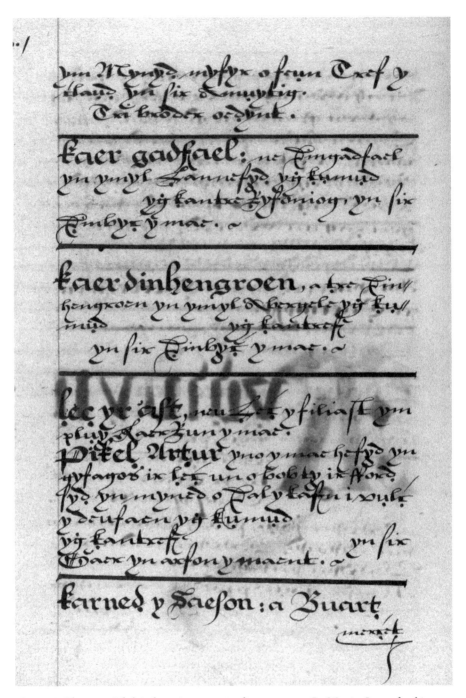

Figure 7. *The name Pikel Arthur, given to a standing stone near Ro Wen in Carnarfonshire, is first attested in NLW Penairth 267, p. 40 written by John Jones of Gellilyfdy (c.1635).*

By permission of Llyfrgell Genedlaethol Cymru / The National Library of Wales.

inaccessible. Access to the library eventually became easier for scholars in the late eighteenth century, leading to a renaissance in Welsh scholarship where the Arthurian arguments of the sixteenth century were tackled afresh.

Edward Lhwyd

Amongst the few scholars who did gain access to the library at Hengwrt, the most notable was Edward Lhwyd (1660–1709). Lhwyd went to Oxford University in 1682 and by 1690 had succeeded Robert Plot as curator of the Ashmolean Museum, an institution he was to be involved with until his death in 1709. Lhwyd was something of a polymath, writing important works on lexicography and fossils early in his career, before moving on to the Celtic languages and the history and antiquities of the Celtic countries. Today he is recognised as one of the most important scholars of the period.[123]

In February 1693 William Nicholson of Carlisle wrote to Edmund Gibson asking whether Lhwyd 'might be prevailed with to undertake Wales in this new edition of Camden'.[124] The publisher of the new edition of Camden's *Britannia* visited Lhwyd in Oxford in May 1693, and Lhwyd initially agreed to undertake the revisions for north Wales, and shortly afterwards finally agreed to do the whole of Wales.[125] In order to gather information for his revisions, Lhwyd formed a network of local correspondents, partly made up of the large contingent of Welsh students at Jesus College. Former students who had become schoolmasters, doctors and clergymen in Wales were all called upon for information and the true scale of this network can be seen by the surviving correspondence.[126] Lhwyd undertook a research trip to Wales in order to gather information for his revisions, leaving Oxford in August 1693, although his publishers thought that this was a waste of time and told him that everything he could possibly need to update the Welsh sections could be found in the libraries of Oxford.[127] Lhwyd submitted his manuscript of revisions to the publishers in September 1694.[128] The work was published the following year, the revisions by Lhwyd printed as 'Additions to' at the end of each county entry.[129] The additions contain items of Arthurian interest that can be traced back either to his correspondents or to notes made on his tour.

The additions for Glamorganshire include a note on the cromlech of Arthur's Stone on the Gower that originates in a letter from John Williams, dated 30 November 1693, in which he states that 'The common people call it Arthur's Stone by a lift of vulgar imagination attributing to yt hero an extravagant size and strength'.[130] Lhwyd had visited the site during his tour in 1694, and the words of John Williams were printed verbatim in the 1695 edition and have been repeated ever since.[131] Another of Lhwyd's correspondents was Erasmus Saunders, who in a letter dated 27 September 1693 described a cromlech in the parish of Llanboidy named Bwrdd Arthur and the now destroyed megalithic site of Buarth Arthur. Once again Lhwyd printed the descriptions almost verbatim and without direct acknowledgment.

'As for the name Bruarth Arthur [sic], 'tis only a nickname of the vulgar, whose humour it is, though not so much (as some have imagin'd) out of ignorance and credulity, as a kind of Rustick diversion, to dedicate many unaccountable monuments to the memory of that Hero; calling some stones of several tun weight his Coits, others his tables, Chairs, etc.' [132]

The reception of the 1695 edition of *Britannia* was mixed, but Lhwyd's revisions were rightly hailed by Thomas Hearne as 'the very best part of all the additions'.[133] Inspired by his work on *Britannia*, and buoyed by the good reviews of his contribution, Lhwyd issued a proposal for *A Design of a British Dictionary, Historical and Geographical: with an Essay entitled 'Archaeologia Britannica'; and a Natural History of Wales*, in November 1695.[134] By the summer of 1696 Lhwyd had secured enough subscriptions to be able to undertake another research trip to Wales. It was during this trip that he met Humphrey Humphreys, 'incomparably the best skill'd in our antiquities of any person in Wales', and also made a brief visit to the library of Hengwrt, 'the most valuable of its guide anywhere extant', where he made a catalogue of the most interesting items.[135] In order to be as thorough as possible in his research, Lhwyd printed 4,000 copies of a three-page questionnaire in December 1696, entitled *Parochial Queries in Order to a Geographical Dictionary, A Natural History &c. of Wales*, and had them distributed across Wales by Jesus College students returning home, who then delivered them to the clergy and gentry of each parish.[136] The *Queries* consist of thirty-one questions requesting information on all manner of subjects, such as the notable houses, castles, antiquities, bridges, churches etc. in each parish. Question 7 is particularly relevant as it asks for the contributors to note any occurrences of

> Roman Ways, Pavements, Stoves, or any Underground Works: Crosses, Beacons, Stones pitched on End in a regular Order; such as Meini hirion in Caernarvonshire, Karn Llechart in Glamorgan and Buarth Arthur in the county of Caermardhin: As also all those rude Stone monuments distinguished by the several Names of Bedh, Gwely, Karnedh, Kromlech, Lhech yr Ast, Lhech y Gawres, Lhech y Wydhan, Koeten Arthur, Kist-vaen, Preseb y Vuwch vrech, &c.[137]

As seen above, both Buarth Arthur and Coetan Arthur had already appeared in the 1695 edition of *Britannia*, and this specific query could perhaps be viewed as a leading question, by referring to names that Lhwyd expected to find. However, countering this is the fact that amidst the returned questionnaires and notebooks kept by Lhwyd, only a few references to Arthurian names exist.[138] The return for the parish of Llandeilo Pertholeu in Monmouthshire, written by a Mr Progers, notes two sites: some stones on the summit of Pen y Val called Cadair Arthur and a stone called Cist Arthur on the hill called Skirrid Fawr.[139] Llys Arthur is given as an alternative name for Caer Gai in Merionethshire, probably under the influence of earlier

Figure 8. *The hillfort of Moel Arthur in Flintshire. This is one of several Arthurian names first attested in the correspondence of Edward Lhwyd during his research for the 1695 edition of William Camden's* Britannia. © Crown Copyright.

editions of *Britannia* and also of Spenser's *Fairie Queene*, which associates Arthur with the site,[140] the hill-fort on the summit of Moel Arthur is mentioned for Nannerch in Flintshire,[141] and the megalithic site of Bedd Arthur, with an accompanying sketch, is recorded for Carmarthenshire.[142] A set of notes, made by Lhwyd during his tours of Wales, is preserved in Cardiff MS 2.59, and these are invaluable, as the original notebook can no longer be traced.[143] They record two sites called Coetan Arthur in Caernarfonshire and another two of the same name in Carmarthenshire.[144] The surviving parochial returns, some 150 in all, cover most of Wales and provide sufficient coverage to show how few Arthurian place names were current at the end of the eighteenth century.

The research of Lhwyd clearly shows that Coetan Arthur was by far the most commonly used term to associate Arthur with a prehistoric megalithic site and it is worthwhile to trace its origin. The earliest reference to *coetan* is found in the 1547 Welsh–English dictionary of William Salesbury, who simply notes that it is the Welsh equivalent of the English word *quoit*, which the *Oxford English Dictionary* (*OED*) traces back to 1366.[145] The *OED* goes on to note that the first association of the word with a megalithic structure in England can be attributed to the mid-eighteenth-century Cornish antiquarian William Borlase. Cornwall is well known for its many megalithic remains with Arthurian names, and it is perhaps surprising that the earliest use of the term Arthur's Quoits here only dates back to 1754. It appears that Borlase

Map 2. *Arthurian names first attested by Edward Lhwyd and his correspondents 1693–7*

was using it as a generic term, most likely influenced by the Merionethshire section of the 1695 *Britannia* that refers to Coetan Arthur, which he quotes.[146] An earlier use of the term can be attested in Wales in the year 1660. It is recorded in the notebooks of the botanist John Ray (a tutor of Lhwyd's at Oxford and one of the four signatories to endorse his *Parochial Queries*) who during a visit to Wales to collect rare plants, notes that

> On a common near Blaynport lie a great many large stones; among the rest, one standing perpendicularly on one End in the Ground, and another large one leaning upon it, and two others, one on each side the leaning stone; these Stones they call *King Arthur's Quoits.*[147]

However, Ray was not the first person to use the term in Wales, as the Pembrokeshire antiquary George Owen of Henllys refers to a cromlech, on the cliffs near St David's, as Arthur's Quoit in 1604.[148] Earlier still, in the 1590s, is a slightly different usage of the term in a poem by the Caernarfonshire poet Morus Dwyfech. In a poem for Robert ap Rhisiart Gruffudd of Anglesey, the poet asks for stones to be sent from Anglesey to a mill near Nefyn to be used as millstones, which are very quoit-like in shape, and refers to,

> Lle mae rhaid, llew mawr ei hur
> Wrthyn' goetenau Arthur.

> Where there is need of the coetan Arthurs, the lion who gives great gifts. [149]

This suggests that the term Coetan Arthur, especially in this instance where it is in the plural, was being used as a term for any large flat stone, rather than for any one site in particular. Returning to George Owen, it is also interesting to note that he had visited the site at Blaenporth over fifty years before Ray, and despite being familiar with the term Arthur's Quoits he refers to the megaliths as Llech yr Ast (Slab of the Greyhound Bitch).[150] Owen also notes the impressive monument at Pentre Ifan and refers to it as 'Maen y Gromlegh' in 1604 (it only briefly acquired the name Coetan Arthur in a letter from Erasmus Saunders in 1693).[151] Despite the term being used to describe a large flat stone, or a capstone to a cromlech, as early as 1600, it does not seem to have become widely used in Wales until the research surrounding the 1695 edition of Camden's *Britannia* was undertaken. By the end of the nineteenth century at least a dozen sites were commonly known by the name, and several more had been occasionally referred to as such. Lhwyd and his correspondents dismiss any Arthurian connection as the product of the 'imagination of the vulgar', and there is also a complete absence of folklore to explain Arthur's connection.

Aside from his topographical works, Lhwyd notes material of Arthurian interest in his catalogue of Welsh manuscripts, printed in the first volume of his *Archaeologia Britannica*, the *Glossography* in 1707.[152] Within two years of the publication of the *Glossography* he died, the remainder of his grand project never realised. His manuscripts were dispersed and later many were tragically destroyed, along with many other important Welsh manuscripts, in two fires, at Hafod in Ceredigion and Covent Garden in London.[153]

Theophilus Evans

One of the first authors to try and associate a site mentioned in a medieval Welsh Arthurian poem with a real location was Theophilus Evans (1693–1767), an Anglican clergyman from Ceredigion, who published his first work, *Drych y Prif Oesoedd*, at the age of just twenty-three.[154] The book was a celebration of the British History, which added the legend of Joseph of Arimathea bringing Christianity to Britain and a Welsh summary of Paul-Yves Pezron's recently published theories on the origins of the Britons and their descent from Gomer, the grandson of Noah.[155] The work was a huge success, providing the Welsh with a history of their country in their own language. It is indicative of the popularity of Arthur at this period that, despite the celebration of the British History in this work, he is mentioned only once. Evans starts his discussion by reprinting the Llongborth stanza from the Black Book of Carmarthen, using Lhwyd's *Archaeologia Britannica* as his source, and then gives the following:[156]

> Some believe that Llanborth commonly called Maes-Glas (blue or grey field) but the old name is Maes Llas, or Maes y Glanas (that is the field of the murder or massacre.) It is very likely that some of Arthur's men were betrayed and put to death here by Medrod. There is another place in this neighbourhood, within the parish of Penbryn, called Perth Geraint (the word gereint signifying kinsmen.) It is also very likely that many of the kinsmen of the commander of Arthur's ships were buried here, as Old Llywarch in another part of his song uses the words Llongborth and Geraint, and with them he speaks of great slaughter.[157]

Evans was no philologist and his theory, rarely mentioned again, has been most recently dismissed by Iwan Wmffre in his work on the place names of Ceredigion.[158]

Lewis Morris

The only other notable additions to the Arthurian topography of Wales in this period were first attested by a native of Anglesey, Lewis Morris (1701–65). Morris spent his early career working for Customs at the port of Holyhead and proposed a detailed hydrographical survey of the Welsh coast as an aid to shipping. After several years of interrupted work, he eventually published eleven charts of the Welsh coast in 1748.[159] Although primarily concerned with maritime features, the charts do refer to notable landscape features visible from the sea, including Round Table Fort on Anglesey. One of the maps, entitled 'The North Entrance of Bardsey Sound and the Roads', carries the following text in its bottom right-hand corner:

> Off of Bardsey I observe a great overfall of the sea on a bank never observd. by any Hydrographer in any Chart, But the place is so well known amongst the neighbours that it has acquired a name among the Antient Britons which it keeps to this day, Gorffrydau Caswennan and one of the antient poets describing the positiveness of his mistress, most Elegantly says

> > Os anodd o Gaswennan
> > Droi ar Lif or dwr i'r Lan
> > Dau anos na mynd yno
> > Troi Bun or Natur y Bo

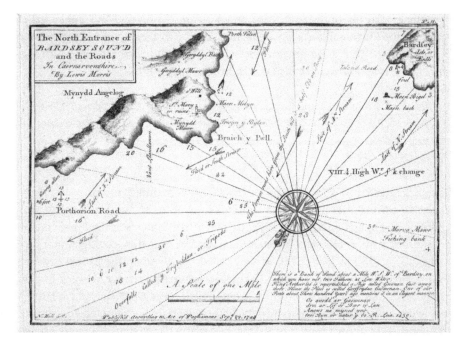

Figure 9. *Map of Bardsey Island from 1748 by Lewis Morris, including a note referring to a reef called Gorffrydiau Caswennan, where Arthur's ship Gwennan was supposedly wrecked.* By permission of Llyfrgell Genedlaethol Cymru / The National Library of Wales.

If it was hard from Caswennan to turn to windward from the water to the shore, twice as hard as that is to change a girl's nature.[160]

Morris dates the poem to around 1450 and mentions the site on several occasions elsewhere in his manuscripts.[161] The sandbank in question is still considered a danger to shipping and is mentioned by several other poets of the fifteenth century, but without the Arthurian connection, which seemingly originates with Morris.[162] An earlier view, by the antiquary Roger Morris, associates the site with the ship of Madog ap Owain Gwynedd, the supposed founder of a Welsh colony in America in the twelfth century, instead of Arthur.[163]

Lewis Morris also noted another Arthurian association with a site previously known by another name. On his 1747 map entitled 'A Plan of the Manor of Perveth Commonly Call'd Cwmmwd y Perveth', Morris refers to an earthwork near Ponterwyd in Ceredigion as Llys Arthur. However, the site is first noted in 1574 under the name Cloddiau Llys.[164] In another manuscript, he also adds that 'It is known locally as *Llys Arthur* and the natives have an abundance of stories about Arthur and Gwenhwyfar,' although if these traditions did exist, they have failed to be recorded elsewhere.[165] The name used by Morris endured until the early nineteenth century, making it onto the first Ordnance Survey maps.

Along with his brothers Richard and William, Lewis was also influential in founding the Honourable Society of Cymmrodorion in London in 1751. The influence of Edward Lhwyd can be clearly seen in its constitution from 1755, which suggests that it would be worthwhile for members to study

> the Carn, Cromlech, Meini Gwyr, Bedd y Wrach, coetan Arthur, rocking Stones, Barrows, Barclodiad y Widdon, Maen Tarw, Maen Arthur, Cader Arthur, Gorsedd, Eisteddfa, din, Dinas, Castell, Caer and other ancient fabrics or erections of stones found in Wales.[166]

The society acted as a focal point for the Welsh community in London and was a conduit for material from Wales finding its way into the hands of English anti-quarians.[167] English antiquaries became increasingly interested in Welsh manu-scripts, but they were inaccessible to them, and even if they could get access to them they could not read them, so they relied heavily upon the Morris brothers for information on Welsh sources. The extensive correspondence between English antiquarians and the Morris brothers brought their ideas about the British History to a wider audience, although occasionally the material they volunteered appeared in published works without acknowledgement. Morris wrote to Thomas Carte (d. 1754) in a letter dated 30 March 1745, in which he discussed the antiquity of *Brut y Brenhinedd* and the reference to the *receptculi Ursus* (Bear's Den) in Gildas, asking, 'Who was this Ursus but Arthur?'[168] Carte used this material in the first volume of his *General History of England* published in 1747 without acknowledging Morris, who noted this fact in several letters and later in life became quite angry at his treatment.[169]

Although he had been unfairly treated by Carte, Lewis Morris remained in touch with other English antiquarians, and it was with the help of one of them, Daines Barrington, that Morris's friend Evan Evans had his important work on Welsh poetry published.[170] Written primarily as a response to Thomas Gray's 'The Bard', published in 1757 and Macpherson's Ossian poems, which had attracted a lot of attention in England, *Some Specimens of Welsh Poetry* was the first serious work on the subject.[171] This was the first time that many outside Welsh antiquarian circles had had the opportunity to read medieval Welsh poems. Evans was deter-mined to show that Welsh poetry had a rightful place in the history of ancient Britain, and to this end he added numerous explanations for English readers and footnoted every proper name.[172] The lack of reference to Arthur anywhere in the work further reinforces the fact that throughout the eighteenth century Arthur was of little importance in Wales.

These important early first steps towards an understanding of medieval Welsh poetry were soon overwhelmed by a view of the past that came to dominate the Welsh psyche for decades. As will be shown in the next chapter, the bardic fictions and Glamorgan-centric view of the Welsh past created by Iolo Morgannwg soon dominated discussion, and the good work done by the Morris brothers and Evan Evans struggled to be heard. A combination of the emergence of the Romantic move-ment and the Napoleonic Wars led to an increase of English visitors, no longer able to go on their European grand tours, to Wales. Brought up on Camden's *Britannia* and Gerald of Wales, they were keen to find evidence of supposedly ancient bards. The figure of Arthur that had formed the centrepiece of works by Leland and Prise had by the late eighteenth century been reduced to a minor literary character, appearing occasionally in English poems and plays, virtually ignored by Welsh antiquarians and worthy of little more than a footnote in the history books.

Notes

1   Gruffydd Aled Williams, 'The Bardic Road to Bosworth: A Welsh View of Henry Tudor', *Transactions of the Honourable Society of Cymmrodorion* (1986), 7–31; and David Rees, *The Son of Prophecy* (London, 1985), pp. 100–9.

2   W. Garmon Jones, 'Welsh Nationalism and Henry Tudor', *Transactions of the Honourable Society of Cymmrodorion* (1917–18), 1–59.

3   Helen Fulton, *Welsh Prophecy and English Politics in the Late Middle Ages* (Aberystwyth, 2008), p. 25; and for a broader discussion see Aled Llion Jones, *Darogan: Prophecy, Lament and Absent Heroes in Medieval Welsh Literature* (Cardiff, 2013).

4   David Carlson, 'King Arthur and Court Poems for the Birth of Arthur Tudor in 1486', *Humanistica Lovaniensia*, 36 (1987), 152.

5   Charles Bowie Millican, *Spenser and the Round Table: A Study in the Contemporaneous Back-ground for Spenser's Use of the Arthurian Legend* (Cambridge, Mass., 1932), pp. 7–36. Edwin Greenlaw, *Studies in Spenser's Historical Allegory* (Baltimore, 1932) is a less detailed work, but pp. 170–80 give a concise overview of this idea. T. D. Kendrick, *British Antiquity* (London, 1950), pp. 34–8 is based largely upon the work of the two Americans.

6   Sydney Anglo, *Spectacle, Pageantry, and Early Tudor Policy*, second edn (Oxford, 1997), p. 61.

7   Sydney Anglo, 'The British History in Early Tudor Propaganda', *Bulletin of the John Rylands Library, Manchester*, 44 (1961–2), 40. An updated version of this paper, but without the detailed account of the genealogical rolls, can be found in Sydney Anglo, *Images of Tudor Kingship* (London, 1992), pp. 40–60.

8   David Starkey, 'King Henry and King Arthur', *Arthurian Literature*, 16 (1998), 171–96, offers a more positivist interpretation of the Tudor interest in Arthur.

9   Ivo Cavellatus (ed.), *Britannie utriusque regum et principum origo et gesta insignia ab Galfrido Monemutensi ex antiquissimis Britannici ...* (Paris, 1508).

10   Denys Hay, *Polydore Vergil: Renaissance Historian and Man of Letters* (Oxford, 1952), p. 2.

11   The work was reprinted in 1541 and again in 1568. D. E. Rhodes, 'The First Edition of Gildas', *The Library*, Sixth Series, 1 (1979), 355–60.

12   Polidoro Virgilio, *Historia Anglica* (Basle, 1534). A second edition appeared in 1546, and a third (with a continuation to 1538) in 1555. An English translation can be found in Henry Ellis (ed.), *Polydore Vergil's English History*, I (London, 1846).

13   F. A. Gasquet, 'Some Materials for a New Edition of Polydore Vergil's "History"', *Transactions of the Royal Historical Society*, New Series, 16 (1902), 11.

14   Ellis, *Polydore Vergil*, pp. 29–30.

15   Ellis, *Polydore Vergil*, pp. 121–2.

16   Kendrick, *British Antiquity*, p. 84.

17   James P. Carley, 'Leland, John (*c.*1503–1552)', *Oxford Dictionary of National Biography* (Oxford, 2004). A detailed discussion of Leland's response to Vergil can be found in James P. Carley, 'Polydore Vergil and John Leland on King Arthur', in Edward Donald Kennedy (ed.), *King Arthur: A Casebook* (London, 2002), pp. 185–204.

18   Thomas Hearne (ed.), *Joannis Lelandi antiquarii de rebus Britannicis collectanea* (Oxford, 1715), V, appendix 1, pp. 2–10.

19   Hearne, *Joannis Lelandi collectanea*, pp. 5–6; Caroline Brett, 'John Leland, Wales and Early British History', *Welsh History Review*, 15/2 (1990), 174–7.

20   John Leland, *Assertio Inclytissimi Arturii Regis Britanniae* (Londoni, 1544); Richard Robinson, *A Learned and True Assertion of the Original, Life, Actes and Death of the Most Noble, Valiant and Renoumed Prince Arthure, King of Great Brittaine* (London, 1582).

21   Carley, 'Polydore Vergil', 189.

22   Juliette Wood, 'Where does Britain end? The reception of Geoffrey of Monmouth in Scotland and Wales', in Rhiannon Purdie and Nicola Royan (eds), *The Scots and Medieval Arthurian Legend* (Cambridge, 2005), p. 15.

23   Thomas Hearne (ed.), *The Itinerary of John Leland. To Which is Prefix'd Mr Leland's New-years Gift*, 9 vols (Oxford, 1710–12).

24   Lucy Toulmin Smith (ed.), *The Itinerary in Wales of John Leland in or about the years 1536–1539* (London, 1906). A new edition of Leland's notes regarding Wales is a desideratum.

25   Smith, *Itinerary*, p. 119; Gazetteer CER Claerddu.

26   Smith, *Itinerary*, p. 11; Leland, *Assertio*, fol. 20r.

27   Smith, *Itinerary*, p. 99.

28   Leslie Alcock, '*By South Cadbury is that Camelot ...': The Excavation of Cadbury Castle 1966–70* (London, 1972), especially pp. 11–23. See also Dai Morgan Evans, '"King Arthur" and Cadbury Castle, Somerset', *The Antiquaries Journal*, 86 (2006), 227–53.

29   Carley, 'Polydore Vergil', p. 196.

30   Ceri Davies (ed. and trans.), *John Prise: Historiae Britannicae Defensio/A Defence of the British History* (Oxford, 2015), pp. xv–xix. See also Glanmor Williams, 'Sir John Pryse of Brecon', *Brycheiniog*, 31 (1998–9), 52–3.

31   Neil Ker, 'Sir John Prise', in A. G. Watson (ed.), *Books, Collectors and Libraries* (London, 1985), pp. 483–95; note in particular the Red Book of Hergest and Vitae Sanctorum Wallia on p. 487. See Davies, *Defensio*, p. xxv, n. 62 for manuscripts not included in Ker's list.

32   Davies, *Defensio* provides a critical text based upon London, British Library, Cotton Titus E.iii, Oxford, Balliol College, MS 260 and the printed edition from 1573.

33   Davies, *Defensio*, pp. 206–9. See also Daniel Huws, 'Gildas Prisei', *National Library of Wales Journal*, 17 (1971–2), 314–20; and David N. Dumville, 'The textual history of the Welsh–Latin *Historia Brittonum*' (unpublished DPhil thesis, University of Edinburgh, 1975), 809–22.

34   Robinson, *Learned and True Assertion*, fol. 3v; Leland, *Assertio*, fol. 3r.

35   Davies, *Defensio*, p. 215.

36   Davies, *Defensio*, pp. 221–3. The charter is printed in J. Gwenogvryn Evans and John Rhys (eds), *The Book of Llan Dâv* (Oxford, 1893), p.77, and referred to again on p. 133. P. C. Bartrum, *Early Welsh Genealogical Tracts* (Cardiff, 1966), p. 10.

37   Davies, *Defensio*, p. 67, referring to London, British Library, Cotton Domitian A.i.

38   Davies, *Defensio*, p. 237.

39   Of the five manuscripts Prise owned containing the works of Gerald, the only one to contain

this material is London, British Library, Cotton Domitian A.i.; Ker, 'Sir John Prise'; p. 486; Lewis Thorpe (trans.), *Gerald of Wales: The Journey through Wales and The Description of Wales* (Harmondsworth, 1978), p. 259.

40 Davies *Defensio*, p. 249: 'Extat item adhuc locus in Venedotia, qui caedis huius memoriam adhuc retinet, lapidemque ingentem nomen huius Huelini praeferentem habet erectum, vt mos erat antiquis, ad huiusmodi rerum memoriam perpetuandam.'

41 Ceridwen Lloyd-Morgan, 'Welsh tradition in Calais: Elis Gruffydd and his biography of King Arthur', in Norris Lacy (ed.), *The Fortunes of King Arthur* (Cambridge, 2005), p. 77. See also Prys Morgan, 'Elis Gruffydd of Gronant – Tudor Chronicler Extraordinary', *Journal of the Flintshire Historical Society*, 25 (1971–2), 9–20.

42 Cardiff, Central Library, MS 3.4, edited in P. C. Bartrum, '*Y Pedwar Ar Hugain A Farnwyd yn Gadarnaf* (The Twenty-Four Kings Judged to be the Mightiest)', *Celtiques*, 12 (1968–71), 157–94.

43 Most of the manuscript remains unedited. A digital copy is now available online at *www.llgc.org.uk/discover/digital-gallery/manuscripts/early-modern-period/elis-gruffudds-chronicle/* (accessed 31 December 2016).

44 The Arthurian section occupies NLW 5276Dii, fols 321r–342r, and although a leaf has been lost between fols 340 and 341, a later transcription in NLW 6209E (pp. 84–7), copied *c*.1700, has preserved the text. Lloyd-Morgan, 'Welsh tradition in Calais', p. 78.

45 R. Wallis Evans, '*Darogan yr Olew Bendigaid* a *Hystdori yr Olew Bendigaid*', *Llên Cymru*, 14 (1981–2), 86–91; and Ceridwen Lloyd-Morgan, '*Darogan yr Olew Bendigaid*: Chwedl o'r Bymthegfed Ganrif', *Llên Cymru*, 14 (1981–2), 64–85.

46 Thomas Jones, 'Chwedl Huail ap Caw ac Arthur', in Thomas Jones (ed.), *Astudiaethau Amrywriol a Glyflwynir i Syr Thomas Parry-Williams* (Cardiff, 1968), pp. 48–66. For further discussion, see Ceridwen Lloyd-Morgan, 'Welsh tradition in Calais'. An edition of the entire Arthurian section is currently in preparation by the same author.

47 Translation my own based on Jones, 'Chwedl Huail', pp. 55–6. 'Ynn y lle amser yma jr yddoedd lawer o ryueddodau ynn y hran hon j'r ynnys, ac yn vnweig ynn yr ynnys j mae'r llyuyr Ffrengick yn I henwi Surloes, yr hon ynn ol prosses yr ysdori a elwir heddiw Ynnys Voon. Ynn yr Amser, megis ac j mae'r ysdori yn dangos, jr yddoedd bont dros Vwnai y[n] ghlych y lle a elwir heddiw Bon y Don, yr hon jr ydoedd serttain o wyr mewn harnais ynn I chadw ynn wasdad. A brenin yr hynnys hon a wnaeth lawer battle greulon yn erbyn Arthur, yr hraoin a vydai ryhir j traethu ar hyn o amser. Neithyr y neb a ch[w]ynnycho darllain yr [y]sdori gwnaed lauur j ddarllain y llyuyr y sydd o gwnckwesd y Sang Reial.'

48 Arnold Taylor, *The Welsh Castles of Edward I* (London and Ronceverte, 1986), pp. 62–5.

49 *Lancelot du Lac*, 2 vols (Rouen and Paris, 1488) and *Lancelot du Lac*, 2 vols (Paris, 1494).

50 Jones, 'Chwedl Huail', p. 56: 'mae ysdori y Sang Real yn i hennwi Kaerhass, yr hon wrth broses yr ysdo[r]i a elwir heddiw Kaerwys.'

51 Elspeth Kennedy (ed.), *Lancelot do Lac: The Non-Cyclic Old French Prose Romance* (Oxford, 1980), I, p.135, l. 16; English translation in Samuel N. Rosenberg and Carleton W. Carroll (trans.), *Lancelot-Grail 3: Lancelot Parts I and II* (Cambridge, 2010), p.106. For further references see G. D. West, *An Index of Proper Names in French Arthurian Prose Romances* (Toronto, 1978), p. 180, under the heading *Karahes*.

52 Translation my own based upon Jones, 'Chwedl Huail', p. 57: '... j varchnad y dre a fferi tori j ben e far y maen a oedd yn gorwedd ar lawr yr heol. Yr hyn a gyulowned ynn ol hir broses. Ac o'r achos yma, j ddwyn koof o'r weithred hon j gelwir y maen hwn jr hyny hyd heddiw Maen Huail'; Gazetter FLI, Maen Huail.

53   Dafydd Johnston (ed.), *Gwaith Lewis Glyn Gothi* (Cardiff, 1995), p. 282, l. 43. For further references to Huail in Welsh poetry see Jones 'Chwedl Huail', pp. 59–60; and Ann Parry Owen, 'Mynegai i Enwau Priod yng Ngwaith Beirdd y Bedwaredd Ganrif ar Ddeg', *Llên Cymru*, 31 (2008), 57.

54   Translation my own based upon Jones, 'Chwedl Huail', p. 57, 'Ac ynn yr amser yma ynn ol hrai o'r ysdoriae j gwnnaeth Arthur lys yn y lle heddiw a elwir Nannerch. Ac etto j gelwir y man Llys Arthur. Ac yvo a ddywedir mae j gappel ef ydoedd yr eglwys, yr hwnn a alwyd ynn hir o amser ynn ol y Kappel Gwial.' See also Lloyd-Morgan, 'Welsh tradition in Calais', p. 85.

55   Rupert Morris (ed.), *Parochialia Being a Summary of Answers to 'Parochial Queries in order to a Geographical Dictionary, Etc., of Wales' issued by Edward Lhuyd*, 3 parts (London, 1909–11), part 1, p. 77.

56   Thorpe, *Gerald of Wales*, p. 259; Rachel Bromwich and Simon D. Evans (eds), *Culhwch and Olwen* (Cardiff, 1992), p. 10; and Hugh Williams (ed. and trans.), *Gildas*, Cymmrodorion Record Series No. 3, 2 vols (London, 1899–1901), II, pp. 400–3.

57   Kennedy, *Lancelot do Lac*, I, pp. 260.32–262.18. Translated in Rosenberg and Carroll, *Lancelot-Grail 3*, pp. 209–10.

58   See Peter Roberts, *The Chronicle of the Kings of Britain* (London, 1811), pp. 361–2 for a translation of the Welsh text.

59   Lloyd-Morgan, 'Welsh tradition in Calais', p. 91.

60   Thomas Jones, 'A sixteenth-century version of the Arthurian Cave legend', in M. Brahmer (ed.), *Studies in Language and Literature in Honour of Margaret Schlauch* (Warsaw, 1966), pp. 175–85.

61   Lloyd-Morgan, 'Welsh tradition in Calais', p. 84.

62   R. Brinley Jones, 'Llwyd, Humphrey (1527–1568)', *Oxford Dictionary of National Biography* (Oxford, 2004).

63   S. Jayne and F. R. Johnson, *The Lumley Library: The Catalogue of 1609* (London, 1956), p. 6.

64   Ieuan M. Williams, *Humphrey Llwyd: Cronica Walliae* (Cardiff, 2002).

65   Williams, *Cronica Walliae*, pp. 4–9.

66   Williams, *Cronica Walliae*, p. 174.

67   Williams, *Cronica Walliae*, p. 71.

68   M. Paul Bryant-Quinn (ed.), *Gwaith Ieuan Brydydd Hir* (Aberystwyth, 2000), p. 25, l. 16 and p. 87, l. 50; Thomas Roberts, 'Y traddodiad am y Brenin Arthur yng Nghaergai', *Bulletin of the Board of Celtic Studies*, 11 (1944), 12–14.

69   London, British Library, Additional MS 59861. See further Ken MacMillan, 'John Dee's "Brytanici Imperii Limites"', *Huntington Library Quarterly*, 64, No. 1/2 (2001), 151–9; Ken MacMillan and Jennifer Abeles (eds), *John Dee: The Limits of the British Empire* (Westport, 2004); and Thomas Green, 'John Dee, King Arthur and the Conquest of the Arctic', *The Heroic Age*, 15 (2012) http://www.heroicage.org/issues/15/green.php (accessed 12 January 2016).

70   Llwyd, *Cronica Walliae*, pp. 167–8.

71   British Library, Harleian MS 473, fol. 16r. For a discussion of this text see Leslie W. Hepple, 'John Dee, Harleian MS 473, and the Early Recording of Roman Inscriptions', *Britannia*, 33 (2002), 177–81.

72   Philip Schwyzer (ed. and trans.), *Humphrey Llwyd: The Breviary of Britain and Selections from the History of Cambria* (London, 2011), p. 16.

73   David Powel, *The Historie of Cambria, now Called Wales* (London, 1584). Powel's additions are shown in a different typeface.

74   Edmund Spenser, *The Fairie Queene* (London, 1590), Book 1, canto IX, verse 4.

75 The work is commonly referred to as David Powel (ed.), *Pontici Virunnii viri doctissimi Britannicae historiae libri sex magna et fide et diligentia conscripti: ad Britannici codicis fidem correcti, & ab infinitis mendis liberati: quibus praefixus est catalogus regum Britanniae* (London, 1585). The different texts appear as follows, *Ponticus Virunnius*, pp. 1–44; *Itinerarium Cambriae*, pp. 49–230; *Cambriae descriptio*, pp. 231–77; and *De Britannica historia*, pp. 278–84.

76 William Lambarde, *A perambulation of Kent conteining the description, hystorie, and customes of that shyre. Collected and written (for the most part) in the yeare 1570* (London, 1576).

77 Brian Ll. James (ed.), *Rice Merrick: Morganiae Archaiographia: A Book of the Antiquities of Glamorganshire* (Barry Island, 1983).

78 James, *Morganiae Archaiographia*, pp. xxviii–xxxiii.

79 James, *Morganiae Archaiographia*, p. 107. See Gazetteer GLA.

80 Kendrick, *British Antiquity*; and F. J. Levy, *Tudor Historical Thought* (San Marino, 1967). See also Q. F. Deakin, 'The early county historians of Wales and western England 1570–1656' (unpublished PhD thesis, University of Wales, Aberystwyth, 1981).

81 William Camden, *Britannia siue Florentissimorum regnorum, Angliae, Scotiae, Hiberniae, et insularum adiacentium ex intima antiquitate chorographica descriptio* (London, 1586).

82 Camden, *Britannia* (1586), pp. 103–4.

83 Camden, *Britannia* (1586), pp. 356–7. The manuscript of the *Historia Brittonum* used by Camden is now lost, although a later copy of it does survive. See Huws, 'Gildas Prisei', 320, n. 12.

84 Levy, *Tudor Historical Thought*, p. 155.

85 William Camden (Philemon Holland trans.), *Britain, or A chorographicall description of the most flourishing kingdomes, England, Scotland, and Ireland, and the ilands adioyning, out of the depth of antiquitie beautified vvith mappes of the severall shires of England Britannia* (London, 1610), p. 666.

86 Angharad Price, 'Rhys, Siôn Dafydd (*b.* 1533/4, *d.* in or after 1620)', *Oxford Dictionary of National Biography* (Oxford, 2004).

87 Joanne Dauide Rhaeso, *Cambrobrytannicae Cymraecaeve Linguae Institutiones et Rudimenta* (London, 1592).

88 The treatise is in NLW Peniarth 118, fols 731–864. The section on giants, fols 803–37, is edited and translated in Chris Grooms, *The Giants of Wales* (Lampeter, 1993), pp. 249–316.

89 Grooms, *Giants of Wales*, pp. 297–316.

90 'Dicebat autem se non inuenisse alium tantae uirtutis postquam Rithonem gigantem in Arauio monte interfecit, qui ipsum ad proeliandum inuitauerat'; Michael Reeve (ed.) and Neil Wright (trans.), *Geoffrey of Monmouth: The History of the Kings of Britain* (Woodbridge, 2007), pp. 226–7.

91 'et Aquila eius super montem Arauium nidificabit. Venedocia rubebit materno sanguine'; Reeve and Wright, *Geoffrey of Monmouth*, p. 147, lines 84–5.

92 Henry Lewis (ed.), *Brut Dingestow* (Cardiff, 1942), p. 170, gives *mynyd Eryri* for *Mons Aravius*.

93 Rupert T. Pickens (trans.), *Lancelot-Grail 2: The Story of Merlin* (Cambridge, 2010), pp. 34, 155 and 171 respectively.

94 Martha Asher (trans.), *Lancelot-Grail 8: The Post-Vulgate Cycle: The Merlin Continuation* (Cambridge, 2010), p. 34; Eugene Vinaver (ed.), *The Works of Thomas Malory*, revised by P. J. C. Field, third edn, 3 vols (Oxford, 1990), I, p. 54.

95 Grooms, *Giants of Wales*, p. 303.

96   Grooms, *Giants of Wales*, pp. 214–18. John Aubrey in his *Monumenta Britannica* (1684) notes a black letter pamphlet, in the hands of Elias Ashmole, describing the entertainment of Queen Elizabeth at Kenilworth in 1575 with a story about a king of north Wales called Ryers who tries to make a cloak of beards. This suggests that the story had established itself in popular culture at least two decades before Rhys wrote his version. See John Fowles (ed.) and Rodney Legg (annotator), *John Aubrey's Monumenta Britannica, Parts One and Two* (Wincanton, 1980), p. 540.

97   John H. Harvey (ed.), *William Worcestre Itineraries* (Oxford, 1969), p. 201. In light of the Mortimer family interest in the Arthurian legend, noted in chapter 2, could the fact that the castle was founded by them have any bearing on this association?

98   Ac yn mhlwybh Penn Ederyn, Dynas gawr a gabhas y ladh gan Arthvr. A'r lhe trigyiei yndaw a 'elwir etto Caer Craic Dynas gawr; Grooms, *Giants of Wales*, p. 312–13.

99   Grooms, *Giants of Wales*, p. 244.

100   Although the work is untitled, it is usually referred to as Christopher Saxton, *[Atlas of the Counties of England and Wales]* (London, 1580).

101   Sarah Tyacke and John Huddy, *Christopher Saxton and Tudor Map-Making* (London, 1980), p. 32, quoting from 'An assistance for Christopher Saxton to survey Wales 10 July 1576', TNA, PC2/11, pp. 44–5.

102   W. R. B. Robinson, 'Dr. Thomas Phaer's Report on the Harbours and Customs Administration of Wales under Edward VI', *Bulletin of the Board of Celtic Studies*, 24 (1972), 502.

103   P. C. Bartrum (ed.), *Welsh Genealogies AD 300–1400*, 8 vols (Cardiff, 1974) and *Welsh Genealogies AD 1400–1500* (Aberystwyth, 1983). The four instances of Arthur are all found in the 1983 work. Arthur ap William Lewis in vol. 16, Gwent and Morgannwg, 7.1128; Arthur Newton the son of Sir Peter Newton of Heighly in Shropshire in vol. 17, Powys, 9.1495; vol. 18, Gwynedd is Conwy; Arthur the son of Robert ap Rhys the Chaplain to Cardinal Wolsey, 8.1332; and Arthur ap Rhys ap Llewelyn, p. 1. At least two of these names show links to the establishment in England and probably reflect the more common use of the name there.

104   P. C. Bartrum, 'Arthuriana from the Genealogical Manuscripts', *National Library of Wales Journal*, 14 (1965), 242.

105   Gazetteer CRD Maen Arthur.

106   The Melville Richards Archive is available at *www.e-gymraeg.co.uk/enwaulleoedd/amr/cronfa_en.aspx* (accessed on 1 April 2015).

107   J. William Hebel (ed.), *The Works of Michael Drayton*, 5 vols (Oxford, 1931–41); vol. IV contains the *Polyolbion*.

108   Andrew Hadfield, 'Spenser, Drayton and the Question of Britain', *The Review of English Studies*, 51 (2000), 582–99; and Richard Utz, '"There Are Places We Remember": Situating the Medieval Past in Postmedieval Cultural Memories', *Transfiguration, Nordic Journal of Christianity and the Arts*, 6/2 (2004), 95.

109   D. R. Woolf, 'Lewis, John (*d.* 1615/16)', *Oxford Dictionary of National Biography* (Oxford, 2004); Francis G. Payne, 'John Lewis, Llynwene, Historian and Antiquary', *Radnorshire Society Transactions*, 30 (1960), 13.

110   John Lewis, *History of Great Britain, From the First Inhabitants thereof, til the Death of Cadwalader Last King of the Britains* (London, 1729). References to the Book of Taliesin can be found on pp. 183 and 195 and elsewhere throughout the work.

111   Richard White, *Historiarum Britanniae Insulae, ab origine Mundi, ad annum Christi octingentesimum, Libri novem priores*, 9 vols (Douai, 1597–1602).

112 Alan MacColl, 'Richard White and the Legendary History of Britain', *Humanistica Lovaniensia*, 51 (2002), 245–57. White is notable for being one of the earliest authors to use endnotes to explain his sources.

113 Alan MacColl, 'The Construction of England as a Protestant "British" nation in the Sixteenth Century', *Renaissance Studies*, 18/4 (2004), 607; Geoffrey Ashe, 'A Certain Very Ancient Book: Traces of an Arthurian Source in Geoffrey of Monmouth's History', *Speculum*, 56 (1981) 301–23, makes no mention of the earlier suggestion by White.

114 Rhiannon Purdie and Nicola Royan (eds), *The Scots and Medieval Arthurian Legend* (Cambridge, 2005) provides a series of excellent essays exploring this tradition.

115 I have a detailed study of this particular issue in preparation.

116 Daniel Huws, *Medieval Welsh Manuscripts* (Cardiff, 2000), p. 288.

117 Huws, *Medieval Welsh Manuscripts*, p. 291.

118 E. D. Jones, 'Camden, Vaughan and Lhuyd and Merionethshire', *Journal of the Merionethshire Record Society*, 2 (1953–6), 224.

119 Gazetteer MER Camlan.

120 Nesta Lloyd, 'John Jones, Gellilyfdy', *Flintshire Historical Transactions*, 24 (1969–70), 5–18.

121 NLW Peniarth 267, p. 40, See Gazetteer CRN, Pikel Arthur.

122 Richard Morgan, 'Robert Vaughan of Hengwrt (1592–1667)', *Journal of the Merionethshire Record Society*, 8 (1977–80), 400.

123 Brynley F. Roberts, 'Lhuyd, Edward (1659/60?–1709)', *Oxford Dictionary of National Biography* (Oxford, 2004). The spelling of his surname has appeared as both Lhuyd and Lhwyd and he used both during his lifetime. Recent publications have given it as Lhwyd which is also the form that he used to sign most of his correspondence and has therefore been adopted here throughout.

124 Frank Emery, 'Edward Lhwyd and the 1695 *Britannia*', *Antiquity*, 32 (1958), 179. The letter survives as Oxford, Bodleian, Ashmole 1816, fol. 468.

125 R. T. Gunther (ed.), *Early Science in Oxford*, XIV: *Life and Letters of Edward Lhwyd* (Oxford, 1945), p. 193.

126 Over 2,000 letters to and from Edward Lhwyd are now indexed online, and many of them are available as transcripts or page images, as part of the Early Modern Letters Online project at Oxford University. *http://emlo.bodleian.ox.ac.uk/forms/advanced?people=lhwyd%2C+edward* (accessed 31 December 2016).

127 Richard Ellis, 'Some Incidents in the Life of Edward Lhuyd', *Transactions of the Honourable Society of Cymmrodorion* (1906–7), 10.

128 Gwyn Walters and Frank Emery, 'Edward Lhuyd, Edmund Gibson and the Printing of Camden's *Britannia*, 1695', *The Library*, Series 5, 32 (1977), 109–37.

129 Edmund Gibson (ed.), *Camden's Britannia Newly Translated into English with Large Additions and Improvements* (London, 1695).

130 F. V. Emery, 'Edward Lhuyd and Some of his Glamorgan Correspondents: A View of Gower in the 1690s', *Transactions of the Honourable Society of Cymmrodorion* (1965), 64. The original is preserved in Oxford, Bodleian, Ashmole 1817b, fol. 292.

131 Gibson, *Britannia*, col. 619.

132 Gibson, *Britannia*, col. 628. The original letter survives in Oxford, Bodleian, Ashmole 1817, fol. 430. See also Edward Parry, 'The Revd Erasmus Saunders', *Journal of the Pembrokeshire Historical Society*, 13 (2004), 35–42.

133 Ellis, 'Some Incidents', 12, quoting from Oxford, Bodleian, Hearne 94, fol. 153.

134 The full proposal can be read in Ellis, 'Some Incidents', 13–15.

135   Gunther, *Life and Letters*, p. 311. Lhwyd's catalogue is preserved in NLW Peniarth 119.

136   Gunther, *Life and Letters*, p. 316.

137   Edward Lhwyd, *Parochial Queries in Order to a Geographical Dictionary, A Natural History &c. of Wales* (Oxford, 1696), p. 1.

138   The returns are gathered together in Morris, *Parochialia*. For an improved index and a map showing the parishes covered, see F. V. Emery, 'A Map of Edward Lhuyd's *Parochial Queries in Order to a Geographical Dictionary, &c., of Wales* (1696)', *Transactions of the Honourable Society of Cymmrodorion* (1958), 41–53.

139   Morris, *Parochialia*, part 3, pp. 72–3. From Oxford, Bodleian, Ashmole 1820a, fol. 157; Gazetteer MON

140   Morris, *Parochialia*, part 2, p. 71. From Peniarth MS 251, p. 146a.

141   Morris, *Parochialia*, part 1, p. 78. From Kinmel Park MS, vol. II (now known as NLW 1506C), p. 34.

142   Morris, *Parochialia*, part 2, p. 97, illustration on p. 98. From Llanstephan MS 185, p. 100.

143   They appear as appendix 4, entitled 'Lhuydiana', in John Fisher (ed.), *Tours in Wales (1804–1813) by Richard Fenton* (London, 1917), pp. 332–49.

144   Gazetteer, CRN, Coetan Arthur in Llangelynin and Llaniestin; CRM Coetan Arthur in Caeo and Llangadog.

145   *Oxford English Dictionary*, online edition, 'quoit'.

146   William Borlase, *Observations on the Antiquities Historical and Monumental, of the County of Cornwall* (Oxford, 1754), p. 211.

147   George Scott (ed.), *Mr Ray's Itineraries* (London, 1760), p. 237.

148   Browne Willis, *A Survey of the Cathedral Church of St. David's, and the Edifices Belonging to it, as they Stood in the Year 1715* (London, 1717), p. 63; Gazetteer PEM.

149   Owen Owens, 'Gweithiau Barddonol Morus Dwyfech' (unpublished MA thesis, Bangor, 1944), 140. I would like to thank Barry Lewis for his help in interpreting this poem.

150   The term has been discussed in Henry Owen (ed.), *The Description of Penbrokeshire by George Owen of Henllys*, 4 vols (London, 1892–1936), I, p. 252. A new study of why this name was used so widely for prehistoric monuments in Wales would be very useful.

151   Owen, *Description of Penbrokeshire*, I, p. 251, also includes an illustration of the monument by Owen. Erasmus Saunders to Edward Lhwyd, Dol Haidd, 20 January 1693/4 from Bodleian MS. Ashmole 1817a, fols 434–5, in Brynley F. Roberts, 'Edward Lhwyd in Carmarthenshire', *Carmarthenshire Antiquary*, 46 (2010), 37–8.

152   Edward Lhuyd, *Archaeologia Britannica: Giving Some Account Additional to what Has Been Hitherto Publish'd, of the Languages, Histories and Customs of the Original Inhabitants of Great Britain*, I: *Glossography* (Oxford, 1707), pp. 254–65.

153   Eiluned Rees and Gwyn Walters, 'The Dispersion of the Manuscripts of Edward Lhuyd', *Welsh History Review*, 7 (1974), 148–78.

154   Geraint H. Jenkins, 'Evans, Theophilus (1693–1767)', *Oxford Dictionary of National Biography* (Oxford, 2004); Theophilus Evans, *Drych y Prif Oesoedd* (Shrewsbury, 1716).

155   P. Pezron, *L'Antiquité de la nation et la langue des Celtes* (Paris, 1703); translated into English as *The Antiquities of Nations More particularly of the Celtae or Gauls taken to be originally the same people as our Ancient Britains* (London, 1706).

156   Lhuyd, *Archaeologia Britannica*, p. 258 (although actually p. 260).

157   Theophilus Evans, *Drych y Prif Oesoedd* (1716), p. 93, and in a slightly different form in the second edn (Shrewsbury, 1740), p. 130. Translation from George Roberts (trans.), *A View of the Primitive Ages* (Llanidloes, 1865), pp. 107–8.

158 Iwan Wmffre, *The Place-Names of Cardiganshire*, 3 vols (London, 2004), p. 131.

159 Lewis Morris, *Plans of Harbours, Bars, Bays and Roads in St Georges Channel* (London, 1748). Available online at *https://www.llgc.org.uk/discover/digital-gallery/maps/nautical-maps/lewis-morris-and-william-morris-sea-charts/plans-of-harbours-bars-bays-and-roads-in-st-georges-channel/* (accessed 31 December 2016).

160 For a discussion of this text see Ceridwen Lloyd-Morgan, 'Narratives and Non-narratives: Aspects of Welsh Arthurian Tradition', *Arthurian Literature*, 21: *Celtic Arthurian Legend* (Cambridge, 2004), pp. 125–6.

161 Lloyd-Morgan, 'Narratives and Non-narratives', pp. 125–8.

162 Lloyd-Morgan, 'Narratives and Non-narratives', p. 126.

163 Lloyd-Morgan, 'Narratives and Non-narratives', p. 128.

164 David Bick and Philip Wyn Davies, *Lewis Morris and the Cardiganshire Mines* (Aberystwyth, 1994), p. 11; Wmffre, *Place-Names of Cardiganshire*, p. 1070.

165 J. Gwenogvryn Evans, *Report on Manuscripts in Welsh*, II, p. 955. From London, British Library, Additional MS 14903, p. 21b.

166 R. T. Jenkins and H. M. Ramage, *A History of the Honourable Society of Cymmrodorion and of the Gwyneddigion and Cymreigyddion (1751–1951)* (London, 1951), p. 242.

167 Saunders Lewis, *A School of Welsh Augustans* (Wrexham, 1924), pp. 24–54.

168 Hugh Owen (ed.), *Additional Letters of the Morrises of Anglesey (1735–86)*, 2 vols (London, 1947–49), I, pp. 144–5. An idea reused in Graham Philips and Martin Keatman, *King Arthur: The True Story* (London, 1992).

169 Thomas Carte, *A General History of England*, 4 vols (London, 1747–55), I, p. 31, for the material supplied by Lewis Morris. For a discussion of this matter see W. J. Hughes, *Wales and the Welsh in English Literature* (Wrexham, 1924), p. 156.

170 Hughes, *Wales and the Welsh*, pp. 160–3.

171 Evan Evans, *Some Specimens of the Poetry of the Antient Welsh Bards* (London, 1764).

172 Sarah Prescott, *Eighteenth-Century Writing from Wales: Bards and Britons* (Cardiff, 2008), pp. 57–83.

FIVE
FROM TOURISTS
TO THE INTERNET

T HIS FINAL CHAPTER will survey the various sources that have contributed a
majority of the Arthurian place names known today. As the chronological list
in Appendix 1 shows, the nineteenth century provides more first attestations of Arthurian place names than any preceding century. The sources printed in this period
were more widely read because of a general rise in literacy levels and the increased
availability of books through libraries. Some place names originate with the earliest
Ordnance Survey drawings and maps, and still appear today. The development of
place-name research during the twentieth century has done much to bring to light
Arthurian names, especially in unpublished sources, but much still remains to be
done in Wales.

The Tourists

The publication of *Anecdotes of British Topography* (1768) and *England Displayed*
(1769) brought together, in gazetteer form by county, a wealth of material from
earlier works.[1] Both works give good coverage for Wales and they provide a useful
indication of the state of topographical writing at the beginning of the Industrial
Revolution. The Arthurian material they contain is limited to references derived
from the printed editions of Geoffrey of Monmouth, Gerald of Wales, Leland, Prise
and Gibson's 1695 edition of Camden's *Britannia*, illustrating the repetitive nature
of references to the Arthurian place names of Wales at this date. By the end of the
century a combination of the Revolutionary (1792–1802) and Napoleonic (1803–15)
Wars on the continent, the development of the road network, the rise of the Romantic movement and a revival in Celticism led to an increased number of visitors to
Wales.[2] From 1770 onwards, the number of visitors began to rise significantly and
the publication of Welsh tours began, slowly at first, until several appeared each year
by the early nineteenth century. An awareness of, and interest in, local legends and

antiquities can be seen in some of these works, but few of the tourists actively sought out Arthurian sites, and when they mention them at all, it is often only incidentally.

Aside from the shorter, early works of Joseph Cradock (1770) and N. Pen-ruddock Wyndham (1775), the first serious work on the topography of Wales was written by Thomas Pennant (1726–98), who in later years was christened the 'the father of Cambrian tourists'.[3] Pennant lived at Downing near Whitford in Flintshire, and, encouraged by the positive reception of his first travel book, *A Tour in Scotland* (1772),[4] wrote *A Tour in Wales*, which appeared in three parts (1778–83).[5] The title is somewhat misleading as the book is exclusively concerned with north Wales, but it quickly became the single most influential Welsh tour and was referred to by nearly all subsequent visitors to the country. Although showing no particular interest in Arthurian matters, Pennant's *A Tour in Wales* is the earliest source for at least one association, and was also responsible for making other sites better known.[6] On his visit to the area around Llangollen in Denbighshire, Pennant refers to the impressive limestone escarpment of the Eglwyseg valley and notes that 'one of the principal of the Glisseg rocks is honoured with the name of Craig Arthur'.[7] This is the earliest source to associate Arthur with the highest cliffs on the escarpment, and later folklore adds a story of Arthur having his stronghold there and killing a giantess on the nearby pass of Bwlch y Rhiwfelen (better known today as the Horseshoe Pass).[8]

Elsewhere in the book, Pennant refers to a monument that was erected over a boundary stone between the counties of Flintshire and Denbighshire and was at the centre of a legal dispute in 1763:[9]

> The decision, which was in favor of the lords of *Mold*, is recorded on an arch over a noted stone, called *Carreg Carn March Arthur*, which was then adjudged to be the boundary of the parish of *Mold* in the country of *Flint*, and of *Llanverres* in that of *Denbigh*.[10]

In the late eighteenth century it became fashionable, for those who could afford it, to pay for an artist to add extra illustrations to large paper editions of printed tours. This process, known as grangerisation, after its greatest exponent, the Rev. James Granger, survives in at least eight extra-illustrated copies of Pennant's *A Tour in Wales*.[11] Amongst the many extra drawings and etchings that adorn these copies, there is a watercolour of Carreg Carn March Arthur drawn by John Ingleby in 1796, making it one of the earliest depictions of a site with an Arthurian association.[12] Pennant also refers briefly to the hill fort of Moel Arthur in the Clwydian Hills as named 'probably in honor of our celebrated prince', and is the first author to name the hill fort at Din Silwy, known since the Tudor period as Round Table Fort, by its Welsh form, Bwrdd Arthur, a name it still bears on modern maps.[13] The change from an earlier English form to a Welsh form is also evident at Bwrdd Arthur, near Llansannan in Denbighshire, which was first referred to as Round Table by Leland in 1538.[14] A further example of this change can be seen at Arthyr Wood in Glamorganshire in 1734, which only

Figure 10. *Carreg Carn March Arthur, a stone marking the border between Flintshire and Denbighshire, from an extra-illustrated edition of Thomas Pennant's* A Tour in Wales.
By permission of Llyfrgell Genedlaethol Cymru / The National Library of Wales.

became Coed Arthur in 1833.[15] The final Arthurian name first attested by Thomas Pennant concerns the cromlech at Lligwy, near Moelfre in Anglesey.

> Not far from the road, in the lands of Llugwy, is a most stupendous Cromlech, of a rhomboid form. The greatest diagonal is seventeen feet six inches, the lesser fifteen; the thickness three feet nine; its height from the ground only two feet: it was supported by several stones. The Welsh, who ascribe everything stupendous to our famous British king, call it Arthur's Quoit.[16]

The increasing number of published tours led to the compilation of works such as *The Cambrian Traveller's Guide and Pocket Companion* (1808) by William Nicholson, which proved a huge success and was reprinted in a much-expanded form in 1813 and again in 1840.[17] The guide was laid out according to geographical regions and compiled together information from the most important tours, providing a compendium of tourist literature for each location, and is a good example of the type of pocket-sized resource available to the traveller in the early nineteenth century. In order to undertake a comprehensive survey of the Arthurian material found in the printed tourist literature from this period, a survey was made of the titles, up to

1830, found in two separate bibliographical lists of Welsh tours: John Anderson's *The Book of British Topography* (1866) and W. J. Hughes's *Wales and the Welsh in English Literature* (1924).[18]

The survey covered nearly a hundred different works and showed that most of the tours contain little original material, relying almost exclusively on earlier works for their information. This fact is nicely illustrated by Henry Skrine, who in the preface to his 1798 tour urges readers to consult

> In points of history, principally as regarding the ancient buildings both religious and civil, Grose's Antiquities, and Mr. Gough's valuable edition of Camden's Britannia, [which] will prove the best guides, together with Mr. Pennant's very accurate and excellent work.[19]

To the above could have been added Powel's 1584 *History of Cambria*, his 1585 edition of Gerald of Wales and the first volume of the periodical *The Cambrian Register* (for 1795, published in 1798), which together provide some of the earliest English discussions and translations of Welsh historical and antiquarian material. Despite the repetitive nature of the Arthurian material in the printed tours, a small number do provide the earliest source for Arthurian names. A good example can be found in *An Historical Tour of Monmouthshire* (1801) by William Coxe, who made the following observation about a meadow at Bassaleg, near Newport: 'Between the encampment and the road, we passed through a pleasant meadow called Maes Arthur, or the field of Arthur; which according to uncertain tradition, derived its appellation from that renowned hero of British fable.'[20] On the tithe map of 1840 the field is named Maes y Saison (Field of the English). The name is not shown on the earliest Ordnance Survey mapping, but does appear on the six-inch map of 1887, whether this was because of the note in Coxe's *Tour* is not certain. Only a small number of the tourists made the effort to consult non-printed sources, notably Thomas Pennant and Richard Fenton (1746–1821), both of whom consulted Edward Lhwyd's papers in pursuit of information about Welsh antiquities.[21] Having surveyed the tourist literature of the period it is clear that the name Arthur is far more likely to appear in the list of subscribers to each book, than in the actual text itself.[22]

By 1800 Welsh writers were unhappy with how Wales was depicted by English tourists as little more than a picturesque land of mountains, full of sullen and superstitious inhabitants. The fightback began with an article published in *The Cambrian Register* in 1799, authored by CYMRO, a pseudonym for Theophilus Jones, who later wrote *A History of the County of Brecknock* (1805).[23] Jones made the valid point that of all the tours that had been published, only one, *A Tour in Wales* by Thomas Pennant, was written by someone with a local knowledge of Wales.[24] The next tour to be published by somebody living in Wales was Richard Fenton's *A Historical Tour through Pembrokeshire* in 1811, and the first by a Welsh speaker, although still in English and posthumously, was *Cambria Depicta: A Tour through North Wales* by Edward Pugh

Figure 11. *Maen Arthur, the name given to a rocking stone near Dolbenmaen, Caernarfonshire, from the unpublished 'Celtic Antiquites of Snowdonia' (1772) by the Rev. Richard Farrington (NLW 1118C, p. 180).*
By permission of Llyfrgell Genedlaethol Cymru / The National Library of Wales.

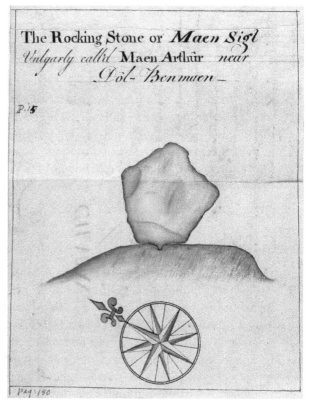

of Ruthin in 1816, a well-illustrated book that portrayed Wales and it inhabitants in a positive light.[25]

Despite the large number of printed tours published from 1770 onwards, a great number remain unpublished in manuscript form. The National Library of Wales has a handlist of over 150 unpublished tours of Wales, and Gwynfryn Walters, in his 1966 thesis on the subject, notes many more examples at different institutions.[26] A detailed survey of these works may reveal further Arthurian material, but the huge effort required would probably discover little based on original observation rather than earlier printed material. One unpublished work known to contain worthwhile material is 'Snowdonia Druidica', which is responsible for the earliest attestation of at least four different Arthurian names. The author was Richard Farrington (1702–72), who entered Jesus College, Oxford in 1720 and ultimately became the chancellor of Bangor Cathedral. Farrington was a friend of Thomas Pennant, who had stayed with him during his tour of Caernarfonshire and corresponded with him on the subject of antiquities.[27]

The work is primarily concerned with the megalithic remains of Caernarfonshire, and it is clear from the three different manuscripts of the work that survive that Farrington had intended to dedicate the work to Pennant.[28] The text in NLW MS 4899 is an early draft of the work dated to 1764 and includes the earliest known Arthurian associations with three megalithic sites in Caernarfonshire. Two relate to cromlechs in the parishes of Llanystumdwy and Clynnog Fawr, and he is also the first to give the now lost rocking stone of Maen Sigl, near Dolbenmaen, the name Maen Arthur.[29] Farrington also used the phrase 'Arthur's Javelins' for standing stones, a phrase which does not seem to have caught on, as it is not mentioned again elsewhere.[30] Two later manuscript copies exist, NLW 1118C and NLW 1119D, and the former contains excellent illustrations of megalithic sites, including Maen Arthur (see Figure 11). The final version of the work in NLW 1119D was intended for publication but never printed, and Farrington's valuable observations and illustrations remain largely unpublished.

When analysed in context it becomes clear that, apart from the few exceptions outlined above, the Arthurian names in the tourist literature are primarily recycled from earlier printed sources and indicate the breadth of the authors' reading, rather than any individual interest in Arthurian matters. Arthur played only a minor role in the writings of the many tourists to visit Wales in the late eighteenth and early nineteenth centuries, but the repetition of the same handful of names has given the impression that Arthurian names were more commonplace than they actually were.[31]

The Silurian Arthur Theory

In 1762 the historian David Hume could write in his *History of England* that King Arthur was a 'prince of the Silures', the Roman name for the British tribe inhabiting south-east Wales.[32] This idea is repeated in numerous works of the time and has caused a great deal of confusion for later writers. It is therefore worthwhile to explain its origin in order to prevent further uncertainty. The theory can ultimately be traced back to the rediscovery of the twelfth-century Book of Llandaf in the sixteenth century. As early as 1545, John Prise had drawn attention to the grant of land to Noe ab Arthur in the Book of Llandaf, but this refers to Arthur ap Pedr of the Harleian genealogies, and despite the name, there is nothing to associate him with the Arthur of legend.[33] However, the Silurian Arthur theory is not built around this individual, but around another name found in the Book of Llandaf. The Latin text provides the name *Athruis fili Mourici* and he is mentioned on twelve separate occasions, one of which refers to him as *Rex Athruis*.[34] The spelling of *Athruis* is consistent throughout the manuscript, and its Welsh form is Athrwys. This *Athruis* was the son of *Mourici* (Meurig), the king of Gwent, and had a son called *Morcant* (Morgan), referred to as *Rex Morcannhuc* (king of Morgannwg).[35] Two further individuals with exactly the same spelling, *Athruis*, are also mentioned elsewhere in the manuscript, suggesting that the name-form was in common usage.

The next reference to the Book of Llandaf, in print, is in a book by Francis Godwin (1562–1633), the bishop of Llandaf from 1601 to 1617, entitled *A Catalogue of the Bishops of England* (1615). Godwin quoted a section from the Life of St Oudoceus concerning the death of *Mouric* at Tintern in Monmouthshire, and later mentions his son *Athruis*.[36] However, in the printed text the name was misspelt as *Arthruis*, and the intrusion of the additional letter r into this name, whether by Godwin or his printers, has been the source of a great deal of later confusion. In 1673 William Dugdale transcribed material from the manuscript when it was in the library of John Selden and also spelt the name as *Arthruis*.[37] Several antiquarians had access to the

Book of Llandaf during the seventeenth century and copied extracts from it, or in the case of Robert Vaughan, the entire contents. Not one of these authors drew any attention to the similarity of *Athruis* to Arthur. The manuscript was in the hands of Robert Davies of Llanerch by 1696 and was then passed down through his family, until reaching Philip Bryan Davies-Cooke of Gwysaney, near Mold in Flintshire, where it was transcribed by J. Gwenogvryn Evans and then printed at Oxford in 1893.[38] It was purchased by the National Library of Wales in 1959, and a digital edition of the manuscript is now available on its website.[39]

At the beginning of the eighteenth century the original manuscript was not easily accessible, but it was still widely discussed amongst historians. The first person to suggest an identification between Athrwys ap Meurig and the King Arthur of legend was Thomas Carte in the first volume of his *General History of England*, published in 1744:

> the ancient register of *Landaff*, among several benefactions made to that church in the times of *Dubricius*, *Teliau*, and *Oudoceus*, the three first bishops of the see, recites at length two grants; one, of the lands of St *Kinmarc* by *Arthruis*, king of Gwent, son of *Mouric*, king of *Glamorgan*, who gave *Moch-ros* to *Dubricius*; the other of *Cair-riow*, by another *Arthruis*, king also of *Gwent*, but the son of *Fernvail*, king of the same country [...] But the language and orthography in which they are written, scarce intelligible now to any of the *Welsh*, but such of the learned as are versed in the writing of *Lowarch* and *Taliessin*, are sufficient vouchers for their antiquity: and the lands were enjoyed by the see of *Landaff*, from the time of its first bishops to that of the reformation. As the times agree, there is little room to doubt but one of these kings of *Gwent*, most probably the former, was the *Arthur* in question; whose death, as it is generally agreed happened A.D. 542.[40]

Carte relied upon the 1615 work by Francis Godwin, with its incorrect spelling of the name, for his information about the material from the *Book of Llandaf*. The identification was subsequently used by David Hume in *A History of England* (1762), John Whitaker in his *A History of Manchester* (1775) and Edward Gibbon in the third volume of his widely read *History of the Decline and Fall of the Roman Empire* (1788), amongst others.[41] Initially few Welsh authors adopted the theory, but William Owen Pughe did concur in his influential *Cambrian Biography* of 1803.[42]

Robert Vaughan's copy of the Book of Llandaf was used as the basis for an edition and English translation of the text by William Rees in 1840, making the work more accessible.[43] In his translation Rees correctly gives the Welsh form of the name as Athrwys, and at no point does he associate him with King Arthur.[44] The association continues to make the occasional appearance in the later nineteenth century: Robert Owen, following William Owen Pughe, in *The Kymry: Their Origin, History, and International Relations* of 1891 accepts the identification, as does Owen 'Morien' Morgan in his *History of Wales*, as late as 1911.[45] However, it never became widely accepted, and it was not until the early 1980s that the idea was resurrected; this is discussed below. The digital version of the manuscript makes it quite clear that the original Latin reading is *Athruis* and not *Arthruis*. The name only became associated with King Arthur through errors in the transcription of the text for publication in 1615 and then a suggestion, based upon those errors, by Thomas Carte in 1744.

Iolo Morganwg

In the late eighteenth century a Romantic view of the past was developed in Wales, based upon a fictional bardic vision that was primarily the work of one man, Edward Williams, better known by his bardic name of Iolo Morganwg. Iolo created his Romantic view of the Welsh past by forging documents and inventing a bardic tradition complete with its own alphabet.[46] His fictions gained a prominent place in Welsh society, his bardic emblem adorned many publications, and his version of Welsh history became widely accepted, with criticism only appearing occasionally.[47] His most enduring creation was the Gorsedd of the Bards, which epitomised his bardic image of the past and survives today in the ceremonies performed at the National Eisteddfod.[48] The attractive version of Welsh history he portrayed became popular, insinuating itself into many of the major works dealing with the history and literature of Wales published in the nineteenth century. For over a century Iolo's invented view of the past cast a shadow over Welsh historians, fuelled by a desire to show that Wales was a distinctly separate nation from England with its own history. The few voices that did express concern about the authenticity of Iolo's works were frequently drowned out by those supporting it. It was not until 1926 that G. J. Williams finally began to untangle the web of Iolo's inventions and show that his Glamorgan-centric bardic view of the past was largely a forgery.[49]

Iolo has little to say about Arthur, but he was convinced by the Silurian theory, as is evident in his 1794 work, *Poems, Lyric and Pastoral*, where he quotes directly from the Thomas Carte extract given above.[50] Iolo was instrumental in the publication of *The Myvyrian Archaiology of Wales* (1801–7), one of the first serious attempts to publish the medieval texts of Wales, including Arthurian material.[51] He used his editorial role to get some of his forgeries included in the volumes, passing them off as authentic medieval sources and causing much confusion to later historians.[52] Amidst Iolo's voluminous manuscripts, only two items of Arthurian material relevant to this work occur. The well-known folk story of a young boy meeting an old man on London Bridge, who gives him a wooden staff and tells him that a cave exists near his home full of treasure, has been associated with different localities all over Wales.[53] Iolo seemingly provides the earliest source (*c.*1800) for Arthur as the guardian of the treasure in a cave within the cliffs of Craig y Dinas, near Neath.[54] The second Arthurian tale to originate with Iolo concerns a short onomastic tale about Arthur leaping from hilltop to hilltop across south Wales, each one becoming known as Arthur's *twmpath* (a mound).[55]

When we consider Iolo's obsession with Wales's distant past, it may appear somewhat surprising that he makes very little mention of Arthur in his works, but knowing, as we do, what he was trying to achieve, this lack of interest is more understandable. The bardic world of Iolo had no place for a hero like Arthur, as most of the available material about him had been discussed thoroughly over the centuries. To integrate the well-established figure of Arthur into his bardic view of the past would have been a near-impossible task and would have undoubtedly brought more scrutiny to bear on his work, making detection of his forgeries more likely. Apart from the occasional reference to 'in the time of Arthur' or 'Arthur's Round Table', Arthur remains a vague figure.[56] As Iolo centred his view of the past on south Wales, it was inevitable that Caerleon should feature in some way and it does play a small part in his mythology. However, it was easier for Iolo to incorporate this site, for apart from its role in Geoffrey of Monmouth, little was known about its post-Roman history, and therefore there was little for him to contradict.[57] Iolo was hugely influential in nineteenth-century Wales, but was primarily concerned with his bards and was able to create a mythology that could run parallel to the Arthurian traditions, without the need to mention them in anything but the vaguest of terms.

The Ordnance Survey

The maps of Wales published by John Speed in 1611 were still being reprinted in the late eighteenth century, and although newer maps of the whole country had appeared in the meantime, few provided any more detail. A similar situation existed across the rest of Britain, and it was not until the Ordnance Survey began its work in the late eighteenth century that things began to change.[58] The Survey produced reliable and accurate maps, published at the scale of one inch to the mile, and coverage for Wales was complete by 1850. Work began in Wales in 1809 with the creation of the first Ordnance Surveyor's Drawing (henceforth OSD), by T. Budgen, for parts of Pembrokeshire and Carmarthenshire, and by 1820 he had surveyed all of south Wales.[59] The drawings for north Wales began in 1816, and the final one, a section of Flintshire, was not finished until 1836.[60]

A comparison between the Arthurian place names shown on the original drawings and those on the final engraved printed maps reveals that some were omitted, some were added and others were changed. At least one Arthurian name found on the OSD for Caernarfonshire: Ffynnon Cegin Arthur, did not make it onto the printed version.[61] A probable reason for this omission is the fact that the printed maps were published at the smaller scale of one inch to the mile, compared to the OSD standard scale of two inches to the mile. Hence there was less space available, especially for a long name that was unlikely to be considered essential.[62] However, this does not explain why at least two Arthurian names on the printed maps are different from those on the earlier OSD; for that it is necessary to understand the revision history of each map before publication:

In the case of the OSDs, the time elapsing between survey and engraving was occasionally as long as thirty years, and delays of fifteen years were commonplace. Thus the publication date of the printed map is frequently misleading. Moreover, the pre-publication revisions habitually made to old surveys serve to differentiate the OSDs still more from their printed derivatives.[63]

A good example of this change can be seen for a dwelling near St Asaph, in Flintshire, named Tyddyn Arthur on the printed map, whereas on the OSD it is called Tyddyn Eithin.[64] The OSD in question, number 309, was drawn by Robert Dawson in 1819–21. There was a gap of nearly twenty years before it was revised in 1838–9 and then finally published in 1840–1.[65] It would seem, therefore, that the change from *Eithin* to Arthur took place during the revisions of 1838–9. Unfortunately the tithe map of the area, dating from 1843, simply refers to the site as 'homestead' and does not help to establish at what point the name may have changed.[66] Another change also involves the word *Eithin*. Pen-y-Graig Eithin, north of Llanddoged in Denbighshire, appears on OSD 312 from 1822, and again on the first printed map of 1840, but on the six-inch map published in 1892 the name has changed to Pen-y-Graig Arthur and the form Pencraig Arthur is still in use on current OS maps. A probable reason behind a change of this nature has been suggested:

> In Wales, as in Gaelic Scotland, the problems faced by English surveyors and cartographers have been greatly compounded by an often alien Celtic language, by unusual complexities in areas of bilingualism and, not least, by the debates and linguistic fads of several generations of scholars.[67]

Eighteen names in the gazetteer have their earliest attestation on the Ordnance Survey maps and drawings and while some of these may yet be shown to have been in use at an earlier date, it suggests that the maps are not always a reliable indication of earlier Arthurian associations.

The Re-emergence of Arthur

The beginning of the Arthurian revival is linked to the publication of two new editions of Malory's *Le Morte Darthur* in 1816 and 1817.[68] The 1817 edition of Malory includes an introduction by Robert Southey, which discusses the sources used by Malory and draws attention to material of Welsh origin. Southey was a long-time correspondent of William Owen Pughe and drew heavily upon his *Cambrian Biography* (1803) in his introduction, which ends with the statement, 'certain it is that many of the Round Table fictions originated in Wales, or Bretagne, and probably might still be traced there.'[69] The revival can also be seen in the arts and literature of the period, including paintings of the Pre-Raphaelite school, epitomised by Edward Burne-Jones, and the first appearance of Tennyson's poem, *The Lady of Shalott* (1832).[70] The same period also saw the posthumous publication of one of the best early attempts to analyse the origins of the Arthurian legend, Joseph Ritson's *The Life of King Arthur* (1825).[71]

Arthurian material was being seriously discussed in Wales by 1802 in *The Bardic Museum* and, perhaps most notably, a little later, in two books by Peter Roberts.[72] *The Chronicle of the Kings of Britain* (1811) was an English translation of the copy of *Brut y Brenhinedd* in Oxford, Jesus College, MS 61, and drew attention to the many differences from the better-known Latin text.[73] Roberts added several appendices printing Arthurian material from other Welsh sources, including material from the Arthurian section of the chronicle of Elis Gruffydd, some of which has not appeared in print since.[74] He continued his study of Welsh traditions in *The Cambrian Popular Antiquities of Wales* (1815), which included a thirty-page section on Arthur that mixed the Galfridian story with references to Malory, *Y Seint Greal* and the chronicle of Elis Gruffydd, although, perhaps surprisingly, with no reference to the medieval Welsh poetry that was readily available in *The Myvyrian Archaiology* and *The Bardic Museum*.[75]

The Welsh texts, with English translations and notes, of the Four Branches of the Mabinogi and eight tales from the Red Book of Hergest were published by Charlotte Guest in seven parts between 1838 and 1845, and then as a three-volume set with a new introduction in 1849.[76] This was the first time that most people, including many in Wales, had seen these tales, and they had a huge influence, most notably on Tennyson.[77] Guest placed an emphasis on the topography of Wales, which to her mind could be used to prove the antiquity of the tales, and her emphasis on the topography and place names of Wales proved to be an attractive approach for subsequent writers. Building on the publication of the most important medieval Welsh texts, based upon their earliest manuscripts, in Skene's *Four Ancient Books of Wales* (1868), John Stuart Glennie penned his *Arthurian Localities* (1869) and 'discovered' over a hundred Arthurian sites in Scotland, as discussed on page 6.[78] His book inspired a similar survey in Wales, albeit on a much smaller scale, in a series of brief notes over a period of three years in *Archaeologia Cambrensis*, the journal of the Cambrian Archaeological Society.[79]

A number of learned journals concerned with the history and antiquities of Wales began to appear at the turn of the nineteenth century and provided forums for the discussion and publication of texts that could reach a large audience. The earliest serious journal was *The Cambrian Register* (1795–1818), followed by *The Cambro-Briton* (1819–22) and *The Cambrian Quarterly* (1829–33). An increasingly academic approach to the history and literature of Wales can be seen in the earliest journals of the Honourable Society of Cymmrodorion which managed to produce printed volumes in 1822 and 1843, but it was not until the appearance of the first volume of *Y Cymmrodor* in 1877 and their *Transactions* in 1893 that volumes appeared regularly. The society was also responsible for the publication of important sources such as Hugh Williams's translation of *De excidio* by Gildas (1899–1901) and the four-volume edition of George Owen's *Description of Penbrokeshire* (1893–1936) with voluminous notes by Egerton Phillimore. The first journal to focus primarily upon the archaeology of Wales was *Archaeologia Cambrensis* (1846–), and its pages contain some of the earliest drawings and descriptions of antiquities in Wales. The Cambrian Archaeological Society also printed important sources, notably the *Parochalia* of Edward Lhwyd (1911–13) and *Fenton's Tours in Wales* (1917). In 1868 the first journal dedicated to the antiquities and history of a single county appeared with the *Montgomeryshire Collections*. Eventually, all the counties in Wales had a historical journal, the last to start being Denbighshire in 1952. The change in emphasis from the national and patriotic *Cambrian Register* through to the emphasis on archaeology in *Archaeologia Cambrensis* and the detailed local studies of the county journals is reflected in the obscurity of the Arthurian names they mention. Whereas the earliest journals frequently repeated material published previously, the later county journals would often publish parish histories with sections on antiquities and draw attention to names of interest preserved in previously unpublished local documents.[80]

The Welsh-language periodicals of the nineteenth century also published articles concerning the antiquities and history of Wales, one of the most useful being *Y Brython* (1858–63), notable for containing the earliest printing of the story of Arthur being killed at Bwlch y Saethau, near Snowdon and of his body being subsequently buried in a cave hidden amongst the massive cliffs of Lliwedd.[81] The essay, entitled 'Hanes Plwyf Beddgelert' and written by William Jones (Bleddyn), shared the first prize at the 1860 Beddglelert eisteddfod with another writer of Welsh folklore, the Rev. Owen Wynne Jones, better known as Glasynys.[82] Allied to these periodicals were the annual transactions of the National Eisteddfod, which frequently held competitions for essays on folklore and antiquities, and then published the winning entries.[83] Smaller, local eisteddfodau also gave prizes to essays on local antiquities; a good example of this is the work on the antiquities of Mynydd Mawr in Carmarthenshire, written in 1863, which is the sole source for the name Coffor Arthur, a stone monument in the parish of Llandybie.[84]

The chronological list in Appendix 1 shows names that have their first attestation in the nineteenth century, many of which can be found in the pages of the periodicals discussed above. The folk motifs familiar to modern readers of King Arthur finding a pebble in his shoe and throwing it across the landscape to form a cromlech, or a prominent stone being named after Arthur because he had thrown it from a nearby hilltop, first appear in this early periodical literature. The earliest example in Wales is found in an article in *The Cambrian Quarterly* (1830) concerning the cromlech known as Coetan Arthur, near Dyffryn Ardudwy in Merionethshire:

> Having come about two hundred yards, we must clamber over the wall on our left, to look at a stone, of about ten feet long, eight feet wide, and about twenty inches thick, recumbent upon other stones, scarcely above the ground. And this is a quoit, which all about will tell you was thrown by Arthur, from the top of Moelvre. 'Surely he must

have made a bad throw, as the mark he sent before must be a good mile from hence. I see some one has actually carved, as it were, the impression of a hand at the edge of the stone.' Carved, indeed! Why, there is not a boy about here but will tell you, that the marks you say are carved, are the real marks of Arthur's fingers, where he took hold of the stone to throw it.[85]

This motif of Arthur throwing rocks from mountain tops is not found in the earliest tourist literature, and it is only after 1830 that it becomes commonplace. The exact reason for this development is not clear. Although Arthur, along with the Devil and innumerable giants, had long been associated with prominent rocks and megalithic sites, there is only the briefest of elaboration in the earlier sources.[86] At some point in the early nineteenth century a seeming need for elaboration developed and well-known sites acquired folk tales explaining the association with Arthur for the first time. It is probable that some tales existed earlier, although how much earlier is difficult to judge, but what is certain is that the tales appear in far greater numbers from the second quarter of the nineteenth century onwards, until by the end of the century such tales are commonplace. This period saw the development of an interest in popular superstitions, the term 'folk-lore' only appearing in 1846, particularly in Britain and in Germany, notably with the work of the Grimm brothers. An important publication on the subject was the two-volume edition of John Brand's *Observations on Popular Antiquities* (1813), with extensive notes by Henry Ellis, which covered a wide array of material but very little about Arthur.[87] This and other early works were examined by Sir Francis Palgrave in the *Quarterly Review* for 1820, and although Welsh Arthurian material is discussed, primarily via the works of William Owen Pughe, there is no reference to the motif of Arthur throwing stones across the landscape.[88] It is difficult to find an exact point of origin for the appearance of this motif, but it seems most likely that it appeared amidst the revival in interest in Arthur following the printing of *Le Morte Darthur* in 1817, at a time when the study of folklore was in its infancy.

The published studies of folklore in Wales consider Arthurian matters with varying degrees of interest. One of the earliest, *Cambrian Superstitions* by William Howells (1831), said, 'the traditions of Beth Celert, Arthur's Chair, and a few others, as they are generally known, I have thought proper to withhold.'[89] Two popular Welsh-language folklore books of the Victorian period, *Cymru Fu* (1864) and *Ysten Sioned* (1882), did provide Arthurian material. *Cymru Fu* reprints *Culhwch and Olwen* and *Iarlles y Fynnon* from the Mabinogion, and also prints a tract called 'Traddodiad Eryri' (Traditions of Snowdonia) written by Glasynys, which draws primarily upon a letter to Edward Lhwyd published in the *Cambrian Journal* of 1859.[90] *Ysten Sioned* (1882) gives only a single page to Arthur but relates the unusual story, first recorded by Iolo Morgannwg, entitled 'Twmpathau Arthur'.[91] The later nineteenth century saw the publication of important collections of Welsh folklore. Wirt Sikes discussed Arthur in less than a page in his *British Goblins* (1880) and is the only source to refer to a stone in the River Sawddwy as Arthur's Pot.[92] Elias Owen won first prize at the National Eisteddfod held in Liverpool in 1887 for his essay entitled 'The Folk-Lore of North Wales', which was subsequently printed in a revised form as *Welsh Folk-Lore* (1896).[93] Owen's work is 400 pages long and deals with all aspects of Welsh folklore, but Arthur is not mentioned once. In contrast, the same cannot be said for the work of one of the judges of Owen's essay, Sir John Rhŷs, who gathered together some earlier articles in a revised form as *Celtic Folklore: Welsh and Manx* (1901).[94]

Celtic Folklore was the culmination of Rhŷs's research into Welsh traditions, which complemented his work on Celtic linguistics and early medieval inscribed stones.[95] The book is still in regular use today and, in contrast to Owen, it contains a great deal of Arthurian material. The earlier publications of Rhŷs suggest a good reason for this difference. He first published on the Arthurian legend in the early volumes of *Y Cymmrodor* in the 1880s and followed this with his book-length study of the subject, *Studies in the Arthurian Legend* (1891).[96] Rhŷs also subsequently wrote the introduction to the Everyman edition of Malory's *Le Morte Darthur* (1906), in which he made available English translations of the medieval Welsh Arthurian poems 'Pa Gur' and 'Preideu Annwfyn'.[97] This introduction was very influential as it bought the earliest Welsh poetry to a much wider audience than previous works had been able to do. Rhŷs was also involved in the publication of the diplomatic editions of the Book of Llandaf and the Red Book of Hergest, containing *Culhwch and Olwen*, *The Dream of Rhonabwy* and a version of the Triads.[98] He was made professor of Celtic at Oxford University in 1877, and amongst his pupils was Sir John Morris-Jones who, as discussed in chapter 3, was influential in the study of the earliest Welsh poetry.[99]

Several Arthurian associations well known today either originate in, or became popular because of, *Celtic Folklore*. Rhŷs was often the first person to translate material that had originated in Welsh-language journals and make it available to a wider audience, the Carnedd Arthur material from *Y Brython* and the Marchlyn Mawr tale from the Welsh newspaper *Llais y Wlad* being two notable examples.[100] He was also responsible for some associations that had no precedent, such as his, probably unintentional, arthurianisation of Llyn Llydaw:

> But the scene suggests a far more romantic picture; for down below was Llyn Llydaw with its sequestered isle, connected then by means only of a primitive canoe with a shore occupied by men engaged in working the ore of Eryri. Nay with the eyes of Malory we seem to watch Bedivere making, with Excalibur in his hands, his three reluctant journeys to the lake ere he yielded it to the arm emerging from the deep. We fancy we behold how 'euyn fast by the banke housed a lytyl barge with many fayr ladyes in hit' which was to carry the wounded Arthur away to the accompaniment of mourning and loud lamentation.[101]

So influential was *Celtic Folklore* that by 1980 Geoffrey Ashe could write, in regard to Llyn Llydaw, that 'Welsh legend locates the casting-away of Excalibur here'.[102] Later in life, Rhŷs continued to be involved in Welsh archaeology through his work as the first chairman of the Royal Commission on the Ancient and Historical Monuments of Wales, from its foundation in 1908 until his death in 1915.

The Royal Commission was given a Royal Warrant to 'make an inventory of the Ancient and Historical Monuments and Constructions connected with or illustrative of the contemporary culture, civilisation and conditions of life of the people in Wales and Monmouthshire from the earliest times, and to specify those which seem most worthy of preservation'.[103] The inventories were divided into parishes and all sites of interest predating 1714 were listed, as well as interesting field names from the tithe maps. By 1925 volumes had been published for Montgomeryshire (1911), Flintshire (1912), Radnorshire (1913), Denbighshire (1914), Carmarthenshire (1917), Merionethshire (1921) and Pembrokeshire (1925).[104] The Pembrokeshire volume was subjected to a scathing review by Mortimer Wheeler, who criticised the standard of recording and the antiquarian approach to the evidence.[105] As a result of this criticism a different style was used for the Anglesey Inventory in 1937, which was far more scientific in approach. One negative aspect of this new approach was that the fieldnames of interest found in the tithe schedule for each parish were no longer published, the emphasis being now on physical remains. The three volumes covering the county of Caernarfonshire were the last to provide a county-wide inventory of all sites, as subsequent volumes for Breconshire and Glamorgan were produced either by historical period, or site type, indicative of their greater detail.

The seven inventories printed by 1925 all contain Arthurian names and are often well documented, but in some instances it appears that the entry in the inventory is the first appearance of a name. This is particularly noticeable in the volume for Carmarthenshire (1917), where Bwrdd Arthur in Llangynog, Carreg Arthur in Bettws and Croes Arthur in Abergwili all appear for the first time.[106] Material for the early inventories was often collected by a single person and for Carmarthenshire the work was entrusted to George Eyre Evans. His fieldwork notebooks from his time with the Royal Commission are archived in the National Library of Wales and allow a fascinating insight into the collection of material for the published inventories.[107] The printed works give no reference to an earlier source for the names, and the notebooks provide no further evidence, Evans simply stating that earlier traditions associated the site with Arthur. No earlier sources for these associations have yet come to light.

A Royal Warrant was similarly granted to the Historical Manuscripts Commission in 1869 with a remit to 'make enquiry as to the existence and location of manuscripts, including records or archives of all kinds, of value for the study of history'.[108] The work of carrying out this enquiry for Welsh manuscripts was undertaken by J. Gwenogvryn Evans, his first report appearing in 1898 and the sixth and final report in 1910.[109] During his comprehensive survey, Evans brought to light Arthurian references that might otherwise have remained unnoticed, notably the earliest mention of Pikel Arthur in a manuscript of John Jones of Gellilyfdy and the Llys Arthur traditions recorded by Lewis Morris in the 1740s.[110]

The early twentieth century saw the appearance of books designed for the general reader, and titles such as *King Arthur in Cornwall* (1900), *The Lost Land of King Arthur* (1909) and *King Arthur's Country* (1926), all focused attention on the landscape element of the Arthurian legend and proved popular.[111] What many consider to be the first modern analysis of the Arthurian legend, *Arthur of Britain* (1927) by E. K. Chambers, also discussed the Arthurian topography of Britain, but it was based primarily on the works mentioned above and made no attempt to discern the earliest attestation of the names.[112] A detailed collection of Welsh folklore appeared in 1930, entitled *Welsh Folk-Lore and Folk Custom*, and like *Celtic Folklore* by Rhŷs, it too was written by an academic who had previously published on Arthur.[113] T. Gwynn Jones was the professor of Welsh literature at Aberystwyth and had published an article in 1927 entitled 'Some Arthurian Matter in Keltic', which gave a very perceptive overview of the state of scholarship in regard to Welsh Arthurian studies at that time.[114] He also wrote the influential Welsh Arthurian poem, *Ymadawiad Arthur* (The Departure of Arthur) in 1902, which was heavily influenced by the works of Tennyson.[115]

The increasing interest in all aspects of the Arthurian legend saw the appearance of the first Arthurian bibliographies, and a meeting of scholars with an interest in Arthurian matters in Truro in 1930 ultimately led to the foundation of the International Arthurian Society in 1948.[116] The society has annual conferences for each national branch and every three years an international conference takes place, bringing together scholars from all over the world. The society's annual *Bibliographical Bulletin* remains an invaluable research tool, especially for works published in foreign languages.[117] Building upon the respectability which publications like the *Bulletin* gave to Arthurian studies, E. R. Harris, the former County Librarian for Flintshire, donated his own collection of Arthurian books in 1952 to form the core of what is now known as The Arthurian Collection. This specialist collection, was housed at Mold in Flintshire before moving to Bangor University in 2015, and consists of over 2,500 items on the Arthurian legend, remaining an invaluable resource.[118]

In the late 1930s the renowned cardiologist G. Arbour Stephens (1870–1945) claimed Arthurian associations with a myriad of sites over south-west Wales in a series of newspaper columns and pamphlets. Titles such as *The County of Merlin as the Provenance of the Perlesvaus, Carmarthenshire and the Glastonbury Legends*, 'King Arthur and Maes-y-Bar, Llansamlet: Swansea Valley and Arthurian Placenames' and 'The Topographical Importance of Kidwelly and the Burry Estuary in connection with the Arthurian Romances' give a good idea of his arguments.[119] These brief articles contain little, if any, substance, no references and rely very heavily upon similar sounding names and wishful thinking. One longer work (twelve pages) is *New Light on the Arthurian Battlefields* (1938), in which he argues that the battles from the *Historia Brittonum* could be located in Gower and Carmarthenshire, culminating with the battle of Badon at Llanbadarn Fynydd in Radnorshire.[120] I mention his work here only for the sake of completeness, as it seems to have made little impact on later writers. Yet despite the weakness of their content these articles do pre-date, by some forty years, the approach taken by the non-academic Arthurian writers discussed below.[121] His claims are all the more remarkable in that he was married to the Arthurian scholar Mary Williams (1883–1977), who was professor of French at Swansea, a prominent member of the International Arthurian Society and from 1961 to 1963 the president of the Folklore Society.[122] We can only wonder if she ever got to read them before they were published.

The appearance of Geoffrey Ashe's *King Arthur's Avalon: The Story of Glastonbury* in 1957 can be seen as the start of a renewed popular interest in the Arthurian legend, in particular its associations with Glastonbury.[123] The following year saw the publication of an important article on the Welsh aspects of the Arthurian legend by Thomas Jones, although it only became widely known through its English translation by Gerald Morgan in 1964.[124] The year 1959 saw the publication of *Arthurian Literature in the Middle Ages*, a large collaborative work edited by Roger S. Loomis, which influenced a generation of scholars and, for non-Welsh speakers, remained one of the few reliable sources of information on Welsh texts.[125] It has subsequently been superseded by a series of collaborative volumes published by the University of Wales Press, *The Arthur of the Welsh* (1991), *The Arthur of the English* (1999), *The Arthur of the Germans* (2000), *The Arthur of the French* (2006), *The Arthur of Medieval Latin Literature* (2011), *The Arthur of the North* (2011), *The Arthur of the Italians* (2014) and *The Arthur of the Iberians* (2015). *The Arthur of the Celtic Literatures*, which will replace *The Arthur of the Welsh*, is in preparation.

In the late 1960s major historical works were still considering Arthur as a vague, but probably historical figure and as Higham notes, 'The idea of a glorious Arthurian age of British achievement against the Saxons passed from the world of literature to that of history, therefore, during the 1960s and had become both extremely popular and widely accepted by the early 1970s.'[126] The two major works which lent an academic credibility to the idea of a historical Arthur were *Arthur's Britain* (1971) by Leslie Alcock and *The Age of Arthur* (1973) by John Morris, both of which remain in print today.[127] Both works were used in television documentaries, and combined with the popular works of Geoffrey Ashe, produced a raised awareness in antiquities, especially megalithic monuments, enhanced by other popular works such as Janet and Colin Bord's *Mysterious Britain* (1972). The appearance of academic respectability made Arthur a hot topic among the general public.[128] From a Welsh academic perspective, Rachel Bromwich revisited Thomas Jones's 1958 article in 1976 and was broadly in agreement with his conclusions.[129] The renewed popular interest in Arthur continued apace, but in academic circles the publication of an article by David Dumville had a major influence. The article, entitled 'Sub-Roman Britain: History and Legend', was published in the journal *History* in 1977 and argued that as the surviving sources were written centuries after the period to which they related, they were an unreliable record.[130]

Dumville's brusque dismissal of Arthur effectively halted the appearance of academic books with such titles as *Arthur's Britain*. The gap left by the professional historians was soon filled by amateur historians, arguing for various 'real' Arthurs. These authors either tried to identify the figure of Arthur with a real historical person from approximately the same time period and explained the difference in name by suggesting that Arthur was a title, or that their 'real' candidate had inspired the stories of Arthur.[131] Candidates ranged from three different people called Artir in sixth-century Scotland, to a British warlord called Riothamus who had fought in Gaul, and as Higham notes,

> There have been numerous recent reconstructions of an historical Arthur in a particular locality, in most instances for reasons which apparently revolve around a search for local identity and validation in the present.[132]

Amateur Historians and King Arthur in Wales

One result of these 'real' Arthur works, was the creation of new Arthurian associations with sites in Wales, where none had previously existed. The first works to have such an impact upon Wales were those of Baram Blackett and Alan Wilson, who self-published their ideas in three large volumes in 1981. One of the three volumes was little more than a reprint of the 1840 Rees edition of the Book of Llandaf, with a new introduction reiterating the identification of Athrwys, here spelt Arthwys, with King Arthur.[133] The second volume, in over 300 quarto pages of confusing text, outlines their research in more detail and made the suggestion that the difficulty in identifying the 'real' Arthur is that there were actually two kings of that name, and that their deeds have become amalgamated. They identify Antun Du, a figure of the fourth century, as their Arthur I, and Athrwys ap Meurig, the sixth-century ruler of Glamorgan mentioned in the Book of Llandaf, as Arthur II, resurrecting the Silurian Arthur theory discussed above.[134] The third volume is a novel based upon their research. The authors place a strong emphasis on the works of Iolo Morganwg and make frequent use of inaccurate Victorian editions of medieval Welsh texts, whilst ignoring most modern editions and discussions.

In 1983 an article in the *Guardian* newspaper reported that the authors claimed to have discovered the burial site of King Arthur in a cave in south Wales at Coed y Mwstyr, a forest in Pencoed, near Bridgend.[135] Following this publicity Chris Barber, who had recently published a photographic book entitled *Mysterious Wales* (1982), was contacted by Blackett and Wilson and asked if he would take photographs for their next book.[136] The year 1986 saw the publication of Barber's popular sequel, *More Mysterious Wales*, as well as Blackett and Wilson's *Artorius Rex Discovered*, which included many of the same photographs.[137] Blackett and Wilson did not publish another book until 1998, when *The Holy Kingdom*, co-authored with Adrian Gilbert, was released and a much wider audience became aware of their theories.[138] The book once again associated Arthur's burial with the cave in Coed y Mwstyr, but also identified the hill fort of Castlefield camp, north of Cardiff, as the location of Camelot, and the hill of Mynydd Baedan near Tondu as the site of the battle of Badon.[139] They also claimed that Arthur had been reburied at the ruined church of St Peter Super Montem, an isolated site on the hills above Llanharan, and that a pile of stones in a nearby field was his final resting place. The most audacious claim by the authors is that they had discovered a stone bearing the inscription REX ARTORIVS FILI MAVRICIVS nearby.[140] This stone obviously attracted interest from the media, but was never accepted as authentic by the academic community. As the editors of *The Arthurian Annals* note, 'Although these amateur historical researchers stirred up considerable attention with their theories and a series of belligerent encounters with critics and the press, they were largely ignored by the scholarly community.'[141]

Chris Barber, in conjunction with David Pykitt, published his own Arthurian volume, *Journey to Avalon* in 1993. Although the book deals with the same sources used by Blackett and Wilson, it is more clearly argued and also draws attention to other works that have attempted to identify Arthur as a real person.[142] Not content with following the identification of Athrwys ap Meurig with King Arthur, they also associate him with St Arthmael, who is culted at Saint Armel des Boschaux in Brittany.[143] They identified the battle of Camlan with Porth Cadlan, near the village of Aberdaron, and Bardsey Island as Ynys Afallach, the Isle of Avalon.[144] Barber and Pykitt published a further work on the subject in 2005 where, although they still associated Bardsey Island with the Isle of Avalon, they no longer mention their identification of Porth Cadlan with Camlan.[145]

The same period also produced Arthurian works relevant to Wales not reliant upon the Silurian Arthur idea. Graham Phillips and Martin Keatman, in *King Arthur: The True Story* (1992), identified Arthur with Owain Ddantgwyn, son of Cuneglasus, on the basis that Cunegalsus was associated with *receptaculi ursi*, 'the Bear's Den' in the sixth-century *De excidio* of Gildas.[146] This 'Bear's Den' has been identified with the hill fort of Dinarth (Din=fort, Arth=bear) near Llandrillo yn Rhos on the north Wales coast, in the area where Owain Ddantgwyn ruled. The book proved to be popular and, unlike those using the Silurian Arthur theory, made some attempt to engage with academic literature. Graham Phillips went on to offer further works which boldly claimed to have located the grave of the Virgin Mary in Anglesey and the Ark of the Covenant in Warwickshire.[147]

Further Arthurian associations with sites in Wales were made by Steve Blake and Scott Lloyd although they made no claim to have found a 'real' Arthur candidate in their two books on the Welsh aspects of the Arthurian legend (2000 and 2002).[148] They emphasised locations associated with names from genealogical works such as *Bonedd y Saint* that could claim a relationship with Arthur and brought together lesser-known material in an attempt to show Arthur's sphere of influence. On the basis that the *Vera historia di morte Arthuri* was probably written at Aberconwy Abbey, they associated the story of Arthur's funeral with that abbey's grange at Rhyd Llanfair, near Pentrefoelas, and noted the nearby Dark Age burial site at Trebeddau as a possible burial site.[149]

All of the titles discussed above suffer from the same basic deficiencies: a lack of proper understanding of the reliability of source materials from different eras, an assumption that Ordnance Survey mapping can be used to reconstruct landscapes from over a thousand years ago and a lack of awareness of the academic literature that could have saved them from many errors. Despite these deficiencies the titles are usually written in an engaging manner, with a sense of discovery that has proved to be very popular and seen sales in the tens of thousands, something rarely achieved by academic works. The increased level of public awareness of these works is self-perpetuating as their claims get featured in the press, with a little help from the publishers' marketing team, and soon find their way into the local tourist literature. They also become source materials for other popular works, and the Arthurian associations they put forward can become established through sheer repetition.[150]

Tourism

An association between the Arthurian legend and tourism has a long history, especially at Glastonbury, which has been receiving visitors since the 'discovery' of Arthur's grave there in 1191. Cornish tourism has also traded on its Arthurian associations, especially at Tintagel, since at least the 1850s, and continues to do so today. However, it is the developments in Scotland that more closely parallel those in Wales. Claims to have identified the real King Arthur with figures from Scottish history are not new, and several titles have repeatedly made this claim. In doing so they have all drawn extensively upon the identifications put forward by Glennie and Skene in 1868 and the small number of medieval references to place names containing the name Arthur.[151] Michael Wood drew attention to the Scottish claims in his 1981 book, *In Search of the Dark Ages* and the accompanying television documentary.[152] D. F. Carroll in his 1996 work, *Arturius – A Quest for Camelot* argued that Arthur was Artuir mac Áedán, making full use of the locations suggested by Glennie and Skene, and placing Camelot at Camelon near Falkirk. He was so confident in his assertion that he issued a $50,000 challenge to anybody who could prove him wrong.[153] The former director of the Edinburgh Fringe festival and chairman of Scottish TV, Alistair Moffat, published *Arthur and the Lost Kingdoms* in 1999 making Arthur a leader of an army in the sixth century, with his centre at Roxburgh in southern Scotland.[154] Simon Andrew Stirling reiterated the Artuir mac Áedán theory and made many breathless claims besides in his *The King Arthur Conspiracy* in 2012, while Robin Crichton created a pocket-sized guide to the Arthurian sites of Scotland, complete with maps and itineraries for his Arthur Trail in *On the Trail of King Arthur* (2013).[155] A detailed critique of the Arthurian place names suggested by Glennie and Skene is much needed.

All of the works discussed above have been the subject of newspaper articles and television news items, giving the various theories a higher profile than any academic books that have appeared in the same time period. Higham encapsulates the academic attitude towards these works in his important book from 2002:

This is a powerful lobby, which has considerable influence over a wide and public debate, operating with the active encouragement of publishers, confident that subject recognition remains high enough to sell almost any number of works on Arthur.[156]

There is little doubt that the popularity of Arthurian books makes them attractive to publishers, as they are easy to market and have a large eager audience waiting for the next claim, the more extravagant the better. The Arthurian connections in Wales have even led to visitor attractions, such as King Arthur's Labyrinth in Corris, which attracts thousands of visitors every year. In 1995 Hollywood came to Wales and constructed a castle on an island in Llyn Trawsfynydd, for the filming of *First Knight*, starring Sean Connery as King Arthur and Richard Gere as Lancelot. The possibility that a new Steven Spielberg film about King Arthur could be made in Britain, led to the bizarre situation during the summer of 2002 of MPs claiming that the film should come to their constituency because of its supposed Arthurian connections.[157]

The popularity of the legend was also used by the Welsh Tourist Board, which made a concerted effort to promote Wales as an Arthurian destination in 2000, with the publication of an A3 fold-out leaflet entitled 'King Arthur: Follow his Legend around Wales'. This was accompanied by a website entitled 'Wisdom and Walks' that detailed places to visit and their associated stories.[158] Although that particular website ceased to be active in 2006, the Visit Wales (the body that replaced that Welsh Tourist Board in 2006) website still promotes Arthurian trails.[159] Another website, developed to make the most of the thousands of visitors to the Ryder Cup in Newport in 2010, entitled 'Home to the Legend of King Arthur', focused upon the Arthurian sites of south-east Wales and included downloadable leaflets, maps and videos promoting sites first noted by Geoffrey of Monmouth, Gerald of Wales and Edward Lhwyd.[160] The fascination of the Arthurian legend remains undiminished for both academic and amateur alike, and the continued claims of Arthurian associations with sites in Wales goes on, allowing us, to some extent, better to understand the process over the centuries.

Notes

1   Richard Gough, *Anecdotes of British Topography* (London, 1768); and Society of Gentlemen, *England Displayed. Being a new, complete, and accurate survey and description of the Kingdom of England, and principality of Wales* (London, 1769).

2   A. H. Dodd, 'The Roads of North Wales, 1750–1850', *Archaeologia Cambrensis*, 80 (1925), 121–48; Esther Moir, *The Discovery of Britain: The English Tourist 1520–1840* (London, 1964), pp. 129–38 for Wales in particular; and Roger Simpson, *Camelot Regained: The Arthurian Revival and Tennyson 1800–1849* (Cambridge, 1990), p. 65.

3   Joseph Cradock, *Letters from Snowdon: descriptive of a tour through the northern counties of Wales. Containing the antiquities, history, and state of the country* (London, 1770); N. Penruddock Wyndham, *A Gentleman's Tour Through Monmouthshire and Wales in 1774* (London, 1775); R. Paul Evans, 'Thomas Pennant (1726–1798): The Father of Cambrian Tourists', *Welsh History Review*, 13 (1987), 395–417.

4   Thomas Pennant, *A Tour in Scotland MDCCLXIX* (Chester, 1771).

5   Thomas Pennant, *A Tour in Wales MDCLXX*, 2 vols in three parts (London, 1778–83).

6   He had previously mentioned Arthur's Oven in his *A Tour in Scotland*, p. 212, and the third edition (Warrington, 1774), adds a reference to Arthur's Round Table in Westmorland, p. 256.

7   Pennant, *Tour in Wales*, I, p. 375; Gazetteer DEN, Craig Arthur.

8   The tale was first printed in Teithydd, 'Ymholiadau Hynafiaethol', *Taliesin* (1860), 285–6, and is translated in Chris Grooms, *Giants of Wales* (Lampeter, 1993), pp. 85–6.

9   Pennant, *Tour in Wales*, I, p. 417.

10   Pennant, *Tour in Wales*, I, p. 390. Also see Gazetteer, FLI, Carreg Carn March Arthur.

11   R. Paul Evans, 'Richard Bull and Thomas Pennant: Virtuosi in the Art of Grangerisation or Extra-Illustration', *National Library of Wales Journal*, 30 (1998), 269–94.

12   NLW PD9149 can be viewed at *http://digidol.llgc.org.uk/METS/ING00001/ingleview-er?item=67&locale=cy* (accessed 4 July 2014).

13   Pennant, *Tour in Wales*, I, p. 412, and II, p. 263 respectively.

14   See Gazetteer, DEN, Bwrdd Arthur (Llansannan)

15   See Gazetteer, GLA, Arthyr Wood.

16   Pennant, *Tour in Wales*, II, pp. 273–4.

17   George Nicholson, *The Cambrian Traveller's Guide and Pocket Companion* (Stourport, 1808; second edn, Stourport, 1813; third edn, London, 1840).

18   John Anderson, *The Book of British Topography* (London, 1866), pp. 334–53; W. J. Hughes, *Wales and the Welsh in English Literature* (Wrexham, 1924), pp. 189–200. A further resource is the online bibliography by Diana Luft, 'English Language Travel Books Dealing with Wales', available at *www.cardiff.ac.uk/special-collections/subject-guides/travel* (accessed 31 December 2016).

19   Henry Skrine, *Two Successive Tours throughout the Whole of Wales, with Several of the Adjacent English Counties ...* (London, 1798), p. xvi.

20   William Coxe, *An Historical Tour of Monmouthshire* (London, 1801), p. 75.

21   Evans, 'Father of Cambrian Tourists', 402; John Fisher (ed.), *Tours in Wales (1804–1813) by Richard Fenton* (London, 1917), pp. 332–49.

22   For further discussion, see Roger Simpson, *Camelot Regained*, pp. 66–71.

23   Hywel M. Davies, 'Wales in English Travel Writing 1791–8: The Welsh Critique of Theophilus Jones', *Welsh History Review*, 23/3 (2007), 65–93.

24   CYMRO, 'Cursory Remarks on Welsh Tours', *The Cambrian Register for 1796* (London, 1799), p. 422.

25   Richard Fenton, *A Historical Tour through Pembrokeshire* (London, 1811); Edward Pugh, *Cambria Depicta: A Tour through North Wales* (London, 1816), p. 37; John Barrell, *Edward Pugh of Ruthin 1763–1813: A Native Artist* (Cardiff, 2013).

26   A. P. Wakelin, 'Tours in Wales: A Handlist of Manuscript Journals Describing Tours Made in Wales from the Collections in The National Library of Wales' (1981) available in the manuscript reading room at the NLW; Gwynfryn Walters, 'The tourist and guide book literature of Wales 1770–1870: a descriptive and bibliographical survey with an analysis of the cartographic content and its context' (unpublished MSc thesis, University of Wales, Aberystwyth, 1966), 4.

27   B. G. Owens, 'Some Unpublished Material of the Reverend Richard Farrington, Rector of Llangybi', *Journal of the Welsh Bibliographical Society*, 5 (1937–42), 16–32; and 'The Reverend Richard Farrington, Rector of Llangybi: A Further Note', *Journal of the Welsh Bibliographical Society*, 5 (1937–42), 241–2.

28   The three versions of the work are NLW MS 4899 (1764), NLW, MS 1118C (1769) entitled 'Snowdonia Druidica, or The Druid Monuments of Snowdon with Plans and Drawings ...' and NLW MS 1119D (1772) entitled 'The Celtick Antiquities of Snowdon Attempted...', which was probably prepared for publication.

29   See Gazetteer CRN, Coetan Arthur (Llanystumdwy), Coetan Arthur (Clynnog Fawr) and Maen Arthur (Dolbenmaen).

30   See Gazetteer CRN, Arthur's Javelins.

31   A notable exception to this is the introduction to Benjamin Heath Malkin, *The Scenery, Antiquities and Biography of South Wales*, 2 vols (London, 1804–7), I, pp. 1–78 which discusses Arthur at some length.

32   David Hume, *The History of England, from the Invasion of Julius Caesar to the Accession of Henry VII*, 2 vols (London, 1762), I, p. 17.

33   John Prise, *Historiae Brytannicae Defensio* (London, 1573), p. 127. The charter is printed in J. Gwenogvryn Evans and John Rhys (eds), *The Book of Llan Dâv* (Oxford, 1893), p.77, and referred to again on p. 133; P. C. Bartrum, *Early Welsh Genealogical Tracts* (Cardiff, 1966), p. 10.

34   Evans and Rhys (eds), *Book of Llan Dâv*, p. 161.

35   Evans and Rhys (eds), *Book of Llan Dâv*, p. 45.

36   Francis Godwin, *A Catalogue of the Bishops of England* (London, 1615), pp. 516–18.

37   William Dugdale (ed.), *Monastici Anglicani: volumen tertium et ultimim* (London, 1673), p. 198.

38   The history of the manuscript is described in detail in Evans and Rhys (eds), *The Book of Llan Dâv*, pp. viii–xvii.

39   *www.llgc.org.uk/discover/digital-gallery/manuscripts/the-middle-ages/the-book-of-llandaff/* (accessed 31 December 2016).

40   Thomas Carte, *A General History of England*, 4 vols (London, 1747–55), I, p. 202.

41   Hume, *The History of England*, I, p. 17; John Whitaker, *A History of Manchester*, 4 vols (1771–5), II, p. 34; and Edward Gibbon, *The History of the Decline and Fall of the Roman Empire* (London, 1788), III, p. 618.

42   William Owen Pughe, *The Cambrian Biography: Or, Historical Notices of Celebrated Men Among the Ancient Britons* (London, 1803), p. 14.

43   William J. Rees (trans.) *The Liber Landavensis: Llyfr Teilo* (Llandovery, 1840).

44   Rees, *Liber Landavensis*, p. 411.

45   Robert Owen, *The Kymry: Their Origin, History, and International Relations* (Carmarthen, 1891), p. 77; Owen 'Morien' Morgan, *A History of Wales from the Earliest Period* (Liverpool, 1911), pp. 118–23.

46   Marion Löffler, *The Literary and Historical Legacy of Iolo Morganwg* (Cardiff, 2007).

47   Löffler, *Literary and Historical Legacy*, pp. 32–4.

48   Löffler, *Literary and Historical Legacy*, pp. 42–51.

49   G. J. Williams, *Iolo Morganwg a Chywyddau'r Ychwanegiad* (Cardiff, 1926).

50   Edward Williams, *Poems, Lyric and Pastoral*, 2 vols (London, 1794), I, p. 195.

51   Owen Jones, Iolo Morganwg and William Owen Pughe (eds), *The Myvyrian Archaiology of Wales*, 3 vols (London, 1801–7).

52   For example, the supposed medieval Welsh chronicle called 'Brut Aberpergwm'.

53   Elissa R. Henken, *National Redeemer: Owain Glyndŵr in Welsh Tradition* (Cardiff, 1996), pp. 80–4. See also Gazetteer MER, Ogof Arthur.

54   NLW MS 13121B, pp. 419–22. This tale was first printed in Elijah Waring, *Recollections and Anecdotes of Edward Williams* (London, 1852), pp. 95–8.

55   This tale was first printed in [D. Silvan Evans (ed.)], *Ysten Sioned* (Aberystwyth, 1882), p. 3, based on NLW MS 13146, p. 316.

56   This conclusion is based upon a survey of the printed material in Taliesin Williams (ed.), *Iolo Manuscripts* (Llandovery, 1848).

57   Williams, *Iolo Manuscripts*, pp. 459 and 625.

58   For an overview of the origins of the Ordnance Survey see Rachel Hewitt, *Map of a Nation: A Biography of the Ordnance Survey* (London, 2010).

59   Yolande Hodson, *Ordnance Surveyors' Drawings 1789–c.1840: The Original Manuscript Maps of the First Ordnance Survey of England and Wales from the British Library Map Library* (Reading, 1989), p. 28. All of the Ordnance Survey Drawings will be referenced by their three-digit number and are now available online at *www.bl.uk/onlinegallery/onlineex/ordsurvdraw/* (accessed 1 June 2014).

60   Hodson, *Ordnance Surveyors' Drawings*, p. 114, OSD 344.

61   See Gazetteer CRN, Ffynnon Cegin Arthur.

62   Hodson, *Ordnance Surveyors' Drawings*, p. 12.

63   Hodson, *Ordnance Surveyors' Drawings*, p. 13. For a more detailed description of the revision process, see pp. 18–19.

64   See Gazetteer FLI, Tyddyn Arthur.

65   Hodson, *Ordnance Surveyors' Drawings*, p. 112.

66   Tithe map for St Asaph, Cilowen, Bodeugon and Rhyllon, number 531 in Robert Davies, *The Tithe Maps of Wales* (Aberystwyth, 1999), p. 228.

67   J. B. Harley and Gwyn Walters, 'Welsh Orthography and Ordnance Survey Mapping 1820–1905', *Archaeologia Cambrensis*, 131 (1982), 98. See also Hewitt, *Map of a Nation*, pp. 191–4.

68   Inga Bryden, *Reinventing King Arthur: The Arthurian Legends in Victorian Culture* (London, 2005), p. 18. See also Roger Simpson, *Camelot Regained*.

69   Robert Southey (ed.), *The Byrth, Lyf and Actes of King Arthur*, 2 vols (London, 1817), I, p. ix. He also mentions the Silurian Arthur theory; Arthur Johnston, 'William Owen Pughe and the Mabinogion', *National Library of Wales Journal*, 10 (1957–8), 325

70   Simpson, *Camelot Regained*, pp. 252–3.

71   Joseph Ritson, *The Life of King Arthur: From Ancient Historians and Authentic Documents* (London, 1825). For a detailed study of this work, see, Annette B. Hopkins, 'Ritson's *Life of King Arthur*', *Proceedings of the Modern Language Association*, 43/1 (March, 1928), 251–87.

72   Edward Jones, *The Bardic Museum of Primitive British Literature* (London, 1802), pp. 20–6. It gives an English translation of the Huail story from the chronicle of Elis Gruffudd, from the copy by John Jones in NLW 6209, p. 22.

73   Peter Roberts, *The Chronicle of the Kings of Britain* (London, 1811).

74   Roberts, *Chronicle of the Kings of Britain*, p. 361 also uses NLW 6209, but prints material not found in *The Bardic Museum*.

75   Peter Roberts, *The Cambrian Popular Antiquities of Wales* (London, 1815), pp. 81–109.

76   Charlotte Guest (ed. and trans.), *The Mabinogion*, 3 vols (London, 1849). She also included the *Ystoria Taliesin*, a text not included in modern editions. Revel Guest and Angela V. John, *Lady Charlotte Guest: An Extraordinary Life* (Stroud, 2007), pp. 248–50.

77   Simpson, *Camelot Regained*, *passim*.

78   William F. Skene, *Four Ancient Books of Wales*, 2 vols (Edinburgh, 1868); and John Stuart Glennie, *Arthurian Localities: Their Historical Origin, Chief Country and Fingalian Relations with a Map of Arthurian Scotland* (Edinburgh, 1869).

79 Anon., 'Arthurian Localities in the Principality and the Marches', *Archaeologia Cambrensis*, (1872), 71–2, continued in (1872), 269–70; (1874), 88–90, 175 and (1875), 290.

80 For examples see Gazetteer FLI, Penbedw Stone Circle and CRM, Carreg Pumsaint.

81 See Gazetteer CRN, Carnedd Arthur and Lliwedd.

82 D. E. Jenkins, *Beddgelert: Its Facts, Fairies and Folklore* (Portmadoc, 1899), p. vii.

83 Two notable folklore collections from the National Eisteddfodau are T. C. Evans (Cadrawd), 'The folklore of Glamorgan', *Eisteddfod Genedlaethol Gymry Cofnodion a Chyfansoddiadau Buddugol Eisteddfod Aberdar, 1885* (Cardiff, 1887), pp. 186–235; and William Davies 'Casgliad o Len-gwerin Meirion', in *Eisteddfod Genedlaethol y Cymry. Cofndion a Chyfansoddiaidau Buddugol Eisteddfod Blaenau Ffestiniog, 1898* (Liverpool, 1900), pp. 84–269.

84 Gomer M. Roberts, 'Mynydd Mawr Traditions', *Carmarthenshire Antiquary*, 1 (1941), 59–60; Gazetteer CRM, Coffor Arthur.

85 Idrison (William Owen Pughe), 'Ardudwy', *The Cambrian Quarterly*, 2 (1830), 12.

86 Leslie V. Grinsell, *Folklore of Prehistoric Sites in Britain* (Newton Abbott, 1976), pp. 20–3.

87 John Brand, *Observations on Popular Antiquities Chiefly Illustrating the Origin of our Vulgar Customs, Ceremonies and Superstitions*, with additional notes by Henry Ellis, 2 vols (London, 1813).

88 Francis Palgrave, 'Popular Mythology of the Middle Ages', *Quarterly Review*, 22 (1820), 348–80.

89 William Howells, *Cambrian Superstitions* (Tipton, 1831), p. 154.

90 [Glasynys], *Cymru Fu* (Wrexham, 1864), pp. 464–80. This is probably the essay that shared first prize with William Jones at the Beddgleert Eisteddfod in 1860. See Gazetteer CRN, Llyn Dinas.

91 [Evans], *Ysten Sioned*, p. 3. Although he is not named on the title page, this work was edited by D. Silvan Evans. See Juliette Thomas, 'The Development of Folklore Studies in Wales 1700–1900', *Keystone Folklore*, 20/4 (1975), 33–52 for further discussion of folklore studies in Wales.

92 Gazetteer CRM, Arthur's Pot.

93 Elias Owen, *Welsh Folk-Lore* (Oswestry, 1896).

94 John Rhŷs, *Celtic Folklore: Welsh and Manx* (Oxford, 1901).

95 Juliette Wood, 'Folk Narrative Research in Wales at the Beginning of the Twentieth Century: The Influence of John Rhŷs (1840–1916)', *Folklore*, 116 (2005), 325–41.

96 John Rhŷs, *Studies in the Arthurian Legend* (Oxford, 1891).

97 John Rhŷs, 'Introduction', *Le Morte D'Arthur*, 2 vols (London, 1906), I, pp. vii–xxvi.

98 Evans and Rhys, *Book of Llan Dâv*; John Rhŷs and J. Gwenogvryn Evans, *The Text of the Mabinogion and Other Welsh Tales from the Red Book of Hergest* (Oxford, 1887).

99 John Fraser, 'Rhŷs, Sir John (1840–1915)', rev. Mari A. Williams, *Oxford Dictionary of National Biography* (Oxford, 2004).

100 Gazetteer CRN, Carnedd Arthur and Marchlyn Mawr.

101 Rhŷs, *Celtic Folklore*, pp. 475–6.

102 Geoffrey Ashe, *A Guidebook to Arthurian Britain* (London, 1980), p. 143.

103 Royal Commission on the Ancient and Historical Monuments of Wales and Monmouthshire, *An Inventory of the Ancient Monuments of Wales and Monmouthshire: I – County of Montgomery* (London, 1911), p. iv.

104 These volumes are now freely available via Google Books.

105 David M. Browne, 'From Antiquarianism to Archaeology: The Genesis and Achievement of the Royal Commission's Anglesey Volume', *Archaeologia Cambrensis*, 156 (2007), 33. The review in question appeared in *Antiquity*, 1 (1927), 245–7.

106   See Gazetteer CRM.

107   NLW MSS 13447–71.

108   *www.nationalarchives.gov.uk/information-management/legislation/hmc-warrant.htm* (accessed 17 May 2014).

109   J. Gwenogvryn Evans (ed.), *A Report on Manuscripts in the Welsh Language*, 2 vols (1898–1910), contains all six reports.

110   See Gazetteer CRN Pikel Arthur and CRD Llys Arthur for details.

111   W. H. Dickinson, *King Arthur in Cornwall* (London, 1900); John Cuming Walters, *The Lost Land of King Arthur* (London, 1909); and F. J. Snell, *King Arthur's Country* (London, 1926).

112   E. K. Chambers, *Arthur of Britain* (London, 1927).

113   T. Gwynn Jones, *Welsh Folk-lore and Folk Custom* (London, 1930).

114   T. Gwynn Jones, 'Some Arthurian Matter in Keltic', *Aberystwyth Studies*, 8 (1927), 37–93.

115   T. Gwynn Jones, *Ymadawiad Arthur a Chaniadau Eraill* (Caernarfon, 1910). The poem had won the chair at the 1902 National Eisteddfod in Bangor.

116   John J. Parry, *A Bibliography of Critical Arthurian Literature for the Years 1922–29* (London, 1929); and John J. Parry and Margaret Schlauch, *A Bibliography of Critical Arthurian Literature for the Years 1930–1935* (London, 1936). Parry continued to publish annual bibliographies in *Modern Language Quarterly* right up until his death in 1963.

117   *Bibliographical Bulletin of the International Arthurian Society* (1949–).

118   *The Arthurian Collection Catalogue* (Clwyd, 1994).

119   I have included a full list of his Arthurian articles in the Bibliography, some of which are newspaper cuttings with no date or provenance. All are available at the National Library of Wales.

120   G. Arbour Stephens, *New Light on Arthurian Battlefields* (Haverfordwest, 1938), pp. 11–12.

121   His work did directly inspire Lewis Edwards in his search for the Pumpsaint Landscape Zodiac, echoing the Glastonbury Zodiac 'discovered' by Katherine Maltwood in 1934. Lewis Edwards, 'The Pumpsaint Temple of the Stars' (unpublished, 1947), Aberystwyth, National Monuments Record of Wales, C20133.

122   Stewart F. Sanderson, 'Obituary: Professor Mary Williams', *Folklore*, 89/1 (1978), 104–5.

123   Geoffrey Ashe, *King Arthur's Avalon: the Story of Glastonbury* (London, 1957).

124   Thomas Jones, 'Datblygiadau Cynnar Chwedl Arthur', *Bulletin of the Board of Celtic Studies*, 17 (1958), 237–52; and 'The Early Evolution of the Legend of Arthur', *Nottingham Medieval Studies*, 8 (1964), 3–21.

125   Roger S. Loomis (ed.), *Arthurian Literature in the Middle Ages* (Oxford, 1959).

126   N. J. Higham, *King Arthur and Myth-Making* (London, 2002), p. 27.

127   Leslie Alcock, *Arthur's Britain: History and Archaeology, A.D. 367–634* (London, 1971); John Morris, *The Age of Arthur* (London, 1973).

128   Janet and Colin Bord, *Mysterious Britain* (London, 1972).

129   Rachel Bromwich, 'Concepts of Arthur', *Studia Celtica*, 10–11 (1975–6), 163–81.

130   David Dumville, 'Sub-Roman Britain: History and Legend', *History*, New Series, 62 (1977), 173–92.

131   Some notable works are Geoffrey Ashe, *The Discovery of King Arthur* (London, 1985), which identified Arthur with Riothamus; Norma Goodrich in *Arthur* (London, 1986) drew upon Skene and Glennie, and located the court of Arthur at Carlisle; and Frank Reno, in *The Historic King Arthur: Authenticating the Celtic Hero of Post-Roman Britain* (Jefferson, 1996), solves the problem by making Aurelius Ambrosius, Riothamus and Arthur all the same person.

132   Higham, *King Arthur: Myth-Making and History*, p. 34.

133 A. T. Blackett and Alan Wilson, *Arthur and the Charters of the Kings* (Cardiff, 1981), p. 23. The copyright statement is dated March 1980.

134 A. T. Blackett and Alan Wilson, *Arthur: King of Glamorgan and Gwent* (Cardiff, 1981), pp. 44–5 and 107–9. They also identify Maelgwn Gwynedd as Sir Lancelot, and place his grave at Nevern in Pembrokeshire, pp. 236–8.

135 *The Guardian*, 23 July 1983, p. 3.

136 Chris Barber, *Mysterious Wales* (Newton Abbot, 1982) and *idem*, *More Mysterious Wales* (Newton Abbot, 1986), Introduction (unpaginated).

137 Barber, *More Mysterious Wales*, pp. 135–45; Baram Blackett and Alan Wilson, *Artorius Rex Discovered* (Cardiff, 1986). Barber later removed any reference to the theories of Blackett and Wilson in his revised single-volume *Mysterious Wales* (Abergavenny, 1999).

138 Adrian Gilbert, Alan Wilson and Baram Blackett, *The Holy Kingdom* (London, 1998).

139 Gilbert, *Holy Kingdom*, pp. 279–82, 228–9 and 236–40.

140 Gilbert, *Holy Kingdom*, pp. 285–6. A brief summary of their excavations is given on pp. 332–5. Their description of finding the stone can be found in *Artorius Rex*, pp. 260–2. I am unaware of any published archaeological report from the dig.

141 Daniel P. Nastali and Phillip C. Boardman, *The Arthurian Annals: The Tradition in English from 1250 to 2000*, 2 vols (Oxford, 2004), I, p. 488.

142 Chris Barber and David Pykitt, *Journey to Avalon* (Abergavenny, 1993), pp. 208–11.

143 Barber and Pykitt, *Journey to Avalon*, p. 34.

144 Barber and Pykitt, *Journey to Avalon*, pp. 141–3.

145 Chris Barber and David Pykitt, *The Legacy of King Arthur* (Abergavenny, 2005), pp.18 and 124–5.

146 Graham Philips and Martin Keatman, *King Arthur: The True Story* (London, 1992); H. Williams, *Gildas* (London, 1899–1901), I, p. 72.

147 Graham Philips, *The Marian Conspiracy* (London, 2000) and *The Templars and the Ark of the Covenant* (Rochester, 2004).

148 Steve Blake and Scott Lloyd, *The Keys to Avalon* (Shaftesbury, 2000) and *Pendragon: The Origins of Arthur* (London, 2002).

149 Blake and Lloyd, *Pendragon: The Origins of Arthur*, pp. 199–204.

150 For a good example of this, see the popular work by Mike Ashley, *The Mammoth Book of King Arthur* (London, 2005), which draws on many of the works discussed in this chapter.

151 Scott Lloyd, 'Arthurian Place Names and Later Traditions', in Ceridwen Lloyd-Morgan and Erich Poppe (eds), *The Arthur of the Celtic Literatures* (Cardiff, forthcoming).

152 Michael Wood, *In Search of the Dark Ages* (London, 1981), pp. 56–9. *In Search of Arthur* was first broadcast on BBC Two on 12 March 1980 and then again on 10 November 1981.

153 D. F. Carroll, *Arturius – A Quest for Camelot* (Goxhill, 1996). The challenge is still posted on his website *www.kingarthurlegend.com/king-arthur-challenge.html* (accessed 10 March 2016).

154 Alistair Moffat, *Arthur and the Lost Kingdoms* (London, 1999).

155 Simon Andrew Stirling, *The King Arthur Conspiracy: How a Scottish Prince Became a Mythical Hero* (Stroud, 2012); Robin Crichton, *On the Trail of King Arthur: A Journey into Dark Age Scotland including Illustrations, Maps and Itineraries* (Edinburgh, 2013).

156 Higham, *King Arthur*, p. 35.

157 See *web.archive.org/web/20050310203228/http://www.newswales.co.uk/?section=Culture&F=1&id=5809* for an overview of Spielberg's proposed investment and the various different MPs who suggested amendments to the Early Day Motion. See *http://edmi.parliament.uk/EDMi/EDMDetails.aspx?EDMID=19799&SESSION=680* (accessed 31 December 2016) for details of Early Day Motion no.1637 from 18 July 2002, which was concerned with this

matter.

158 The site is no longer active and can only be viewed via the Internet Archive's Wayback
     Machine, *https://web.archive.org/web/20060818214406/http://www.wisdom-and-walks.co.uk/*
     (accessed 22 March 2016).

159 *www.traveltrade.visitwales.com/en/content/cms/itineraries/sample-itineraries/king-arthur-
     in-wales/king-arthur/* (accessed 22 March 2016).

160 The site is no longer active and can be only partially viewed via the Internet Archive's
     Wayback Machine, *http://idl.newport.ac.uk/kingarthur/index.htm* (accessed 22 March 2014).

CONCLUSION

THIS BOOK SET OUT to explore the earliest attestation for each Arthurian place name in Wales and examine the sources in which the earliest note of the name appeared. The survey of the available material has shown to what extent earlier sources have influenced later ones and how some names, first recorded in the medieval period, dropped out of use and have only been recovered during the place-name research of the twentieth century.

The *Historia Brittonum* remains the earliest securely dated reference to Arthur, and its list of battles is the founding text for the Arthurian legend as we know it today. It is unlikely that Geoffrey of Monmouth could have made Arthur such a central figure in his *Historia regum Britanniae* without it. Alongside the two entries in the *Annales Cambriae*, the battle list remains the most important text for the study of the earliest origins of the Arthurian legend, for both those who consider him to be historical and those who consider him mythical in origin. The *Mirabilia* are the earliest source to claim that Arthur (or more accurately his dog and son) was directly responsible for a landscape feature in Wales, and with the exception of one name provided by Gerald of Wales, there is little else to show that this sort of association was widespread in Wales in the twelfth century. The Latin *vitae* of the Welsh saints contain the earliest reference to Arthur as a legendary king, and he is used as a figure to give credence to claims of ecclesiastical land ownership, although Maelgwn Gwynedd, a sixth-century king with stronger historical credentials, is also used in a similar role. The name Arthur also appears in connection with boundary markers in late twelfth century sources, for example Vadumi Arthuri, near Cardigan and Ffynnon Arthur, near Merthyr Tydfil are both found in documents associated with monastic houses; it is impossible to know for certain if the Arthur used in these instances is the figure of legend, but the scarcity of the name in medieval Wales suggests that it could be a possibility. The fame of Arthur grew throughout the twelfth century and many of these names more likely reflect this popularity rather than any long-held memory of a sixth-century leader.

The *Historia regum Britanniae* (*HRB*) of Geoffrey of Monmouth is the earliest source to provide a narrative of Arthur's life, but apart from the Roman town of Caerleon, Wales has no part to play in this narrative, his battles and adventures taking place in England or on the continent. The image of Arthur portrayed in *HRB* came to influence Welsh thinking in the later Middle Ages but its impact was not instant. Another writer of the twelfth century who had an influential role to play in the depiction of Arthur in a Welsh context was Gerald of Wales. Aside from his references to Caerleon, inspired by Geoffrey, Gerald added his much-quoted reference to Arthur lending his name to Cadair Arthur, a col between two summits in the Brecon Beacons. Gerald's works were frequently quoted throughout the Middle Ages, especially his description of the discovery of Arthur's body at Glastonbury.

The large numbers of Arthurian romance manuscripts that survive in various European languages are a testament to the popularity of the genre in the Middle Ages. Some of the place names in the romances can be securely identified, such as Cardigan and Caerleon, but the remainder are often vague and romanticised, with only references to Norgales and the river Severn giving any indication of location. The fact that both regions saw considerable contact between the Marcher lords and the Welsh ruling dynasties, including frequent conflicts, is unlikely to be a coincidence and further study of the proper names in French Arthurian romances may show some parallels with contemporary events. An interest in Arthurian material is evident in works associated with the powerful Mortimer family of the Welsh Marches, especially the Middle English material produced at Ludlow in the fourteenth century. Wales never produced an equivalent to Malory's *Le Morte Darthur*, and although there is little evidence that the people of Wales viewed themselves in any sort of Arthurian context, to those who read the Arthurian romances Wales was portrayed as a land where Arthurian knights could go on quests, fight all manner of strange enemies and seek the Holy Grail.

The amount of scholarly attention given to the small number of medieval Welsh texts that mention Arthur can give the impression that Arthur played a prominent role in the medieval literature of Wales. One of the main reasons for this attention has been the theory that some of these Welsh texts predated the publication of *HRB* in 1138, but the arguments for this position have been challenged by more recent scholarship. The linguistic arguments of an older generation of scholars, such as Ifor Williams and Idris Foster, on which so much of the pre-Geoffrey dating rested, now look increasingly insecure.[1] A clearer understanding of the development of the Welsh language in the medieval period has evolved since the publication of the *Cyfres Beirdd y Tywysogion* corpus and the results of this new understanding have been applied to the difficult task of dating prose texts and *cynfeirdd* poetry. The argument that the Welsh texts depicted a more primitive form of Arthur because they showed no influence from *HRB*, and should therefore be dated from before 1138, has also been shown to be flawed. Geoffrey's text may have had an almost immediate effect on Latin and Anglo-Norman literature, but it was not until it was translated into

Welsh as *Brut y Brenhinedd* in the early thirteenth century, that it started to have an impact upon Welsh literature. In effect, this has left a window of some sixty years in which texts, long thought to have been written before 1138, may have originated. One intriguing outcome of this reassessment is that the development of the Arthurian legend in Wales now more closely mirrors that happening elsewhere. The late twelfth and early thirteenth century saw an explosion of Arthurian texts in England, France and across the continent, and the Welsh material should, perhaps, be more usefully seen as Wales's contribution to this development. Future research needs to focus more on the influence that continental material had upon Welsh Arthurian sources, rather than viewing them as representative of an insular tradition untouched by these outside influences.

The very small number of references to the Welsh prose tales *Culhwch and Olwen* and *The Dream of Rhonabwy* in the poetry of the medieval period, suggests that these tales were only known to a small literary circle and that they do not represent a widely known earlier Arthurian tradition. The place names associated with Arthur in both tales are not mentioned elsewhere until the rediscovery of the texts in the early nineteenth century. In medieval Welsh poetry (1100–1500) there is only one possible association of Arthur with an identifiable location and even that is doubtful. The poetry makes no mention of the 'well-known' tradition of Arthur's return as the *mab darogan* (son of prophecy), the role being filled primarily by Owain Lawgoch and Owain Glyndŵr; Arthur is notable only by his absence. The lack of a role for Arthur in the propaganda written during the Gwynedd dynasty's attempt to gain hegemony over the whole of Wales in the thirteenth century illustrates the minor role he appears to have played in the national consciousness of medieval Wales. It is only when the authenticity of Geoffrey of Monmouth's *HRB* was called into question in the early sixteenth century that Welsh authors, fired by a renewed sense of nationalism under the Tudor dynasty, began to take more interest in the figure of Arthur.

The first works to emphasise a link between King Arthur and Wales in the early modern period were produced in response to the criticism of Geoffrey of Monmouth's view of the past. They show how ingrained *HRB* had become to the national identity of Wales, which is all the more remarkable when we remember that it was not until the turn of the thirteenth century that it was incorporated into Welsh literature at all, and another century before it began to become a dominant factor. John Leland gathered together evidence for Arthur's existence, and Sir John Prise refined this approach to make it more relevant to Wales. Both authors have been much quoted in this respect over the centuries, but it is worth noting that one of the main reasons for this is the lack of any other similar works to draw upon. Elis Gruffydd, in his unpublished chronicle, drew upon the French sources and the oral traditions of north Wales to compile his biography of Arthur. Aside from the wide reading of Gruffydd evident in his chronicle, the story of Huail is notable for being the only piece of Arthurian folklore in Wales to show a continuation of a theme found in three separate twelfth-century sources. When we take into account the fact that *Maen Huail*, the focus of the tale, is also recorded elsewhere in the sixteenth century it is the most widely attested Arthurian folk tale associated with Wales.

The use of Arthur in a nationalistic sense in Wales had practically disappeared by the end of the sixteenth century, and he was subsequently only dealt with briefly, the change perhaps reflecting a change in attitudes following the Act of Union (1536). The depiction of Arthur also begins to change at this time with the focus shifting from regarding him as a pseudo-historical king towards viewing him as a more legendary character. Increasing numbers of Arthurian place names are first attested in Wales as the seventeenth century progresses, but this seems to have little to do with any increased interest in the legend. The fact that Arthur was a very rare name in medieval Wales goes some way to explaining the small number of place names that can be first attested in the medieval period. This fact, combined with the increased level of documentation produced following the Act of Union, is certainly a factor in the increase of Arthur place names first attested in the early modern period. Many of these names did not remain in use long enough for inclusion onto the earliest Ordnance Survey maps or tithe schedules, and have only been recovered as a result of place-name research in the twentieth century.

Coetan Arthur is the best example of how a term, initially used to explain the appearance of a megalithic monument, later became widespread and the focus of many folk tales. It was used occasionally in the seventeenth century, but it was only after the appearance of the term in Edward Lhwyd's additions to the 1695 edition of Camden's *Britannia* that it gained widespread currency in Wales and subsequently elsewhere. Once it became established as the generic term for a megalithic monument, it is perhaps not surprising that these monuments began to acquire folk tales to explain the name, though it is notable that there seem to be no recorded examples of this before the early nineteenth century.

By the turn of the nineteenth century the tourist literature concerning Wales frequently mentioned sites of Arthurian interest, but nearly all of the references were derived from either the 1695 edition of Camden's *Britannia* or Thomas Pennant's *A Tour in Wales* (1778–83). The widespread circulation of this tourist literature raised the profile of monuments with Arthurian names, and following the publication of a new edition of Malory's *Le Morte Darthur* in 1816 there was an increased interest in such sites. An important milestone in this increased interest, from a Welsh perspective, was the publication of the three-volume edition of *The Mabinogion* by Charlotte Guest in 1849. She encouraged the study of topographical names in both her introduction and the notes that accompanied each tale. The topic gained further popularity with the publication of *Arthurian Localities* by John Stuart Glennie in 1869, which, although focused primarily on Scotland, encouraged a similar, albeit briefer, study for names in Wales.[2]

The first comprehensive parish-by-parish survey of antiquities since the *Parochalia* of Edward Lhwyd in 1696 was undertaken by the Royal Commission on the Ancient and Historical Monuments of Wales, with the first volume, covering

Montgomeryshire, appearing in 1911. All of the early inventories contain Arthurian material, and the appearance of Arthurian names in such esteemed works lent them an air of credibility, even if several of them only appear for the first time within their pages. As the twentieth century progressed, academic interest in the legend continued, but it was the non-academic works that created new Arthurian place names. The popularity of these works far exceeded anything published academically on the subject, and they have done much to emphasise the idea of Wales as an Arthurian landscape. Their uncritical use of source material, however, frequently misleads the general reader and irritates the academic.

The Arthurian legend was popular across Europe throughout the medieval period, and the fact that it is still not possible to give a straightforward answer to the question, 'Did Arthur exist?' is one of the major reasons why the legend remains so popular. A fact that deserves to be emphasised is that the origin of the legend can be traced back to a work produced in north Wales in the ninth century. We are unsure who the author of the work was, or where he got the name Arthur from, but the nomenclature of the Welsh landscape would be very different without him.

The gazetteer of this book, in Appendix 2, provides a comprehensive checklist of the Arthurian place names of Wales for the first time, and Appendix 1 provides a chronological list of the earliest references to each site. Those undertaking future research will now be able to assign a date to the first attestation of an Arthurian name, instead of labelling it as 'traditional'. Bedwyr Lewis Jones was the first to make a plea for a scholarly discussion of Arthurian place names in Wales that would 'help to suppress a whole lot of nonsense', and I hope that this work has made some small contribution towards that discussion.[3]

Notes

1   In particular see, G. Isaac, 'Scholarship and Patriotism: The Case of the Oldest Welsh Poetry', *Studi Celtici*, 1 (2002), 67–81.

2   Anon, 'Arthurian Localities in the Principality and the Marches', *Archaeologia Cambrensis* (1872), 71–2.

3   Bedwyr Lewis Jones, 'Arthurian Place-Names: An End to Nonsense', *Amazing Quests: The Journey into Growth. A Special Issue of The Journal of Myth, Fantasy and Romanticism*, 4 (The Mythopoeic Literature Society of Australia, 1996), 9.

APPENDIX ONE

A CHRONOLOGICAL LIST OF THE FIRST ATTESTATIONS OF ARTHURIAN NAMES IN WALES

Site Name	County	Date	Grid Ref	Community
Corngafallt	BRE	1100	SN 94316441	Llanwrthwl
Bochrhiw Carn	GLA	1100	SO 09960494	Bedlinog
Rhyd Gwrthebau	MON	1100	ST 3894	Llanhennock
Tredunnock	MON	1100	ST 37889480	Llanhennock
Llanbadarn Fawr	CRD	1120	SN 59908101	Llanbadarn Fawr
Caerleon	MON	1138	ST 3390	Caerleon
Vadum Arthuri	CRD	1165	SN 23634888	Y Ferwig
Cardigan	CRD	1172	SN 177459	Cardigan
Garth Grugyn	CRD	1175	SN 62997456	Llanilar
Aber Tywi	CRM	1175	SN 3610	Llansteffan
Llwch Ewin	CRM	1175	SN 7028	Llangadog
Cwm Cerwyn	PEM	1175	SN 1031	Boncath
Mynyw	PEM	1175	SM 753253	St Davids
Cadair Arthur	BRE	1188	SO 00942141	Glyn Tarell
Fontem Arthur	RAD	1200	SO 05987855	Llanbadarn Fynydd
Ffynnon Arthur	GLA	1203		
Foel Fenlli	DEN	1258	SJ 16296009	Llanbedr Dyffryn Clwyd
Arthur Street	MTG	1300	SO 22219650	Montgomery
Cerrig Arthur	ANG	1306	SH 393678	Llangadwaldr
Ffynnon Arthur	MTG	1309	SJ 09811552	Llanfihangel yng Ngwynfa
Maen Arthur	PEM	1326	SM 747269	St Davids
Penarthur	PEM	1326	SM 74792649	St Davids
Arthur's Gate	MTG	1336	SO 22259698	Montgomery

Site Name	County	Date	Grid Ref	Community
Perthi Arthur	FLI	1347	SJ 1478	Whitford
King Arthur's Round Table	MON	1405	ST 33829035	Caerleon
Caer Gai	MER	1450	SH 87753147	Llanuwchllyn
Knucklas Castle	RAD	1478	SO 24937453	Bugeildy
Round Table	DEN	1536	SH 96046722	Llansannan
Claerddu	CRD	1536	SN 79206896	Ystrad Fflur
Maen Huail	DEN	1550	SJ 12365826	Ruthin
Caerwys	FLI	1550	SJ 128729	Caerwys
Capel Y Gwail	FLI	1550	SJ 16666967	Nannerch
Llys Arthur	FLI	1550	SJ 1669	Nannerch
Rounde Table	ANG	1562	SH 586814	Llanfihangel-din-Sylwy
Melin Maen Arthur	CRD	1566	SN 738726	Llanfihangel yn Creuddyn
Maen Arthur	CRD	1568	SN 7372	Ysbyty Ystwyth
Camlan	MER	1571	SH 8511	Mawddwy
Ffynnon Arthur	DEN	1574	SJ 244406	Llangollen Rural
Bwlch y Gyfylchi	GLA	1578	SS 807955	Glyncorrwg
Crug Tor y Bedol	GLA	1578	SS 82399900	Michaelstone-Super-Avon
Arthur's Butts Hill	GLA	1580	ST106836	Pentyrch
Llech Arthur	CRM	1581		Trelech a'r Betws
Maes Arthur	MER	1592	SN 6099	Botalog
Tyddyn Arthur	MER	1592	SH 77442074	Llanfachreth
Caer Craig Dinas Gawr	GLA	1597	SN 9103	Penderyn
Castell Cribawr	GLA	1597	SS 841826	Llangewydd, now Cefn Cribwr
Bwlch-y-Groes	MER	1597	SH 913232	Llanuwchllyn
Llwyn y Meini Hirion	MTG	1597		Pennant Melangell
Coetan Arthur	PEM	1600	SM 72532805	St Davids
Tir Llech Arthur	GLA	1602	SN 7205	Llangiwg
Tir Arthur	BRE	1606	SO 0942	Crickadarn
Eisteddfa Arthur	PEM	1607	SN 10153508	Nevern
Acre Arthur	DEN	1610	SJ 1062	Llanynys
Craig Arthur	FLI	1610	SJ 09687871	Trelawnyd
Croes Arthur	MON	1611	SO 408197	Cross Ash
Tir Person Arthur	ANG	1615	SH 2484	Pentraeth
Pen Arthur	CRM	1618	SN 71632370	Llangadog
Cae Maen Arthur	ANG	1633	SH 37059035	Llanfechell
Tref Arthur	ANG	1633	SH 260798	Trearddur

Site Name	County	Date	Grid Ref	Community
Pikel Arthur	CRN	1635	SH 73557164	Caerhun
Cae Carreg Arthur	DEN	1636		Tre'r Castell
Arthur's Chair	RAD	1656	SO 1644	Painscastle
King Arthur's Quoits	CRD	1662	SN 2648	Blaenporth
Cae Arthur	ANG	1681	SH 2484	Pentraeth
Llyn Dinas	CRN	1693	SH 610493	Beddgelert
Arthur's Stone	GLA	1693	SS 49139055	Llanrhidan Lower
Bryn Arthur	MER	1693	SJ 059429	Llangar
Coetan Arthur	PEM	1694	SN 09943702	Nevern
Moel Arthur	FLI	1694	SJ 145661	Nannerch
Buarth Arthur	CRM	1695	SN 14162659	Llandyssilio East
Bwrdd Arthur	CRM	1695	SN 17052565	Llanboidy
Gwern Arthur	MTG	1695	SJ 093012	Llanwyddelan
Coetan Arthur	CRM	1696	SN 656348	Caeo
Gwely Arthur	CRM	1696	SN 170256	Llanboidy
Coetan Arthur	CRN	1696	SH 601103	Llangelynin
Coetan Arthur	CRN	1696	SH 264341	Llaniestin
Cadair Arthur	MON	1697	SO 272187	Llantilio Pertholey
Cist Arthur	MON	1697	SO 331182	Llantilio Pertholey
Bedd Arthur	PEM	1697	SN 13053251	Mynachlog Ddu
Llanborth	CRD	1716	SN 29615216	Penbryn
Gardd Arthur	CRN	1717		Bangor
Pen Gwely Arthur	FLI	1721	SJ 0983	Gronant
Carreg Carn March Arthur	FLI	1725	SJ 20246266	Mold Rural
Arthyr Wood	GLA	1734	ST 038714	Llancarfan
Cist Arthur	FLI	1737	SJ 146658	Nannerch
Gorffrydiau Caswennan	CRN	1742	SH 1321	
Ffynnon Arthur	PEM	1745	SN 250314	Clydau
Llys Arthur	CRD	1747	SN 78658251	Blaenrheidol
Coetan Arthur	ANG	1750	SH 46428460	Llanfihangel tre'r Beirdd
Coetan Arthur	ANG	1762	SH 25868056	Holyhead Rural
Coetan Arthur	CRN	1764	SH 41594867	Clynnnog Fawr
Coetan Arthur	CRN	1764	SH 49884131	Llanystumdwy
Maen Arthur	CRN	1764	SH 5143	Dolbenmaen
Arthur's Javelins	CRN	1772	SH 498413	Llanystumdwy
Craig Arthur	DEN	1780	SJ 223470	Llangollen Rural
Arthur's Quoit	ANG	1783	SH 50138603	Penrhos Lligwy

Site Name	County	Date	Grid Ref	Community
Cadair Arthur	MER	1789	SH 711130	Llanfihangel-y-Pennant
King Arthur's Hall	MON	1789	SO 54611559	Whitchurch
Merlin's Hill	CRM	1791	SN 454215	Abergwili
Bwrdd Arthur	DEN	1795	SJ 07733462	Llanarmon Dyffryn Ceiriog
Coetan Arthur	MER	1795	SH 60312281	Dyffryn Ardudwy
Maes Arthur	MON	1798	ST 267861	Coedkernew
Dinas Arthur	MON	1799		Cwm Iou
Ffynnon Cegin Arthur	CRN	1800	SH 55486488	Llanddeiniolen
Craig-y-Dinas	GLA	1800	SN 91450808	Ystradfellte
Carn Arthur	PEM	1810	SN 13403223	Mynachlog Ddu
Arthur's Hill	FLI	1815	SJ 3165	Hawarden
Coetan Arthur	ANG	1818	SH 39248168	Tref Alaw
Coetan Arthur	CRN	1821	SH 22973454	Penllech
Nant Arthur	CRD	1829	SN 74267485	Pontarfynach
Carn March Arthur	MER	1834	SN 65049821	Tywyn
Carreg Arthur	MTG	1836	SJ 135051	Manafon
Melin Arthur	MTG	1836	SJ 10740166	Manafon
Tyddyn Arthur	FLI	1840	SJ 06147330	Waen
Maen Arthur	ANG	1840	SH 36849025	Llanfechell
Glyn Arthur	DEN	1840	SJ 13546566	Llangwyfan
Cae Arthur	MTG	1840	SO 20579455	Llandyssil
Parc Arthur	CRN	1841	SH 57736771	Pentir
Coetan Arthur	CRM	1842	SN 738227	Llangadog
Sylvaen	MER	1852	SH 63171888	Barmouth
Ogof Arthur	ANG	1859	SH 33167072	Aberffraw
Carnedd Arthur	CRN	1860	SH 614542	Beddgelert
Ogof Llanciau Eryri	CRN	1860	SH 6253	Beddgelert
Arthur's Quoit	ANG	1861	SH 43268575	Llandyfrydog
Coffor Arthur	CRM	1863	SN 5815	Llandybie
Cae Arthur	FLI	1865	SJ 0377	Criccin
Carnedd Trystan	CRN	1866	SH 68916419	Llanllechid
Cerrig Arthur	MER	1868	SH 58852284	Llanenddwyn Dyffryn Ardudwy
Parcarthur	FLI	1871	SJ 20756273	Gwernymynydd
Cefn Arthur	CRM	1872	SN 834335	Llandovery
Coetan Arthur	PEM	1872	SN 06033935	Newport
Penbedw Stone Circle	FLI	1873	SJ 17116793	Nannerch

Site Name	County	Date	Grid Ref	Community
Marchlyn Mawr	CRN	1880	SH 615615	Llandegai
Pwll Arthur	GLA	1885	ST 11247761	St Fagans
Ty Arthur	MON	1885	SO 206056	Abertillery
Banc Pen Arthur	CRM	1887	SN 711237	Llangadog
Coetan Arthur	CRN	1888	SH 536621	Llanrug
Llain Arthur	CRD	1891	SN 62688227	Faenor
Glyn Arthur	CRN	1891	SH 547649	Llanddeiniolen
Bryn Arthur	PEM	1891	SN 14612943	Mynachlog Ddu
Pen-y-Graig Arthur	CRN	1892	SH 81306494	Maenan
Ogo'r Dinas	CRM	1893	SN 612165	Llandybie
Llys Arthur	CRN	1893	SH 4352	Clynnog
Cerrig Meibion Arthur	PEM	1898	SN 11823102	Mynachlog Ddu
Ogof Arthur	MER	1901		
Bryn Arthur	ANG	1901	SH 422943	Amlwch
Llyn Llydaw	CRN	1901	SH 6253	Beddgelert
Caerleon cave at,	MON	1901	ST 3291	Caerleon
Bwrdd Arthur	CRM	1912	SN 337162	Llangynog
Bwrdd Arthur	CRM	1913	SN 485133	Llangyndeyrn
Carreg Arthur	CRM	1913	SN 66541211	Bettws
Cerrig Arthur	MER	1913	SH 63171888	Llanaber
Croes Arthur	CRM	1917	SN 46602585	Abergwili
Cerrig Pen Arthur	CRM	1917	SN 723244	Llangadog
Coetan Arthur	CRD	1922	SN 609674	Llangwyryfon
Pant Arthur	CRD	1922	SN 6067	Llangwyryfon
Dinas Bran	DEN	1932	SJ 22264306	Llangollen Urban
Arthur's Parlour	FLI	1938	SJ 146716	Ysceifiog

Map 3. *The pre-1974 county boundaries of Wales used in the Gazetteer*

Map 4. *The modern county boundaries of Wales*

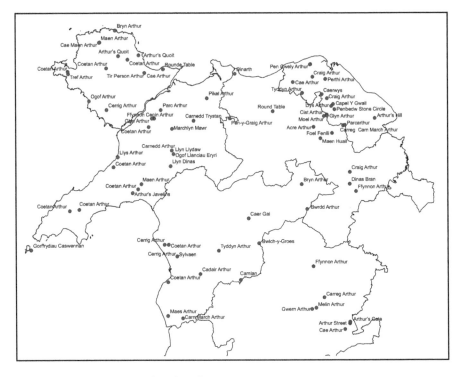

Map 5. *The Arthurian sites of north Wales*

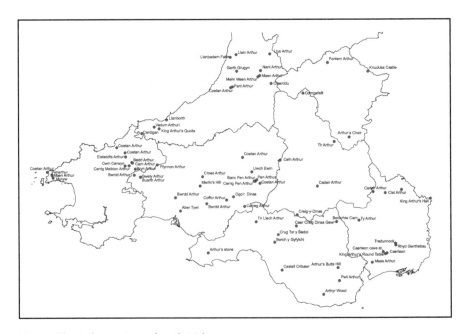

Map 6. *The Arthurian Sites of south Wales*

A GAZETTEER OF ARTHURIAN SITES IN WALES

T HIS GAZETTEER DETAILS all of the places in Wales either associated with the figure of Arthur or containing the name. The sites are divided into the thirteen pre-1974 counties of Wales, primarily for convenience, as trying to list sites based upon the current twenty-two counties would leave some empty and at the time of writing further boundary changes seem inevitable. The information for every site provides references in their short form (Author, date, page number), and full details can be found in the Bibliography.

Sites that cannot be securely identified, to at least a county level, such as the battle list from the *Historia Brittonum* have not been included in this Gazetteer. The names from the Boar Hunt episode in *Culhwch and Olwen* have been discussed in detail elsewhere (Bromwich and Evans, 1992), and only those directly associated with Arthur are given here. Based upon the discussion of the dating of this text in Chapter Three, and for the purposes of the chronological list in Appendix One, I have assigned them all a conservative date of 1175. The headings to each site contain the following information.

Site Name	Community	National Grid Reference	Earliest Date
Arthur's Quoit	(Llandyfrydog	SH 433857)	**1869**

Grid references will be given as 8 figures where possible, for example when referring to a monument that is still extant. Six-figure references allow for a little more ambiguity and four- figure references are often only given as an approximate location and should be used as such. Sites that are associated with a county but cannot be located more closely do not have a grid reference. Please note that inclusion in this list does not mean that a site is accessible; many are situated on private land. For further information on many of the historic sites listed here the most convenient starting point is the Historic Wales Portal at *historicwales.gov.uk*. This website provides detailed modern and older mapping of Wales and access to the database records of the four Welsh archaeological trusts, National Museum Wales, CADW and the National Monuments Record of Wales. For access to other mapping the following sites are invaluable:

- *www.bl.uk/onlinegallery/onlineex/ordsurvdraw/* enables access to all of the Ordnance Survey Drawings (OSD), georeferenced onto Google Earth. All references to the dates of the map revisions between the OSD and the first printed edition are derived from Hodson (1989).

- *www.visionofbritain.org.uk/maps/* provides access to the first series one-inch to the Mile Ordnance Survey mapping for the whole of Wales, dating from the 1830s onwards.

- *http://cynefin.archiveswales.org.uk/* provides access to all of the 1,091 tithe maps and apportionment schedules for Wales

- The Melville Richards Archive (MRA) is an invaluable aid to the research of Welsh place names and is available at *www.e-gymraeg.co.uk/enwaulleoedd/amr/*

As with any gazetteer of this sort, mistakes and oversights are inevitable. Any new information or corrections would be gratefully received.

Abbreviations

MRA	Melville Richards Archive
OS	Ordnance Survey
OSD	Ordnance Survey Drawings (these pre-date the printed maps)
RCAHMW	Royal Commission on the Ancient and Historical Monuments of Wales
TNA	The National Archives

ANGLESEY (ANG)

Arthur's Quoit (Llandyfrydog SH 43268575)   **1861**
A glacial erratic on the top of a small rocky eminence widely referred to as Maen Chwyf (Rocking Stone). The site is named Gorseddau on OSD 317 and then as Maen Chwyf on the first series one-inch map of 1840. The first association with Arthur can be attributed to a travel guide from 1861: 'Llwydiarth, the beautifully wooded demesne of the Lloyd family. In the grounds is a famous Maen Chwyf or rocking stone, called locally Arthur's Quoit' (Murray, 1861, 51). This identification was used by Glennie (1869, xxiv), but the stone was always referred to as Maen Chwyf by antiquarian writers who visited Anglesey (Baynes, 1911, 54).

Arthur's Quoit (Penrhos Lligwy SH 50138603)   **1783**
The earliest writer to associate the well-known burial chamber at Lligwy with Arthur
is Thomas Pennant, who states:

> Not far from the road, in the lands of Llugwy, is a most stupendous Cromlech, of
> a rhomboid form. The greatest diagonal is seventeen feet six inches, the lesser fif-
> teen; the thickness three feet nine; its height from the ground only two feet: it was
> supported by several stones. The Welsh, who ascribe every thing stupendous to our
> famous British king, called it Arthur's Quoit. (Pennant 1783, II, 273–4)

Bryn Arthur (Amlwch SH 422943)   **1901**
The name of a house that first appears on the second edition, six-inch OS map, from
1901. It is absent from the first edition of 1891.

Bwrdd Arthur
See **Rounde Table**.

Cae Arthur (Pentraeth SH 2484)   **1681**
The schedule for Bangor University, Bodorgan MS 559 notes the following parcels of
land in an Indenture of release, dated February 1681/2: 'Cae Arthur, Cae Wrth gefn y
ty and Llain y pant, all in the parish of Pentraeth'. None of these three names can be
found on the tithe schedule and their exact location is uncertain. See also **Tir Parson
Arthur** below.

Cae Maen Arthur (Llanfechell SH 37059035)   **1633**
Bangor University, Baron Hill MS 4703, dated 1633, notes the name Cae Maen Arthur.
The name later appears on the tithe schedule as field number 135, and then on the six-
inch first series OS map from 1888 as that of a farmhouse. See the nearby **Maen Arthur**.

Cerrig Arthur (Bodorgan SH 393678)   **1306**
The name given to 'a tiny Episcopal Free vill in Malltraeth commote. Probably located
near Llanfeirian in Llangadwaladr' (Jones, Glanville R. J, 1955, 96.) The earliest form
recorded is Crec Arthur in 1306 (Roberts, Tomos, 1976–7, 53) and it appears on a
survey map of the Bodorgan estate (1724) as Careg Arthur, NNE of Bodorgan Hall
(Bangor University, Bodorgan MS 1579, 2).

Coetan Arthur (Holyhead Rural SH 25868056)   **1762**
An otherwise unnamed site situated on the summit of a low rocky outcrop, that was
long thought to be a cromlech. The earliest printed appearance of the name can be
found in (Anon., 1775, 37), but an earlier manuscript, on which at least parts of this
book was based, provides the earliest reference to this name: 'There was another dru-
idical altar or Cromlech within about a quarter of a mile of the town of Holyhead,

called Coiten Arthur, i.e. Arthur's quoit, but the upper or flat stone is now removed to an adjoyning hedge' (Bangor University, MS 7866, 31). The Holyhead section, from which this extract is taken, was originally written by Rev. John Thomas in 1762 (Williams, T. P. T., 2006, 22–4).

Coetan Arthur (Llanfihangel tre'r Beirdd SH 46428460)   **1750**
A cromlech on the southern slopes of Mynydd Bodafon marked as Cromlech on OSD 317 (1818) and on the first series six-inch OS map (1868). It was destroyed in 1871 during the building of a new road over the mountain (Baynes, 1911, 13). The monument is depicted as Coetan Arthur on a map of the area (c.1750) by Lewis Morris in British Library, Additional MS 14929 fols 43v–44r (Owen, Hugh, 1951, 49).

Coetan Arthur (Tref Alaw SH 39248168)   **1818**
The name of a cromlech that first appears on OSD 317 (1818) as Coytan Arthur and appears on modern maps as Coetan Arthur.

Craig Arthur
See **Cerrig Arthur.**

Crug Arthur
See **Cerrig Arthur.**

Maen Arthur (Llanfechell SH 36849025)   **1840**
A natural erratic boulder, south of Llanfechell, not named on the OSD. It appears on the first edition one-inch map of 1840 suggesting that it was added during the revision of 1836–8. The nearby Cae Maen Arthur, suggests the name may be older.

Ogof Arthur (Llangwyfan SH 33167072)   **1859**
This name, associated with a cave in a sea cliff, first appeared in (Anon., 1859, 138). The article is primarily concerned with the treasure that the cave is supposed to contain, but also notes:

> Un o'r pethau nesaf yr ymdriniaf ychydig arno yw Ogof Arthur, yr hon sydd ar yr ochr ddeheuol I fynydd y Cnwc; ac y mae hen draddodiad fod Arthur wedi bod yn llechau yn yr ogof yma pan oedd mewn rhyfel a'r Gwyddelod.

> One of the next things I deal a little on is Arthur's Cave, which is on the south side of Mynydd y Cnwc; and there is an old tradition that Arthur had hidden in the cave when he was at war with the Irish.

The name is shown on the second edition, six-inch map (1886) and became more widely known through its appearance in (Rhŷs, 1901, 457–8).

Rounde Table (Llanfihangel-din-Sylwy SH 586814) **1562**
The Iron Age hill fort better known as Din Sylwy is first referred to as 'Rounde Table' by Dr Thomas Phaer in 1562 (Robinson, W. R. B., 1972, 502). The Welsh form **Bwrdd Arthur**, by which the site is still known today, can only be traced back to (Pennant, 1781, II, 264). (Jones, Glanville R. J., 1955, 96) refers to an unidentified medieval hamlet called 'Bwrdd Arthur'in the vill of Cremlyn. He derived this name from the form *Botarthuar* in the printed edition of the *Extent of Anglesey*.The original fourteenth-century text (Bangor University, Baron Hill MS 6714) came to light in the 1930s and gives the name as *Bodiordderch* (Carr, 1971–2, 246). This name has been discussed in (Richards, Melville, 1973, 43); it has nothng to do with Arthur, and the confusion can be traced back to the 1955 article.

Tir Person Arthur (Pentraeth SH 2484) **1615**
A small tenement located in the parish of Pentraeth, associated with John Arthur, the rector of Llangadwaladr from 1615 onwards. It is probable that the Arthur family is also responsible for the name **Cae Arthur** in the same parish, and possibly some of the other names in the vicinity (Richards, T., 1940, 63).

Tref Arthur (Trearddur SH 260798) **1633**
This small community is named Treffyarddr in 1409 (TNA, SC 6/1233/1), and the form Trefarthur first appears in 1633 (NLW, Carreg-Lwyd MS, Series I/1371). It appears as Trei Arthur on OSD 317 (1818) and Tre Arthur on the first edition one-inch map (1840), before settling on the modern form Trearddur Bay.

BRECONSHIRE (BRE)

Bann Arthur
See **Cadair Arthur**.

Cadair Arthur (Glyn Tarell, SO 00942141) **1188**
A name given to the col between the two highest summits of the Brecon Beacons by Gerald of Wales in 1188, discussed on p. 28. In the introduction to his 1592 Welsh grammar, Siôn Dafydd Rhys notes that the names **Bann Arthur** and **Moel Arthur** were also used for this mountain (Rhaeso, 1592, on the penultimate page of unpaginated introductory section headed 'At y Cymry'). A much later tradition exists, no doubt inspired by the name, concerning Arthur holding a Round Table with his knights on the summit:

> Among the many remarkable traditions concerning the Round Table is that which survives in Wales that Arthur assembled his followers on the heights of the Brecknockshire Beacons, and there made known his design to establish a knighthood and to found a Table Round. On the summit of Pen-y-Van may yet be seen huge stones

and rock fragments which the superstitious regard as the broken relics of the Table, to the real existence of which far more attention has been given than to its allegorical significance. (Walters, 1909, 144)

Corngafallt (Llanwrthwl SN 94316441)   **1100**
A hill two miles south-west of Rhayder, mentioned in the *Mirabilia* as the site of a stone bearing the paw-print of Arthur's dog, discussed on p. 15.

Moel Arthur
See **Cadair Arthur**.

Tir Arthur (Crickadarn SO 0942)   **1606**
The Calendar of Deeds and Documents, The Quaritch Deeds (Aberystwyth, 1922), describes NLW Quaritch MS 695 as a 'Bond dated 30 Aug 1606 concerning the messuage called Tir yr Eskyr in Krukadern extending in length from a brook called Klettowr to the land late of John Thomas Griffith and in breadth from a brook called Nantllynwrnoll to Tir Arthur.' The river Clettwr flows into the river Wye near the village of Erwood. The exact location is uncertain.

CAERNARFONSHIRE (CRN)

Arthur's Javelins (Llanystumdwy SH 498413)   **1772**
Richard Farrington refers to these standing stones in his unpublished 'Snowdonia Druidica'. See **Coetan Arthur** (Llanystumdwy) for an earlier mention of the same stones, but without the name: 'We can only presume they are not of a different species and might in former times go under the name of Arthur's Javelins, for the grand triple cromlech called Coetan Arthur is not so far distant from them' (NLW 1119D, p. 85).

Carnedd Arthur (Beddgelert SH 614542)   **1860**
The folk tale of Arthur fighting on the flanks of Snowdon is first noted in a Welsh essay written for the Beddgelert eisteddfod in 1860 by William Jones and printed in (Anon., 1861, 331). Carnedd Arthur is situated on Bwlch y Saethau, the pass between the summits of Snowdon and Lliwedd: 'To this day there remains in the middle of this pass a large heap of stones, which is called "Carnedd Arthur" (Arthur's Cairn), and this marks the spot where the great British prince takes his rest' (Jenkins, 1899, 256). The tale became more widely known following its appearance in (Rhŷs, 1901, 473–9). The exact cairn in question is uncertain, as several mounds of stone exist at Bwlch y Saethau

Carnedd Trystan (Llanllechid SH 68916419)   **1866**
A cairn of this name existed on the slopes of Carnedd Llewelyn (Hughes, Hugh Derfel, 1866, 52), and it can probably be identified with the cairn marked on the modern

OS maps at this grid reference. The site became more widely known from its inclusion in (Rhŷs, 1901, 480), but the name is no longer in use.

Cegin Arthur
See **Ffynnon Gegin Arthur**.

Coetan Arthur (Llanrug SH 536621)   **1888**
The name given to a possible cromlech by an informant of John Rhŷs (Rhŷs, 1888, 58). The name is not used today.

Coetan Arthur (Penllech SH 22973454   **1821**
A cromlech on the slopes of Mynydd Cefn Amwlch, on OSD 300 (1816), but by 1821 known as Coetan Arthur (Williams, Peter, 1821, 168). A later article notes the following folklore:

> The group goes by the name of 'Coiten Arthur' (Arthur's Quoit) from a tradition that Arthur Gawr (Arthur the Giant) cast it from Carn Madryn, a mountain a few miles off, and that his wife brought the three other stones in her apron, and placed them as supporters or props to the Coiten. (T. L. D. J. P., 1847, 97)

Coetan Arthur (Llanystumdwy SH 49884131)   **1764**
The site is first mentioned by Richard Farrington in his unpublished 'Snowdonia Druidica':

> There is a stone wall near a haggard not far from the farmhouse [Ystumcegid], which runs up toward the rock above it in which wall, near the entrance into the next field there are three uncommon shaped pillars erect, with tops resembling the heads of Javelins. No account can be given of them, unless they were either symbols or notices of the grand Tripple Cromlech not far off them; that, to this day goes by the name of Coetan Arthur. (NLW MS 4899, 234).

A later version of this tract provides an illustration of the site (NLW MS 1118C, 174). It is also later mentioned by Fenton who simply refers to it as a cromlech with no reference to the name Coetan Arthur (Fisher, 1917, 253).

Coetan Arthur (Llaniestin SH 264341)   **1696**
The following note appears under the heading 'Coetan Artur' in Cardiff MS 2.59, a notebook of Edward Lhwyd: 'Tre Garnedd in Llanjestin Parish is about 3 yards long, and 2 and half broad, and is a monument of that kind they call heathen Altars, and not of the cromlech kind. About 4 yards to the west of this is a very small tumulus, like a large grave' (Fisher, 1917, 334). The monument in question no longer survives, but was located in the vicinity of the house called Tregarnedd.

Coetan Arthur (Clynnnog Fawr SH 41594867)   **1764**
Richard Farrington first notes the name in 1764: 'the field it is in is called Cae y
Coetan to this day, meaning Arthur's Quoit, as before, ie the vulgar fabulous name of
most cromlechs' (NLW 4899, 232). Evidence for the monument survives at this grid
reference, albeit much damaged (RCAHMW, 1964, 128).

Coetan Arthur (Llangelynin SH 601103)   **1696**
The following note appears under the heading 'Coetan Artur' in Cardiff MS 2.59,
a notebook of Edward Lhwyd, perhaps associated with the standing stones at
Gwastadgoed, but the exact site is uncertain:

> Yng Hae'r Goeten in Celynin parish a Cromlech, very smooth underneath, but of
> an uneven testudineous kind of form above like that at Bodowyr, in Anglesey. It is
> supported by 3 stones, about 3 feet in height, but there's a 4th not near so high. The
> entry into it is almost towards the East. Many rude stones near, some down others
> pitched on end. (Fisher, 1917, 333)

Ffynnon Gegin Arthur (Llanddeiniolen SH 55486488)   **1800**
The site of a once-frequented well, renowned for its healing properties (Williams, A.
Wyn, 1858). It first appears in (Evans, John, 1800, 181) and on OSD 306 (1816), but
not on the published one-inch map of 1836. An earlier reference to a 'Cegin Arthur',
c.1400 appears in a poem entitled 'I'r Niwl' (NLW Llanstephan MS 135, 85), but it is
not clear that it is referring to this, or any other particular site (Lewis, Henry, 1925,
218, line 27).

Gardd Arthur (Bangor)   **1717**
The schedule for Bangor University, Penrhyn MS 1637 mentions a site of this name
in Bangor. Could there be a connection with **Parc Arthur**?

Glyn Arthur (Llanddeiniolen SH 547649)   **1891**
(RCAHMW, 1960, 181) states that there is a much-destroyed cairn on a hill of this
name at 430 ft above sea level. The name is not found on early OS maps and first
appears on the six-inch map of 1891. The MRA also notes a Glan Arthur in the same
area, but gives no source and it is most likely a variant spelling.

Gorffrydiau Caswennan (SH 1321)   **1742**
A chart entitled 'The North entrance of Bardsey Sound and the roads in Caernarvonshire' notes a sandbank near Bardsey Island of this name and Caswennan is identified
as the ship of Arthur (Morris, L., 1748, plate 11); see page 112. Elsewhere Morris
notes 'When I was upon my survey of that Island of Bardsey, for the Admiralty A.D.
1742, the inhabitants gave me the same name and account, with the above, of those
sholes' (London, British Library, Add MS 14,903, 5). Although Lewis identifies the

sandbank as being WSW of Bardsey Island the location of six wrecks in close proximity at SH1321 suggests this may have been the site intended.

Llyn Dinas (Beddgelert SH 610493)   1693
A letter from Edward Lhwyd in the possession of Robert Williams, dated 1693, was printed in 1859; the accompanying translation is given below:

> On the banks of Llyn Dinas there are three graves, called the graves of the three youths, three men, or three soldiers (that is, the soldiers of Arthur), or the graves of the tall men; and two graves, called the graves of the fiddler and his servant, or the graves of the black fiddler and his servant. And between Dinas and the lake is the grave of Sir Owen Maxen, who had been fighting against the giant with steel balls; there are depressions in the ground, where each stood, to be seen still. Others say that it was with arrows they fought, and that the depressions now seen were places that they dug to defend themselves. Neither of them however got over the affair. When the knight perceived that there was no hope of his living much longer, he was asked where he wished to be buried; he requested that an arrow should be shot skyward, and where it fell, that they should make his grave there. (Williams, Robert, 1859, 213–14)

The letter suggests that the graves were situated somewhere in the vicinity of the house named Beudy Bedd Owen on modern maps, but the site is uncertain.

Llyn Llydaw (Beddgelert SH 6253)   1901
In the twentieth century several authors note Llyn Llydaw as a possible site for the casting away of Excalibur. In his 1980 study of Arthurian Britain, Geoffrey Ashe says of Llyn Llydaw that, 'Welsh legend locates the casting-away of Excalibur here' (Ashe, 1980, 160), but the true source of this tradition originates with John Rhŷs in 1901 (Rhŷs, 1901, 475–6).

Llys Arthur (Clynnog SH 4352)   1893
The name of a farm (*Royal Commission on Land*, III, 1893, 576). The exact site is uncertain, but it may have had some association with **Coetan Arthur** in the same parish.

Maen Arthur (Dolbenmaen SH 5143)   1764
Richard Farrington mentions this rocking stone and includes an impressive illustration of it in his unpublished manuscript (NLW 1118C, 180); see figure 11:

> It is found above a farm house called Dolewgan and did before it was thrown off its axis rest upon its center and admitted of motion to and again the mover was disposed. But now the umbilicus is out of its socket and no force can affect it. It is some tuns in weight and goes under the title of Maen Arthur, as all Druid monuments are denominated by the vulgar. (NLW 4899, 242)

The site was better known as Maen Sigl, (Anon., 1849, 3). It is not named on any OS map and the exact site is now uncertain.

Marchlyn Mawr (Llandegai SH 615615)   **1880**

This folk tale according to (Rhŷs, 1883, 183) was 'published not long ago, in *Llais y Wlad* (Bangor, North Wales), and in the *Drych* (Utica, United States)', as part of a series of articles on the folklore of Caernarfonshire. I have been unable to view the original newspaper sources and as Rhŷs wrote in 1883, a date of *c*.1880 is likely:

> The Marchlyn Mawr is surrounded by rocks terrible to look at, and tradition relates how one of the sons of the farmer of Rhiwen, once on a time, when helping a sheep that had fallen among the rocks to get away discovered a tremendous cave there; he entered, and saw that it was full of treasures and arms of great value; but, as it was beginning to grow dark, and as clambering back was a difficult matter even in the light of day, he went home that evening, and next morning with the grey dawn he set out again for the cave, when he found it without much trouble. He entered, and began to look about him at the treasures that were there. In the center of the cave stood a huge table of pure gold, and on the table lay a crown of gold and pearls. He understood at once that they were the crown and treasures of Arthur. He approached the table, and as he stretched forth his hand to take hold of the crown he was frightened by an awful noise, the noise, as it were, of a thousand thunders bursting over his head, and the whole place was as dark as Tartarus. He tried to grope and feel his way out as fast as he could. When he had succeeded in reaching to the middle of the rocks, he cast his eye on the lake, which had been stirred all through, while its white crested waves dashed through the jagged teeth of the rocks up to the spot where he stood. But as he continued looking at the middle of the lake he beheld a coracle containing three women, the fairest that the eye of man ever fell on. They were being quickly rowed to the mouth of the cave; but the dread aspect of him who rowed was enough to send thrills of horror through the strongest of men. The youth was able to escape home, but no health remained in his constitution after that, and even the mere mention of the Marchlyn in his hearing used to be enough to make him insane. (Rhŷs, 1883, 183–6)

Ogof Llanciau Eryri (Beddgelert SH 6253)   **1860**

For the earlier part of this story see **Carnedd Arthur**:

> In the steep precipice on the left, near the upper end of Llyn Llydaw, is a cave turned into a remarkably sacred use, which is called the 'Cave of the Youth of Eryri' [Ogof Llanciau Eryri]. We are told that after King Arthur was slain at Bwlch y Saethau, and had been buried under the huge stone mound at that pass, all his men ascended the peak of Lliwedd, and descended thence to an immense cave in one of the steep ascents of Cwm Dyli. When all had entered into this hiding-place, the mouth of the

cave was closed with the loose stones and turf within, a small hole being left, so that no one except by the merest accident could discover it. The men then gave themselves over to sleep, leaning on their shields, so that they might be in an attitude ready for the second coming of Arthur; for he is expected to return again and restore the British Crown to the original Britans, from whom it was taken by Alien forces. This expectation is embodied in an old saw.

> The Youth of Eryri, stout of Heart
> Shall win their crown again.

Very many years ago, as the several shepherds of this part were collecting their flocks on Lliwedd, one of the sheep fell on to a ledge of this precipice. The shepherd of Cwm Dyli ventured down to bring it back again, and to his astonishment he saw the mouth of the secret cave close to the very ledge to which the sheep had fallen. A light was burning within, and he ventured to peep into the mysterious cavity, and behold! A numberless host of soldiers all asleep, and leaning on their shilds, and ready at any moment for the word of command. Seeing them fast asleep, he thought he shoulod like to go in and have a look at them. But, as he was pushing his way in, he knocked his head against a bell which was hanging in the entrance, and this rattled until every corner of the cave was resounding deafeningly. The soldiers to a man immediately woke up, and as they awoke gave forth a terrific shout. The shepherd got such a fright that he was never well again; and no one has ever since dared to approach even the mouth of the cave. (Jenkins, D. E., 1899, 300–1, translating from Anon., 1861, 371, which prints an essay written in 1860)

Parc Arthur (Pentir SH 57736771)   1841
OSD 312 (1822) names this earthwork 'Ancient Fort', so the name 'Parc Arthur' must have been added to first edition one-inch map (1841) during the revision of 1838. It is not named on the later, larger-scale six-inch map.

Pen-y-Graig Arthur (Maenan SH 81306494)   1892
This house is named as Pen-y-Graig Eithin on OSD 309 (1819) and also on the first series OS map from 1840. The change from Eithin to Arthur first appears on the first edition six-inch map that was surveyed 1875–87, but not published until 1892. The exact reason for this change is unclear.

Pikel Arthur (Caerhun SH 73557164)   1635
A standing stone near Ro Wen, first referred to as Pikel Artur in a collection of Welsh historical miscellanea put together by John Jones of Gellilyfdy, whilst he was in debtors' prison in Fleet Street from 1635 to 1641. The text reads: 'Pikel Artur yno y mae hefyd yn gyfagos ir Llech obob tu ir ffordd o Tal y Cafn i Fwlch y Deufaen yn lumud yg llantel […] yn fir acer yn arfon y maent' (NLW Peniarth 267, 40).

CARMARTHENSHIRE (CRM)

Aber Tywi (Llansteffan SN 3610)   **1175**
The mouth of the river Tywi, near the village of Llansteffan, where Arthur slew Cynlas ap Cynan and Gwilenhin, the king of France, in *Culhwch and Olwen* (Bromwich and Evans, 1992, 38, l. 1128).

Arthur's Pot
See **Crochan Arthur**.

Banc Pen Arthur (Llangadog SN 711237)   **1887**
The name given to the high ground, west of **Pen Arthur** (Llangadog) on the first edition, six-inch OS map from 1887.

Buarth Arthur (Llandyssilio East SN 14162659)   **1695**
Noted by Edward Lhwyd in his additions to Gibson's 1695 edition of Camden's *Britannia*:

> But Buarth Arthur or Meineu Gwyr, on a mountain near Kil y maen lhwyd, is one of that kind of circular stone-monuments our English historians ascribe to the Danes [...] As for the name Buarth Arthur, 'tis only a nickname of the vulgar, whose humour it is, though not so much (as some have imagin'd) out of ignorance and credulity, as a kind of Rustick diversion, to dedicate many unaccountable monuments to the memory of that Hero; calling some stones of several tun weight his Coits, others his tables, Chairs, etc.' (Gibson, 1695, 628).

Lhwyd had received his information about the monument from Erasmus Saunders in a letter dated 27 November 1693 (Bodl. MS Ashmole 1817a, fol. 430r, in Roberts, B. F., 2010, 40). However, Saunders makes no reference to the name Buarth Arthur and it would appear that Lhwyd came across this name on his tour of south Wales between 14 August and early October 1693 (Roberts, B. F., 2010, 25). This monument is better known today as Meini Gwyr.

Bwrdd Arthur (Llanboidy SN 17052565)   **1695**
The cromlech better known as Gwal y Viliast, first mentioned by Edward Lhwyd in 1695.

> Gwal y viliast or Bwrdh Arthur in Lhan Boudy parish, is a monument in some respect like that which we have described at this barrow [previous entry is for Kings Barrow], viz a rude stone about ten yards in circumference, and above three foot thick, supported by four pillars, which are about two foot and a half in height. (Gibson, 1695, 628)

Bwrdd Arthur (Llangyndeyrn SN 485133)   **1913**

A name first recorded by George Eyre Evans during fieldwork for the Carmarthen-shire Inventory in April 1913:

> Between the farmhouses of tan y banc and Glan Hiriaeth are the remains of a ruined Cromlech, which is known by the names of 'Bwrdd Arthur' and 'Gwal y viliast'. [...] The name of Arthur was associated with the site before the limits of the memory of the oldest inhabitant, and has doubtless descended from the middle ages. On Mynydd Llangyndeyrn. Meetings of an eisteddfodic nature used to be held here each spring, but have long since ceased. (RCAHMW, 1917, 165)

Bwrdd Arthur (Llangynog SN 337162)   **1912**

First recorded in a field notebook kept by George Eyre Evans whilst working on the Royal Commission Inventory for Carmarthenshire:

> Bwrdd Arthur. About 100 yards to the W. of Ebenezer cromlech is a fine oval stone with a perectly flat surface known locally as 'Bwrdd Arthur'. It is hard not to believe it has been so placed by man, on the other hand its size seem to forbid such placing. It measures 12ft in length; 9 ft in breadth & stands some 4ft out of ground. (NLW 13456A, 1 August 1912)

Carreg Arthur (Bettws SN 66541211)   **1913**

First recorded in a field notebook kept by George Eyre Evans whilst undertaking fieldwork for the Royal Commission inventory volume for Carmarthenshire.

> Carreg Arthur – This is about 300 yards E. of the above carin [Bodyst]. It has every appearance of being a detached point of an adjoining outcrop. Its flat top is 12' by 11'. Part of the ground underneath it slopes away, the height above the surface is 2 ft 6 in. It is a naturally placed stone. Through it run 5 parallel streaks of [spar?] longitudinally. According to local tradition when King Arthur and his men were crossing from Mynyd Du to Mynyd Bettws, at this spot King Arthur could not walk in consequence of a stone in his shoe which irritated his foot & this is the stone he then removed. (NLW 13466A, under 8 July 1913)

Cefn Arthur (Llandovery SN 834335)   **1872**

(Anon., 1872, 270), refers to 'Cefn Arthur (?Cefn Erthan) on the border of this county, four miles north-west of Llywel'. All mapping refers to the ridge as Cefn Arthen, or Erthen, and any reference to Arthur appears to be wishful thinking.

Cerrig Pen Arthur (Llangadog SN 723244)   **1917**

The notebook of George Eyre Evans from his fieldwork for this site refers to 'Stones at Pen Arthur Isaf. Three natural drift stones' (NLW MS 13462A, under 3 April 1914), but in the printed inventory the stones have acquired the name Cerrig Pen Arthur:

At the farm of Pen Arthur issa are three boulders which are known as Cerrig Pen Arthur (the head stones of Arthur) or (the stones of Arthurs head). They doubtless represent a demolished cromlech, though how its members became so widely separated is not easily explained. (RCAHMW, 1917, 142)

Nearby are **Pen Arthur** and **Banc Pen Arthur.**

Coetan Arthur (Llangadog SN 738227)   **1842**
This site first appears in Guest's notes to her translation of *Culhwch and Olwen*, where Coetan Arthur is described as 'one of two large rocks in the bed of the Sawdde river' (Guest, 1842, 364). 'Arthurian Localities' (*Archaeologia Cambrensis*, 1874, 89) adds a little more information: 'a large rock in the river Sawddwy, Carmarthenshire, which our hero is said to have flung to its present position from Pen Arthur, a distance of about a mile'.

For **Pen Arthur** see below. The site seems also to have occasionally been called **Grafelyn Arthur** (Owen, Henry, 1936, IV, 416).

Coetan Arthur (Caeo SN 656348)   **1696**
Mentioned by Edward Lhwyd in his notebook from 1696, 'Coitane Arthyr ar Waun Cwm luogwen' (Fisher, 1917, 343). Rhos Cwm Luogwen appears on the tithe schedule, situated to the north of a farm called Cwm Liog, thereby narrowing down the likely location of the site (Grooms, 1993, 124).

Coffor Arthur (Llandybie SN 5815)   **1863**
First appears in an essay written *c.*1863 for a local eisteddfod competition. The lake in question is Llyn Llech Owen, but the exact site is uncertain:

> Y mae Carnedd o gerrig ar yr ochr dwyreiniol i'r llyn, uwchben Castell y Graig yn ei ganol y mae un garreg fawr, yr hon elwir coffor Arthur.

> A stone cairn on the eastern side of the lake, above Castell y Graig has in the middle of it a large stone that was called Coffor Arthur. (Roberts, Gomer M., 1941, 60; translation mine).

Crochan Arthur
See **Gwely Arthur.**

Croes Arthur (Abergwili SN 46602585)   **1917**
An earthwork forming an irregular parallelogram: 'locally the camp is known as that of Croes Arthur, the fields within the ramparts being called Gwastad y Groes, the level of the cross' (RCAHMW, 1917, 2–3). The name is still used today.

Dyffryn Amanw   1175
The valley of the river Aman, between Brynaman and Pontardawe, where Arthur and
his men killed the two pigs Banw and Benwig in *Culhwch and Olwen* (Bromwich and
Evans, 1992, 40, line 1149).

Dyffryn Llychwr   1175
The valley of the river Loughor, which runs from Pontardulais up to Ammanford and
then north-east into the Black Mountains, where Arthur came following the slaying
of huntsmen by the pigs Grugyn Gwallt Ereint and Llwydawg in *Culhwch and Olwen*
(Bromwich and Evans, 1992, 39, line 1136).

Grafelyn Arthur
See **Coetan Arthur** (Llangadog).

Gwely Arthur (Llanboidy SN 170256)   1696
'In the bed of the river Tav, and just below the cromlech, is a stone known as "Crochan Arthur" "Arthur's Kettle" from a curious cavity in its surface which has doubtless been caused by natural agencies' (RCAHMW, 1917, 73). An alternative name for
this stone is **Arthur's Pot**:

> This is under a cromlech at Dolwilim, on the banks of the Tawe and in the stream itself
> when the water is high; it is a circular hole of considerable depth, accurately bored in
> the stone by the action of water. This hole is called Arthur's Pot, and according to local
> belief was made by Merlin for the hero king to cook his dinner in. (Sikes, 1880, 369)

The earliest name is from a reply to Lhwyd's *Parochial Queries*:

> in the midst of the river Tafe is a great stone about the bignesse of LL: y: fst [Llech
> y Filiast] but halfe a yard narrow called Gwely Arthur which rude monuments &
> severall other called by his name in other prets (omitting the ignorant stories of the
> vulgar). (Emery, 1975, 108)

Llech Arthur (Trelech a'r Betws)   1581
MRA notes the name *llech arthyr* in the parish of Trelech a'r Betws, in a rental document from 1581 in TNA SC 12/29/8.

Llwch Ewin (Llangadog SN 7028)   1175
Arthur and his men met the pigs Grugyn Gwallt Ereint and Llwydawg at this site, and
Echel Big-hip and Arwyli ap Gwyddaeg Gwyr were killed by them (Bromwich and
Evans, 1992, 40, l. 1152). The location is uncertain, but *castellum Lluchewin* (identi-
fied as Llangadog Castle) appears twice in the B-text of the *Annales Cambriae*, under
the years 1205 and 1208, making it a strong candidate (ab Ithel, 1860, 66).

Merlins Hill (Abergwili SN 454215)   1791
A note from a tour, undertaken in 1791, states that 'Arthur is asleep under Merlins Hill at Carmarthenshire' (Morgan, M., 1795, 189).

Mynydd Amanw   1175
The mountain where the River Aman has its source and where Arthur and his men killed one of the piglets of Twrch Trwyth in *Culhwch and Olwen* (Bromwich and Evans, 1992, 39, l. 1145).

Ogo'r Dinas (Llandybie SN 612165)   1893
A letter sent to John Rhŷs in 1893 refers to a tradition of Arthur sleeping in a cave called Ogo'r Dinas, near Llandybie, although the site is more often associated with Owain Lawgoch (Rhŷs, 1901, 468). The cave is better known as Ogof Cil-yr-Ychen (Roberts, Gomer, 1939, 247–59). Arthur is most likely a later addition.

Pen Arthur (Llangadog SN 71632370)   1618
The name given to a farmhouse and also the hillside above it. Charlotte Guest provides the following:

> On the Llangadock side of the Black mountain, we meet with fresh reminiscences of the Britsh Monarch in Pen Arthur, and Coiten Arthur. The latter is one of two large rocks in the bed of the Sawdde river, said to have been the hero's quoit, which he flung from the summit of Pen Arthur to its present position; a distance of about a mile. The rock beside the Coitan was thrown into the stream from the same eminence by a lady of those days being a pebble in her shoe which gave her some annoyance. (Guest, 1842, 364)

The MRA notes the form Tir Pen Arthur in 1618, but does not give an exact source.

Peuliniog   1175
The easternmost commote of Cantref Gwarthaf, situated between Narberth and Carmarthen, where Arthur and his men caught up with the Twrch Twyth, who had slain three of his men in *Culhwch and Olwen* (Bromwich and Evans, 1992, 39, ll. 1125–6).

CEREDIGION (CRD)

Cardigan (Cardigan SN 177459)   1172
The town is first named as the site of Arthur's Court in the French verse romance *Erec et Enide* by Chrétien de Troyes (1172) and is discussed in Chapter Two.

Claerddu (Ystrad Fflur SN 79206896)   1536
A tradition linked to this site was first recorded by John Leland in 1536:

The first river be side Tyue that I passid over was Clardue, that is to say Blak Clare, no great streame but cumming thoroug cragges. In the farther side of hit I saw ii. veri poore cotagis for somer dayres for catel, and hard by were ii. hilettes, thorough the wich Clarduy passith, wher they fable that a gigant striding was wont to wasch his hondes, and that Arture killid hym. The dwellers say also that the giant was buried therby, and shew the place.' (Smith, L. T., 1906, 119)

The river Claerddu flows through a small gorge near an old farm called Claerddu, and a platform for two small cottages survives. The mound where the giant was buried is identified by Grooms as being situated just west of the cottage platform (Grooms, 1993, 89–90).

Coetan Arthur (Llangwyryfon SN 609674)   1922
See **Pant Arthur** for details.

Garth Grugyn (Llanilar SN 62997456)   1175
An earthen mound, near Llanilar, where Arthur and his men fought against the Twrch Trwyth. Eli, Trachmyr and Grugyn were killed at this location in *Culhwch and Olwen* (Bromwich and Evans, 1992, 40, l. 1160).

King Arthur's Quoits (Blaenporth SN 2648)   1662
The site is first mentioned by George Owen in 1604 as Llech yr Ast (Owen, Henry, I, 251–2) but it is John Ray who during his travels in Wales in 1662 first records the Arthurian name:

> On a common near Blaynport lie a great many large stones; among the rest, one standing perpendicularly on one End in the Ground, and another large one leaning upon it, and two others, one on each side the leaning stone; these Stones they call King *Arthur's Quoits*. (Scott, 1760, 237)

The site was destroyed in the mid-nineteenth century (Houlder, 1994, 116–17).

Llain Arthur (Faenor SN 62688227)   1891
The cottage of Llain Arthur first appears on the first edition, six-inch OS map published in 1891.

Llanbadarn Fawr (Llanbadarn Fawr SN 59908101)   1120
The church of St Padarn in Llanbadarn Fawr, where King Arthur came into conflict with the saint according to the *Vita Paterni* (Wade-Evans, 1944, 261).

Llanborth (Penbryn SN 29615216)   1716
Theophilus Evans was the first to try and associate this site with the battle of Llongborth mentioned in *The Black Book of Carmarthen*, discussed on page 112.

Llys Arthur (Blaenrheidol SN 78658251)   **1747**
British Library, Additional MS 15,566 contains a copy of *Brut y Brehinedd* transcribed in the first quarter of the sixteenth century, and is interleaved throughout by Lewis Morris. One of the notes on p. 21 reads:

> At Dyffryn Castell near Eisteddva Gurig in Cwmwd Pervedd, Cardiganshire, are some mounds or banks of earth about 40 yards square, and seemingly the ruins of an old camp. It is known locally as Llys Arthur and the natives have an abundance of stories about Arthur and Gwenhwyfar. (Evans, J. G., 1898–1910, II, 955)

The name also appears on a map by Lewis Morris entitled 'A Plan of the Manor of Perveth commonly call'd cwmmwd y perveth', which dates to 1747 (Wmffre, 2004, 1070). The site, a low lying square earthwork, is still marked on current OS maps.

Maen Arthur (Ysbyty Ystwyth SN 7372)   **1568**
A note in the hand of Lewis Morris, in British Library, Additional MS 14,903, p. 21, states that 'Maen Arthur is on the river Ystwith near Pont rhydy groes' (Evans, J. G., 1898–1910, II, 955). The earliest form of the name is Manarthyr, found in NLW Crosswood Deeds, 13 (Wmffre, 2004, 908). The place in question appears to be an indeterminate point in the rocky outcrops that form the gorge through which the river Ystywth runs, near the village of Pontrhydygroes.

Melin Maen Arthur (Llanfihangel yn Creuddyn SN 738726)   **1566**
A site that probably takes its name from **Maen Arthur**, first noted in NLW Crosswood Deeds, 28, written in 1566 (Wmffre, 2004, 908).

Nant Arthur (Pont-rhyd-y-groes SN 74267485)   **1829**
The name of a house one-mile north of Pont-rhyd-y-groes, on the B4343, first recorded in the parish register. Wmmfre notes that the name 'seems to have been suggested by Maen Arthur' (Wmffre, 2004, 910).

Pant Arthur (Llangwyryfon SN 6067)   **1922**
A collection of notes by the local headmaster, James James, sent to David Thomas for his rural lore collection project, contains the following passage under the title, 'The Antiquities on Mynydd Bach and about Llyn Eiddwen', dated Saturday 14 October 1922:

> The tradition concerning Beddau'r Milwyr is that they are the burial places of Arthur's knights or soldiers. Coetanau Arthur are big stones in Pant Arthur which probably were cromlechs and it is said in the district that the quality of the stone in them is different to any stones in the surrounding rocks. (NLW David Thomas Collection, B45: Llangwyryfon)

The exact site is uncertain and the name is otherwise unknown.

Rhyd Arthur
See **Vadum Arthuri**.

Vadum Arthuri (Y Ferwig SN 23634888)   1165
A confirmation of grants made to Chertsey abbey by the Clare lords and witnessed
by Rhys ap Gruffydd contains the following:

> Scilicet ecclesiam Sancte Marie de Cardygan cum capella Sancti Petri de castello et
> cum duabus carucatis terre ad eam pertinentibus que iacent ab aquilonari parte vie
> que ducit versus Blaenporth et Canclauas usque ad vadum Arthuri et cum terra extra
> cimiterium ecclesie Sancte Marie de burgagia. (Pryce, 2005, 168)

> Namely St Mary's Church, Cardigan, with the castle chapel of St Peter and the two
> carucates of land pertaining to it north of the road leading towards Blaen-porth,
> Canllefaes up to Arthur's Ford and land beyond the cemetery of St Mary's church for
> establishing burgages.

Egerton Phillimore notes that 'Rhyd Arthur seems to be the place now called Rhyd
Fach, on a branch of the brook which joins the Teifi at Cardigan' (Owen, Henry, IV,
461), but (Wmffre, 31) considers the ford near Penbont to be more likely.

DENBIGHSHIRE (DEN)

Acre Arthur (Llanynys SJ 1062)   1610
MRA records the form Ackyr Arthur as a field name in the parish of Llanynys, from
a NLW Bachymbyd manuscript, but gives no further details. The name is also found
in a NLW Maenan MS from 1730, but it is not in the tithe schedule, suggesting it had
fallen out of use by 1840. The exact location is uncertain.

Bwrdd Arthur (Llanarmon Dyffryn Ceiriog SJ 07733462)   1795
A boulder, near the summit of Cadair Bronwen, on the border between Denbighshire and Merionethshire. The earliest reference is: 'Bwrdd Arthur, Arthur's Table,
a very large flat stone or cromlech, on Berwyn Mountain – Llandrillo' (Anon.,
1795, 292).

Bwrdd Arthur (Llansannan)
See **Round Table**.

Cae Carreg Arthur (Tre'r Castell)   1636
MRA notes the name Kay Carreg Arthir in NLW Wynnstay 82/69 dated to 1636. The
field can no longer be identified.

Clogwyn Arthur
See **Craig Arthur**.

Craig Arthur (Llangollen Rural SJ 223470)   **1780**
The name is first recorded by (Pennant, 1778–81, I, 375). A later folk tale concerning a giantess and St Collen briefly mentions 'Arthur the giant' and 'his fortress in the Eglywesg rocks' (Teithydd, 1860 and Grooms, 1993, 85–6). The name **Clogwyn Arthur** appears in (*Archaeologia Cambrensis*, 1874, 88) and is almost certainly to be identified with Craig Arthur.

Dinas Bran (Llangollen Urban SJ 22264306)   **1932**
The remains of this, impressively sited, thirteenth-century castle were first associated with the Grail Castle of Corbenic in (Loomis, 1932). The site has also been identified with the Chastiel Bran in the thirteenth-century Anglo-Norman tale *Fulk le Fitz Waryn* (Hathaway et al, 1975, 4 and 66).

Ffynnon Arthur (Llangollen Rural SJ 244406)   **1574**
Named in a document from 1574 (NLW Chirk Castle MS (F) 5) as Ffynnon Arthyr. One of the returns to the *Parochial Enquiries* of Edward Lhwyd notes, 'Nant Alis o Fynnonne Arthur ag i dhowrdwy vilhdir a chwarter is na'r dre' (Morris, 1912, part 2, 43). Nant Alis survives today in Cwm Alis farm. A reference to 'Ffynnon Arthur in Berwyn' in (*Archaeologia Cambrensis*, 1874, 88) is almost certainly the same site.

Foel Fenlli (Llanbedr Dyffryn Clwyd SJ 16296009)   **1258**
The Iron Age hill fort on the summit of Foel Fenlli is referred to as Caer Fenlli in a poem by Bleddyn Fardd (1258–84), discussed on page 66.

Glyn Arthur (Llangwyfan SJ 13546566)   **1840**
A house on the slopes of Moel Arthur, mistakenly said to be on Moel Famma in (*Archaeologia Cambrensis*, 1874, 88). The name does not appear on OSD 322 (1821), but is on the first printed map from 1840 and probably added during the revision of 1838.

Maen Huail (Ruthin SJ 12365826)   **1550**
A large boulder that sits on the town square in Ruthin, mentioned by Elis Gruffydd in his Chronicle, completed *c*.1550. The site is discussed in more detail on page 96.

Round Table (Llansannan SH 96046722)   **1536**
A natural feature noted by John Leland in 1536:

> There is in the paroch of Llansannan in the side of a stony hille a place where ther be
> 24. holes or places in a roundel for men to sitte in, but sum lesse and sum bigger, cutte

out of the mayne rok by mannes hand, and there children and young men cumming to seke their catelle use to sitte and play. Sum calle it the round table. Kiddes use ther communely to play and skip from sete to sete. (Smith, Lucy Toulmin, 1906, 99)

John Speed was the first to call it Arthur's Round Table in his notes on Denbighsire (Speed, 1611, 119). The site is named Arthurs Table on OSD 307 (1818), but Bwrdd Arthur on the published map of 1840, the name still in use today.

FLINTSHIRE (FLI)

Arthur's Hill (Hawarden SJ 3165)   1815
According to (Owen, Hywel Wyn, 1993, 70), the name appears in 'Survey of the Parish of Hawarden in the County of Flint, 1815' (Clwyd Record Office, D/BJ/346). There is no tradition about the name and it no longer appears on any maps.

Arthur's Parlour (Ysceifiog SJ 146716)   1938

> This is at the bottom of the parish of Ysceifiog, but is now hidden by a lake which was created recently. The late Mr J. E. Jones, Melin-y-Wern, Nannerch, told Mr Lewis Hughes that he had been in the cave many times when he was young. It was a big, long cave and at the far end was a chamber called Arthur's Parlour. The tradition is that Arthur Fawr, after the battle of Caer Moel Arthur, rested in his cave. (Isaac, 1938, 111)

(Coleman, 1956, 7) locates the cave at the nearby Craig y Shiagus, a limestone outcrop near the shores of the lake. Compare with the **Penbedw** material below.

Cae Arthur (Criccin SJ 0377)   1865
MRA records the form Cae Arthur in NLW Bodrhyddan MS B928.

Caerwys (Caerwys SJ 128729)   1550
Elis Gruffydd in his Chronicle identifies Carahis of the *Prose Lancelot* with Caerwys. See page 96.

Capel Y Gwail (Nannerch SJ 16666967)   1550
The name given to Arthur's chapel in Elis Gruffydd's Chronicle. The name was still known in 1697; see page 96.

Carreg Carn March Arthur (Mold Rural SJ 20246266)   1725
A stone inscribed with the judgement from a law case over the boundary between Flintshire and Denbighshire, mistakenly referred to as Maen Arthur in (Glennie, 1869, p. xxiii). A document entitled 'Presentment on Walking the Boundaries of

Mold 1725' refers to it as 'Carn March Arthur between Llanverras and Hendrebife' (Anon., 1922, 98). By 1869 the site had acquired the following folk tale:

> When Arthur reigned in Britain, like all monarchs, he had enemies to contend with, and the tale runs that – one day, being hard pressed, and retreating over these hills, his life was saved by the fleetness of his stead, which coming to an abrupt precipice, had to jump for his life; and it was from one of these surrounding hills he leaped, and alighted on this spot with such force, that his two fore feet left their impressions on the solid rock some inches in depth. (Leslie, 1869, 35)

Cist Arthur (Nannerch SJ 146658)   1737

'A copy of the Survey of the Lordship of Ruthin, 1737' details a walk around the boundary of the Lordship of Ruthin and contains the following line: 'to the top of the hill called *Moel Arthur* and from thence directly down to *Cist Arthur* and from thence to the top of *Bwlch ffraink*" (Fisher, 1914, 440). This corresponds with the southern slope of Moel Arthur. The exact site of this cist is not clear and some quarrying has taken place on the southern slope of the hill, perhaps destroying it in the process. See **Moel Arthur** below.

Craig Arthur (Trelawnyd SJ 09687871)   1610

A small limestone outcrop that has been partly quarried, near the southern boundary of the parish:

> The River Ffydhion runs through ye parish: having its first rise on Tegan mount, and joyns itself with ye streams of severall wells in ye parish: called by ye names of Ffynnonen Craig Arthyr, but why Craig Arthur is so call'd I could not learn. (Morris, R., 1909–11, part 1, 60)

The nearby farm is also known as Craig Arthur and in the recusant roll, PRO Wales 4 975/6 (8 James I), Certificate of Richard, bishop of St Asaph, 28 September 1610, under the parish of Relevenwyd (modern Trelawnyd) mentions 'Elizabeth Davies of Craig Arthur, widow' (Jones, E. Gwynne, 1945, 129).

Llys Arthur (Nannerch SJ 1669)   1550

Mentioned by Elis Gruffudd in his chronicle as being near Nannerch, but cannot be identified; see page 96.

Moel Arthur (Nannerch SJ 145661)   1694

The name first appears in a letter from Richard Mostyn to Edward Lhwyd dated February 28, 1694:

> There are abundance of entrenchments at the tops of our hills especially near the

borders of Lordshipps, there is one fair one above my house, that looks over the vale of Clwyd with a treble trench of one side & a single one to the precipice tis calld Moel Arthur. (Lloyd, Nesta, 1971–2, 44–7)

A document of 1873 states that 'Another legend is that Arthur's sword "Ex Calibur" was buried under some rocks near the top of the Bwlch [pass] just under Moel Arthur' (Lewis, J. B., 1971–2, 125). See also **Cist Arthur**. MRA notes the form Moel Iarthur for the site in 1567, which suggests that Moel Iarddur, a well-attested personal name, may have been the original name.

Parcarthur (Gwernymynydd SJ 20756273)   1871
Parcarthur Farm first appears on the six-inch OS map surveyed in 1871 and likely derives from its close proximity to **Carreg Carn March Arthur**.

Penbedw Stone Circle (Nannerch SJ 17116793)   1873
The Penbedw papers are in the Flintshire Record Office. D/B/221, dated 1873, gives 'reasons why Penbedw may probably be the site of King Arthur's 8th battle'. The document suggests that the battle of Guinnion from the *Historia Brittonum* should be understood as Gwynedd, and as the largest hill fort in Gwynedd is Penycloddiau then that is the most likely place for the battle! The author also notes the proximity of Moel Arthur, Cefn y Gadfa (Ridge of Battle) on Moel Fammau, and the remains of a stone circle in the park of the house of Penbedw. He then claims that 'There is a legend that the women and children witnessed a great battle from the encampment at Penycloddiau, when it was going on in the narrow valley that leads down to Nannerch.' The document ends with the statement:

> That Arthur's 8th battle was fought in this neighbourhood, and that the stone circle and maenhir in Penbedw Park were erected in memory of the event and in honour of those who were slain. It has in other instances been known that the body of the chief man was buried at the foot of the maenhir, and those of inferior rank within the circle. (Lewis, J. B., 1971–2, 124–5)

Pen Gwely Arthur (Gronant SJ 0983)   1721
A parcel of land in Gronant, mentioned in a mortgage from 1721 (Denbighshire Record Office, Allington Hughes & Bate, 1199).

Penycloddiau
See **Penbedw Stone Circle**.

Perthi Arthur (Whitford SJ 1478)   1347
MRA records the name Perthi Arthur from a document dated 1347, although frustratingly the exact source is uncertain and the site cannot be identified.

Tyddyn Arthur (Waen SJ 06147330)   **1840**
A small dwelling on the first series OS map (1840), but on OSD 309 (1818) the same
place is called Tyddyn Eithin; see page 134.

GLAMORGAN (GLA)

Arthur's Butts Hill (Pentyrch ST 106836)   **1580**
The name first appears on Christopher Saxton's map of Glamorgan (Saxton, 1580)
as 'Arthors buttes hill'. The modern name for the site is Garth Hill, near Pentyrch,
Llantrisant, and the older name has passed from usage.

Arthur's stone (Reynoldstone SS 49139055)   **1693**
This well-known monument, also known as Maen Ceti, was first associated with
Arthur by John Williams in a letter to Edward Lhwyd dated 30 November 1693 (MS
Ashmole 1817b, fols 292–3): '… the Common people call it Arthur's Stone by a lift of
vulgar imagination attributing to yt hero an extravagant size and strength' (Emery,
1965, 63–4).

Arthyr Wood (Llancarfan ST 038714)   **1734**
Arthyr Wood first appears in a document from 1734 (Clark, 1866, 395). The Welsh
form, Coed Arthur, first appears on the first series one-inch OS map from 1833.

Bochrhiw Carn (Bedlinog SO 09960494)   **1100**
A hilltop where Arthur, Cai and Bedwyr play dice in the *Vita Cadoci* (Wade-Evans,
1944, 27). The site corresponds to the hill top known to modern maps as Mynydd
Fochrhiw, near the village of Fochrhiw, three miles east of Merthyr Tydfil; see page 20.

Bwlch y Gyfylchi (Michaelstone-Super-Avon SS 807955)   **1578**
First mentioned by Rees Merrick in 1578, 'At a place called Bwlch y Gyfylchi stand
two stones distant [...] foot between which it is said that one of Arthur's knights was
buried' (James, 1983, 107). The exact location uncertain, but it was probably in the
vicinity of the house called Gyfylchi on modern maps, which is near a pass between
two valleys.

Caer Craig Dinas Gawr (Penderyn SN 9103)   **1597**
A hill fort where Arthur killed a giant, according to Siôn Dafydd Rhys in his tract on
Welsh giants (Grooms, 1993, 313).

Castell Cribawr (Cefn Cribwr SS 841826)   **1597**
The name given to the hill-fort of Pen-y-Castell, where Arthur killed three giantesses
and the giant Cribawr according to Siôn Dafydd Rhys in his treatise on Giants in
Wales (Grooms, 1993, 311).

Coed Arthur
See **Arthyr Wood**.

Craig-y-Dinas (Ystradfellte SN 91450808)   **1800**
The folk tale known as 'the Welshman on London Bridge', in which a young Welshman meets a stranger on London Bridge and is told about a cave near his home in
Wales which contains treasure and is guarded by a sleeping King Arthur, has been
told in its basic form using a variety of different locations for the cave, but the earliest
printed version is in (Waring, 1850, 95–8). This is based upon the earlier manuscript
version by Iolo Morganwg, written *c*.1800 (NLW 13121B, 419–22).

Crug Tor y Bedol (Michaelstone-Super-Avon SS 82399900)   **1578**
A mound marking the burial of a tyrant killed by Arthur, according to Rice Merrick
in 1578:

> It is said that a tyrant named Pedolhearn was slain by Arthur within this parish,
> where a great heap of earth is at this day to be seen, called thereof Crug Tor y Bedol,
> upon the top of a mountain named Mynydd Tor y Bedol, so also named of the
> slaughter of this tyrant, of some termed a giant. (James, 1983, 107)

The site can be identified with a tumulus on a mountain area called Banwen Torybe-
tel (Grooms, 1993, 213).

Ffynnon Arthur   **1203**
This name appears in an agreement between the Cistercian houses of Caerleon and
Margam concerning the division of lands between the rivers Neath and Taf, preserved in British Library, Harleian Charter 75 A. 32 (dated 1203). The name is not
otherwise known and the exact site is uncertain.

> Scilicet quod sicut Rotheni Maur a primo capite suo cadit in fluvium Taph. Et ab illo
> capie in directum usque ad Fennaun Arthur. Et a fennaun Arthur usque ad Magnam
> Polam. Et ab illa pola sicut aqua de Wrelec cadit in Fluvium de Neht. (Clark, 1910,
> II, 289)

> From the source of the Rhondda Mawr to its fall into the Taff, and from that point to
> Fynnon Arthur. And from Ffynnon Arthur to Magna Pola [Llyn Fawr?], thence to
> the point where the Gwrelych falls into the Neath.

Pwll Arthur (St Fagans ST 11247761)   **1885**
A small pool near St Fagans named on the first edition of the six-inch OS map, published in 1885.

Tir Llech Arthur (Llangiwg SN 7205)   1602

MRA notes a conveyance (Glamorgan Record Office, D/D Yc 398) dated 28 September 1602 for the transfer of two parcels of land in the parish of Llangiwg, one of which is named Tire Leach Arthur.

MERIONETHSHIRE (MER)

Bryn Arthur (Llangar SJ 059429)   1693

A field mentioned in a letter from John Lloyd to Edward Lhwyd dated 29 December 1693 (NLW, Peniarth MS 427, fol. 31r):

> Not far from hence near Plas issa where Ken Eyton lives (who was with me this journey, as you shall hear from him) is Rhyd y Saeson, where a battle was fought, but I know not when. The English fought on one side of the way & the Welsh on the other. That field is called Bryn Arthur, & the next behind it Maes y Llaes & not far off Llwyn Cadwgan or Caewgan. Some say Dymma lle doed ô hyd ir Saeson, as if they were pursued so far. (Lloyd, John, 1851, 56)

The field is probably situated on Nant Rhyd y Saeson, near Plas-isaf.

Bwlch-y-Groes (Llanuwchllyn SH 913232)   1597

A localised folk tale, ultimately based upon an episode from the *Historia regum Britanniae* of Geoffrey of Monmouth written in 1138 (Reeve and Wright, 2007, 226), is associated with this location by Siôn Dafydd Rhys in 1597. For a further discussion see page 101:

> Itto the giant, calling himself the king of Gwynedd in the time of Arthur, sent to Arthur to ask for his beard. And Arthur denied it to him. And as a result of that they met on the top of a hill called Bwlch-y-Groes between Mawddwy and Penllyn in the country of Meirionydd. And in the meeting at Itto's wish they cast their weapons away from them in order to prove their strength. And at last they struggled and by rolling, they came to the valley bottom, the place called Blaen Cynllwyd, having pulled each other's beards. And in memory to that, that hill is called Rhiw y Barfau. And after that, they fought with their swords and Arthur killed the giant, in which place the grave of Itto is still to be seen today at the foot of the slope. (Grooms, 1993, 303)

Cadair Arthur (Llanfihangel y Pennant SH 711130)   1789

The 1789 edition of Camden's *Britannia* (Gough, 1789, 540), in relation to the summit of Cadair Idris, notes that 'near another lake on the top is the supposed chair of Arthur, a natural cavity in the rock.' The name is rarely mentioned in later sources.

Caer Gai (Llanuwchllyn SH 87753147) **1450**
The remains of a Roman Fort associated with Arthur's childhood by some writers. The name is first found in a poem by Ieuan Brydydd Hir in 1450 (Bryant-Quinn, 2000, 25). The site was also known as Llys Arthur in the late seventeenth century (Morris, 1909–11, part 2, 71). The site is discussed in more detail in (Roberts, Thomas, 1944, 12–14) and on page 98.

Camlan (Mawddwy SH 8511) **1571**
The name Camlan first appears in the A-text of the *Annales Cambriae* as the site of the final battle of Arthur, and also the place where Mordred fell; see page 105. The name Camlan is given to a small vill, or township, in the medieval lordship of Mawddwy and is first attested in NLW Bronwydd MS 2224, a document dated 26 September 1571, and according to the schedule is a 'Release of lands and tenements called Dolykoll and Maes broyn lying between the streams called Y kwm byghan and Nant yr esgolion in the vill of Kamlan within the lordship of Mowthoy'. It also appears in a document from 1598 entitled 'The Mowddwy Composcision' (*Royal Commission on Land Minutes of Evidence*, IV, 1898, 955b). The name is no longer in administrative use, but survives on modern maps in the following names:

Camlan Isaf	SH 8513 1123
Camlan Uchaf	SH 8580 1195
Bron Camlan	SH 8546 1180
Maes y Camlan	SH 8568 1325

Camlan is also shown on modern mapping near the pass of Bwlch Oerddrws, on the main A470 road between the village of Dinas Mawddwy and Dolgellau. It is attractive to think that the name should be attached to this strategic pass between north and south Wales, but it is not found associated with this location on the OSD and there is no earlier documentary evidence to support the association. Also of note is Afon Gamlan, a river that runs down from Cwm Camlan and into the river Eden north of Dolgellau. According to MRA, the form Afon Gamlan can be found in Bangor University, Nannau MS 180 from 1592, and another document form the same year preserves the form Afon Gamlon (TNA SC 12/30/24, fol. 42).

Carn March Arthur (Tywyn SN 65049821) **1834**
A stone bearing this name first appears on OSD 338 (1834). An explanation of the name appeared in 1853:

> Be that as it may, King Arthur and his war horse have the credit amongst the mountaineers here of ridding them of the monster, in place of Hu the mighty, in proof of which is shown an impression on a neighbouring rock bearing a resemblance to those made by the shoe or hoof of a horse, as having been left there by his charger

when our British Hercules, was engaged in this redoubtable act of prowess, and this impression has been given the name of Carn March Arthur, the hoof of Arthur's horse, which it retains to this day. (Pughe, John, 1853, 202)

Carreg Arthur (Llanddwywe is y Graig)
See **Coetan Arthur** (Llanddwywe is y Graig).

Cerrig Arthur (Llanaber SH 63171888)   1913
First recorded by A. N. Palmer during his fieldwork in August 1913 for the Merionethshire inventory volume for the Royal Commission. The name cannot be traced back any earlier:

> About 200 yards north-east of Fron Wen farm House, now appurtenant to the farm called Sylvaen are two standing stones, 4 feet apart which are known locally as the Druids Stones but by the occupier of the farm they are called Cerrig Arthur, Arthur's Stones. (RCAHMW, 1921, 43)

Cerrig Arthur (Llanenddwyn Dyffryn Ardudwy SH 58852284)   1868
A name occasionally given to two cromlechs situated next to each other, better known as the Dyffryn Ardudwy chambered tombs. The earliest note of an association with Arthur is in (*Archaeologia Cambrensis*, 1868, 468): 'One or both of these cromlechs is associated, as usual, with the name of Arthur.' The earliest source actually to use the name Cerrig Arthur is: 'These cromlechau are traditionally connected with Arthur, who is fabled to have thrown the stones from the top of Moelfre; they are sometimes called Cerrig Arthur and sometimes Coetan Arthur' (RCAHMW, 1921, 99).

Coetan Arthur (Dyffryn Ardudwy SH 60312281)   1795
The name given to the capstone of a cromlech that first appears in the *Cambrian Register* (1795, 295): 'Coetan Arthur, Arthur's Quoit, a cromlech near Llanddwywau having the print of a large hand dexterously carved on the side of it, as if sunk in from the weight of holding it'. See pages 136–7.

Coetan Arthur (Llanenddwyn Dyffryn Ardudwy)
See **Cerrig Arthur** (Llanenddwyn Dyffryn Ardudwy).

Llys Arthur
See **Caer Gai**.

Maes Arthur (Botalog SN 6099)   1592
MRA notes the name Mayse Arthur from 1592 (TNA, LR 2/236, 73), but from 1633 onwards it is called Maes Erthyr.

Ogof Arthur   **1901**
The earliest reference to this name is in a variant of the London Bridge story, for
which see **Craig y Dinas** under Glamorganshire:

> To return to Iolo's yarn, one may say that there are traces of his story as at one time
> current in Merionethshire, but with the variation that the Welshman met the wizard
> not on London Bridge but at a fair at Bala, and that the cave was somewhere in Meri-
> oneth: the hero was Arthur, and the cave was known as Ogof Arthur. Whether any
> such cave is still known I cannot tell. (Rhŷs, 1901, 464)

The association of the tale with Bala is found earlier in a book written for children
(Edwards, O. M., 1894), but the name Ogof Arthur does not appear.

Sylvaen (Barmouth SH 63171888)   **1852**
A brief notice in (*Archaeologia Cambrensis*, 1852, 70–1) states that

> Mr Ffoulkes exhibited a rubbing of a large figure resembling the blade of a sword, of which
> there are a pair sculptured upon a rock, in an inclosure called 'The Field of the Swords'
> on a farm named Sylvaen between Barmouth and Dolgellau. An account of this sculp-
> ture, with its accompanying legend, affirming it to have been produced by King Arthur's
> throwing his sword against the rock, may be expected by the readers of *Arch. Camb.*

However, no such tale is given and it seems to have recieved little notice since.

Tyddyn Arthur (Llanfachreth SH 77442074)   **1592**
MRA notes the name Tyddyn Arthur from 1592 in (TNA LR 2/236). The name also
appears on OSD 303 (1819) and on all subsequent OS mapping.

MONMOUTHSHIRE (MON)

Arthur's Round Table
See **King Arthur's Round Table**.

Cadair Arthur (Llantilio Pertholey SO 272187)   **1697**
A name given to some stones on the summit of Sugar Loaf mountain, 'It [parish of
Llantilo Bertholey] is bounded on the W with the Mountaine called fforest Moel (the
sumit or top of which mountain is called Pen y Val, where are certain stones called
Cadeir Arthur' (Morris, R., 1909–11, part 3, 72).

Caerleon (ST 3390)   **1138**
The court of Arthur according to Geoffrey of Monmouth in his *Historia regum
Britanniae*, which describes it as being 'admirably positioned on the river Usk not far

from the mouth of the River Severn in Glamorgan' (Reeve and Wright, 2007, 208). Frequently mentioned in later romances and no doubt referring to the remains of the Roman fortress on the site.

Caerleon, cave at (Caerleon ST 3291)   **1901**
John Rhŷs gives a variant on the **Craig y Dinas** in Glamorganshire story, placing the cave, which contains the soldiers of Arthur, in a wood near Caerleon (Rhŷs, 1901, 462–4).

Cist Arthur (Llantilio Pertholey SO 331182)   **1697**
A stone, the exact location of which is uncertain. 'There upon Skerrid Fawr a great stone shaped like a house called Cist Arthur, in English Arthur's Chest, as Cadeir Arthur is Arthur's Chair' (Morris, R., 1909–11, part 3, 73).

Croes Arthur (Cross Ash SO 408197)   **1611**
A boundary stone called Crosse Arthur, between the manor of Skenfrith and Manor of Monmouth, is noted in the Book of Surveys in the office of the Duchy of Lancaster, dated 5 July 1611 (Rees, W, 1953, 92).

Dinas Arthur (Cwm Iou)   **1799**
(Bradney, I, 235) mentions a sale of land by Edward fifth Earl of Oxford in 1799, and one of the entries in the sale catalogue reads: 'Dinas Arthur, 9 acres, let to William Price at £8.' The name no longer exists and the exact site is uncertain.

King Arthur's Hall (Whitchurch SO 54611559)   **1789**
A well-known cave on the hill called Little Doward, and the earliest reference to the name is found in (Gough, 1789, II, 448).

Maes Arthur (Coedkernew ST 267861)   **1798**
A meadow half a mile south of Bassaleg, first mentioned by William Coxe during a tour in the area in 1798, discusssed on page 128.

Rhyd Gwrthebau (Llanhennock ST 3894)   **1100**
A ford on the River Usk, where Arthur received his tribute of cattle from St Cadog, according to the Vita Cadoci (Wade-Evans, 1944, 72), dicussed on page 21.

Round Table (Caerleon ST 33829035)   **1405**
The remains of the Roman amphitheatre at Caerleon and, according to (Gough, 1789, I, 480), 'the inhabitants call it King Arthur's Round Table.' Gough is the earliest definite reference to the name, but there is an earlier possible mention in the *Chronicles of Enguerrand de Monstrelet* for the year 1405, written during the Glyndŵr rebellion:

Thence they marched into the country of Linorquie [pays de Morganie], went to the Round Table, which is a noble abbey, and then took the road to Worcester, where they burnt the suburbs and adjoining country. (Johnes, 1840, I, 28; French text in Buchon, 1857, I, 82)

The site is almost certainly Caerleon, and the nearby abbey in question Llantarnam. It is an interesting early example of Arthur being associated with a landscape feature by an author from outside Wales.

Tredunnock (Llanhennock ST 37889480)   **1100**
A village on the west bank of the river Usk associated with Arthur in the *Vita Cadoci*; see **Rhyd Gwerthebau** above.

Ty Arthur (Abertillery SO 206056)   **1885**
A property near Roseheyworth colliery in Abertillery, that first appears on the six-inch map printed in 1885. The property has since been consumed by the expansion of the colliery (Olding, 1987).

MONTGOMERYSHIRE (MTG)

Arthur's Gate (Montgomery SO 22259698)   **1336**
One of the four medieval gates in the town walls of Montgomery, noted by John Leland in 1536: 'Great ruines of the waulle yet apere ad vestigial of iiii. Gates thus cawlyd, Kedewen Gate, Chyrbyry Gate, Arturs Gate, Kery Gate' (Smith, L. T., 1906, 11). However, the name appears in 1336 as *portam Arthury* in NLW Powis Castle MS 16255 (Richards, M., 1965, 182).

Arthur Street (Montgomery SO 22219650)   **1300**
The street that ran to **Arthur's Gate** in Montgomery is first recorded as Arturestret in NLW Powis Castle MS 16272 (Richards, M., 1965, 182).

Cae Arthur (Llandyssil SO 20579455)   **1840**
A field name on the tithe schedule (1840) for the parish of Llandyssil, field number 734.

Carreg Arthur (Manafon SJ 135051)   **1836**
A natural boulder standing on the edge of the upland district called Y Byrwydd that appears on the first edition one-inch OS map from 1836. There is seemingly no tradition associated with it.

Ffynnon Arthur (Llanfihangel yng Ngwynfa SJ 09811552)   **1309**
The medieval township of Finnoun Arthur, near Llanfihangel yng Ngwynfa, is first recorded in a document from 1309 entitled 'Inquisitio post mortem Griffini de la Pole' (Inq. 2 Edw, II no. 79; printed in Bridgeman, 1868, 157). The only attempt to

identify a specific site clearly describes the well, situated at SJ10291737 on earlier OS maps, as that known to the local populace as Ffynnon Arthur (Owen, E., 1898).

Gwern Arthur (Llanwyddelan SJ 093012)   **1695**
NLW Powis Castle MS 12775, dated 1695, gives: 'in the parish of Llanwythelan, a messauge and land called Gwerne Arthur in the same passage' (Charles, B. G., 1972, III, 18). This should probably be identified with the field called Wern Arthur, numbered 894 on the tithe schedule.

Llwyn y Meini Hirion (Pennant Melangell)   **1597**
Siôn Dafydd Rhys in his treatise on giants in Wales notes that a giant named Ceimiad was killed at a site marked by two standing stones called Llwyn y Meini Hirion in the parish of Pennant Melangell (Grooms, 1993, 316). The name no longer survives, and Grooms identifies the site with the remains of a burial mound (SJ 13802486) and a standing stone (SJ 13692482), but these seem to be a long way from Pennant Melangell (Grooms, 1993, 152–3).

Melin Arthur (Manafon SJ 10740166)   **1836**
This name first appears on the first series one-inch OS map in 1836. It appears on modern maps as Lower Mill.

Porth Arthur
See **Arthur's Gate**.

PEMBROKESHIRE (PEM)

Bedd Arthur (Mynachlog Ddu SN 13053251)   **1697**
A stone circle on the Prescelli hills, first named in the notebook of Edward Lhwyd with an accompanying illustration (Morris, 1909–11, part 2, 97–8).

Bryn Arthur (Mynachlog Ddu SN 14612943)   **1891**
A house that first appears on the first edition, six-inch OS map (1891).

Carn Arthur (Mynachlog Ddu SN 13403223)   **1810**
A natural outcrop of rock on the Prescelli hills that is first referred to as Carn Arthur on OSD 185 (1810) and is still marked on modern maps.

Cerrig Meibion Arthur (Mynachlog Ddu SN 11823102)   **1898**
Two standing stones in Cwm Cerwyn, in the parish of Mynachlog Ddu. The earliest reference to this name appears in (*Archaeologia Cambrensis*, 1898, 74): 'two of these stones we see from Clysaithmaen are called the stones of the sons of Arthur.' Later works associate these stones with the Boar Hunt episode from *Culhwch and Olwen*

and give them the Welsh name still in use today. There is no evidence that the name existed before the publication of that tale in 1842. See **Cwm Cerwyn** below.

Coetan Arthur (Newport SN 06033935)   **1872**
A well-known cromlech in the parish of Newport first linked with Arthur by R. W. Barnwell in 1872, who notes that 'it is called "Careg Coetan", and is associated with the name of Arthur' (Barnwell, 1872, 140).

Coetan Arthur (St David's SM 72532805)   **1600**
A well-known cromlech situated on the cliff top at St David's Head. The monument is referred to as Arthur's Quoit in a manuscript probably written by George Owen *c.*1600 (Willis, 1717, 63).

Coetan Arthur (Nevern SN 09943702)   **1694**
The impressive and well-known cromlech of Pentre Ifan. The earliest reference to this site is in George Owen's *Description of Penbrokeshire* (1604) where he notes that 'they call it *Y Gromlech*' (Owen, Henry, 1892–1936, I, 252). The name Coetan Arthur is first associated with the monument in a letter dated 20 January 1694 by Erasmus Saunders to Edward Lhwyd (Roberts, B. F., 2010, 37–8). The Arthurian name is otherwise unknown for this monument, suggesting that it is was being used generically.

Cwm Cerwyn (Boncath SN 1031)   **1175**
In the tale *Culhwch ac Olwen* this is the location where Arthur and his men confront the Twrch Trwyth. The boar kills four of his warriors and then in a second attack slays four more, including Gwydre the son of Arthur (Bromwich and Evans, 1992, 39, l. 1112). The name survives in the hill Foel Cwmcerwyn, the highest point in the Prescelly hills (Charles, B. G., 1992, 125).

Eisteddfa Arthur (Nevern SN 10153508)   **1607**
The name is associated with a collection of stones and the earliest name for the site is recorded as Jestethva in 1506. In 1607 the name Ysteddva Arthyr appears for the first time and still appears on modern maps (Charles, B. G., 1992, 137).

Ffynnon Arthur (Clydau SN 250314)   **1745**
A letter from David Lewes to the antiquarian Lewis Morris, dated 4 July 1745, provides the following note:

> As for the storie of King Arthur killing Howell ap Naw the brother of Gildas menconed by Bishop Usher in his book de *Britt Eclesiarum Primordiis* I had the like storie from an ancient man but that the action was near Clydey in the County of Pembroke, the difference was he was named Owen instead of Howell, there is a place in the parish called ffynnon Arthur. (Owen, Hugh, 1947, I, 161)

The story of the killing of Huail by Arthur is discussed on page 96. The source for the informant's story is (Ussher, 1639, 677). The name Park Ffynnon Arthur appears on the tithe schedule for the parish of Clydau (1849, no. 1009) and is most likely the site in question.

Ffynnon Penarthur
See **Penarthur.**

Maen Arthur (St David's SM 747269)   **1326**
The name Maynarthr first appears attached to a parcel of land in *The Black Book of St David's* from 1326 (Willis-Bund, 1902, 54). It seems to have influenced the name of the nearby farm, **Penarthur**, and several important inscribed stones have been found in the area (Edwards, N., 2007, 451–4). One of these stones was referred to in the early seventeenth century as standing in a field called Arthur's Stone (Willis, B., 1717, 65). For a further discussion on the development of the name see (Charles, B. G., 1992, 296).

Nyfer, river   **1175**
In the tale of *Culhwch and Olwen*, Arthur ranged his warriors on both side of the river Nyfer (Bromwich and Evans, 1992, 39, l. 1109). The river Nyfer has its source on the hill of Frenni Fawr, near the village of Crymych and flows westwards into Cardigan Bay at Newport.

Penarthur (St David's SM 74792649)   **1326**
Closely associated with **Maen Arthur**. The earliest form known is Panthar from 1326 (Willis-Bund, 1902, 62), and the form 'Maenarthyr Ycha alias PenArthur' is mentioned in 1608. Charles suggests that the 'original name was probably Pen Maen Arthur' (Charles, B. G., 1992, 297). He also draws attention to the fact that a person called Thomas Arthur is named in the *Black Book of St David's*. This may account for the name, rather than the legendary Arthur. The name is still on modern OS maps as Penarthur farm, and nearby is **Pont Penarthur** (SM 753264) and a small lake called **Ffynnon Penarthur** (SM 753265).

Pont Penarthur
See **Penarthur.**

Porth Cerddin   **1175**
In the tale of *Culhwch and Olwen*, Arthur and his men disembark on their return from Ireland at a place called Porth Cerddin in Dyfed (Bromwich and Evans, 1992, 37, ll. 1055–6). The exact location of Porth Cerddin in Dyfed is uncertain. The name translates as 'the Harbour of the rowan tree', and it might be Porth Mawr near St David's Head (SM 731268), or Pwll Crochan five miles west of Fishguard (SM

885364), both of which fit the available evidence. Before moving on to the next task there is a short line that states: 'And Mesur-y-Peir is there.' The name means 'Measure of the Cauldron', and presumably it was situated at, or very close to, Porth Cerddin (Foster, 1940, 30–1).

Mynyw (St David's SM 753253)   1175
In the tale Culhwch and Olwen, Arthur spends a night in Mynyw, the Welsh name for St David's, after arriving from Ireland (Bromwich and Evans, 1992, 38, ll. 1098–9).

RADNORSHIRE (RAD)

Arthur's Chair (Painscastle SO 1644)   1656
The only reference to this monument is found in the *Monumenta Britannica* by John Aubrey (1684):

> Anno 1656, as I rode from Brecknock to Radnor, on top of a mountain (I think not far from Painscastle) is a monument of stones like a sepulcher, but much bigger than that at Holyhead [Trifigneth]; the stones were great and rudely placed. I think they called it Arthur's Chair or such a name (query Sir John Hoskyns for this), but this monument did no more belong to him, [than] did that called Round Table in Cumberland. See Ortelius – Arthur Cadahyr in Brecknockshire, 1570 *Theatrum Orbis Terrarum*. (Fowles and Legg, 1980, 826)

Aubrey might be giving the monument its name retrospectively, inspired by the **Cadair Arthur** in Brecoshire, originating with Gerald of Wales, that appeared on Humphrey Llwyd's map (Ortelius, 1570). Probably a monument on The Begwns, south of Painscastle.

Fontem Arthur (Llanbadarn Fynydd SO 05987855)   1200
A boundary marker in a charter for Cwm-Hir Abbey dated 1200. The site is possibly the well shown on modern maps as St David's Well (Charles, B. G., 1970, 72).

Knucklas Castle (Bugeildy SO 24937453)   1478
Arthur is first associated with Knucklas castle by William of Worcester: 'Knucklas Castle 1½ miles from the town of Knighton and 3 miles from Clun, is said to have been founded by King Arthur' (Harvey, J. H., 1969, 201). A possible reason for this association is the known Arthurian interests of the Mortimer dynasty who built the castle; see page 50. The castle was also the site of a folk-tale recorded by Siôn Dafydd Rhys in 1597 (Grooms, 1993, 316).

BIBLIOGRAPhY

Ab Ithel, J. Williams (ed. and trans.), *Annales Cambriae* (London, 1860).

Ackerman, W., *An Index of Arthurian Names in Middle English* (Stanford, 1952).

Alcock, Leslie, *Arthur's Britain: History and Archaeology, A.D. 367–634* (London, 1971).

—— *'By South Cadbury is that Camelot ...', The Excavation of Cadbury Castle 1966–70* (London, 1972).

Anderson, John, *The Book of British Topography* (London, 1866).

Andrews, R. M., Costigan, N. G. (Bosco), James, Christine, Lynch, Peredur I., McKenna, Catherine and Owen, Morfydd E. (eds), *Gwaith Bleddyn Fardd a Beirdd Eraill Ail Hanner y Drydedd Ganrif Ar Ddeg* (Cardiff, 1996).

Anglo, Sydney, 'The *British History* in Early Tudor Propaganda – with an Appendix of the Manuscript Pedigrees of the Kings of England, Henry VI to Henry VIII', *Bulletin of the John Rylands Library Manchester*, 44 (1961–2), 17–48.

—— *Images of Tudor Kingship* (London, 1992).

—— *Spectacle, Pageantry, and Early Tudor Policy*, second edn (Oxford, 1997).

Anon., *A History of Anglesey* (London, 1775).

—— 'Topography of Wales', *The Cambrian Register* (1795).

—— 'Rhyl MSS. – Celtic Antiquities no. II', *Archaeologia Cambrensis* (1849), 1–6.

—— 'Hynafiaethau Llangwyfan, Mon', *Y Brython*, 2 (July, 1859), 138–9.

—— 'Plwyf Beddgelert', *Y Brython*, 4 (1861), 329–36.

—— 'Arthurian Localities in the Principality and the Marches', *Archaeologia Cambrensis*, (1872), 71–2.

—— 'Presentment on Walking the Boundaries of Mold 1725', *Flintshire Historical Society Publications*, 9 (1922), 98.

Anscombe, A., 'Local Names in the 'Arthuriana' in the "Historia Brittonum"', *Zeitschrift für Celtische Philologie*, 5 (1904), 103–23.

The Arthurian Collection Catalogue (Clwyd, 1994).

Ashe, Geoffrey, *King Arthur's Avalon: The Story of Glastonbury* (London, 1957).

—— *A Guidebook to Arthurian Britain* (London, 1980).

—— 'A Certain Very Ancient Book: Traces of an Arthurian Source in Geoffrey of Monmouth's History', *Speculum*, 56 (1981) 301–23.

—— *The Discovery of King Arthur* (London, 1985).

—— *The Traveller's Guide to Arthurian Britain* (Glastonbury, 1997).

Asher, Martha (trans.), *Lancleot-Grail 8: The Post-Vulgate Cycle: The Merlin Continuation* (Cambridge, 2010).

Ashley, Mike, *The Mammoth Book of King Arthur* (London, 2005).

Aurell, Martin, 'Henry II and Arthurian Legend', in Christopher Harper-Bill and Nicholas Vincent (eds), *Henry II: New Interpretations* (Woodbridge, 2007), pp. 362–94.

Babington, C. and Lumby, J. R. (eds), *Polychronicon Ranulphi Higden monachi Cestrensis*, 9 vols, Rolls Series, 41 (1865–86).

Bachellery, E. (ed. and trans.), *L'oeuvre poétique de Gutun Owain*, 2 vols (Paris, 1950–1).

Barber, Chris, *Mysterious Wales* (Newton Abbot, 1982).

—— *More Mysterious Wales* (Newton Abbott, 1986).

—— and David Pykitt, *Journey to Avalon* (Abergavenny, 1993).

—— and David Pykitt, *The Legacy of King Arthur* (Abergavenny, 2005).

Barber, Richard, 'The *Vera Historia de Morte Arthuri* and Its Place in Arthurian Tradition', *Arthurian Literature*, 1 (1981), 62–78.

—— Addendum on the *Vera Historia de Morte Arthuri*', in James P. Carley (ed.), *Glastonbury Abbey and the Arthurian Tradition* (Cambridge, 2001), pp. 143–4.

Barnwell, E. L., 'On Some South Wales Cromlechs', *Archaeologia Cambrensis* (1872), 81–143.

Barrell, John, *Edward Pugh of Ruthin 1763-1813: A Native Artist* (Cardiff, 2013).

Barron, W. R. J. (ed.), *Sir Gawain and the Green Knight* (Manchester, 1998).

—— (ed.), *The Arthur of the English*, revised edn (Cardiff, 2001).

—— and Weinberg, S. C. (eds), *Lawmans Brut* (Harlow, 1995).

Bartlett, Robert, *Gerald of Wales: A Voice of the Middle Ages* (Stroud, 2006).

Bartrum, P. C., 'Arthuriana from the Genealogical Manuscripts', *National Library of Wales Journal*, 14 (1965), 242–45.

—— (ed.), *Early Welsh Genealogical Tracts* (Cardiff, 1966).

—— 'Y Pedwar Ar Hugain A Farnwyd Yn Gadarnaf* (The Twenty-Four Kings Judged to be the Mightiest)', *Études Celtiques*, 12 (1968–71), 157–94.

—— *Welsh Genealogies AD 300-1400*, 8 vols (Cardiff, 1974).

—— *Welsh Genealogies AD 1400-1500*, 18 vols (Aberystwyth, 1983).

—— *A Welsh Classical Dictionary* (Aberystwyth, 1993).

Baumgartner, Emmanuèle, 'The Prose *Tristan*', in Glyn S. Burgess,and Karen Pratt (eds), *The Arthur of the French* (Cardiff, 2006), pp. 325–41.

Baynes, E. Neil, 'The Megalithic Remains of Anglesey', *Transactions of the Honourable Society of Cymmrodorion* (1910–11), 2–91.

The Bibliographical Bulletin of the International Arthurian Society, (1949–).

Bick, David and Davies, Philip Wyn, *Lewis Morris and the Cardiganshire Mines* (Aberystwyth, 1994).

Bieler, Ludwig (ed. and trans.), *The Patrician Texts in the Book of Armagh*, Scriptores Latini Hiberniae, 10 (Dublin, 1979).

Blackett, A. T. and Wilson, Alan, *Arthur: King of Glamorgan and Gwent* (Cardiff, 1981).

—— *Arthur and the Charters of the Kings* (Cardiff, 1981).

Blackett, Baram and Wilson, Alan, *Artorius Rex Discovered* (Cardiff, 1986).

Blake, Steve and Lloyd, Scott, *The Keys to Avalon* (Shaftesbury, 2000).

—— *Pendragon: The Origins of Arthur* (London, 2002).

Boardman, Steve, Davies, John Reuben and Williamson, Elia (eds), *Saints' Cults in the Celtic Worlds* (Woodbridge, 2009).

Bollard, John, 'Traddodiad a Dychan yn *Breudwydd Rhonabwy*', *Llên Cymru*, 13 (1985), 155–63.

— and Anthony Griffiths, *Tales of Arthur: Legend and Landscape of Wales* (Llandysul, 2010).

Bord, Janet and Bord, Colin, *Mysterious Britain* (London, 1972).

Borlase, William, *Observations on the Antiquities Historical and Monumental, of the County of Cornwall* (Oxford, 1754).

Bradney, Joseph Alfred, *A History of Monmouthshire: From the Coming of the Normans into Wales down to the Present Time*, 4 vols (London, 1904–33).

Brand, John, *Observations on Popular Antiquities Chiefly Illustrating the Origin of our Vulgar Customs, Ceremonies and Superstitions*, with additional notes by Henry Ellis, 2 vols (London, 1813).

Brault, Gérard J., 'Arthurian Heraldry and the Date of *Escanor*', *Bibliographical Bulletin of the International Arthurian Society*, 11 (1959), 81–8.

Breeze, Andrew, 'The The Historical Arthur and Sixth Century Scotland', *Northern History*, 52 (2015), 158–81

Brett, Caroline, 'John Leland, Wales and Early British History', *Welsh History Review*, 15/2 (1995), 169–82.

Bridgeman, G. T. O., 'The Princes of Upper Powys', *Montgomeryshire Collections*, 1 (1868), 1–194.

Bromwich, Rachel (ed.), *The Beginnings of Welsh Poetry: Studies by Sir Ifor Williams* (Cardiff, 1972).

— 'Concepts of Arthur', *Studia Celtica*, 10–11 (1975–6), 163–81.

— (ed. and trans.), *Trioedd Ynys Prydein*, third edition (Cardiff, 2006).

— and D. Simon Evans (eds), *Culhwch ac Olwen: Testun Syr Idris Foster* (Cardiff, 1988).

— and D. Simon Evans (eds), *Culhwch and Olwen: An Edition and Study of the Oldest Arthurian Tale* (Cardiff, 1992).

— and A. O. H. Jarman and Brynley F. Roberts (eds), *The Arthur of the Welsh* (Cardiff, 1991).

Brooke, Christopher N. L., *The Church and the Welsh Border in the Central Middle Ages* (Woodbridge, 1986).

Brown, Arthur C. L., 'Welsh Traditions in Layamon's "Brut"', *Modern Philology*, 1 (1903), 95–103.

Browne, David M., 'From Antiquarianism to Archaeology: The Genesis and Achievement of the Royal Commission's Anglesey Volume', *Archaeologia Cambrensis*, 156 (2009), 33–49.

Brugger, E., 'Beiträge zur Erklärung der arthurischen Geographie: I Estregales', *Zeitschrift für Französische Sprach und Litteratur*, 27 (1904), 69–116.

Bryant, Nigel (trans.), *The High Book of the Grail: Perlesvaus* (Woodbridge, 1978).

— (trans.), *The Complete Story of the Grail: Chrétien de Troyes' Perceval and Its Continuations* (Cambridge, 2015).

Bryant-Quinn, M. Paul (ed.), *Gwaith Ieuan Brydydd Hir* (Aberystwyth, 2000).

Bryden, Inga, *Reinventing King Arthur: The Arthurian Legends in Victorian Culture* (London, 2005).

Buchon, J. A. (ed.), *Chroniques d'Enguerrand de Monstrelet: en deux livres, avec pièces justificatives (nouvelle édition)*, 6 vols (Paris, 1857–62).

Bullock-Davies, Constance, 'Chrétien de Troyes and England', *Arthurian Literature*, 1 (1981), 1–61.

Burgess, Glyn S. and Pratt, Karen (eds), *The Arthur of the French* (Cardiff, 2006).

Busby, K. (ed.), *Chrétien de Troyes, Le Roman de Perceval ou Le Conte du Graal: édition critique d'après tous les manuscrits* (Tübingen, 1993).

The Calendar of Deeds and Documents, The Quaritch Deeds (Aberystwyth, 1922).

Calendar of Inquisitions Post Mortem, V (London, 1898).

Camden, William, *Britannia siue Florentissimorum regnorum, Angliae, Scotiae, Hiberniae, et insularum adiacentium ex intima antiquitate chorographica descriptio* (London, 1586).

—— (Philemon Holland, trans), *Britain, or A chorographicall description of the most flourishing kingdomes, England, Scotland, and Ireland, and the ilands adioyning, out of the depth of antiquitie beautified vvith mappes of the severall shires of England Britannia* (London, 1610).

Carley, James P. (ed.), *Glastonbury Abbey and the Arthurian Tradition* (Cambridge, 2001).

—— 'Polydore Vergil and John Leland on King Arthur', in Edward Donald Kennedy (ed.), *King Arthur: A Casebook* (London, 2002), pp. 185–204.

—— 'Leland, John (*c.*1503–1552)', *Oxford Dictionary of National Biography* (Oxford, 2004).

Carlson, David, 'King Arthur and Court Poems for the Birth of Arthur Tudor in 1486', *Humanistica Lovaniensia*, 36 (1987), 147–83.

Carman, J. Neale, 'The *Perlesvaus* and the Bristol Channel', *Research Studies*, 32 (1964), 85–105.

—— 'South Welsh geography and British history in the *Perlesvaus*', in Norris J. Lacy (ed.), *A Medieval French Miscellany: Papers of the 1970 Kansas Conference on Medieval French Literature* (Kansas, 1972), pp. 37–59.

—— *A Study of the Pseudo-Map Cycle of Arthurian Romance* (Kansas, 1973).

Carr, A. D., 'The Extent of Anglesey, 1352', *Transactions of the Anglesey Antiquarian Society* (1971–2), 150–272.

Carroll, D. F., *Arturius – A Quest for Camelot* (Goxhill, 1996).

Carte, Thomas, *A General History of England*, 4 vols (London, 1747–55).

Cavellatus, Ivo (ed.), *Britannie utriusque regum et principum origo et gesta insignia ab Galfrido Monemutensi ex antiquissimis Britannici ...* (Paris, 1508).

Chadwick, Nora K., 'Early culture and learning in north Wales', in Nora K. Chadwick, Kathleen Hughes, Christopher Brooke and Kenneth Jackson (eds), *Studies in the Early British Church* (Cambridge, 1958), pp. 29–120.

Chambers, E. K., *Arthur of Britain* (London, 1927).

Charles, B. G., 'An Early Charter of the Abbey of Cwmhir', *Radnorshire Society Transactions*, 40 (1970), 68–74.

—— *A Schedule of Powis Castle Deeds and Documents*, 5 vols (Aberystwyth, 1971–3).

—— *The Place-Names of Pembrokeshire*, 2 vols (Aberystwyth, 1992).

Charles-Edwards, T. M., 'The Date of the Four Branches of the Mabinogi', *Transactions of the Honourable Society of Cymmrodorion* (1970–1), 263–98.

—— 'The Date of Culhwch ac Olwen', in W. McLeod, A. Burnyear, D. U. Stiùbhairt, T. O. Clancy and R. O. Maolalaigh (eds), *Bile ós Chrannaibh: A Festschrift for William Gillies* (Ceann Drochaid, 2010), pp. 45–56.

—— *Wales and the Britons 350–1064* (Oxford, 2013).

Chase, Carol (trans.), *Lancelot-Grail 1: The History of the Holy Grail*, (Cambridge, 2010).

Chibnall, Marjorie, 'Matilda (1102–1167)', *Oxford Dictionary of National Biography* (Oxford, 2004).

Clancy, Joseph P., *Medieval Welsh Poems* (Dublin, 2003).

Clancy, Thomas (trans.), *The Triumph Tree: Scotland's Earliest Poetry AD 550–1350* (Edinburgh, 1998).

Clark, G. T., 'Contribution towards a History of the Parish of Llantrithyd in Glamorgan', *Archaeologia Cambrensis* (1866), 389–97.

—— (ed.), *Cartae et alia munimenta quae ad dominium de Glamorgancia pertinent*, 6 vols (Cardiff, 1910).

Clarke, Basil, (ed. and trans.), *Life of Merlin* (Cardiff, 1973).
Coe, Jonathan Baron, 'The Place-Names of the Book of Llandaf' (unpublished PhD thesis, University of Wales, Aberystwyth, 2001).
Coleman, Stanley Jackson, *Lore and Legend of Flintshire* (Douglas, 1956).
Colgrave, B. and Mynors, R. A. B. (eds), *Bede's Ecclesiastical History of the English People* (Oxford, 1992).
Collingwood, W. G., 'Arthur's Battles', *Antiquity*, 3 (1929), 292–8.
Coxe, William, *An Historical Tour of Monmouthshire* (London, 1801).
Cradock, Joseph, *Letters from Snowdon: descriptive of a tour through the northern counties of Wales. Containing the antiquities, history, and state of the country* (London, 1770).
Crichton, Robin, *On the Trail of King Arthur: A Journey into Dark Age Scotland including Illustrations, Maps and Itineraries* (Edinburgh, 2013).
Crick, Julia, *Historia Regum Britannie of Geoffrey of Monmouth*, III: *A Summary Catalogue of the Manuscripts* (Cambridge, 1989).
—— 'The British Past and the Welsh Future: Gerald of Wales, Geoffrey of Monmouth and Arthur of Britain', *Celtica*, 23 (1999), 60–75.
—— 'Monmouth, Geoffrey of (d. 1154/5)', *Oxford Dictionary of National Biography*, (Oxford, 2004).
Crouch, David, 'The Slow Death of Kingship in Glamorgan, 1067–1158', *Morgannwg*, 29 (1985), 20–41.
Crump, J. J., 'The Mortimer Family and the Making of the March', *Thirteenth Century England*, 6 (1997), 117–26.
CYMRO, 'Cursory Remarks on Welsh Tours', *The Cambrian Register for 1796* (London, 1799), pp. 421–54.

Dalton, Paul, 'The Topical Concerns of Geoffrey of Monmouth's *Historia Regum Britannie*: History, Prophecy and Peacemaking, and English Identity in the Twelfth Century', *Journal of British Studies*, 44 (2005), 688–712.
Dames, Michael, *Merlin and Wales: A Magician's Landscape* (London, 2002).
Daniel, Iestyn, Haycock, Marged, Johnston, Dafydd and Rowland, Jenny (eds), *Cyfoeth y Testun: Ysgrifiau ar Lenyddiaeth Gymraeg yr Oesoedd Canol* (Cardiff, 2003).
Daniel-Tyssen, J. R., *Royal Charters and Historical Documents Relating to the Town & County of Carmarthen and the Abbeys of Talley and Tygwyn-ar-Daf* (Carmarthen, 1878).
Davenport, Tony, 'Wales and Welshness in Middle English romances', in Ruth Kennedy and Simon Meecham-Jones (eds), *Authority and Subjugation in Writing of Medieval Wales* (New York, 2008), pp. 137–58.
Davies, Ceri (ed. and trans.), *John Prise: Historiae Britannicae Defensio / A Defence of the British History* (Oxford, 2015).
Davies, Ellis, *Flintshire Place-Names* (Cardiff, 1959).
Davies, Hywel M., 'Wales in English Travel Writing 1791–8: The Welsh Critique of Theophilus Jones', *Welsh History Review*, 23/3 (2007), 65–93.
Davies, John Reuben, 'The saints of south Wales and the Welsh Church', in A. Thacker and R. Sharpe (eds), *Local Saints and Local Churches in the Early Medieval West* (Oxford, 2002), pp. 361–95.
—— *The Book of Llandaf and the Norman Church in Wales* (Woodbridge, 2003).
—— 'Bishop Kentigern amongst the Britons', in Steve Boardman, John Reuben Davies and Elia Williamson (eds), *Saints' Cults in the Celtic Worlds* (Woodbridge, 2009), pp. 66–90.

Davies, R. R., 'Law and national identity in thirteenth-century Wales', in R. R. Davies, Ralph
    A. Griffiths, Ieuan Gwynedd Jones and Kenneth O. Morgan (eds), *Welsh Society and
    Nationhood* (Cardiff, 1984), pp. 51–69.
—— *Conquest Co-existence and Change* (Cardiff, 1987).
Davies, Robert, *The Tithe Maps of Wales* (Aberystwyth, 1999).
Davies, Sioned (trans.) *The Mabinogion* (Oxford, 2007).
—— and Thomas, Peter Wynn (eds), *Canhwyll Marchogion: Cyd-destunoli Peredur* (Cardiff,
    2000).
Davies, Wendy, *The Llandaff Charters* (Aberystwyth, 1979).
Davies, William, 'Casgliad o Len-gwerin Meirion', *Eisteddfod Genedlaethol y Cymry. Cofndion
    a Chyfansoddiaidau Buddugol Eisteddfod Blaenau Ffestiniog, 1898* (Liverpool, 1900),
    pp. 84–269.
Day, Mildred Leake (ed. and trans.), *Latin Arthurian Literature* (Cambridge, 2005).
Deakin, Q. F., 'The early county historians of Wales and western England 1570–1656'
    (unpublished PhD thesis, University of Wales, Aberystwyth, 1981).
Dickinson, W. H., *King Arthur in Cornwall* (London, 1900).
Dimock, James F., (ed) *Giraldi Cambrensis Opera, VI: Itinerarium Kambriae et Descriptio
    Kambriae* (London, 1868).
Diverres, A. H., Review of *French Arthurian Prose Romances. An Index of Proper Names* by
    G. D. West, *French Studies*, 35 (1981), 63–4.
Dodd, A. H., 'The roads of north Wales, 1750–1850', *Archaeologia Cambrensis*, 80 (1925),
    121–48.
Dover, Carol (ed.), *A Companion to the Lancelot-Grail Cycle* (Woodbridge, 2003).
Dugdale, William (ed.), *Monastici Anglicani. Volumen tertium et ultimim* (London, 1683).
Dumville, David N., 'The Corpus Christi "Nennius"', *Bulletin of the Board of Celtic Studies*, 25
    (1972–4), 369–80.
—— 'Some aspects of the chronology of the *Historia Brittonum*', *Bulletin of the Board of Celtic
    Studies*, 25 (1972–4), 439–45.
—— 'The textual history of the Welsh-Latin *Historia Brittonum*' (unpublished DPhil thesis,
    University of Edinburgh, 1975).
—— 'An Irish Idiom Latinised', *Éigse: A Journal of Irish Studies*, 16 (1975–6), 183–6.
—— 'The Textual History of "Lebor Bretnach": A Preliminary Study', *Éigse: A Journal of Irish
    Studies*, 16 (1975–6), 255–73.
—— 'Sub-Roman Britain: History and Legend', *History*, New Series, 62 (1977), 173–92.
—— 'Celtic-Latin Texts in Northern England c.1150–c.1250', *Celtica*, 12 (1977), 19–49.
—— (ed.), *Celtic Britain in the Early Middle Ages* (Woodbridge, 1980).
—— (ed.), *The Historia Brittonum, 3: The Vatican Recension* (Cambridge, 1985).
—— 'The Historical Value of the *Historia Brittonum*', *Arthurian Literature*, 6 (1986), 1–26.
—— *Histories and Pseudo-Histories of the Insular Middle Ages* (Aldershot, 1990).
—— '*Historia Brittonum*: an Insular History from the Carolingian age', in Anton Scharer
    and Georg Scheibelreiter (eds), *Historiographie im frühen Mittelalter*, Institut für
    Österreichische Geschichtsforschung, Veröffentlichungen, 32 (Vienna, 1994), 406–34.

Eadie, J., 'Sir Gawain's Travels in North Wales', *The Review of English Studies*, 34 (1983),
    191–5.
Echard, Sian, *Arthurian Narrative in the Latin Tradition* (Cambridge, 1998).
Edwards, Cyril (trans.), *Parzival with Titurel and the Love Lyrics: Wolfram von Eschenbach*
    (Cambridge, 2004).
Edwards, Huw Meirion (ed.), *Gwaith Madog Dwygraig* (Aberystwyth, 2006).

Edwards, Lewis, 'The Pumpsaint Temple of the Stars' (unpublished, 1947), Aberystwyth, National Monuments Record of Wales, C20133.

Edwards, O. M. *Llyfrau Ystraeon Hanes* (1894).

Ellis, Henry (ed.), *Registrum vulgariter nuncupatum 'The Record of Caernarvon': a codice msto Harleiano 696 descriptum* (London, 1838).

—— (ed.), *Polydore Vergil's English History*, I (London, 1846).

Ellis, Richard, 'Some Incidents in the Life of Edward Lhuyd', *Transactions of the Honourable Society of Cymmrodorion* (1906-7), 1–51.

Emanuel, Hywel D., 'The Latin Life of St Cadoc: a textual and lexicographical study' (unpublished MA dissertation, University of Wales, 1950).

—— 'An Analysis of the Composition of the "Vita Cadoci"', *National Library of Wales Journal*, 7 (1951–2), 217–27.

—— 'Geoffrey of Monmouth's *Historia regum Britannie*: A Second Variant Version', *Medium Ævum*, 35 (1966), 103–8.

Emery, Frank, 'Edward Lhwyd and the 1695 *Britannia*', *Antiquity*, 32 (1958), 179–82.

—— 'A Map of Edward Lhuyd's *Parochial Queries in Order to a Geographical Dictionary, &c.*, of Wales (1696)', *Transactions of the Honourable Society of Cymmrodorion* (1958), 41–53.

—— 'Edward Lhuyd and some of his Glamorgan Correspondents: a View of Gower in the 1690s', *Transactions of the Honourable Society of Cymmrodorion* (1965), 59–114.

—— 'A New Reply to Lluyd's *Queries* (1696): Llanboidy, Carmarthenshire', *Archaeologia Cambrensis*, 124 (1975), 102–10.

Evans, Andrew J., Nettleship, John and Perry, Steven, '*Linn Liuan / Llynn Llyw*: The Wondrous Lake of the *Historia Brittonum's de Mirabilibus Britanniae* and *Culhwch ac Olwen*', *Folklore*, 119/3 (2008), 295–318.

[Evans, D. Silvan] (ed.), *Ysten Sioned, neu y Gronfa Gymmysg* (Aberystwyth, 1882).

Evans, Dai Morgan, '"King Arthur" and Cadbury Castle, Somerset', *The Antiquaries Journal*, 86 (2006), 227–53.

Evans, Evan, *Some Specimens of the Poetry of the Antient Welsh Bards* (London, 1764).

Evans, J. Gwenogvryn, *Report on Manuscripts in the Welsh Language*, 2 vols (London, 1898–1910).

—— *The White Book Mabinogion* (Pwllheli, 1907).

—— *The Book of Taliesin* (Llanbedrog, 1910).

—— *Poems from the Book of Taliesin* (Llanbedrog, 1915).

—— *The Book of Aneirin* (Llanbedrog, 1922).

—— 'Taliesin or the Critic Criticized', *Y Cymmrodor*, 34 (1924).

—— and John Rhys (eds), *The Text of the Book of Llan Dâv* (Oxford, 1893).

Evans, John, *A Tour through parts of North Wales in the year 1798 and at other times* (London, 1800).

Evans, R. Paul, 'Thomas Pennant (1726–1798): The Father of Cambrian Tourists', *Welsh History Review*, 13 (1987), 395–417.

—— 'Richard Bull and Thomas Pennant: Virtuosi in the Art of Grangerisation or Extra-Illustration', *National Library of Wales Journal*, 30 (1998), 269–94.

Evans, R. Wallis, '*Darogan yr Olew Bendigaid a Hystdori yr Olew Bendigaid*', *Llên Cymru*, 14 (1981–2), 86–91

Evans, T. C. (Cadrawd), 'The folklore of Glamorgan', in *Eisteddfod Genedlaethol Gymry Cofnodion a Chyfansoddiadau Buddugol Eisteddfod Aberdar, 1885* (Cardiff, 1887), pp. 186–235.

Evans, Theophilus, *Drych y Prif Oesoedd* (Shrewsbury, 1716).

—— *Drych y Prif Oesoedd*, second edn (Shrewsbury, 1740).

Evans-Gunther, Charles, 'Arthur: The Clwyd Connection', *Journal of the Pendragon Society*, 24/1 (1994), 4–7.

Fairburn, Neil, *Traveller's Guide to the Kingdoms of Arthur* (London, 1983).
Faletra, Michael A., 'Narrating the Matter of Britain: Geoffrey of Monmouth and the Norman Colonization of Wales', *Chaucer Review*, 35 (2000), 60–85.
— *Wales and the Medieval Colonial Imagination: The Matters of Britain in the Twelfth Century* (London, 2014).
Faral, E., (ed.), *La légende arthurienne: études et documents, les plus anciens textes*, 3 vols (Paris, 1929).
Fenton, Richard, *A Historical Tour through Pembrokeshire* (London, 1811).
Field, P. J. C., 'Malory and Cardiff', *Arthuriana*, 16/2 (2006), 45–8.
Fisher, John, 'The Lordship of Ruthin: Its Survey, with Some Extracts from the Records', *Archaeologia Cambrensis* (1914), 440.
— (ed.), *Tours in Wales (1804–1813) by Richard Fenton* (London, 1917).
Foerster, Wendelin (ed.), *Erec und Enide von Christian von Troyes* (Halle, 1890).
Foster, Idris, 'Astudiaeth o Chwedl Culhwch ac Olwen' (unpublished MA dissertation, University of Bangor, 1935).
— 'The Irish influence on some Welsh personal names', in John Ryan (ed.), *Féil-sgríbhinn Eóin Mhic Néill: Essays and Studies Presented to Professor Eoin MacNeill on the Occasion of his Seventieth Birthday, May 15th 1938* (Dublin, 1940), pp. 28–36.
— '*Culhwch* and *Olwen* and *Rhonabwy's Dream*', in Roger S. Loomis (ed.), *Arthurian Literature in the Middle Ages* (Oxford, 1959), pp. 31–43.
Fowles, John (ed.) and Legg, Rodney (annotator), *John Aubrey's Monumenta Britannica, Parts One and Two* (Wincanton, 1980).
Fraser, John, 'Rhŷs, Sir John (1840–1915)', rev. Mari A. Williams, *Oxford Dictionary of National Biography* (Oxford, 2004).
French, Walter Hoyt and Brockway, Charles (eds), *Middle English Metrical Romances* (New York, 1930).
Fulton, Helen., 'Cyd-destun Gwleidyddol *Breudwyt Ronabwy*', *Llên Cymru*, 22 (1999), 42–56.
— 'The *Mabinogi* and the education of princes in medieval Wales', in Helen Fulton (ed.), *Medieval Celtic Literature and Society* (Dublin, 2005), pp. 230–47.
— *Welsh Prophecy and English Politics in the Late Middle Ages* (Aberystwyth, 2008).

Gale, Thomas (ed.), *Historiae Britannicae, Saxonicae, Anglo-Danicae scriptores XV* (Oxford, 1691).
Gasquet, F. A., 'Some Materials for a New Edition of Polydore Vergil's "History"', *Transactions of the Royal Historical Society*, New Series, 16 (1902), 1–17.
Gibbon, Edward, *The History of the Decline and Fall of the Roman Empire*, 6 vols (London, 1776–89).
Gibson, Edmund (ed.), *Camden's Britannia Newly Translated into English with Large Additions and Improvements* (London, 1695).
Giffin, Mary E., 'Cadwalader, Arthur and Brutus in the Wigmore Manuscript', *Speculum*, 16 (1941), 109–20.
— 'The Date of the *Dream of Rhonabwy*', *Transactions of the Honourable Society of Cymmrodorion* (1958), 33–40.
Gilbert, Adrian, Wilson, Alan and Blackett, Baram, *The Holy Kingdom* (London, 1998).
Gildea, J. (ed.), *Durmart le Galois, roman arthurien du treizième siècle*, 2 vols (Villanova, 1965–6).

Gillingham, John, 'The Context and Purposes of Geoffrey of Monmouth's *History of the Kings of Britain*', *Anglo-Norman Studies*, 13 (1990), 99–118.

—— 'Henry II, Richard I and the Lord Rhys', *Peritia*, 10 (1996), 225–36.

[Glasynys], *Cymru Fu* (Wrexham, 1864).

Glennie, John S. Stuart, 'A Journey through Arthurian Scotland', *Macmillan's Magazine* (December, 1867), 161–74.

—— *Arthurian Localities: Their Historical Origin, Chief Country and Fingalian Relations with a Map of Arthurian Scotland* (Edinburgh, 1869).

Godwin, Francis, *A Catalogue of the Bishops of England* (London, 1615).

Goetinck, Glenys (ed.), *Historia Peredur vab Efrawc* (Cardiff, 1976).

Goodrich, Norma, *Arthur* (London, 1986)

Gough, Richard (ed.), *Anecdotes of British Topography* (London, 1768).

—— (ed.), *Britannia: or, a Chorographical Description of the Flourishing Kingdoms of England, Scotland, and Ireland, and the Islands Adjacent; from the Earliest Antiquity. By William Camden*, 3 vols (London, 1789).

Grabowski, Kathryn and Dumville, David (eds), *Chronicles and Annals of Mediaeval Ireland and Wales* (Woodbridge, 1984).

Grant, Angela, 'Gwenogvryn Evans and Cyfraith Hywel', *The National Library of Wales Journal*, 36 (2014) (*www.llgc.org.uk/collections/activities/research/nlw-journal/* accessed 31 December 2016).

Green, Thomas, *Concepts of Arthur* (Stroud, 2007).

—— *Arthuriana: Early Arthurian Tradition and the Origins of the Legend* (Lincoln, 2009).

—— 'John Dee, King Arthur and the Conquest of the Arctic', *The Heroic Age*, 15 (2012) (*www.heroicage.org/issues/15/green.php/* accessed 18 May, 2013).

Greenlaw, Edwin, *Studies in Spenser's Historical Allegory* (Baltimore, 1932).

Greenway, Diana (ed. and trans.), *Henry, Archdeacon of Huntingdon, Historia Anglorum: The History of the English People* (Oxford, 1996).

Gresham, Colin, 'Archbishop Baldwin's Journey through Merioneth in 1188', *Journal of the Merioneth Historical and Record Society*, 10 (1985–9), 186–204.

Griffith, Richard R., 'The authorship question reconsidered', in Toshiyuki Takamiya and Derek Brewer (eds), *Aspects of Malory* (Woodbridge, 1981), pp. 159–77.

Griffiths, Margaret Enid, *Early Vaticination in Welsh with English Parallels* (Cardiff, 1937).

Griffiths, Ralph A. and Thomas, Roger S., *The Making of the Tudor Dynasty* (Gloucester, 1985).

Grinsell, Leslie V., *Folklore of Prehistoric Sites in Britain* (Newton Abbot, 1976).

—— 'Notes on the Folklore of Prehistoric Sites in Britain', *Folklore*, 90/1 (1979), 66–70.

Grooms, Chris, *The Giants of Wales: Cewri Cymru* (Lampeter, 1993).

Grosjean, P., 'Vie de Saint Cadoc par Caradoc de Llancarfan', *Analecta Bollandiana*, 60 (1942), 35–67.

Gruffydd, R. Geraint, 'Canu Cadwallon ap Cadfan', in Rachel Bromwich and R. Brinley Jones (eds), *Astudiaethau ar yr Hengerdd: Studies in Old Welsh Poetry* (Cardiff, 1978), pp. 25–43.

Guest, Charlotte (ed. and trans.), *Kilhwch and Olwen* (Llandovery, 1842).

—— (ed. and trans.), *Breuddydd Rhonabwy* (Llandovery, 1843).

—— (ed. and trans.), *The Mabinogion from the Llyfr Coch o Hergest and Other Ancient Welsh Manuscripts with an English Translation and Notes*, 3 vols (London, 1849).

Guest, Revel and John, Angela V., *Lady Charlotte Guest: An Extraordinary Life* (Stroud, 2007).

Gunn, Rev. W., (ed. and trans.), *The "Historia Brittonum" commonly attributed to Nennius, from a manuscript lately discovered in the library of the Vatican Palace at Rome; edited in the tenth century by Mark the Hermit; with an English version* (London, 1819).

Gunther, R. T. (ed.), *Early Science in Oxford*, XIV: *Life and Letters of Edward Lhwyd* (Oxford, 1945).

Guy, Ben, 'The Origins of the Compilation of Welsh Historical Texts in Harley 3859', *Studia Celtica*, 49 (2015), 21–56.

Gwynn, Edward J. (ed. and trans.), *The Metrical Dindshenchas*, 4 vols (1903–6).

Hadfield, Andrew, 'Spenser, Drayton and the Question of Britain', *The Review of English Studies*, 51 (2000), 582–99.

Harley, J. B. and Walters, Gwyn, 'Welsh Orthography and Ordnance Survey Mapping 1820–1905', *Archaeologia Cambrensis*, 121 (1982), 98–135.

Harris, Silas M., 'The Calendar of the Vitae Sanctorum Wallensium', *Journal of the Historical Society of the Church in Wales*, 3 (1953), 3–53.

Harvey, John H. (ed.), *William Worcestre Itineraries* (Oxford, 1969).

Hathaway, E. J., Ricketts, P. T., Robson, C. A. and Wilshere, A. D. (eds), *Fouke le Fitz Waryn*, Anglo-Norman Text Society, 26–8 (Oxford, 1975).

Hay, Denys, *Polydore Vergil: Renaissance Historian and Man of Letters* (Oxford, 1952).

Haycock, Marged (ed. and trans.), *Legendary Poems in the Book of Taliesin* (Aberystwyth, 2007).

—— *Prophecies from the Book of Taliesin* (Aberystwyth, 2013).

Hearne, Thomas (ed.), *The Itinerary of John Leland. To Which is Prefix'd Mr Leland's New-years Gift*, 9 vols (Oxford, 1710–12).

—— *Joannis Lelandi antiquarii de rebus Britannicis collectanea*, 6 vols (Oxford, 1715).

Hebel, J. William (ed.), *The Works of Michael Drayton*, 5 vols (Oxford, 1931–41).

Henken, Elissa R., *Traditions of the Welsh Saints* (Woodbridge, 1987).

—— *National Redeemer: Owain Glyndŵr in Welsh Tradition* (Cardiff, 1996).

Hepple, Leslie W., 'John Dee, Harleian MS 473, and the Early Recording of Roman Inscriptions in Britain', *Britannia*, 33 (2002), 177–81.

Hewitt, Rachel, *Map of a Nation: A Biography of the Ordnance Survey* (London, 2010).

Heyworth, P. L., 'Sir Gawain's Crossing of Dee', *Medium Ævum*, 41 (1972) 124–7.

Higham, N. J., *King Arthur: Myth-Making and History* (London, 2002).

Hodson, Yolande, *Ordnance Surveyors' Drawings 1789–c.1840: The Original Manuscript Maps of the First Ordnance Survey of England and Wales from the British Library Map Library* (Reading, 1989).

Holden, Brock W., *Lords of the Central Marches: English Aristocracy and Frontier Society, 1087–1265* (Oxford, 2008).

Hopkins, Annette B., 'Ritson's *Life of King Arthur*', *Proceedings of the Modern Language Association*, 43/1 (March, 1928), 251–87.

Hopkinson, Charles and Speight, Martin, *The Mortimers, Lords of the March* (Logaston, 2002).

Houlder, C. H. 'The Stone Age', in J. L. Davies and D. P. Kirkby (eds), *Cardiganshire County History*, I: *From the Earliest Times to the Coming of the Normans* (Cardiff, 1994), pp. 107–23.

Howells, William, *Cambrian Superstitions* (Tipton, 1831).

Howlett, R. (ed.), *Chronicles of the Reigns of Stephen, Henry II and Richard I*, 4 vols (London, 1884–9).

Hughes, Hugh Derfel, *Hynafiaethau Llandegai a Llanllechid* (Bethesda, 1866).

Hughes, Ian (ed.), *Math Uab Mathonwy* (Dublin, 2013).

Hughes, Kathleen, 'The Welsh Latin Chronicles: *Annales Cambriae* and related texts', in David Dumville (ed.), *Celtic Britain in the Early Middle Ages* (Woodbridge, 1980), pp. 67–85.

—— 'British Library MS. Cotton Vespasian A. XIV (*Vitae Sanctorum Wallensium*): its purpose and provenance', in David Dumville (ed.), *Celtic Britain in the Early Middle Ages* (Woodbridge, 1980), pp. 53–66.

Hughes, W. J., *Wales and the Welsh in English Literature* (Wrexham, 1924).

Hume, David, *The History of England, from the Invasion of Julius Caesar to the Accession of Henry VII*, 2 vols (London, 1762).

Huws, Daniel, 'Gildas Prisei', *National Library of Wales Journal*, 17 (1971–2), 314–20.

—— *Medieval Welsh Manuscripts* (Aberystwyth, 2000).

—— 'Llyfr Coch Hergest', in Iestyn Daniel, Marged Haycock, Dafydd Johnston and Jenny Rowland (eds), *Cyfoeth y Testun: Ysgrifiau ar Lenyddiaeth Gymraeg yr Oesoedd Canol* (Cardiff, 2003), pp. 1–30.

—— *Repertory of Welsh Manuscripts and Scribes* (Forthcoming).

Idrison [William Owen Pughe], 'Ardudwy', *The Cambrian Quarterly*, 2 (1830), 9–18.

Isaac, Evan, *Coelion Cymru* (Aberystwyth, 1938).

Isaac, G. R., 'The History and Transmission of the 'Gododdin'', *Cambrian Medieval Celtic Studies*, 37 (1999), 55–78.

—— 'Scholarship and Patriotism: The Case of the Oldest Welsh Poetry', *Studi Celtici*, 1 (2002), 67–81.

Jackson, Kenneth, 'Once Again Arthur's Battles', *Modern Philology*, 43 (1945), 44–57.

—— 'Arthur in early Welsh Verse', in Roger Loomis (ed.), *Arthurian Literature in the Middle Ages* (Oxford, 1959), pp. 12–19.

—— (trans.), *The Gododdin: The Oldest Scottish Poem* (Edinburgh, 1969).

James, Brian Ll. (ed.), *Rice Merrick: Morganiae Archaiographia: A Book of the Antiquities of Glamorganshire* (Barry Island, 1983).

Jankulak, Karen, 'Carantoc alias Cairnech? British saints, Irish saints, and the Irish in Wales', in Karen Jankulak and Jonathan M. Wooding (eds), *Ireland and Wales in the Middle Ages* (Dublin, 2007), pp. 116–48.

Jarman, A. O. H., *Llyfr Du Caerfyrddin* (Cardiff, 1982).

—— 'Llyfr Du Caerfyrddin: the Black Book of Carmarthen', *Proceedings of the British Academy*, 71 (1985), 333–56.

Jayne, S. and Johnson, F. R., *The Lumley Library: The Catalogue of 1609* (London, 1956).

Jenkins, D. E., *Beddgelert: Its Facts, Fairies and Folklore* (Portmadoc, 1899).

Jenkins, Geraint H., 'Evans, Theophilus (1693–1767)', *Oxford Dictionary of National Biography* (Oxford, 2004).

Jenkins, Manon Bonner, 'Aspects of the Welsh prophetic verse tradition'(unpublished PhD thesis, University of Cambridge, 1990).

Jenkins, R. T. and Ramage, H. M., *A History of the Honourable Society of the Cymmrodorion and of the Gwyneddigion and Cymreigyddion (1751–1951)* (London, 1951).

Johnes, Thomas (trans.), *The Chronicles of Enguerrand de Monstrelet: containing an account of the cruel civil wars between the houses of Orleans and Burgundy*, 2 vols (London, 1853).

Johnston, Arthur, 'William Owen Pughe and the Mabinogion', *National Library of Wales Journal*, 10 (1957–8), 323–8.

Johnston, Dafydd (trans.), *Iolo Goch Poems* (Llandysul, 1993).

—— (ed.), *Gwaith Lewis Glyn Gothi* (Cardiff, 1995).

—— et al. (eds), *Cerddi Dafydd ap Gwilym* (Cardiff, 2010).

Jones, Aled Llion, *Darogan: Prophecy, Lament and Absent Heroes in Medieval Welsh Literature* (Cardiff, 2013).

Jones, Bedwyr Lewis, 'Arthurian Place-Names: An End to Nonsense', *Amazing Quests: the Journey into Growth. A Special Issue of the Journal of Myth, Fantasy and Romanticism*, 4 (The Mythopoeic Literature Society of Australia, 1996), 1–9.

Jones, Brinley R., 'Llwyd, Humphrey (1527–1568)', *Oxford Dictionary of National Biography* (Oxford, 2004).

Jones, E. D., 'Camden, Vaughan and Lhwyd and Merionethshire', *Journal of the Merionethshire Record Society*, 2 (1953–6), 209–27.

Jones, Edward, *The Bardic Museum of Primitive British Literature* (London, 1802).

Jones, E. Gwynne, 'Catholic Recusancy in the Counties of Denbigh, Flint and Montgomery 1581–1625', *Transactions of the Honourable Society of Cymmrodorion* (1945), 114–33.

Jones, Evan D., 'Melwas, Gwenhwyfar, a Chai', *Bulletin of the Board of Celtic Studies*, 8 (1937), 203–8.

Jones, Glanville R. J., 'The Distribution of Medieval Settlement in Anglesey', *Transactions of the Anglesey Antiquarian Society* (1955), 27–96.

Jones, Nerys Ann, 'An Index to the Discussions on Place-Names by Henry Owen and E. J. Phillimore in *The Description of Penbrokshire* by George Owen of Henllys', *Studia Celtica*, 26–7 (1991/92), 214–25.

— and Owen, Ann Parry (eds), *Gwaith Cynddelw Brydydd Mawr I* (Cardiff, 1991).

— and Owen, Ann Parry (eds), *Gwaith Cynddelw Brydydd Mawr II* (Cardiff, 1995).

— and Pryce, Huw (eds), *Yr Arglwydd Rhys* (Cardiff, 1996).

Jones, Owen, Morganwg, Iolo and Pughe, William Owen (eds), *The Myvyrian Archaiology of Wales*, 3 vols (London, 1801–7).

Jones, R. Brinley, 'Llwyd, Humphrey (1527–1568)', *Oxford Dictionary of National Biography* (Oxford, 2004).

Jones, T. Gwynn, *Ymadawiad Arthur a Chaniadau Eraill* (Caernarfon, 1910).

— 'Some Arthurian Matter in Keltic', *Aberystwyth Studies*, 8 (1927), 37–93.

— *Welsh Folk-Lore and Folk Custom* (London, 1930).

Jones, Thomas, *Brut y Tywysogyon Peniarth MS. 20* (Cardiff, 1941).

— (ed.), *Cronica de Wallia and Other Documents from Exeter Cathedral Library MS. 3514* (Cardiff, 1946).

— (ed. and trans.), *Brut y Tywysogyon or The Chronicle of the Princes; Peniarth MS 20 Version* (Cardiff, 1952).

— (ed. and trans.), *Brut y Tywysogyon or the Chronicle of the Princes: Red Book of Hergest Version* (Cardiff, 1955).

— 'Datblygiadau Cynnar Chwedl Arthur', *Bulletin of the Board of Celtic Studies*, 17 (1958), 237–52.

— 'The Early Evolution of the Legend of Arthur', *Nottingham Medieval Studies*, 8 (1964), 3–21.

— 'A sixteenth-century version of the Arthurian Cave legend', in M. Brahmer (ed.), *Studies in Language and Literature in Honour of Margaret Schlauch* (Warsaw, 1966), pp. 175–85.

— 'The Black Book of Carmarthen "Stanzas of the Graves"', *Proceedings of the British Academy*, 53 (1967), 97–136.

— 'Chwedl Huail ap Caw ac Arthur', in Thomas Jones (ed.), *Astudiaethau Amrywriol a Glyflwynir i Syr Thomas Parry-Williams* (Cardiff, 1968), pp. 48–66.

— (ed.), *Ystoryaeu Seint Greal: Rhan I, Y Keis* (Cardiff, 1992).

Jones, W. Garmon, 'Welsh Nationalism and Henry Tudor', *Transactions of the Honourable Society of Cymmrodorion* (1917–18), 1–59.

Kelly, Thomas E., 'Fouke fitz Waryn', in Thomas H. Ohlgren (ed.), *Medieval Outlaws: Ten Tales in Modern English* (Stroud, 1998), pp. 106–67.

Kendrick, T. D., *British Antiquity* (London, 1950).

Kennedy, Elspeth (ed.), *Lancelot do Lac The Non-Cyclic Old French Prose Romance*, 2 vols (Oxford, 1980).

Kennedy, Ruth and Meecham-Jones, Simon (eds), *Authority and Subjugation in Writing of Medieval Wales* (New York, 2008).

Ker, Neil, *English Manuscripts in the Century after the Norman Conquest: The Lyell Lectures 1952–3* (Oxford, 1960).

— 'Sir John Prise', in A. G. Watson (ed.), *Books, Collectors and Libraries* (London, 1985), pp. 471–96.

Keynes, Simon and Lapidge, Michael (trans.), *Alfred the Great, Asser's Life of King Alfred and Other Contemporary Sources* (Harmondsworth, 1983).

Koch, John T., *The Celtic Heroic Age* (Malden, 1995).

— *The Gododdin of Aneurin: Text and Context from Dark-Age North Britain* (Cardiff, 1997).

Lacy, Norris J. (ed.), *The Fortunes of King Arthur* (Cambridge, 2005).

Lagorio, Valerie M., 'The evolving legend of St Joseph of Glastonbury', in James P. Carley (ed.), *Glastonbury Abbey and the Arthurian Tradition* (Cambridge, 2001), pp. 55–81.

Lambarde, William, *A perambulation of Kent conteining the description, hystorie, and customes of that shyre. Collected and written (for the most part) in the yeare. 1570*, (London, 1576).

Lancelot du Lac, 2 vols (vol 1, Rouen; vol 2, Paris, 1488).

Lancelot du Lac, 2 vols (Antoine Verard, Paris, 1494).

Lapidge, M., 'The *Vera Historia de Morte Arthuri*: a new edition', in James P. Carley (ed.), *Glastonbury Abbey and the Arthurian Tradition* (Cambridge, 2001), pp. 115–41.

Latimer, Paul, 'Henry II's Campaign against the Welsh in 1165', *Welsh History Review*, 14 (1988), 523–52.

Leland, John, *Assertio Inclytissimi Arturii Regis Britanniae* (Londoni, 1544).

Le Saux, Françoise, *Layamon's Brut: The Poem and its Sources* (Woodbridge, 1989).

Leslie, Charles Henry, *Rambles around Mold* (Mold, 1869).

Levy, F. J., *Tudor Historical Thought* (San Marino, 1967).

Lewis, Henry (ed.), *Brut Dingestow* (Cardiff, 1942).

— and Thomas Roberts and Ifor Williams (eds), *Cywyddau Iolo Goch ac Eraill 1350–1450* (Bangor, 1925).

Lewis, J. B., 'An Account of the Penbedw Papers in the Flintshire Record Office', *Journal of the Flintshire Historical Society*, 25 (1971–2), 124–52.

Lewis, John, *History of Great Britain, From the First Inhabitants thereof, til the Death of Cadwalader Last King of the Britains* (London, 1729).

Lewis, Saunders, *A School of Welsh Augustans* (Wrexham, 1924).

Lhuyd, Edward, *Archaeologia Britannica: Giving Some Account Additional to what Has Been Hitherto Publish'd, of the Languages, Histories and Customs of the Original Inhabitants of Great Britain*, I: *Glossography* (Oxford, 1707).

Lhwyd, Edward, *Parochial Queries in Order to a Geographical Dictionary, A Natural History &c. of Wales* (Oxford, 1696).

Lieberman, Max, *The Medieval March of Wales: The Creation and Perception of a Frontier, 1066–1283* (Cambridge, 2010).

Lloyd, John, 'Letters from and to Edward Lhwyd', *Archaeologia Cambrensis* (1851), 52–8.

Lloyd, John E., *A History of Wales: From the Earliest Times to the Edwardian Conquest*, third edn, (London, 1939).

Lloyd, Nesta, 'John Jones, Gellilyfdy', *Journal of the Flintshire Historical Society*, 24 (1969–70), 5–18.

— 'The Correspondence of Edward Lhuyd and Richard Mostyn', *Journal of the Flintshire Historical Society*, 25 (1971–2), 31–61.

Lloyd, Scott, 'Arthurian Place Names and Later Traditions' in Ceridwen Lloyd-Morgan and Erich Poppe (eds), *The Arthur of the Celtic Literatures* (Cardiff, forthcoming).

Lloyd-Morgan, Ceridwen, 'A study of *Y Seint Greal* in relation to *La Queste del Saint Graal* and *Perlesvaus*'(unpublished DPhil thesis, Oxford University, 1978).

— 'The Peniarth 15 Fragment of *Y Seint Greal*: Arthurian Tradition in the Late Fifteenth Century', *Bulletin of the Board of Celtic Studies*, 28 (1978), 73–82.

— 'Nodiadau Ychwanegol ar yr Achau Arthuraidd a'u Ffynonellau Ffrangeg', *National Library of Wales Journal*, 21 (1980), 329–39.

— '*Darogan yr Olew Bendigaid*: Chwedl o'r Bymthegfed Ganrif', *Llên Cymru*, 14 (1981–2), 64–85.

— 'Breuddwyd Rhonabwy and later Arthurian literature', in Rachel Bromwich, A. O. H. Jarman, and Brynley F. Roberts (eds), *The Arthur of the Welsh* (Cardiff, 1991), pp. 183–208.

— 'French texts, Welsh translators', in Roger Ellis (ed.), *The Medieval Translator*, II (London, 1991), pp. 45–63.

— 'Narratives and Non-narratives: Aspects of Welsh Arthurian Tradition', *Arthurian Literature*, 21 (Cambridge, 2004), 115–36.

— 'Medieval Welsh Tales or Romances? Problems of Genre and Terminology', *Cambrian Medieval Celtic Studies*, 47 (2004), 41–58.

— 'Welsh tradition in Calais: Elis Gruffydd and his biography of King Arthur', in Norris Lacy (ed.), *The Fortunes of King Arthur* (Cambridge, 2005), pp. 77–91.

— 'Crossing the borders: literary borrowing in Wales and England', in Ruth Kennedy and Simon Meecham-Jones (eds), *Authority and Subjugation in Writing of Medieval Wales* (New York, 2008), pp. 159–73.

— and Erich Poppe (eds), *The Arthur of the Celtic Literatures* (Cardiff, forthcoming).

Löffler, Marion, *The Literary and Historical Legacy of Iolo Morganwg* (Cardiff, 2007).

Loomis, Roger S., '"Chastiel Bran", "Dinas Bran", and the Grail Castle', in Mary Williams and James A. de Rothschild (eds), *A Miscellany of Studies in Romance Languages & Literatures Presented to Leon E. Kastner* (Cambridge, 1932), pp. 342–50.

— *Arthurian Tradition and Chrétien de Troyes* (New York, 1949).

— 'Edward I, Arthurian Enthusiast', *Speculum*, 28 (1953), 114–27.

— *Wales and the Arthurian Legend* (Cardiff, 1956).

— (ed.), *Arthurian Literature in the Middle Ages* (Oxford, 1959).

Luard, H. R. (ed.), *Annales Monastici*, 4 vols. (London, 1864–9).

Lyte, H. C. Maxwell (ed.), *A Descriptive Catalogue of Ancient Deeds in the Public Record Office*, 6 vols (London, 1890–1915).

McClure, Judith and Collins, Roger (ed. and trans.), *Bede: The Ecclesiastical History of the English People, The Greater Chronicle and Bede's Letter to Egbert* (Oxford, 1994).

MacColl, Alan, 'Richard White and the Legendary History of Britain', *Humanistica Lovaniensia*, 51 (2002), 245–57.

— 'The Construction of England as a Protestant "British" Nation in the Sixteenth Century', *Renaissance Studies*, 18/4 (2004), 582–608.

MacMillan, Ken, 'John Dee's "Brytanici Imperii Limites"', *Huntington Library Quarterly*, 64 1/2 (2001), 151–9.

—— and Abeles, Jennifer (eds), *John Dee: The Limits of the British Empire* (Westport, 2004).

Malkin, Benjamin, *The Scenery, Antiquities, and Biography of South Wales* (London, 1804–7).

Maltwood, K. E., *A Guide to Glastonbury's Temple of the Stars: Their Giant Effigies Described from Air Views, Maps, and from "The High History of the Holy Grail"* (London, 1934).

Mann, Kevin, 'The March of Wales: A Question of Terminology', *Welsh History Review*, 18 (1996), 1–12.

Matheson, Lister M., 'The Arthurian Stories of Lambeth Palace Library MS 84', *Arthurian Literature*, 5 (1985), 70–91.

Merlet, Lucien (ed.), *Cartulaire de l'abbaye de la Sainte-Trinité de Tiron*, 2 vols (Chartres, 1882–3).

Middleton, Roger 'Studies in the textual relationships of the Erec/Geraint stories' (unpublished DPhil thesis, Oxford University, 1976).

—— 'Manuscripts of the *Lancelot-Grail* cycle in England and Wales: some books and their owners', in Carol Dover (ed.), *A Companion to the Lancelot-Grail Cycle* (Woodbridge, 2003), pp. 219–35.

—— 'The manuscripts', in Glyn S. Burgess and Karen Pratt (eds), *The Arthur of the French* (Cardiff, 2006), pp. 1–92.

Millican, Charles Bowie, *Spenser and the Round Table: A Study in the Contemporaneous Background for Spenser's Use of the Arthurian Legend* (Cambridge, Mass., 1932).

Moffat, Alistair, *Arthur and the Lost Kingdoms* (London, 1999).

Moir, Esther, *The Discovery of Britain: The English Tourist 1520–1840* (London, 1964).

Mommsen, Theodor (ed.), *Monumenta Germaniae Historica, Auctores Antiquissimi, xii, Chronica Minora saec. IV, V, VI, VII*, vol. III (Berlin, 1898).

Morgan, Mrs Mary, *A tour to Milford Haven, in the year 1791* (London, 1795).

Morgan, Owen 'Morien', *A History of Wales from the Earliest Period* (Liverpool, 1911).

Morgan, Prys, 'Elis Gruffydd of Gronant – Tudor Chronicler Extraordinary', *Journal of the Flintshire Historical Society*, 25 (1971–2), 9–20.

Morgan, Richard, 'Robert Vaughan of Hengwrt (1592–1667)', *Journal of the Merionethshire Record Society*, 8 (1977–80), 397–408.

—— *A Study of Montgomeryshire Place-Names* (Llanrwst, 2001).

Morgan, T. J., 'Dadansoddi'r Gogynfeirdd (1)', *Bulletin of the Board of Celtic Studies*, 13 (1948–50), 169–74

—— 'Dadansoddi'r Gogynfeirdd (2)', *Bulletin of the Board of Celtic Studies*, 14 (1950–2), 1–8.

Morris, John, (ed.), *Nennius, the British History and the Welsh Annals* (Chichester, 1980).

Morris, Lewis, *Plans of Harbours, Bars, Bays and Roads in St George's Channel* (London, 1748).

Morris, Rosemary, 'Aspects of Time and Place in the French Arthurian Verse Romances', *French Studies*, 42 (1988), 257–77.

Morris, Rupert (ed.), *Parochialia Being a Summary of Answers to 'Parochial Queries in order to a Geographical Dictionary, Etc., of Wales'* issued by Edward Lhuyd, 3 parts (London, 1909–11).

Morris-Jones, John, 'Taliesin', *Y Cymmrodor*, 28 (1918).

Murray, John, *Handbook for Travellers in North Wales* (London, 1861).

Mynors, R. A. B, Thomson, R. M. and Winterbottom, M. (eds), *William of Malmesbury: Gesta Regvm Anglorvm, The History of the English Kings*, I (Oxford, 1998).

Nash, David, *Taliesin or the Bards and Druids of Britain* (London, 1858).

Nastali, Daniel P. and Boardman, Phillip C., *The Arthurian Annals: The Tradition in English from 1250 to 2000*, 2 vols (Oxford, 2004).

Nicholson, George, *The Cambrian Traveller's Guide and Pocket Companion* (Stourport, 1808).
Nicholson, Helen, 'Following the Path of the Lionheart: The *De Ortu Walwanii* and the *Itinerarium Peregrinorum et Gesta Regis Ricardi*', *Medium Ævum*, 69 (2000), 21–33.
Nitze, William A. and Jenkins, T. A. (eds), *Le Haut Livre du Graal: Perlesvaus*, 2 vols (Chicago, 1932–7).
Norris, Ralph, *Malory's Library: The Sources of Morte Darthur* (Woodbridge, 2008).

Ohlgren, Thomas H. (ed.), *Medieval Outlaws: Ten Tales in Modern English* (Stroud, 1998).
ÓhÓgáin, Dáithí, *Fionn mac Cumhail Images of a Gaelic Hero* (Dublin, 1988).
Olding, Frank, 'Gwent and the Arthurian Legend', *Gwent Local History: The Journal of the Gwent Local History Council*, 63 (Autumn, 1987), 23–9.
Ortelius, Abraham, *Theatrum Orbis Terrarum* (Antwerp, 1570).
Owen, Ann Parry, 'Mynegai i Enwau Priod ym Marddoniaeth Beirdd y Tywysogion', *Llên Cymru*, 20 (1997), 25–45.
—— 'Mynegai i Enwau Priod yng Ngwaith Beirdd y Bedwaredd Ganrif Ar Ddeg', *Llên Cymru*, 31 (2008), 35–89.
Owen, D. D. R. (trans.), *Chrétien de Troyes, Arthurian Romances* (London, 1993).
Owen, Elias, *Welsh Folk-Lore* (Oswestry, 1896).
—— 'Montgomeryshire Folk-Lore: Holy Wells in the Parish of Llanfihangel Ynghwnfa, Montgomeryshire', *Montgomeryshire Collections*, 30 (1898), 307–10.
Owen, Henry (ed.), *The Description of Penbrokeshire by George Owen of Henllys*, 4 vols (London, 1892–1936).
Owen, Hugh (ed.), *Additional Letters of the Morrises of Anglesey (1735–86)*, 2 vols (London, 1947–9).
—— (ed.), *The Life and Works of Lewis Morris (Llewelyn Ddu o Fon 1701–1765)* (Llangefni, 1951).
Owen, Hywel Wyn, *The Placenames of East Flintshire* (Cardiff, 1993).
—— and Morgan, Richard, *Dictionary of the Place-Names of Wales* (Llandysul, 2007).
Owen, Morfydd. E., 'Royal propaganda: stories from the law-texts', in T. M. Charles-Edwards, Morfydd E. Owen and Paul Russell (eds), *The Welsh King and his Court* (Cardiff, 2000), pp. 224–54.
Owen, Robert, *The Kymry: Their Origin, History, and International Relations* (Carmarthen, 1891).
Owens, B. G., 'Some Unpublished Material of the Reverend Richard Farrington, Rector of Llangybi', *Journal of the Welsh Bibliographical Society*, 5 (1937–42), 16–32.
—— 'The Reverend Richard Farrington, Rector of Llangybi: A Further Note', *Journal of the Welsh Bibliographical Society*, 5 (1937–42), 241–2.
Owens, Owen, 'Gweithiau Barddonol Morus Dwyfech' (unpublished MA thesis, University of Bangor, 1944).

Padel, O. J., 'Geoffrey of Monmouth and Cornwall', *Cambridge Medieval Celtic Studies*, 8 (1984), 1–28.
—— 'Some south-western sites with Arthurian associations', in Rachel Bromwich, A. O. H. Jarman, and Brynley F. Roberts (eds), *The Arthur of the Welsh* (Cardiff, 1991), pp. 229–48.
—— 'The Nature of Arthur', *Cambrian Medieval Celtic Studies*, 27 (1994), 1–31.
—— *Arthur in Medieval Welsh Literature* (Cardiff, 2000).
—— 'Geoffrey of Monmouth and the Merlin Legend', *Cambrian Medieval Celtic Studies*, 51 (2006), 37–65.

Palgrave, Francis, 'Popular Mythology of the Middle Ages', *Quarterly Review*, 22 (1820), 348–80.

Parry, Edward, 'The Revd. Erasmus Saunders', *Journal of the Pembrokeshire Historical Society*, 13 (2004), 35–42.

Parry, John J., *A Bibliography of Critical Arthurian Literature for the Years 1922–29* (London, 1929).

— and Schlauch, Margaret, *A Bibliography of Critical Arthurian Literature for the Years 1930–1935* (London, 1936).

Parsons, John Carmi, 'The second exhumation of King Arthur's remains at Glastonbury, 19 April 1278', in John P. Carley (ed.), *Glastonbury Abbey and the Arthurian Tradition* (Woodbridge, 2001), pp. 179–83.

Payne, Francis G., 'John Lewis, Llynwene, Historian and Antiquary', *Radnorshire Society Transactions*, 30 (1960), 4–16.

Pennant, Thomas, *A Tour in Scotland. MDCCLXIX.* (Chester, 1771).

— *A Tour in Wales MDCCLXX*, 2 vols (London, 1778–83).

Pezron, P., *L'Antiquité de la nation et la langue des Celtes* (Paris, 1703).

— *The Antiquities of Nations More particularly of the Celtae or Gauls taken to be originally the same people as our Ancient Britains* (London, 1706).

Philips, Graham, *The Marian Conspiracy* (London, 2000).

— *The Templars and the Ark of the Covenant* (Rochester, 2004).

— and Keatman, Martin, *King Arthur: The True Story* (London, 1992).

Phillimore, Egerton, 'The *Annales Cambriae* and Old Welsh Genealogies from *Harleian MS. 3859*', *Y Cymmrodor*, 9 (1888), 141–83.

Pickens, Rupert T. (trans.), *Lancelot-Grail 2: The Story of Merlin* (Cambridge, 2010).

— Busby, Keith and Williams, Andrea M. L., 'Perceval and the Grail', in Glyn S. Burgess and Karen Pratt (eds), *The Arthur of the French* (Cardiff, 2005), pp. 222–47.

Piggott, Stuart, 'The Sources of Geoffrey of Monmouth', *Antiquity*, 15 (1941), 269–86.

Ponceau, Jean-Paul (ed.), *L'Estoire del Saint Graal*, 2 vols (Paris, 1997).

Poppe, Erich and Reck, Regine, 'A French Romance in Wales: *Ystorya Bown o Hamtwn*. Processes of Medieval Translations. [Part I]', *Zeitschrift für Celtische Philologie*, 55 (2006), 122–180 and [Part II], *Zeitschrift für Celtische Philologie*, 56 (2008), 129–64.

Potter, K. R. (ed. and trans.), *Gesta Stephani* (Oxford, 1976).

Powel, David, *The Historie of Cambria, now called Wales* (London, 1584).

— (ed.), *Pontici Virunnii viri doctissimi Britannicae historiae libri sex magna et fide et diligentia conscripti: ad Britannici codicis fidem correcti, & ab infinitis mendis liberati: quibus praefixus est catalogus regum Britanniae* (London, 1585).

Prescott, Sarah, *Eighteenth-Century Writing from Wales: Bards and Britons* (Cardiff, 2008).

Price, Angharad, 'Rhys, Siôn Dafydd (*b.* 1533/4, *d.* in or after 1620)', *Oxford Dictionary of National Biography* (Oxford, 2004).

Prise, John, *Historiae Brytannicae Defensio* (London, 1573).

Pritchard, Emily M., *The History of St. Dogmaels Abbey: Together with her Cells, Pill, Caldey and Glascareg and the Mother Abbey of Tiron* (London, 1907).

Pryce, Huw, 'The Context and Purpose of the Earliest Welsh Law Books', *Cambrian Medieval Celtic Studies*, 39 (2000), 39–63.

— 'British or Welsh? National Identity in Twelfth-Century Wales', *English Historical Review*, 115 (2001), 775–801.

— (ed.), *Acts of the Welsh Rulers 1120–1283* (Cardiff, 2005).

Pugh, Edward, *Cambria Depicta: A Tour through North Wales* (London, 1816).

Pughe, John, 'Gwragedd Annwn – The Dames of Elfin Land, A Legend of Llyn Barfog', *Archaeologia Cambrensis* (1853), 201–5.

Pughe, William Owen, *The Cambrian Biography: Or, Historical Notices of Celebrated Men Among the Ancient Britons* (London, 1803).

Purdie, Rhiannon and Royan, Nicola (eds), *The Scots and Medieval Arthurian Legend* (Cambridge, 2005).

Ralegh Radford, C. A. and Swanton, Michael J., *Arthurian Sites in the West* (Exeter, 2002).

Rees, David, *The Son of Prophecy* (London, 1985).

Rees, Eiluned and Walters, Gwyn, 'The Dispersion of the Manuscripts of Edward Lhuyd', *Welsh History Review*, 7 (1974), 148–78.

Rees, Una (ed.), *The Cartulary of Haughmond Abbey* (Cardiff, 1985).

Rees, William (ed.), *A Survey of the Duchy of Lancaster Lordships in Wales 1609–1613* (Cardiff, 1953).

Rees, William J. (trans.), *The Liber Landavensis: Llyfr Teilo* (Llandovery, 1840).

Reeve, Michael D. (ed.) and Wright, Neil (trans.), *Geoffrey of Monmouth: The History of the Kings of Britain: An Edition and Translation of De Gestis Britonum [Historia Regum Britanniae]* (Woodbridge, 2007).

Reiss, Edmund, 'The Welsh Versions of Geoffrey of Monmouth's *Historia*', *Welsh History Review*, 4 (1968), 97–127.

Remfry, Paul Martin (trans.), *Annales Cambriae: A Translation of Harleian 3859: PRO E. 164/1: Cottonian Domitian, A1: Exeter Cathedral Library MS. 3514 and MS Exchequer DB Neath, PRO E. 164/1* (n.p., 2007).

Reno, Frank, *The Historic King Arthur: Authenticating the Celtic Hero of Post-Roman Britain* (Jefferson, 1996).

Revard, Carter, 'Courtly romances in the Privy Wardrobe', in Evelyn Mullally and John Thompson (eds), *Court and Cultural Diversity* (Woodbridge, 1997), pp. 297–308.

Rhaeso, Joanne Dauide, *Cambrobrytannicae Cymraecaeve Linguae Institutiones et Rudimenta* (Londini, 1592).

Rhodes, D. E., 'The First Edition of Gildas', *The Library*, Sixth Series, 1 (1979), 355–60.

Rhŷs, John, 'Welsh Fairy Tales', *Y Cymmrodor*, 6 (1883), 155–221.

—— 'Coetan Arthur Cromlech near Caernarvon', *Archaeologia Cambrensis* (1888), 58.

—— *Studies in the Arthurian Legend* (Oxford, 1891).

—— 'Notes on the Hunting of the Twrch Trwyth', *Transactions of the Honourable Society of Cymmrodorion* (1894–5), 1–34 and 146–8.

—— *Celtic Folklore: Welsh and Manx* (Oxford, 1901).

—— 'Introduction', *Le Morte D'Arthur* (London, 1906).

—— and J. Gwenogvryn Evans, *The Text of the Mabinogion and Other Welsh Tales from the Red Book of Hergest* (Oxford, 1887).

Richards, Melville, *Breudwyt Ronabwy* (Cardiff, 1948).

—— 'Arthur's Gate at Montgomery', *Archaeologia Cambrensis*, 114 (1965), 181–2.

—— 'Arthurian Onomastics', *Transactions of the Honourable Society of Cymmrodorion*, (1969), 250–64.

—— 'Hafoty (Llansadwrn)', *Transactions of the Anglesey Antiquarian Society* (1973), 39–54.

Richards, Thomas, 'U.C.N.W. Library, Special Collections', *Transactions of the Anglesey Antiquarian Society* (1940), 62–75.

Rickard, P., *Britain in Medieval French Literature 1100–1500* (Cambridge, 1956).

Ritson, Joseph, *The Life of King Arthur: from Ancient Historians and Authentic Documents* (London, 1825).

Roberts, Brynley F., 'Astudiaeth destunol o'r tri chyfieithiad Cymraeg cynharaf o Historia

Regum Britanniae Sieffre o Fynwy: ynghyd ag "argraffiad" beirniadol o destun Peniarth
44' (unpublished PhD thesis, University of Wales, Aberystwyth, 1969).
— 'Ymagweddau at *Brut y Brenhinedd* hyd 1890', *Bulletin of the Board of Celtic Studies*, 24
(1971), 122–38.
— *Brut y Brenhinedd* (Dublin, 1971).
— 'The Treatment of Personal Names in the Early Welsh Versions of *Historia Regum
Britanniae*', *Bulletin of the Board of Celtic Studies*, 25 (1972–4), 274–90.
— 'Fersiwn Dingestow o *Brut y Brenhinedd*', *Bulletin of the Board of Celtic Studies*, 27
(1977), 331–61.
— 'The Red Book of Hergest Version of *Brut y Brenhinedd*', *Studia Celtica*, 12/13 (1977/8),
147–86.
— *Brut Tysilio* (Swansea, 1980).
— 'Culhwch ac Olwen, The Triads, Saints' Lives', in Rachel Bromwich, A. O. H. Jarman and
Brynley F. Roberts (eds), *The Arthur of the Welsh* (Cardiff, 1991), pp. 73–95.
— 'Where were the Four Branches of the Mabinogi written?', in Joseph Falaky Nagy (ed.),
The Individual in Celtic Countries: CSANA Yearbook 1 (Dublin, 2001), pp. 61–73.
— 'Lhuyd, Edward (1659/60?–1709)', *Oxford Dictionary of National Biography* (Oxford,
2004).
— 'Edward Lhwyd in Carmarthenshire', *Carmarthenshire Antiquary*, 46 (2010), 24–43.
Roberts, George (trans.), *A View of the Primitive Ages* (Llanidloes, 1865).
Roberts, Glyn, *Aspects of Welsh History* (Cardiff, 1969).
Roberts, Gomer M., *Hanes Plwyf Llandybie* (Cardiff, 1939).
— 'Mynydd Mawr Traditions', *Carmarthenshire Antiquary*, 1 (1941), 59–60.
Roberts, Peter, *The Chronicle of the Kings of Britain* (London, 1811).
— *The Cambrian Popular Antiquities of Wales* (London, 1815).
Roberts, Ruth Eloise, 'Welsh place-names in the earliest Arthurian texts' (unpublished DPhil
thesis, Columbia University, 1957).
Roberts, Thomas, 'Y Traddodiad am y Brenin Arthur yng Nghaergai', *Bulletin of the Board of
Celtic Studies*, 11 (1944), 12–14.
Roberts, Tomos, 'Enwau lleoedd, 1. safle Capel Mair o Ddindryfwl 2. safle Cerrigarthur',
Transactions of the Anglesey Antiquarian Society (1976–7), 51–3.
Robinson, Richard, *A Learned and True Assertion of the Original, Life, Actes and Death of the
Most Noble, Valiant and Renoumed Prince Arthure, King of Great Brittaine* (London, 1582).
Robinson, W. R. B., 'Dr. Thomas Phaer's Report on the Harbours and Customs
Administration of Wales under Edward VI', *Bulletin of the Board of Celtic Studies*, 24
(1972), 485–503.
Rodway, Simon, 'A Datable Development in Medieval Welsh', *Cambrian Medieval Celtic
Studies*, 36 (1998), 71–94.
— 'Absolute Forms in the Poetry of the Gogynfeirdd: Functionally Obsolete Archaisms or
Working System?', *Journal of Celtic Linguistics*, 7 (1998), 63–84.
— 'The Red Book Text of *Culhwch and Olwen*: A Modernising Scribe at Work', *Studi
Celtici*, 3 (2004), 93–161.
— 'The Date and Authorship of *Culhwch ac Olwen*: A Reassessment', *Cambrian Medieval
Celtic Studies*, 49 (2005), 21–44.
— 'The Where, Who, When and Why of Medieval Welsh Prose Texts: Some
Methodological Considerations', *Studia Celtica*, 41 (2007), 47–89.
— *Dating Medieval Welsh Literature: Evidence from the Verbal System* (Aberystwyth, 2013).
Rosenberg, Samuel N. and Carroll, Carleton W. (trans.), *Lancelot-Grail 3: Lancelot Parts I and
II* (Cambridge, 2010).

Rowlands, I. W., 'King John and Wales', in S. D. Church (ed.), *King John: New Interpretations* (Woodbridge, 1999), pp. 273–87.

—— 'The 1201 Peace between King John and Llywelyn ap Iorwerth', *Studia Celtica*, 34 (2000), 149–66.

Royal Commission on Land in Wales and Monmouthshire. Minutes of Evidence Taken before the Royal Commission on Land in Wales and Monmouthshire; with Appendix of Documents, 5 vols (London, 1894–6).

Royal Commission on the Ancient and Historical Monuments of Wales, *An Inventory of the Ancient Monuments of Wales and Monmouthshire: I – County of Montgomery* (London, 1911).

—— *An Inventory of the Ancient Monuments of Wales and Monmouthshire: V – County of Carmarthen* (London, 1917).

—— *An Inventory of the Ancient Monuments of Wales and Monmouthshire: VI – County of Merioneth* (London, 1921).

—— *An Inventory of the Ancient Monuments in Anglesey* (London, 1937).

—— *An Inventory of the Ancient Monuments in Caernarvonshire Volume II: Central: The Cantref of Arfon and the Commote of Eifionydd* (London, 1960).

—— *An Inventory of the Ancient Monuments in Caernarvonshire Volume III: West: The Cantref of Lleyn* (London, 1964).

Rushton, Cory James, 'Malory's divided Wales', in Ruth Kennedy and Simon Meecham-Jones (eds), *Authority and Subjugation in Writing of Medieval Wales* (New York,   2008), pp. 175–89.

Russell, Paul, 'Texts in Contexts: Recent Work on the Medieval Welsh Prose Tales', *Cambrian Medieval Celtic Studies*, 45 (2003), 60–72.

Salter, H. E., 'Geoffrey of Monmouth and Oxford', *English Historical Review*, 34 (1919), 382–5.

Sanderson, Stewart F., 'Obituary: Professor Mary Williams', *Folklore*, 89/1 (1978), 104–05.

Saxton, Christopher, *[Atlas of the Counties of England and Wales]* (London, 1580).

Schichtman, Martin and Finke, Laurie, 'Profiting from the Past: History as Symbolic Culture in the *Historia Regum Britanniae*', *Arthurian Literature*, 12 (1993), 1–35.

Schmolke-Hasselmann, Beate, 'The Round Table: Ideal, Fiction, Reality', *Arthurian Literature*, 2 (1983), 41–75.

—— *The Evolution of Arthurian Romance: The Verse Tradition from Chrétien to Froissart* (Cambridge, 1998).

Schwyzer, Philip (ed. and trans.), *Humphrey Llwyd: The Breviary of Britain and Selections from the History of Cambria* (London, 2011).

Scott, George (ed.), *Mr Ray's Itineraries* (London, 1760).

Sharpe, Richard and Davies, John Reuben, 'Rhygyfarch's Life of St David', in J. Wyn Evans and Jonathan M. Wooding (eds), *St David of Wales: Cult, Church and Nation* (Woodbridge, 2007), pp. 107–55.

Short, Ian (ed. and trans.), *Estoire des Engleis: History of the English* (Oxford, 2009).

Sikes, Wirt, *British Goblins: Welsh Folk-Lore, Fairy Mythology, Legends and Traditions* (London, 1880).

Simpson, Roger, *Camelot Regained: The Arthurian Revival and Tennyson 1800–1849* (Cambridge, 1990).

Sims-Williams, Patrick, 'The early Welsh Arthurian Poems', in Rachel Bromwich, A. O. H. Jarman and Brynley F. Roberts (eds), *The Arthur of the Welsh* (Cardiff, 1991), pp. 33–71.

—   'Clas Beuno and the Four Branches of the Mabinogion', in Bernard Maier and Stefan
      Zimmer with Christine Bakte (eds), *150 Jahre "Mabinogion": Deutch-Walische
      Kulturbeziehungen* (Tübingen, 2001), pp. 111–27.
—   *Rhai Addasiadau Cymraeg Canol o Sieffre o Fynwy* (Aberystwyth, 2011).
Skene, William F., *The Four Ancient Books of Wales*, 2 vols (Edinburgh, 1868).
Skrine, Henry, *Two Successive Tours throughout the Whole of Wales, with Several of the
      Adjacent English Counties …* (London, 1798).
Smith, J. Beverley, 'Magna Carta and the Charters of the Welsh Princes', *English Historical
      Review*, 99 (1984), 344–62.
—   *Llywelyn ap Gruffudd Prince of Wales* (Cardiff, 1998).
Smith, Lucy Toulmin, *The Itinerary in Wales of John Leland in or about the Years 1536–1539*
      (London, 1906).
Snell, F. J., *King Arthur's Country* (London, 1926).
Society of Gentlemen, *England Displayed. Being a new, complete, and accurate survey and
      description of the Kingdom of England, and principality of Wales* (London, 1769).
Southey, Robert (ed.), *The Byrth, Lyf and Actes of King Arthur*, 2 vols (London, 1817).
Speed, John, *The Theatre of the Empire Great Britaine* (London, 1611).
Spenser, Edmund, *The Fairie Queene,* (London, 1590).
Spittal, Jeffrey and Field, John, *A Reader's Guide to the Place-Names of the United Kingdom*
      (Stamford, 1990).
Starkey, David, 'King Henry and King Arthur', *Arthurian Literature*, 16 (1998), 171–96.
Stephens, G. Arbour, 'Llangwyryfon and Certain Placenames in Cardiganshire', *Transactions
      of the Honourable Society of Cymmrodorion* (1929–30), 114–30.
—   'Merlin and the Valley of Darnantes', *Swansea Guardian* (1937).
—   'The Romance of Tinopolis', *Swansea Guardian* (10 June 1938).
—   *New Light on Arthurian Battlefields* (Haverfordwest, 1938).
—   'The Topographical Importance of Kidwelly and the Burry Estuary in Connection with
      the Arthurian Romances', *The Carmarthen Journal* (November 25, 1938).
—   *Carmarthenshire and the Glastonbury Legends: Was the Isle of Avalon in the Lordship of
      Kidwelly* (n.p., 1939)
—   'Carmarthen and a Legend: Does "Merlin's Tree" Mark the Site of Merlin's Burial-Place?',
      The Carmarthen Journal (29 March 1940).
—   *The County of Merlin as the Provenance of the Perlesvaus* (1941)
—   'Caerlleon in Carmartheshire', *The Carmarthen Journal* (August 27, 1943).
—   'King Arthur and Maes-y-Bar, Llansamlet: Swansea Valley and Arthurian Placenames',
      newspaper cutting (n.d.)
Stevenson, Joseph (ed.), *Nennii Historia Britonum ad fidem codicum manuscriptorum*
      (London, 1838).
Stevenson, William Henry (ed.), *Asser's Life of King Alfred* (Oxford, 1959).
Stirling, Simon Andrew, *The King Arthur Conspiracy: How a Scottish Prince Became a
      Mythical Hero* (Stroud, 2012).
Swanton, Michael (ed. and trans.), *The Anglo-Saxon Chronicle* (London, 1996).

Tatlock, J. P. S., *The Legendary History of Britain* (Berkeley, 1950).
Taylor, Arnold, *The Welsh Castles of Edward I* (London and Ronceverte, 1986).
Teithydd, 'Ymholiadau Hynafiaethol', *Taliesin* (1860), 285–6.
Tennant, W. C., 'Croes Naid', *National Library of Wales Journal*, 7 (1951–2), 102–15.
Thomas, Charles and Howlett, David, 'Vita Sancti Paterni: The Life of Saint Padarn and the
      Original Miniu', *Trivium*, 33 (2003).

Thomas, Graham and Williams, Nicholas, *Bewnans Ke: The Life of St Kea* (Exeter, 2007).
Thompson, John J., 'Authors and audiences', in W. R. J. Barron (ed.), *The Arthur of the English* (Cardiff, 2001), pp. 371–95.
Thomas, Juliette, 'The Development of Folklore Studies in Wales 1700–1900', *Keystone Folklore*, 20/4 (1975), 33–52.
Thomson, R. L. (ed.), *Owein or Chwedyl Iarlles y Ffynnawn* (Dublin, 1986).
—— *Ystorya Gereint uab Erbin* (Dublin, 1997).
Thorn, Frank and Caroline (eds), *Domesday Book, XVII: Herefordshire* (Chichester, 1982).
Thornton, David Ewan, 'A Neglected Genealogy of Llywelyn ap Gruffudd', *Cambrian Medieval Celtic Studies*, 23 (1992), 9–23.
Thorpe, Lewis (trans.), *Gerald of Wales: The Journey through Wales and The Description of Wales* (Harmondsworth, 1978).
T. L. D. J. P., 'Cromlech on Mynydd Cefn Ammwlch, Caernarvonshire', *Archaeologia Cambrensis* (1847), 97–9.
Tolstoy, Nikolai, 'Nennius, Chapter Fifty-Six', *Bulletin of the Board of Celtic Studies*, 19 (1960–2), 118–62.
Trachsler, Richard (ed.), *Girart d' Amiens, Escanor: roman arthurian en vers de la fin du XIIIe siècle*, 2 vols (Geneva, 1994).
Trevelyan, Marie, *Folk-Lore and Folk-Stories of Wales* (London, 1909).
Trotter, D. A., *Medieval French Literature and the Crusades (1100–1300)* (Geneva, 1987).
Turner, Sharon, *A Vindication of the Genuineness of the Ancient British Poems of Aneurin, Taliesin, Llywarch Hen, and Merdhin, with Specimens of the Poems* (London, 1803).
Turvey, Roger, *Llywelyn the Great: Prince of Gwynedd* (Llandysul, 2007).
Tyacke, Sarah and Huddy, John, *Christopher Saxton and Tudor Map-Making* (London, 1980).

Ussher, James, *Britannicarum Ecclesiarum Antiquitates* (Dublin, 1639).
Utz, Richard, '"There Are Places We Remember": Situating the Medieval Past in Postmedieval Cultural Memories', *Transfiguration, Nordic Journal of Christianity and the Arts*, 6/2 (2004), 89–108.

Vale, Juliet, 'Arthur in English society', in W. R. J. Barron (ed.), *The Arthur of the English* (Cardiff, 2001), pp. 185–96.
Vinaver, Eugene (ed.), *The Works of Thomas Malory*, revised by P. J. C. Field, third edition, 3 vols (Oxford, 1990).
Virgilio, Polidoro, *Historia Anglica* (Basle, 1534).
Vitt, Anthony M., 'Peredur vab Efrawc: Edited Texts and Translations of the MSS Peniarth 7 and 14 Versions' (unpublished MPhil Thesis, Aberystwyth University, 2010).

Wade-Evans, A. W., *Nennius's History of the Britons* (London, 1938).
—— (ed. and trans.), *Vitae Sanctorum Britanniae et Genealogiae* (Cardiff, 1944; reprint edn Cardiff, 2013).
Wakelin, A. P., 'Tours in Wales: A Handlist of Manuscript Journals Describing Tours Made in Wales from the Collections in The National Library of Wales' (unpublished, 1981).
Walters, Gwyn and Emery, Frank, 'Edward Lhuyd, Edmund Gibson and the Printing of Camden's *Britannia*, 1695', *The Library*, Series 5, 32 (1977), 109–37.
Walters, Gwynfryn, 'The tourist and guide book literature of Wales 1770–1870: a descriptive and bibliographical survey with an analysis of the cartographic content and its context' (unpublished MSc thesis, University of Wales, Aberystwyth, 1966).
Walters, J. Cuming, *The Lost Land of King Arthur* (London, 1909).

Ward, Charlotte, 'Arthur in the Welsh Bruts', in Cyril J. Byrne, Margaret Harry and Padraig O'Siadhail (eds), *Celtic Peoples and Celtic Languages: Proceedings of the Second North American Congress of Celtic Studies Held in Halifax, August 16–19, 1989* (Halifax, 1992), pp. 383–90.

Waring, Elijah, *Recollections and Anecdotes of Edward Williams* (London, 1850).

Warren, Michelle A., *History on the Edge: Excalibur and the Borders of Britain, 1100–1300* (Minneapolis, 2000).

Webster, K. T., *Guinevere: A Study of Her Abductions* (Milton, Mass., 1951).

Weiss, Judith (ed.), *Wace's Roman De Brut: A History of the British: Text and Translation* (Exeter, 1999).

West, G. D., *An Index of Proper Names in French Arthurian Verse Romances 1150–1300* (Toronto, 1969)

—— *An Index of Proper Names in French Arthurian Prose Romances* (Toronto, 1978).

Whitaker, J., *The History of Manchester*, 4 vols (London, 1771–5).

White, Richard, *Historiarum Britanniae insulae, ab origine Mundi, ad annum Christi octingentesimum, Libri novem priores*, 9 vols (Douai, 1597–1602).

Wilkinson, Louise J., 'Joan, Wife of Llywelyn the Great', *Thirteenth Century England*, 10 (2005), 81–93.

Williams, A. Wynn, *King Arthur's Well, Llanddeioniolen, near Caernarfon, A Chalybeate Spring* (Caernarvon, 1858).

Williams, David H., *Atlas of Cistercian Lands in Wales* (Cardiff, 1990).

Williams, Edward, *Poems, Lyric and Pastoral*, 2 vols (London, 1794).

Williams, G. J., *Iolo Morganwg a Chywyddau'r Ychwanegiad* (Cardiff, 1926).

—— and Jones, E. J., *Gramedegau'r Penceirddiaid* (Cardiff, 1934).

Williams, Glanmor, 'Sir John Pryse of Brecon', *Brycheiniog*, 31 (1998–9), 49–63.

Williams, Gruffydd Aled, 'The Bardic Road to Bosworth: A Welsh View of Henry Tudor', *Transactions of the Honourable Society of Cymmrodorion* (1986), 7–31.

Williams, Hugh (ed. and trans.), *Gildas*, Cymmrodorion Record Series No. 3, 2 vols, (London, 1899–1901).

Williams, Ieuan M., *Humphrey Llwyd: Cronica Walliae* (Cardiff, 2002).

Williams, Ifor, *Canu Aneirin* (Cardiff, 1938).

—— *Canu Taliesin* (Cardiff, 1958).

Williams, J. E. Caerwyn, 'Yr Arglwydd Rhys ac "Eisteddfod" Aberteifi 1176', in Nerys Ann Jones and Huw Pryce (eds), *Yr Arglwydd Rhys* (Cardiff, 1996), pp. 94–128.

—— and Lynch, Peredur I. (eds), *Gwaith Meilyr Brydydd a'i Ddisgynyddion* (Cardiff, 1994).

Williams, John Godfrey, *Arthur, Prehistoric Sites & Place-Names* (Hay-on-Wye, 1993).

Williams, Peter Bayley, *A Tourists Guide through the County of Caernarvonshire* (Caernarvon, 1821).

Williams, Robert, 'Legends of Wales', *The Cambrian Journal* (1859), 208–16.

—— (ed. and trans.), *Y Seint Greal* (London, 1876).

Williams, T. P. T., 'The "Dodsley" History of Anglesey re-visited', *Transactions of the Anglesey Antiquarian Society* (2006), 15–33.

Williams, Taliesin (ed.), *Iolo Manuscripts* (Llandovery, 1848).

Willis, Browne, *A Survey of the Cathedral Church of St. David's, and the Edifices Belonging to it, as they Stood in the Year 1715* (London, 1717).

Willis-Bund, J. W. (ed.), *The Black Book of St David's* (London, 1902).

Winterbottom, Michael (ed. and trans.), *Gildas: The Ruin of Britain and Other Documents* (London, 1978).

Wmffre, Iwan, *The Place-Names of Cardiganshire*, 3 vols (Oxford, 2004).

Wood, Juliette, 'Where does Britain end? The reception of Geoffrey of Monmouth in Scotland and Wales', in Rhiannon Purdie and Nicola Royan (eds), *The Scots and Medieval Arthurian Legend* (Woodbridge, 2005), pp. 9–23.

—— 'Folk Narrative Research in Wales at the Beginning of the Twentieth Century: The Influence of John Rhŷs (1840–1916)', *Folklore*, 116 (2005), 325–41.

Wood, Michael, *In Search of the Dark Ages* (London, 1981).

Woolf, D. R., 'Lewis, John (*d.* 1615/16)', *Oxford Dictionary of National Biography* (Oxford, 2004).

Wright, Neil (ed.) *Historia Regum Britannie of Geoffrey of Monmouth I: Bern, Burgerbibliothek, MS 568* (Cambridge, 1985).

—— *Historia Regum Britannie of Geoffrey of Monmouth II: The First Variant Version: A Critical Edition* (Cambridge, 1988).

—— 'The place of Henry of Huntingdon's *Epistola ad Warinumin* in the text-history of Geoffrey of Monmouth's *Historia regum Britannie*: a preliminary investigation', in Jondorf, Gillian and Dumville, David N. (eds), *France and the British Isles in the Middle Ages* (Woodbridge, 1991), pp. 71–113.

Wyndham, N. Penruddock, *A Gentleman's Tour Through Monmouthshire and Wales in 1774* (London, 1775).

Zhao, Xiezhen, 'Arthurian personal names in medieval Welsh Poetry' (unpublished MPhil thesis, Aberystwyth University, 2015).

INDEX